DEC 2009

JAYHAWKERS

JAYHAWKERS

The Civil War Brigade of
James Henry Lane

Bryce D. Benedict

UNIVERSITY OF OKLAHOMA PRESS : NORMAN

Library of Congress Cataloging-in-Publication Data

Benedict, Bryce D., 1955–
　　Jayhawkers : the Civil War brigade of James Henry Lane / Bryce D. Benedict.
　　　p.　　cm.
　　ISBN 978-0-8061-3999-9 (hardcover : alk. paper)
　　1. United States. Army. Lane's Brigade (1861–1862) 2. Kansas—History—Civil War, 1861–1865—Regimental histories. 3. United States—History—Civil War, 1861–1865—Regimental histories. 4. Lane, James Henry, 1814–1866. 5. Kansas—History—Civil War, 1861–1865—Campaigns. 6. Missouri—History—Civil War, 1861–1865—Campaigns. 7. United States—History—Civil War, 1861–1865—Campaigns. I. Title.
　　E508.4.B46 2009
　　973.7'481—dc22
　　　　　　　　　　　　　　　　　　　　　　　　　　　　　　2008033602

The paper in this book meets the guidelines for permanence and durability of the Committee on Production Guidelines for Book Longevity of the Council on Library Resources, Inc. ∞

Copyright © 2009 by the University of Oklahoma Press, Norman, Publishing Division of the University. Manufactured in the U.S.A.

All rights reserved. No part of this publication may be reproduced, stored in a retrieval system, or transmitted, in any form or by any means, electronic, mechanical, photocopying, recording, or otherwise—except as permitted under Section 107 or 108 of the United States Copyright Act—without the prior permission of the University of Oklahoma Press.

1　2　3　4　5　6　7　8　9　10

*To my wife,
Kelly,
one hot chick*

Can you not send us re-enforcements; with it, we could play hell with Missouri in a few days.

James H. Lane, August 25, 1861

The Kansas troops would have been kept on this side of the line and our neighbors left to take care of themselves, had not [the Missouri] plundering bands come among us, killing our citizens, plundering our villages and threatening our camps. . . . The chastising which followed, was given with reluctance, but it was necessary to teach them that they could not invade the soil of Kansas with impunity.

Chaplain H. H. Moore,
Third Regiment Kansas Volunteers, December 18, 1861

Contents

List of Illustrations	xi
Terminology and Scope	xiii
Introduction	3
1. Bleeding Kansas	13
2. The Blast of War	25
3. A Fighting Brigade Is Born	33
4. "We Could Play Hell with Missouri"	56
5. Drywood and Osceola	72
6. Frémont's Grand Army	109
7. Lane the Liberator	147
8. Visitations of Mercy	165
9. Monotony and Mutiny	190
10. Dissolution	202
11. The Great Southern Expedition	219
Conclusion	239
Appendix A. Necrology	251

Appendix B	Brigade Staff	259
Appendix C	Brigade Casualties	261
Notes		267
Bibliography		321
Index		333

Illustrations

FIGURES

Senator James H. Lane	135
"Battle of Booneville, or the Great Missouri 'Lyon' Hunt"	136
Sterling Price	137
James Montgomery	138
Fort Lincoln	139
Thomas Moonlight	140
James G. Blunt	141
John Ritchie	142
Samuel D. Sturgis	143
"General" Lane on cover of *Harper's Weekly*	144
Henry Wager Halleck	145
David Hunter	146

MAP

Lane's Brigade Area of Operations, 1861	2

Terminology and Scope

Throughout this work the soldiers in Kansas units are referred to as "jayhawkers," while those on the Southern side are "secesh," "secessionists," or "rebels." To have referred to the men in the Kansas units as Kansans would be inaccurate, as a considerable number of men within Lane's Brigade came from other Northern states and many others were refugees from Missouri. Similarly, using the term "Confederate" to describe the other side is inadequate as most of the forces arrayed against Lane were guerillas or local militia or belonged to the Missouri State Guard before that organization was incorporated into the Confederacy.

Another term frequently used is "contrabands," originally coined by Benjamin F. Butler, who described escaped slaves held by the Union army as "contraband of war." During the Civil War, the word was quickly adapted to describe any escaped slave and eventually was even applied to free blacks.

The companies in Lane's Brigade are generally referenced by the name of the company commander rather than the letter assigned to the company. This is because in the early stages of these companies' existence, something of a game of musical chairs was carried on in which the companies were given new letter designations within regiments that were then swapped between regiments.

An example of this is Captain James M. Williams's company, which began as Company B of the Third Regiment, was transferred to the Fifth Regiment as Company K, and then redesignated as Company F. Merely referring to a unit as Company B, Third Regiment, would lead to unnecessary confusion.

The focus of this work is the Third, Fourth, and Fifth Kansas Volunteer Regiments, which made up the core of Lane's Brigade. Other units, such as the Sixth Kansas and Charles Jennison's regiment, are included to the extent they cooperated with Lane and are needed to illuminate the events along the Kansas-Missouri border.

This book is not a biography of Lane. Only the most cursory background information has been provided to give a fair sense of the man and how he came to Kansas. To those persons interested in a biography, I recommend Wendell Holmes Stephenson's *The Political Career of General James H. Lane*. While somewhat dated, it is well researched and balanced in its approach. Unfortunately, it is long out of print and hard to find.

Finally, I have used *sic* sparingly, preferring to retain wherever possible the original spelling and punctuation of direct quotations.

JAYHAWKERS

Lanes's Brigade area of operations, 1861

Introduction

As civil war descended on the United States in April 1861, Kansas—which had achieved statehood only three months before—was threatened by armed secessionists in Missouri. Although the federal government placed no requisition on Kansas for troops, Kansas governor Charles Robinson nonetheless tendered two regiments for military service. These regiments joined the Union forces of Brigadier General Nathaniel Lyon in his pursuit of the secessionist Missouri State Guard, thus effectively denuding Kansas of troops.

Into this vacuum stepped James Henry Lane, who had received authority directly from President Abraham Lincoln to raise and command two volunteer regiments. Lane would come to command three regiments, which he called the Kansas Brigade, more popularly known as Lane's Brigade. The brigade operated along Missouri's western border, putting into practice Lane's belief that the best place to defend Kansas was from within Missouri and that the best way to crush the rebellion was to destroy slavery. In its brief existence, the brigade would fight one pitched battle and numerous skirmishes, liberate hundreds of slaves, and join Major General John C. Frémont's October 1861 campaign against the Missouri State Guard. In its various marches, the brigade seized private property, sometimes to deprive the enemy of its use, sometimes as a punitive measure, and sometimes merely to line the pockets of its soldiers. The brigade also burned large portions of four towns and murdered, under the guise of a drum-head court martial, six men.

The brigade was hailed both as the savior of Kansas and as the terror of Missouri. Although operating in the backwater of the far-western frontier, the brigade, and especially Lane, garnered national praise as heroic victors. However, the admiration was not universal. Major General Henry W. Halleck, commander of the Department of the Missouri, which then encompassed Kansas, despised Lane. Halleck asserted: "The conduct of our troops during the Fremont campaign, and especially the course pursued by those under Lane and [Charles R.] Jennison, has turned against us many thousands who were formerly Union men. A few more such raids, in connection with the ultra speeches made by leading men in Congress, will make [Missouri] as unanimous against us as Eastern Virginia."[1]

Halleck claimed that various outrages in Missouri had been committed by three classes of persons: rebel guerillas, a segment of the Federal volunteer troops, and the Kansas "jayhawkers." The third class, "the Kansas jayhawkers, or robbers, . . . [was] organized under the auspices of Senator Lane," Halleck wrote. "They wear the uniform of and it is believed received pay from the United States. Their principal occupation for the last six months seems to have been the stealing of negroes, the robbing of houses, and the burning of barns, grain, and forage. The evidence of their crimes is unquestionable." In short, the brigade was accused of engaging, to a degree, in what has come to be known as "total war."[2]

Authorities have offered different interpretations of the phrase "total war," embraced by the Union army. In the following discussion, I adopt the definition offered by Major Jeffrey Addicott, a former senior instructor in the International Law Division of the U.S. Army's Judge Advocate School, in describing Major General William T. Sherman's "march to the sea" in 1864: "The targeting of defenseless civilian populations. . . . The soldiers were allowed to rob, pillage, and burn in a swath of horror. . . . Sherman illegally directed his ferocity toward innocent and helpless civilians."[3]

Modern warfare is regulated by the law of war (also known as the law of armed conflict), which encompasses both written law and widely recognized customs. For the U.S. Army, written law includes Field Manual 27-10, *The Law of Land Warfare*, and the Geneva Convention. The Union army in 1861 had no such written law and relied on customary law. Customary law derived from studying the past conduct of armies in the field in order to discern what conduct seemed to be universally approved and what conduct was condemned. Customary law, as taught in the 1860s at the U.S. Military Academy at West Point, was included in an ethics course. The text used in that course concluded that "a war between the governments of two nations, is a war between all the individuals of the one, and all the individuals of which the other nation is composed." This definition would seem to allow unrestricted warfare against civilians. Yet it also held that "the general usage now is not to touch private property upon land, without making compensation, unless in special cases dictated by the necessary operations of war."[4] The second, and probably less important, source of customary law was the institutional knowledge of the U.S. Army. During the Revolutionary War, Creek and Seminole wars, and U.S.-Mexican War, the army had limited experience with operations against enemy civilians.[5]

Whatever lessons the army had learned regarding its operations in occupied territory apparently were not widely disseminated and were lost with the death or retirement of the officers who had participated in such campaigns. However, even if such knowledge had been shared within the officer corps, it was not necessarily of great help when the Civil War began. The pool of regular army officers who might have had some knowledge of the law of war was quite small; a paltry 638 West Point graduates "already had regular army commissions, returned to the regular army from civilian life, or accepted commissions in volunteer regiments." Lincoln's call for 75,000 volunteers in April 1861 included a need for 3,549 officers. Few of these new volunteer officers had any knowledge of the customary laws of war. No schools existed for these officers to learn their craft, and although they could avail themselves of texts by

Winfield Scott or William Hardee that detailed tactics and maneuvers, nothing similar explained how to act in occupied territory.[6] Not until April 1863 did the War Department, in an effort to set out the ethical limits of warfare, issue formal guidelines to field commanders. Prior to that date the various theater and department commanders issued their own orders on this subject.[7]

Nor could commanders look to Congress for guidance. In August 1861 Congress passed the Confiscation Act, an unwieldy instrument with which to suppress rebellion. The act provided that property used to support the rebellion could be seized if the owner had consented to such use. Even if such consent could be proven, the property had to be seized and a condemnation action initiated in a U.S. district court. This process might have proved satisfactory in cases in which the property was securely within Union lines, but in 1861 Missouri a county might be in the hands of the Union one week and occupied by rebel forces the next. Sherman complained from Memphis in September 1862: "We have no District Court here, and none of the machinery whereby to put in motion the Confiscation act—we take the property of Rebels & use it, but the title remains undisturbed." Such lack of guidance presented a dilemma for the Federal commander who on a scout came across a supply of goods that was likely to fall into the hands of rebel cavalry, or found a mill grinding grain for rebel bread.[8]

If the government gave Lane no law, he was largely free to make his own. Lane's central tenet for the prosecution of the war was that the slaves must be freed: "Withdraw [slavery], and this Rebellion falls of its own weight. The masters will not work, and they must eat. . . . March your splendid armies into the heart of their Confederacy; win one victory; oppose kindness to cruelty, and as the peasantry of France rallied to the standard of Napoleon on his return from Elba, so will the slaves with one impulse flock to ours." While freeing slaves was seen as the most direct way to cripple the enemy, Lane also endorsed the destruction of civilian property to weaken the enemy.[9]

In freeing slaves, Lane's Brigade was not hobbled by any official Federal policy. Although passage of the Fugitive Slave Act in 1850 required returning slaves to loyal owners, some believed this law should not be extended to disloyal owners. The government sanctioned Major General Benjamin F. Butler for retaining slaves who had escaped from rebels as "contraband of war" but stopped short of declaring them free. Brigadier General William S. Harney, in St. Louis, replied to a civilian's inquiry about the government's policy on slavery. "I have no special instructions on this head from the War Department," wrote Harney on May 14, but he agreed it was not the government's intention to interfere with "the institution of negro slavery." Congress's Crittendon-Johnson Resolution of July expressed the sentiment that the war was not being prosecuted to overthrow or interfere with the rights or "established institutions" of the states in rebellion. "Established institutions" clearly was a reference to the institution of slavery. However, sentiment was not law. The Confiscation Act of early August would allow for the freeing of slaves, but only after a court proceeding. Later that month Lincoln revoked Frémont's attempt to issue an emancipation proclamation in Missouri. In Kentucky, Brigadier General William T. Sherman advised a subordinate on November 8, "I have no instructions from Government on the subject of Negroes." Halleck danced around the issue by ordering on November 20 that fugitive slaves were to be excluded from Union camps. One commander outdanced Halleck by claiming that the "negroes" in his camp "all stoutly asserted that they were free" and that such persons were authorized to be in his camp as they were all officially employed as "officer's servants, teamsters, and hospital attendants." By January 1862 Lincoln still had no settled policy. As to slaves, he told Lane: "The only difference between you and me is that you are willing to surrender fugitives to loyal owners in case they are willing to return, while I do not believe the United States government has any right to give them up in any case. And if it had, the people would not permit us to exercise it." Regardless of whether they lacked the legal authority to emancipate slaves, in practical terms the men of Lane's Brigade would do so by sending them into Kansas.[10]

Lane wanted secessionists to feel the pain of treason. One brigade soldier, Lieutenant Joseph Trego, noted in October 1861: "Lane said he meant to make the secessionists in Missouri feel the difference between being loyal and disloyal citizens and he is doing it. We have camped where there was secession farms on one side and Union farms on the other, when we would leave[,] the secession farms were stripped of every thing like crops & fencing while the others remained untouched." A Missourian who professed neutrality had little security. Trego claimed "neutral men are just about all of them secessionists in principle." As Trego wrote this, his men were happily feasting on mutton and chickens, and feeding their horses the corn and oats left on the farm of "a red-mouthed secessionist who took his negroes, stock, family and himself off south about two weeks ago."[11]

Whatever judgment may be made concerning Lane's Brigade, one thing is certain—the brigade was a direct reflection of its commander, who was not an officer but a U.S. senator from Kansas. In the first ten years of Kansas's existence, first as a territory and then as a state, no person within it exerted greater influence than Jim Lane, and no person excited greater emotion. Lane's fame, or infamy, derived from his oratorical skills, his boundless energy, and some would also say from a flexibility of action attained by not being chained to any moral rock. Historian Lloyd Lewis commented:

> In the 1850's and 1860's there was a simple formula for stump oratory: Get up, say that somebody had said something about you, repeat it twice, and then say "it ain't so." Lane took that common formula, made himself the king of Kansas—he took that formula and went to the United States senate. He would get up on a box or endgate of a wagon anywhere on the plains, and cry "They say Jim Lane is illiterate," and then disprove it by the eloquent and touching statement that his mother had come from Connecticut. He would shout, "They say Jim Lane is a murderer," and then refute it by asking people to remember how he had given his only horse to the ladies of Lawrence to start a public library.[12]

Albert D. Richardson witnessed Lane speaking in Kansas in 1856. He remembered Lane "contorting his thin, wiry form, and uttering bitterest denunciations in deep, husky gutturals . . . defying every recognized rule of rhetoric and oratory, at will he made men roar with laughter, or melt into tears, or clinch their teeth in passion."[13]

Lane tailored his speaking style to his auditors. To a sophisticated audience, or when on the floor of the Senate, he spoke as an educated man. When speaking to common people, Lane modified his style, which was described by a contemporary Kansan, J. J. Ingalls:

> He writhes himself into more contortions than Gabriel Ravel in a pantomime; his voice is a series of transitions from the broken scream of a maniac to the hoarse rasping gutturals of a Dutch butcher in the last gasp of inebriation; the construction of his sentences is loose and disjointed; his diction is a pudding of slang, profanity and solecism; and yet the electric shock of his extraordinary eloquence shrills like a blast of a trumpet; the magnetism of his manner, the fire of his glance, the studied earnestness of his utterance, find a sudden response in the will of his audience, and he sways them like a field of reeds shaken in the wind.[14]

In addition to style, Lane also modified the substance of his speeches. Wendell Holmes Stephenson, Lane's preeminent biographer, wrote: "Lane often adapted his speech to suit the audience. In Washington he was a radical, in St. Louis a conservative, in Waterbury the son of a Connecticut school teacher, in the North a Hoosier, in the South a Kentuckian."[15]

A certain sartorial flair added to his persona. Photographs of the man suggest he never made the acquaintance of a comb; one suspects he deliberately maintained a slightly uncivilized look. In Lawrence, Kansas, on a cold December day in 1855, he punctuated his outdoor speech by dramatically tossing aside in turn his cloak, hat, coat, vest, and necktie, finally unbuttoning his shirt and rolling up his sleeves "as he paced, like some wild animal . . . the perspiration standing in great beads upon his face." Six years later Lane would find himself in Washington when war broke out. As captain of an ad hoc militia company, not dressing his best for a dinner with

Lincoln's private secretary, John Hay, and a general with his wife might be excused, but again his dramatic arrival and unkempt appearance appears to have been calculated to create a definite impression. "A gaunt, tattered, uncombed and unshorn figure appeared at the door and marched solemnly up to the table," wrote Hay. "He wore a rough overcoat, a torn shirt and suspenderless breeches. His neck was innocent of collar, guileless of necktie. His thin hair stood fretful-porcupine-quill-wise upon his crown. He sat down and gloomily charged upon his dinner." That his militia company had been in existence for less than a week, and was living in relative comfort, makes it more likely that Lane's tattered look was a politician's showmanship.[16]

J. J. Ingalls claimed Lane was "devoid of those qualities of character which excite esteem and cement the enduring structure of popular regard," though he "overcomes the obstacles in the path of achievement by persistent effort and indomitable will." William Phillips would have agreed with Ingalls's characterization of Lane's energy. He noted that Lane "can't sit still long enough to write anything, if he can write at all," and "is great on 'turning up,'—is here, there, and everywhere at the same time—to-day at the bottom, to-morrow at the top of the heap; always on the strongest side; a great lover of excitement, and will have it; a great lover of office, and will have it; will always be a favorite with the people, and will be true to them—so long as they are true to him."[17]

Lloyd Lewis wrote that to those seeking his help, Lane "would make preposterous promises, and then when unable to fulfill them, would tell the outraged victims that he loved them still, and they would forgive him because they had a strong suspicion it was true." Not all people forgave such shortcomings out of a natural fondness for Lane. As Lane gained power and influence, or appeared to, he was always surrounded by sycophants seeking favors. Lane needed those people, and they needed him; a promise broken by Lane today might yet be redeemed tomorrow.[18]

An example is the ordeal of Abelard Guthrie, delegate to Congress from the Nebraska Territory in 1862. He sought Lane's help on several matters, and Lane promised his assistance. After learning

Lane had neglected a matter, Guthrie wrote, "The cool ingratitude and heartless stolidity of this man astounds me! And yet I must not tell him what I think of his conduct!" As Lane continued to promise help without delivering, Guthrie was at a loss to understand such behavior, at one time concluding that Lane "is insane, or his extraordinary moral obliquity at least produces effects so nearly like it that one is in doubt as to the true origin of his aberration of mind." And yet despite his disdain for Lane and clear evidence that Lane promised him one thing while doing another, Guthrie, like so many others in similar circumstances, nonetheless continued to ask Lane for favors.[19]

Historian Albert Castel accused Lane of using the influence he would gain during the Civil War for personal profit to include taking kickbacks on government contracts. Biographer Stephenson, however, claimed Lane "cared nothing for money, for he dreamed of power, not of wealth. He would give away his last dollar, but if he paid a hotel bill it was the occasion for special comment." A man who wrote of seeing Lane in Lawrence in 1863 would have disputed the prior sentiment. The senator was riding about town on a "splendid" horse, "gaily caparisoned with a hundred and twenty-five dollar set of harness." He reported that Lane "lives in the finest residence in the city, owns over twelve hundred acres of heavy, timbered land across the river," had a farm at nearby Clinton, and had purchased a mansion in Washington.[20]

Real estate records, and Lane's probate estate opened after his death in 1866, suggest Lane did care about money. His 1866 probate estate (Lane, the lawyer, died without having made a will) contained an inventory of his real and personal property. The inventory of his personal property—items procured after fire destroyed his home in August 1863—was modest indeed. It was a mundane listing of such items as twelve sheets, fourteen blankets, three landscape paintings, thirty-six plates, and one wagon. No cash was listed, but Lane held notes payable from over a dozen persons for relatively small amounts, averaging about $200 each. As to real estate holdings, a different picture appears. He owned town lots in Emporia, Lecompton, and Grasshopper Falls, and a several block area in Lawrence known as

"Lane's Addition." He also owned two parcels of "R.R. Lands" valued at $15,000. Real estate records show that in 1862 and 1863 Lane acquired several parcels of rural land in Douglas County, and lots in Lane's Addition were being sold by Lane and his wife in early 1863.[21]

Lewis came to the conclusion that "Lane did believe in two things—perhaps only two in the whole realm of life—Kansas and freedom." As I was working on this project, I came across this contemporary comment about Lane in the *New York Times*—"his faith in himself is illimitable and irrepressible."[22] It was Jim Lane's central belief in himself that would lead the soldiers of his brigade to give him their unshakable faith.

The legend of Jim Lane long survived his death. In the 1950s a researcher traveled the rural Ozarks, recording the folk songs of the elderly. "Old Jim Lane" was sung by Mrs. Lon Jones of Mountain Home, Arkansas, on July 17, 1952:

> Here sits a young man in his sad station
> To mourn the loss of his own true love.
> It has been said that she was slain
> All by the hand of old Jim Lane.
>
> Oh no no, 'tis not so!
> She's come back to be his beau.
> Oh no no, 'tis not so!
> She's come back to be his beau.
>
> Here sits a young lady in her sad station
> To mourn the loss of her own true love.
> It has been said that he was slain
> All by the hand of old Jim Lane.
>
> Oh no no, 'tis not so!
> He's come back to be her beau.
> Oh no no, 'tis not so!
> He's come back to be her beau.[23]

CHAPTER 1

Bleeding Kansas

In the popular imagination, Kansas consists of featureless flat plains, yet this characterization is only somewhat accurate, and then only for its western parts. The eastern third, occupied by the first white immigrants, is, as one 1857 observer noted, "a rolling prairie, with no timber of any kind except along the rivers, creeks, and ravines, [where] bottomland is heavily timbered with walnut, oak, hickory, ash, cottonwood, elm lyn & c."[1]

In 1854 the southeastern corner of Kansas Territory was taken up by the Cherokee Neutral Lands and a sliver of land south of it called the Quapaw strip. The Neutral Lands, approximately fifty miles from north to south and twenty-five miles in width, had been given to the Cherokees by an 1835 treaty. By 1860 two thousand whites had settled there illegally, some without knowing they were on Cherokee land. In October of that year the Cherokee agent, aided by U.S. troops, began driving these settlers out. Seventy-five to one hundred houses were burned before a temporary reprieve was granted to the remaining settlers. Appeals were made to Washington and to the Cherokee Nation to allow the settlers to remain. The settlement issue was complicated by intermarriage of whites and Cherokees, which may have entitled them to settle there. No further eviction efforts were made until after the war, when the Cherokees were forced out.[2]

To the west of the Neutral Lands, the Osage reservation extended over half the length of the territory. South of the reservation was a narrow, almost inconsequential strip of land (2.46 miles north to south) that was part of the Cherokee Strip. This feature came about when the southern boundary of the Kansas Territory, as fixed by the Kansas-Nebraska Act of 1854, inadvertently intruded upon Cherokee lands in the Indian Territory. The territory's far western border would be moved eastward, from the Rocky Mountain Front Range to its present location, when the territory was admitted to statehood in 1861. Other than a few missionaries, traders, and soldiers who lived in the territory, the area was occupied by American Indians before the 1850s. Large sections of land in the eastern part of the territory had been nominally set aside as reservations for tribes displaced from eastern states; to the west were the yet-unconquered tribes of Pawnee, Wichita, Kansas (or Kaw), Cheyenne, Arapahoe, Comanche, and Kiowa.[3]

Kansas had three army forts—Leavenworth, Riley, and Scott. None was stockaded or otherwise surrounded by defensive works. All were open collections of barracks, storehouses, and stables. Fort Scott was abandoned and its buildings sold to civilians in 1855. The adjacent town of Fort Scott remained, but the post was reactivated when the Civil War began. The posts at Leavenworth and Riley were joined in 1859 by Camp Alert on the Santa Fe Trail. Originally consisting only of tents and dugouts, Camp Alert was moved and renamed Fort Larned during the war.[4]

The Kansas-Nebraska Act, signed into law by President Franklin Pierce on May 30, 1854, opened Kansas Territory to settlement by whites with the proviso that "popular sovereignty" would decide whether Kansas became a slave state. Immediately, pro-slavery and free state camps encouraged their followers to emigrate to establish Kansas as either slave or free. Although thousands did move into the territory and make land claims, most people were lured more by cheap land and financial opportunity than by politics. Legal title was a significant problem, ignored by the settlers and the federal government alike. The failure to negotiate treaties with resident Indian tribes meant that, as one prominent historian has put it, "not an acre of land was available for pre-emption or purchase." The delay in negotiating treaties and the lack of land surveys led to uncertainty and conflict among settlers.[5]

When the time came in November 1854 to vote for a delegate to the U.S. House of Representatives, hundreds if not thousands of Missouri "border ruffians" crossed into Kansas to vote illegally —a scene repeated the following March in elections for the territorial legislature. If a poll judge questioned the Missourians' qualifications to vote, a revolver or bowie knife was often presented as credentials. In some locations the same credentials were used to dissuade free state men from voting. Missouri slaveholders had legitimate concerns that, as a free state, Kansas would become a haven for fugitive slaves. However, most of the Missourians who crossed over to vote fraudulently were not slave owners and had less of a direct interest in the matter. As a result, free state men in Kansas regarded the territorial legislature elected in March as bogus. Proclaiming they would ignore the pro-slavery laws enacted by the "bogus legislature," they set out to establish a parallel free state government.[6]

It was in this swirl of events that James Henry Lane arrived in Kansas in April 1855. Although he had accomplished much in his forty years, there was little to distinguish him from the homesteaders, traders, speculators, or other opportunists flooding into Kansas. No one then would have predicted that he would rise to national prominence. Six years later, a *New York Times* correspondent described him as beguiling but generally unassuming:

> Lane is a man of some 50 years of age, of medium height, and at first sight rather unprepossessing. His figure is slight, his head wide at the top and narrowing down to the jaw, like an inverted pyramid; his brow wide and high; his eyes small, black and overhung by cliff-like eyebrows, his mouth sensual, and combined with a gleam of fun in his eyes, has an expression of great good humor and enjoyment that wins one irresistibly to the conclusion that he is the best fellow in the world. His hair is thin, slightly tinged with gray, and shoved away from his head in every direction, as if he had just come

in from running bareheaded against a strong wind. In conversation he is ready, full of a rollicking sort of humor.⁷

Lane was born on June 22, 1814, in either Indiana or Kentucky—the record is unclear on this point. His father was Amos Lane, who served Indiana as a state legislator and as a representative in Congress. James studied law in Indiana and was admitted to the bar at age twenty-six. When the war with Mexico broke out, he organized a company of volunteers in Dearborn County, Indiana, and in 1846 was elected colonel of the Third Indiana Volunteer Regiment. The unit saw action at the battle of Buena Vista on February 22–23, 1847, and distinguished itself under Lane's leadership. At one point it came to the aid of another volunteer regiment, the Mississippi Rifles, commanded by Jefferson Davis, who would become U.S. secretary of war and then president of the Confederate States of America. Lane later raised another Indiana regiment, the Fifth, which performed occupation duties in Mexico City.⁸

A Democrat, Lane was elected lieutenant governor of Indiana in 1849 and served until January 1853. Elected a U.S. representative the preceding October, he left state office for Washington, D.C. His term in Congress was undistinguished, however. No advocate of slavery, he nonetheless voted for the Kansas-Nebraska bill, declaring he would uphold constitutional rights and promising to crush any agitation that was "calculated to disturb the harmony of the Union." Declining to stand for reelection in 1854, Lane instead emigrated to the Kansas Territory.⁹

After reaching Kansas in 1855 with his wife, Mary, and four children (Ellen, eleven years old; James H., Jr., nine; Anna, about five; and Jane, four) Lane staked out a land claim near Lawrence. Anna died that first year, and Lane's marriage did not survive the move to Kansas. Writing later for a friendly Kansas newspaper, Lane put the breakup in the best light: "Mrs. Lane found it difficult to endure the hardships, annoyances and inconveniences of a pioneer's lot," and "an estrangement was the result . . . without, however, acrimonious feelings on the part of either." This was less than honest. Mary had filed for divorce in April 1856 in Indiana, alleging abandonment and nonsupport, a fact already publicized by an anti-Lane newspaper. The couple's lawyers negotiated a judgment entered two weeks after the suit was filed.[10]

Lane quickly enmeshed himself in Kansas territorial politics and in the conflict known as Bleeding Kansas. In June 1855 he was involved in the attempt to organize a Democratic party, which endorsed the 1852 national platform and the Kansas-Nebraska Act. This failed to attract any great following, however, and Lane, sensing there was little future as a Democrat in Lawrence, soon insinuated himself into the Free State Party.[11]

Lane's transformation from conservative Democrat to radical Free State man came about gradually. Lane was astute enough to realize that Free State men would view any sudden conversion with suspicion. At an August 1855 Free State convention in Lawrence, Lane advocated "moderation, moderation, moderation." Although he announced he would still vote for the Kansas-Nebraska Act, he said he desired Kansas to be a free state. At that convention a contemporary (and later admirer), John Speer, opposed Lane as a delegate to the Free State convention to be held in Big Springs, because Lane was a "Black law" man—namely, an adherent of the proposed policy to bar all blacks from the territory.[12]

Despite Speer's opposition, Lane was elected as a delegate. Quickly rising to prominence, he was appointed to chair the committee on the party platform. In line with the prevailing attitude of Free State men, the platform denied it was an abolitionist organization and proposed excluding all blacks once statehood was achieved. In a later election, Free State men voted nearly 3 to 1 in favor of the proposal, and in December they adopted a constitution that instructed the first state legislature to exclude free blacks. Lane's political star continued to rise with his selection for several important positions within the Free State Party, including the presidency of its constitutional convention in October.[13]

Outside events intervened to hasten Lane's transformation into a radical. In November 1855 armed Free Staters rescued a man arrested by a pro-slavery sheriff and took him to Lawrence. The acting territorial governor declared that a state of insurrection existed and called out the militia. Lawrence was subsequently besieged not by the Kansas militia but by Missouri border ruffians who threatened to sack the abolitionist town. During this crisis, which became known as the Wakarusa War, no Free State man was more prominent than Lane. A committee of safety anointed Lane with the grandiose title of brigadier general; he directed the construction of earthen fortifications and led the town defenders in military drill. The Missourians were not enthusiastic about attacking a defended town, and they willingly agreed to a "peace treaty" when the new territorial governor arrived on the scene. Lane gained stature for negotiating the peace. As Wendell Holmes Stephenson, an early Lane biographer, noted, the Wakarusa war seemed "a turning point in [Lane's] career." Lane, Stephenson wrote, "was essentially a conservative until that crisis presented a proper background for radical leadership. For in battle array the belligerent Lane was in his element."[14]

Lane was again in battle array in August 1856. Within a week's time, Free State forces led by Lane attacked and forced the surrender of pro-slavery posts at Franklin, Fort Saunders, and Fort Titus— "fort" being an extravagant description of the latter two places, which were fortified homes. Lane followed this by marching the free state militia on the pro-slavery territorial capitol at Lecompton, where a number of Free State leaders were imprisoned. U.S. Army dragoons from Fort Leavenworth intervened and prevented an attack, but as a concession the prisoners were released. Lane's subsequent siege of pro-slavery men at Hickory Point was raised only by another timely arrival of dragoons.[15]

The new territorial governor, John Geary, exerted a strong hand in suppressing violence. What neither side could now win by force would be settled at the ballot box. The continuing influx of settlers resulted in Free State men overwhelming the number of pro-slavery supporters. The legislative elections in October 1857 produced a solid Free State victory, signaling the end of the fight for political supremacy in Kansas. The Free State–dominated legislature elected Lane as major general of the Kansas militia. In that capacity he took the militia to southeastern Kansas in December 1857 to quell local disturbances between Free State and pro-slavery men.[16]

As the struggle over Kansas moved from the battlefield to the ballot box, former enemies came together to pursue a new goal—profit. As one Free State settler wrote, "These same men who were leaders in marauding excursions are the first to take us by the hand and the most anxious to induce the 'Northern Vagabonds' and 'Nigger Thieves' to settle in this place." A Missourian complained of prominent pro-slavery men "and the notorious Lane lying down together, 'hail fellows well met' and partners in trade; growing fat in their purses and persons by speculations in town sites; eating roasted turkeys and drinking champagne." The discovery of gold in the Rocky Mountains resulted in a small wave of emigration in 1858.[17]

With most of the battle over slavery won, Lane returned to a more conventional life. He and Mary remarried in 1857, and in May 1858 he entered into a law partnership with James Christian in Lawrence. The following month, however, Lane shot and killed Gaius Jenkins, a prominent Free State man who held an adjoining land claim, in a dispute over access to a well. It was never established who shot first, and an inquest failed to find Lane at fault. James Christian would later reveal a story explaining how a simple land dispute could have escalated into homicide among supposed allies. According to Christian, Lane's daughter Anna, who died in 1855, was buried on the Kansas claim. When Lane returned to his land in 1857 after having been out of the territory for some time, he discovered that Jenkins had plowed up and cultivated the land on which the grave was located. Lane and Christian spent several days trying in vain to locate any sign of the grave or the child's body. Lane said of Jenkins, "Such a God damn ghoul is not fit to live! If I was only certain that he dug up my child out of revenge on me, I would kill him at first sight." Christian added that Lane, "until the day of his death, believed that Jenkins dug up the child and threw it away. . . . Lane, with all his faults, was a loving and an affectionate father, passionately fond of his children."[18]

Following this violence and attendant controversy, Lane largely disappeared from public life. But the resurrection of his political career began in December 1859 when Mark Delahay invited him to meet presidential candidate Abraham Lincoln, then making a short campaign swing through Kansas. Afterward, Lane campaigned for Lincoln in the Northern states.[19]

Although most Kansans had renounced force as a political tool, southeast Kansas now saw a reprise of violence. The first settlers in Linn and Bourbon counties were pro-slavery in sentiment. Free State men who settled among them were largely driven out in 1856–57, their land claims squatted upon by pro-slavery men. With the return of peace to the territory, Free State immigration increased in the spring of 1857. When legal disputes arose over various land claims, Free State men spurned the local courts, which were dominated by pro-slavery federal appointees who favored pro-slavery men. In response Free State men formed extralegal "claims associations" and a "squatter's court" to adjudicate land claims, with officers appointed to enforce the orders of the squatter's court. When such enforcement actions became odious to federal authorities at Fort Scott, the marshal mounted a raid on the squatter's court located in the home of Oliver P. Bayne in December 1857. Although the raid came to naught, Bayne and James Montgomery, who later became one of Lane's regimental commanders, raised companies to protect Free State settlers. Among Bayne's men was Jeremiah Goldsmith Anderson, who would accompany John Brown on his December 1858 raid into Missouri and his later attack on Harpers Ferry in Virginia.[20]

Montgomery quickly became the bane of pro-slavery men in southeast Kansas. Born in Ohio in 1814, he moved to Kentucky with his parents in 1830. He tried teaching school for a time, took up carpentry, and became a Campbellite preacher. While in Kentucky he married twice, the first marriage ending within a few years with his wife's untimely death. His second wife bore seven children, the first, a girl, born around 1844. Montgomery emigrated to Pike County, Missouri, in 1852, then on to Jackson County the next year to await the opening of the Kansas Territory. In 1854 he purchased two claims in what became Linn County. He occupied a log house built by a pro-slavery Missourian who Montgomery said "was unexpectedly compelled to leave the country" and thus took possession of it until the man returned. He explained that his self-described guerilla company had to "subsist on the enemy. Therefore we feed ourselves at Pro-slavery larders and our horses at Pro-slavery corn-cribs." In his actions against pro-slavery men, Montgomery firmly believed God was on his side. Albert D. Richardson met Montgomery and described him as "that most formidable of characters: a praying fighter. He held daily religious worship in his family." Consistent with being an agent of God's will, Montgomery accepted the personal responsibility of carrying out his duties: "Although believing in a general providence, I believe it my duty to so plan and arrange my acts, as if every thing depended on my own individual act." He prohibited profanity or pilfering, and gave away to needy Free State men the horses he seized, once no longer needed by his men.[21]

When Lane traveled to southeast Kansas in December 1857, in his capacity as major general of the militia, violence quickly subsided, probably due to the arrival of U.S. troops. In his report of his activities, Lane wrote that "peace being fully restored, we disbanded the command, retaining two companies in the field—some 30 men—with orders to protect the inhabitants." Those two companies were those of Montgomery and Bayne—not necessarily the most prudent choice. An uneasy peace lasted until February 11, 1858. On that day Montgomery and Bayne marched their companies into Fort Scott and took control of the town. Fort Scott was where the federal court and land office were located, both offices being held by appointees of the pro-slavery federal administration. In the following months Montgomery, aided by Free State men such as Charles R. "Doc" Jennison and John E. Stewart, were active in driving pro-slavery men out of the territory by threat or by force. While pro-slavery men had been forced to leave before, it had usually been because of disputed land claims; now the evictions were political in nature. Bates and Cass counties in Missouri witnessed a flood of refugees from Kansas Territory.[22]

One of the refugees came back to exact revenge. Charles Hamilton crossed over into Kansas on May 19, 1858, with an armed party. Making a sweep through Linn County, they rounded up eleven men and took them to a ravine near the Marais des Cygnes River. The prisoners were lined up and on the command of Hamilton were shot down. Five were killed, five wounded, and one man unscathed as he feigned death.[23]

In the wake of this round of violence, hundreds of settlers, both Free State and pro-slavery, left Linn and Bourbon counties. The governor arranged for federal troops and a separate posse to be stationed in the troubled area. This reestablished some measure of peace; horse stealing became the biggest concern for the remaining settlers. After these troops were withdrawn in November, Montgomery again began forcing pro-slavery men out of the territory. Attempts to arrest Montgomery failed, then on December 16 Montgomery directly confronted federal authorities by again invading Fort Scott to release two Free State men imprisoned there. A man named John Little was killed after he unwisely fired upon the invaders.[24]

A few months previous, John Brown had made his appearance in Linn County, remaining relatively quiet until December. He would have joined Montgomery's raid on Fort Scott, but he abandoned the project when he learned Montgomery would not agree to burn the town. On the night of December 20, 1858, Brown led a raid into Vernon County, Missouri. He split his force into two groups, each heading for the house of a slave owner. The party Brown led captured the slave owner, liberated ten slaves, and made off with a quantity of horses, oxen, wagons, and food. The other party killed the slave owner and freed a pregnant slave who gave birth in Kansas soon thereafter. About ten days later Jennison and Eli Snyder raided into Missouri and burnt the home and store of Jeremiah Jackson. Snyder would have been one of the victims of Hamilton's Marais des Cygnes massacre, but when called on to surrender, he grabbed a shotgun and drove off Hamilton's men in an exchange of gunfire that wounded Snyder's son.[25]

Although Montgomery was unapologetic for his activities against pro-slavery men, he distanced himself from Brown's Missouri raid. Apparently Montgomery had engaged in some behind-the-scenes negotiations, for twice in January 1859 he surrendered to authorities at Lawrence to face outstanding criminal charges—something he was unlikely to do if he felt imprisonment would result. Each time he was released on bail. Then on February 12 the governor signed the Amnesty Act, which gave amnesty for crimes committed in six southeastern counties that arose out of political differences. Montgomery was never called to account for his acts.[26]

Just as people could finally look forward to peace and prosperity, a drought hit Kansas in June 1859 and lasted until November 1860. As creeks dried up and crops failed, some thirty thousand settlers gave up and left. Relief efforts were organized, and a citizens' meeting at Big Springs in September 1860 published an "appeal for assistance to those whom a bountiful Providence has blessed with abundant harvests":

> We are without bread, and without any means of obtaining it; for there is no money in the country, as every dollar has been absorbed in paying for our lands, which were prematurely forced into market. There are many who must perish, if relief is not afforded them; for the people generally are in no better condition, as it regards clothing, than they are for bread. Few, very few, have clothing to protect them from the inclemencies of the approaching winter. . . . We feel we are making no exaggerated statement, when we say that the combined effects of want and exposure to cold in the enfeebled condition induced by insufficient food must prove fatal to many.[27]

By the time the drought broke, more than eight million pounds of food, seed, and clothing had been distributed to needy Kansans, as well as over $80,000.[28]

In a last spasm of political violence, in November 1860 in Linn County, Jennison orchestrated the hanging of Samuel Scott and Russell Hinds, two pro-slavery men. Hinds had been accused of returning an escaped slave to Missouri. Although not involved in the act, Montgomery approved of it: "He was a drunken border ruffian, worth a great deal to hang, but good for nothing else. He had caught a fugitive slave, and carried him back to Missouri for the sake of a reward. He was condemned by a jury of twelve men, the law being found in the 16th verse of Exodus, xxi. *And he that stealeth a man, and selleth him, or if he be found in his hand he shall surely be put to death.*" A few days later Jennison took a party of men to the home of L. D. Moore, another pro-slavery man, and shot and killed him. Federal troops sent into the area prevented further violence, although Jennison was not caught.[29]

On the Missouri side of the border, Jennison's latest actions—Montgomery being blamed as well—created great alarm, so much so that a militia, known as the Southwest Battalion, which consisted of four companies and an artillery battery, was raised by the state and sent into southwest Missouri to guard against a jayhawker invasion. No invasion was forthcoming, so, as noted by one of the militiamen, they spent their time "in the consumption of their rations and inordinate quantities of 'red-eye whisky'" and drilled just to keep from freezing. The owner of the local "doggery" sold whisky to the men, "and this filled the guard tent with prisoners. Then a sentry was placed in front of his doggery. Result, a drunken sentry and increased traffic." When the stock of red-eye gave out, the Missourians drank "200 bottles of Jayne's Expectorant and 100 of India Cholagogue, then went dry until the thaw!" Then they went home.[30]

CHAPTER 2

The Blast of War

On January 29, 1861, Kansas was admitted as the thirty-fourth state in the Union, with Charles Robinson as its first governor. Its white population was around 107,000, 11,000 of whom had been born in the territory in the previous six years. Of the immigrants, 55,000 came from the Northern states of Ohio, Indiana, Illinois, Pennsylvania, and Iowa; Missouri provided 11,356 and Kentucky 6,556. Kansas had a miniscule number of free blacks. Although slavery had been legal in the territory, few slaves had been brought in, and all had been removed before statehood came with its constitution outlawing slavery. The celebration of statehood was muted by events occurring elsewhere in the nation. South Carolina had voted to secede from the Union in December, and in January so too did Mississippi, Florida, Alabama, Georgia, and Louisiana, followed by Texas on February 1. At Charleston, South Carolina, the federal garrison at Fort Sumter was under siege.[1]

In the midst of this crisis, Lane wrote to the Lawrence *Republican*: "Should war actually ensue . . . the contest must on account of the weakness of the one and the overwhelming power of the other, be brief." He proposed that the Kansas legislature appoint a commission to confer with the Missouri legislature to preserve peace in the event of war. "We could become rich by selling our surplus produce to the bloody combatants," Lane wrote.[2]

As the possibility of war grew, a number of citizens in Missouri and Kansas were concerned about what might transpire between the former antagonists. Worry was particularly high among residents of southeast Kansas and southwest Missouri, where the last battles of "Bleeding Kansas" had been fought. In Bourbon County, Kansas, public meetings were held at which the citizens expressed a wish for peace with Missouri. Lane was invited to come to Fort Scott and make a peace speech. He spoke to a large crowd in March: "He advised the belligerent portion of the Kansas people to 'get a bag of meal under the bed, a ham in the cellar, and a dress for the baby,' before engaging in a war which would be certain to desolate and impoverish the whole country." A few days later he gave a similar speech in Barnesville, Kansas, to the citizens of Bourbon and Linn counties of Kansas, and Vernon County, Missouri.[3]

The first legislature of the new state of Kansas convened on March 26 in Topeka. Among its responsibilities was the election of Kansas's first two U.S. senators. Lane, nearly impoverished, was in town to actively campaign for one of the seats. In a contentious election Lane and Samuel C. Pomeroy were elected on April 4, following which both men hastened to Washington, although their terms would not start until the special session in July.[4]

Fort Sumter surrendered on April 14; the following day Lincoln called for 75,000 volunteer soldiers to put down the rebellion. In Virginia a convention to consider secession had yet to vote on the issue, but public enthusiasm over the victory at Fort Sumter, coupled with anger over Lincoln's call for volunteers, prompted a vote for an ordnance of secession on April 17, which was quickly followed by the seizure of the Harpers Ferry arsenal by Virginia militia.[5]

There were very few troops in Washington that April, and within the city there was fear of an attack from Virginia. Ad hoc volunteer companies were quickly formed from men on hand and distributed as guards throughout the city; among these were companies raised by Lane and former senator Cassius M. Clay. Lane's was called the "Frontier Guard"; Clay commanded the "Clay Guard."

Lane was not unknown to Lincoln. During Lincoln's presidential campaign, Mark Delahay had written to Lincoln from Kansas, soliciting funds to recruit Lincoln delegates for the upcoming convention in Chicago. Delahay wrote that he and Lane would give personal notes guaranteeing repayment of these funds, with interest. Lane appended a note to Lincoln: "I have never met you and yet I feel that you are an old acquaintance and I may add friend—In the movement now on foot under the lead of Col Delehay I cooperate." After Lincoln was elected, Lane wrote him, offering "1000 true Kansans armed & organized" to protect his inauguration. As the lead signatory on a letter from several Kansas men calling themselves the "Army of Freedom in Kansas," Lane suggested organizing "a corps of volunteers (say three regiments)" that could be "ready in active service in the field in thirty days" to aid Lincoln's administration "to the bitter end in maintaining the Union of these States."[6]

The Frontier Guard had seventy-eight members, half of whom were Kansans, many of them office seekers. Lane was its captain; his fellow senator-elect, Samuel Pomeroy, was but a private, as was Mark Delahay. On the evening of April 18, Major David Hunter instructed the Frontier Guard to take up a post in the East Room of the White House. One of the Frontier Guard recorded the following:

> We took up our quarters. The company were furnished with arms, ammunition, and equipments, and "put through" a short drill by Lieut. Stockton. One of the events of the evening was the presentation of a sword to Gen. James H. Lane, by Major Hunter. The affair occasioned immense applause by the company, and three rousing cheers were given for the recipient of the gift, and as many more for the generous donor. It was amusing to see most of the members of the company put on their cartridge boxes, belts, equipments, &c. Their efforts to don the "habiliments of war" betrayed their innocence of military affairs, and showed that their education on such subjects had been sadly neglected. A number of our corpulent comrades were obliged to splice their belts. I observed Hon. Thomas Ewing, Jr., looking at his belt,

probably discussing inwardly whether he would not have to hire some one to put it on for him. How he succeeded in equipping himself I cannot say, as Bailey fixed the Judge's accoutrements, with a view to test his military knowledge, and perhaps enjoy a joke at his expense.[7]

For several days the Frontier Guard remained in the East Room, even sleeping there. Then on April 24 Secretary of War Simon Cameron asked Lane and Clay to perform guard duty with their companies at the U.S. Navy Yard that night. The companies continued to guard the Navy Yard each succeeding night, as well as bridges over the Potomac. One night Lane sent Job Stockton with a detachment into Virginia to make a reconnaissance toward a rebel force that reportedly was planning to capture a drawbridge over the Potomac. No armed rebels were found, but the men did capture a rebel flag flying over a private home, which was then proudly put on display at Lane's headquarters at Willard's Hotel. Among the exploits of the Frontier Guard was to terrorize Arnold Harris, publisher of the *States*, a Washington newspaper described by Harris as "not surpassed in the vigor of its attack on the usurpations of Lincoln by any in the Confederate States." Harris wrote that publication of his newspaper was discontinued only "on account of the threats of Lane's Kansas company that the office should be mobbed, the press and types thrown in the canal, and the editors and supporters hung at the lamp-posts." The arrival of volunteer regiments obviated the need for the further service of the Frontier Guard, and the company was disbanded on May 3.[8]

The sight of a secession flag flying across the Potomac incensed Lane. He proclaimed to Carl Schurz on April 29, "We have got to whip these scoundrels like hell," adding that the North was "a-howling for blood, and they'll have it." Lane now adopted a less conciliatory tone toward Missouri than he had previously expressed. There were rumblings in that state that it too might secede. On April 20 armed secessionists seized muskets and cannons from the U.S. arsenal at Liberty, Missouri, and, according to one Kansan, "with the arms, under command of Jeff Thompson, established a camp at St. Joseph. Rebel ensigns floated defiantly at Independence, Kansas City, Platte City, Weston and Iatan, under which were rapidly being enlisted soldiers for the Rebellion, threatening communications and the safety of Kansas." Two weeks later another party of armed secessionists seized ordnance stores in Kansas City and took 148 weapons and 34,000 cartridges. In Topeka on May 10 Lane urged the occupation of the Missouri towns of Kansas City, Weston, St. Joseph, and Cameron if secession became a reality. Two days later at Lawrence he averred that any blockade of the Missouri River or the interruption of the Hannibal & St. Joseph Railroad would justify an armed invasion from Kansas.[9]

Claiborne Fox Jackson, Missouri's pro-Southern governor, had earlier called for a convention to consider secession but was disappointed when the convention overwhelmingly rejected the notion. Nonetheless, Jackson refused to honor Lincoln's call for troops. He did not give up his hope for secession and intentionally heightened tensions by calling out the state militia—known to be dominated by pro-slavery men—for a week of drill throughout the state. The encampment just outside St. Louis proved particularly galling by flying the Confederate flag. Captain Nathaniel Lyon, the Federal commander in St. Louis, rashly determined to capture the camp without waiting for the week of drill to end and the militiamen to go home.[10]

Lyon surrounded the camp with overwhelming numbers, forced its surrender on May 10, and marched his prisoners away. A large portion of Lyon's troops were German Americans of St. Louis, who were viewed as foreigners by many Missourians and whom Lyon had recruited against the wishes of Governor Jackson. Street fighting broke out between Lyon's men and civilians in town, with the result that twenty-eight civilians were killed and another seventy-five wounded. William Tecumseh Sherman, who as a civilian witnessed the events, sagely observed that "this incident will be used at Jefferson City to precipitate secession for it was a direct attack on State authority—[the Missouri State Guard] being in camp, by orders of the Governor."

This affair provoked the Missouri legislature into authorizing Jackson to mobilize the militia to repel any invasion, and thousands of outraged Missourians reported to the militia camps.[11]

Jackson met with Lyon on June 11, purportedly to discuss a peaceful resolution of the situation; his intent was probably only to buy time. Lyon, now a brigadier general, would hear nothing of any proposal to limit Federal authority. He ended the meeting by declaring, "Better, sir, far better, that the blood of every man, woman, and child within the limits of the State should flow, than that she should defy the federal government. This means war. In an hour one of my officers will call for you and conduct you out of my lines."[12]

Jackson retreated to the state capitol at Jefferson City and prepared for war. His only force was the poorly armed and poorly organized Missouri State Guard, although he was secretly asking the Confederate states for military assistance. Lyon played into Jackson's hands by initiating hostilities. On June 15 he landed his army at Jefferson City; the Missouri State Guard retreated to Boonville, where Lyon routed it two days later. Civil war had descended upon Missouri.[13]

In addition to hostile forces to the east, the western settlements of Kansas worried about raids by Plains Indians. An additional threat arose to the south, where Federal forts in the Indian Territory had been evacuated and occupied by Confederate troops. The Confederacy then began negotiating treaties of alliances with the so-called Five Civilized Tribes in the territory—the Cherokee, Choctaw, Chickasaw, Creek, and Seminole. Kansas was essentially devoid of federal troops; its defense would rely upon whatever volunteers and militia could be raised locally. Throughout Kansas, scores of military companies were being raised, both for home defense and for active service in response to Lincoln's call for volunteers. Although the Federal government had imposed no quota for troops on Kansas, Governor Robinson had obtained authority to raise three volunteer regiments. Not atypical was the experience of one company raised at Fort Scott. This unit, naming itself the Frontier Guard (different from Lane's volunteer unit by the same name) had Charles O. Judson as its drill master; Judson's qualification for this was having served three years at the Naval Academy at Annapolis. Judson was subsequently elected second lieutenant of the company and Charles W. Blair its captain. When Blair marched the company to Fort Leavenworth to be mustered in, Judson was one of the men who declined the opportunity for active service and remained behind to serve in the local militia. At the end of June he was elected second lieutenant of the Frontier Guard No. 2 company; William T. Campbell was its captain.[14]

Two of the regiments raised under Robinson's authority were the First Kansas Infantry, commanded by Colonel George W. Deitzler, and the Second Kansas Infantry, under Colonel Robert B. Mitchell. Robinson's choice of the man to raise a third regiment, James Montgomery, was a curious one, given a lack of any obvious affinity between the two men. From Mound City on May 8 Montgomery wrote to Bostonian George Luther Stearns: "I have organized a Regt. and hope soon to increase it to a Brigade. I have accepted a position on the Govs Staff, with the rank of Col. . . . We have an Artillery Company in our Fort, officered by men who served in the Mexican War." He asked Stearns to send him two small breech-loading guns in Lawrence, noting that although the guns were without carriages, these could be manufactured locally. Whatever allegiance Montgomery had toward Robinson was soon transferred to Lane.[15]

Despite the preparations for war, the people of southeast Kansas still hoped for peace in their neighborhood. Citizens at a mass meeting at Fort Scott on May 23 resolved: "We entertain the kindest feelings of friendship and regard for our neighbors bordering on the line in Vernon county, Missouri, and all other good and patriotic citizens of that state." A similar meeting in Vernon county agreed to appoint a committee to meet with the citizens of Kansas to cultivate peaceable relations.[16]

Such noble sentiments barely lived beyond their being uttered.

Three years earlier Montgomery's campaign of violence drove pro-slavery men out of southeast Kansas, many of whom sought refuge in the Missouri border counties. Now it was the turn of Union men in Missouri to be persecuted and driven from their homes. By the first week of June, ninety-eight families from Missouri and Texas had taken refuge in Fort Scott or fled through that town. A few weeks later a Fort Scott man noted that hundreds had sought refuge in the immediate vicinity, bringing reports of murders and other horrible outrages. A harbinger of this had been seen the previous October amidst the secession crisis: "Twelve families, numbering some sixty or seventy persons, arrived in [Mound City] on Wednesday last, directly from Texas, driven away by the terrible destruction of human life which is now being carried forward there by the proslavery demons. . . . The accounts which they give of the condition of Texas is deplorable—the slaughters which they recounted are terrible." Missouri secessionists might have shown more mercy had they contemplated the retribution that would be coming from Kansas.[17]

CHAPTER 3

A Fighting Brigade Is Born

In Washington, Lane lobbied for a military command. Lincoln advised Secretary of War Simon Cameron on June 20: "We need the services of such a man out there at once; that we better appoint him a brigadier general of volunteers to-day, and send him off with such authority to raise a force (I think two regiments better than three, but as to this I am not particular) as you think will get him into actual work quicker. Tell him when he starts to put it through not to be writing or telegraphing back here, but put it through." That same day Cameron wrote to Lane announcing the government would accept two regiments. Allowing Lane to raise regiments intruded upon the prerogative of Kansas governor Charles Robinson, as the normal practice was for governors to raise regiments and to commission the officers of those regiments. This would exacerbate the tension between Lane and Robinson, who were already political rivals.[1]

Lincoln's words suggested he was intending to cloak Lane with something more than mere authority to raise troops. There was no need for Lane to be a brigadier general unless he was to have a command. A month before Lincoln penned instructions to Cameron, Lane was publicly suggesting he had been given authority to raise troops and command them in an expedition to recapture Federal forts in Arkansas and the Indian Territory. It is probable that Lane had pitched this venture to Lincoln, and this may have been what Lincoln contemplated when authorizing Lane's appointment as a brigadier general. There was otherwise no pressing need for troops to be raised in Kansas. Although the Federal government had imposed no requisition upon the young state for troops, Governor Robinson had already organized two infantry regiments, which were then encamped at Kansas City. The military situation in Missouri seemed under control; Nathaniel Lyon had captured Jefferson City on June 15 and routed the Missouri State Guard at Boonville on June 17.[2]

Lincoln's words also revealed that he wanted a commander who would *act* and not spend his time calling for more reinforcements and explaining why he could not advance. In April 1862 Lincoln, exasperated by Major General George McClellan's failure to advance the huge Army of the Potomac, wrote McClellan and urged him to act. By June 1862 things were not much better. As noted by historian James McPherson, "McClellan was sending a steady stream of telegrams to Washington explaining why he was not quite ready to launch his own offensive: the roads were too wet; his artillery was not all up; it took time to reorganize the divisions crippled in the Seven Pines/Fair Oaks fighting." Lincoln's frustration at the inaction of the Army of the Potomac became such that he once referred to it as "General McClellan's body-guard." In Ulysses S. Grant, Lincoln would find the antithesis of McClellan. McPherson wrote: "When a prominent Pennsylvania Republican went to Lincoln and said that Grant was incompetent, a drunkard, and a political liability to the administration, the president heard him out and replied: '*I can't spare this man; he fights.*'" As long as Lane was in the field and not the telegraph office, he could expect little censure from Lincoln.[3]

Lane wasted no time in announcing his military appointment. The following appeared in several Kansas newspapers:

> LEAVENWORTH, June 25, '61.
> MR. EDITOR:—On the 20th inst., I was duly appointed a Brigadier General in the volunteer force of the U.S., and thereupon received the following order:

WAR DEPARTMENT, June 20, 1861.
GEN. JAMES H. LANE:
Dear Sir:—This department will accept two regiments for three years or during the war, in addition to the three regiments the Department has already accepted from the Governor of Kansas, to be raised and organized by you in Kansas. Orders will be given to muster the same into service immediately on being ready to be mustered; and on being mustered, the requisite arms, &c., will be furnished on the requisition of the mustering officer, who is hereby authorized to make the same.
By order of the President.
SIMON CAMERON, Secretary of War.

Lane accompanied this announcement with an entreaty to the "Fellow Citizens of Kansas and adjoining States and Territories," stating the president had authorized him to form a brigade of *five* regiments, and asked for volunteers. The missive was signed "JAMES H. LANE, Brig. Gen."[4]

This was the last time Lane signed himself as brigadier general. Although a commission had been extended to him, he had neglected to formally accept it. To do so would have cost him his seat in the Senate, for by law he could not be both senator and general officer. In his future dispatches Lane was careful not to hold himself out as an officer, instead signing his correspondence as "James H. Lane, Commanding." If others referred to him as general, he did not correct them; he had been a general in the Kansas militia, so as a matter of etiquette, being called general was at least socially appropriate.

When Lane returned to Washington for the opening of the special session of Congress on July 4, his right to his seat was challenged by Frederick P. Stanton. Stanton testified that when Robinson learned of Lane's appointment, Robinson concluded that the appointment vacated Lane's seat and appointed Stanton to replace Lane. Stanton did not immediately accept Robinson's appointment and instead made further inquiry to the secretary of war, who advised Stanton by telegraph on July 2 that Lane was appointed a brigadier general and had accepted. Upon receipt of this, Stanton accepted Robinson's appointment.[5]

Lane's defense was that although appointed to brigadier general, he had not accepted. In the Senate on July 12 he explained he had been presented a paper from the secretary of war indicating his intention to appoint him a brigadier general in the volunteer service. Lane had replied that he would consider accepting a commission from the government once his brigade was full and then only if the men of the brigade wanted him in command. He later produced a letter from the adjutant general's office dated July 26, which reminded him that although he had been appointed a brigadier general of volunteers, he had never signified his acceptance as was required. Lane's reply, dated July 28, was that he would respond at such time as the brigade was full and the men of it signified their desire to have him as their commander, and further requested that no brigadier be appointed to command the brigade until then. To this letter was appended the signatures of the Kansas congressional delegation, Samuel C. Pomeroy and Martin F. Conway, giving their concurrences.[6]

As to the announcement in the Kansas newspapers that he was a brigadier, Lane blamed this on William Weer, whom Lane had chosen to help raise troops and command one of the two regiments. Lane stated before the Senate Judiciary Committee that he had merely drawn up a rough draft of the announcement and gave it, unsigned, to Weer to take back to Kansas for publication. He claimed that Weer, on his own initiative, added the language that Lane was a brigadier; Weer later gave a statement confirming this. Lane requested more time to present evidence in his behalf, the Judiciary Committee asked Lincoln to provide documents relative to the dispute, and the matter was carried over to the next session, which would convene in December.[7]

Northern newspapers, especially Horace Greeley's *New York Tribune*, and any number of congressmen, had been crying for the Union army to advance and prevent the Confederate Congress from meeting in Richmond on July 20. The Army of the Potomac finally moved and met the Confederate army at Manassas, Virginia, on July 21. A number of Washingtonians came out to watch what became known in the north as the Battle of Bull Run; among them were Lane and two companions, Senators Benjamin F. Wade and Henry Wilson. An artillery captain advised the three men not to go any closer to the front, but Lane announced he wanted a hand in the fighting. Being reminded he was unarmed did not dissuade him. "I can easily find a musket on the field," Lane replied. "I have been there before and know that guns are easily found where fighting is going on." With that, the senators headed off in the direction of the firing. Later that day, during the rout of the Union army, the artillery captain spotted Lane again: "Lane was the first to pass me; he was mounted barebacked on an old flea-bitten gray horse. . . . Across the harness lay his coat, and on it was a musket which, sure enough, he had found. . . . He was long, slender and hay-seed looking. His long legs kept kicking far back to the rear to urge his old beast to greater speed, and so he sped on."[8]

In the Senate four days later, Lane voted in favor of the Crittenden-Johnson Resolution, which declared that the war was not being waged to interfere with the rights or institutions of those states in rebellion, but only to preserve the Union. Yet when a bill was proposed stating that the army or navy would not be used in "abolishing or interfering with African slavery in any of the States," Lane proposed adding the language, "unless a military necessity shall exist for enforcing the laws or maintaining the Constitution of the Union." This amendment was voted down by a vote of 24 to 11.[9]

When Lane spoke on the floor of the Senate, he gave a clear indication of how troops under his command would operate: "I disavow any intent upon the part of the government or its Army to war against the institution of slavery. I said that the effect of marching an army on the soil of any slave State will be to instill into the slaves a determined purpose to free themselves. . . . There will be a colored army marching out of the slave States while the army of freedom was marching in. . . . I do not propose to make myself a slave catcher for traitors and return them to their masters.[10]

This speech was nothing less than a thinly veiled declaration of Lane's intent to take the slave property of Southern civilians. As a war measure, to weaken the Southern economy, it was arguably defensible. But Lane did not content himself with speaking only in the cold mathematics of the South minus its slaves equaled a defeated South. His inflammatory—and wildly exaggerated—rhetoric on the Senate floor justified retribution upon Missouri: "It was [the slave oligarchy of Missouri's] daily practice to murder unarmed, helpless prisoners, and to tear from rocking heads the scalps of their yet living victims. It was their common practice to take free-State men who were from slave States, tie them to trees, and demanding of them to recant their free-State principles, to cut off finger by finger, until the hands were fingerless, and tie them to stakes and riddle them to death with bullets."[11]

There is little evidence such remarks in Washington were widely reprinted on the Kansas-Missouri border, but they would be sure to strike fear into the heart of any rebel Missourian who contemplated Lane commanding troops there. However, Missouri secessionists didn't need any prompting to fear Lane. Lane's actions during the territorial days had already made him a minor legend. Lane, and the Free State men under his command, had been accused of theft, murder, and destruction. His name became a terror to pro-slavery men. "When it was reported that [Lane] was actually approaching a proslavery town," wrote the secretary of Kansas territorial governor John Geary, "a general panic and stampede was the result." But not all of the criticism came from Southerners. The New Haven, Connecticut, *Register* described Lane's appointment as "a burning disgrace" and that Lane and Montgomery were "two as deep-dyed scoundrels as ever went unhung. The murders and robberies committed by these fellows during the troubles in Kansas are known to the whole country."[12]

Of no less concern to secessionists was word that James Montgomery was to have a command. For his actions in the Kansas Territory, he had already achieved notoriety for murder, robbery, and abolitionist fanaticism that spread beyond Kansas and Missouri. Now rumor had him raiding as far south as Fort Ouachita on the Texas border.[13]

In Kansas, Weer established recruiting stations at Leavenworth and Lawrence, and his efforts resulted in the formation of the

Fourth Kansas Volunteers, of which he became its colonel. Weer, an attorney from Wyandotte, had served as territorial attorney general from March 13, 1857, to June 5, 1858. The Fourth was raised primarily from men living north of or along the Kansas River. Montgomery, who held a commission from Robinson, set up headquarters in Mound City, where he began organizing what would become the Third Kansas Volunteers, which he would command. The Third was consisted mostly of men from southeast Kansas and refugees from Missouri.[14]

The Fifth regiment was organized independent of Lane's recruiting efforts. Its genesis lay in the raising of an independent company of cavalry by Hamilton P. "Hamp" Johnson of Leavenworth. Born in Ohio, Johnson had moved to Kentucky where he taught school, became a Methodist preacher, and practiced law. He raised a company for service in the Mexican War and marched with it to Vera Cruz. Returning to Kentucky, he married a woman who owned slaves; he brought the slaves with him when he moved to Kansas, where he joined the Free State Party. What happened to the slaves is unknown. Johnson wrote to Lincoln in February 1860, extending his support to Lincoln's campaign. Specifically, he offered to have his friends in Ohio and Pennsylvania "express their preferences through the medium of their local news papers." It is unknown whether Lincoln responded. In a July 1861 newspaper advertisement, Johnson held himself out as lieutenant colonel of the Third and that he had mustered in one company of mounted men and part of another. In the advertisement, Johnson solicited men to join his command at Camp Lane in Leavenworth. Johnson continued recruiting in an effort to raise an entire regiment, making swings through Kansas, southern Iowa, and northern Missouri. By August 10 he had assembled ten companies.[15]

Men who longed for lesser commands recruited companies and tendered their services to the government. The process was relatively simple. A prominent member of the community would organize a body of infantry or cavalry; when the requisite number of recruits was met, an election was held for company officers. If the captain-to-be was popular, he was elected, following which the governor issued a commission for the office. This method could result in the bravest, most competent man being made captain, or the command could fall to one who seemed least likely to be a disciplinarian. In some instances men singly or in groups simply reported to a camp to join companies in the process of forming. A number of companies were not even recruited in Kansas; William R. Allen's company of the Third was recruited in Ohio and Iowa, and William Rose's company of the Fourth came from Illinois. The Fifth had Elijah E. Harvey's Iowa recruits, and Greenville Watson and Garrett Gibson brought men from Iowa and northern Missouri. John R. Clark's company of the Fifth included many Missourians, and Samuel C. Thompson's company of the Fifth, mustered into service in November, was raised in Iowa.

Noteworthy parallels are found in Clark and Gibson, as well as their companies. Both commanders had served during the Mexican War in separate companies of the Indian Battalion, Missouri Mounted Volunteers, which was part of General Sterling Price's division that fought Indians in the New Mexico Territory. Both men had lived in Mercer County, Missouri, with Gibson moving to southern Iowa in 1860. Gibson's company included men mainly from Mercer County and southern Iowa; Clark's was recruited in Mercer County and its vicinity. Clark's company had initially been raised in Mercer County for service in the Eighteenth Missouri Infantry, but Colonel Hamilton P. Johnson persuaded them to join his Kansas regiment instead.[16]

Why men in these companies did not serve in their home states is unclear. Some may have faced the situation confronting that of a company of Illinois men: their state's quota was met, no more troops were accepted, so they left for Kansas to serve in Jennison's regiment as Company D. Some participated in abolitionist crusades. William R. Allen of Jefferson, Ohio, was an acquaintance of John Brown, Jr. William H. H. Dickinson, of Salem, Ohio, was a private in Allen's company. He was an abolitionist and before the war had joined a secret anti-slavery society known as the Liberty League. Twelve other Salem men joined Allen's company. Salem had a reputation as an abolitionist town. The *Anti-Slavery Bugle* was printed there, an annual Anti-Slavery Fair raised money for the abolitionist cause, and townspeople were active in helping slaves escape. A few months later eight like-minded men from Iowa came west to join Allen's company, but taking a liking to Captain John Foreman, joined his company instead. Among them was Thaddeus Maxson. In the winter of 1857–58, nine followers of John Brown lived at the Springdale, Iowa, home of Maxson's father, where they drilled in military tactics in order to return to Kansas and endeavor to make Kansas a free state.[17]

During this time another force was organized under Federal authority in southeastern Kansas, namely, home guard companies. The July 5 skirmish between Price's Missouri State Guard and Brigadier General Franz Sigel's Federals at Carthage, Missouri, brought home to the citizens of Fort Scott how close the war was. Several representatives from Fort Scott traveled to meet Lyon on his march to Springfield and ask for authority to raise a home defense force; Lyon gave permission for Wyllis C. Ransom to raise three companies of home guards. Three infantry companies were quickly formed, with Ransom, William T. Campbell, and Zacheus Gower as captains, and William R. Judson as major of the battalion. The companies were not mustered into U.S. service until early August. At the same time Captain William E. Prince at Fort Leavenworth ordered that one hundred muskets be forwarded from that post, and Montgomery was directed to supply the balance necessary to equip the remainder of the battalion. These companies formed the nucleus of what would later become the Sixth Kansas Cavalry. Although this unit had no official connection with Lane, it would at least follow his orders.[18]

Also operating out of Mound City was the independent command of Jennison. He was captain of a company he called the "Southern Kansas Jay-Hawkers," which he had organized without state or federal authority. In early July, Captain Prince rebuffed Jennison's offer to muster his company into U.S. service, suggesting he try one of Lane's two regiments instead. Instead of submitting to Lane, Jennison operated as he saw fit, and he saw fit to raid Missouri. No authorities worried too much about Jennison's lack of a legal organization as long as he seemed to be furthering the war effort. The authorities had more to worry about than one renegade band of Unionists, and they lacked the manpower to otherwise police the Kansas-Missouri border. Montgomery, Jennison, and the Fort Scott home guards were the only military force in southeast Kansas.[19]

Montgomery on June 21 wrote to George Luther Stearns in Boston:

> An invasion of Southern Kansas is threatened from South West Missouri, and Western Arkansas, and besides this, they are endeavoring to arm and enlist the Indians against us. They have been driving the Union men out of Missouri, but they have changed the programme now, and refuse to allow any more Union men to leave on the contrary, they compel them to swear allegiance to the State of Missouri, and draft them into the rebel army. In this state of things the Union men have called on me to aid them; and I have promised to do so. I am going down with an active force to join them, and in so doing, I hope to keep them [the rebels] from our doors, by giving them something to do at home.[20]

Montgomery marched into Missouri on June 27 to organize a regiment of loyal Missouri and Kansas men and then to tender this regiment's service to the United States for the duration of the war. He started from Mound City with 180 infantry and cavalry and proceeded to Ball's Mill. There he attacked and routed an enemy company; his casualties were one man wounded and one horse killed; one prisoner was taken. The rebels had no time to mount their horses and fled into the brush. Montgomery's men without horses appropriated the abandoned mounts. Leonard J. Swingley from Mansfield in Linn County, and who was not present for the skirmish, wrote that he had been informed Montgomery's men then "commenced stealing. They made the lady of the house get them something to eat. . . . After they was through eating they broke the [marble-top] table all to pieces stole every thing that was of any account." The following day a detachment of Montgomery's men, acting in concert with Missouri Unionists, attacked rebels on Walnut Creek in Bates County. Several secesh were reported killed, and two more were reported killed in another skirmish before the men returned to

Mound City. Swingley noted that Montgomery came back with fifty horses and that sometime between then and July 7 fourteen Kansas men crossed the border, killed three Missourians, and took their horses and property. Sometime between July 5 and July 10 Montgomery made another march into Missouri and "offered battle" to the enemy in his "fortified camp." But, as an anonymous trooper noted, the enemy had "evacuated," and Montgomery's men "burned his works." This story may be the same one reported in another source, in which Montgomery took two hundred men into Missouri and skirmished with the secesh, having one of his men wounded but making off with twenty horses. After retreating back into Kansas, Montgomery recrossed the border, this time raiding into Cedar County.[21]

One deficiency throughout the brigade's campaign was that the men inadequately characterized the enemy they encountered. In this they cannot be entirely faulted, for it was not always clear who was shooting back, especially as few of the enemy wore uniforms. The rebels they met included units of the Missouri State Guard, recruits being assembled for the Missouri State Guard, local militia, and ad hoc armed bands of dubious legality; at no time did the brigade come up against regular Confederate troops.

One of Montgomery's captains was Eli Snyder of Osawatomie, who had raised an infantry company. Before the war Snyder had been an ally of John Brown. Two months after the Marais des Cygnes massacre, Snyder led a party into Missouri and captured a man who allegedly had been with Charles Hamilton. The lucky man was not killed on the spot and escaped after being imprisoned in Kansas. Snyder returned to Missouri in December 1858 in the company of Jennison, again in pursuit of one of Hamilton's men. That man was not found, but his home and store were burned. For his actions Snyder was ordered placed under arrest by the Federal judge at Fort Scott, but he was never apprehended.[22]

In late March 1861 Snyder sought the arrest of a young man named William Clarke Quantrill who had become an annoyance on the border with his criminal ways. Quantrill had come to Kansas from Ohio. He briefly taught school in Lykins County but abandoned this to take up petty crime. Snyder and a dozen of his men were deputized to assist in the arrest. Quantrill was surrounded in a cabin where he was staying and taken without incident. On the return trip Snyder tried to goad the disarmed Quantrill into a fight but was unsuccessful. He then tried to shoot Quantrill, but this too failed when someone knocked Snyder's gun aside and the shot went wide. The appearance of seventeen heavily armed border ruffians from Paola helped convince the local probate judge to rule in favor of Quantrill's habeas corpus petition, and he was released.[23]

Snyder enlisted forty men into a militia company on April 1, 1861; he and his lieutenants received their commissions from Governor Robinson on April 6. Snyder didn't limit the operations of his militia company to Kansas. The first week of July he took his command into Bates County to assist Union men there. The town of West Point was captured along with one "contraband." Snyder's independent actions were curtailed when the state called his company into active duty on May 7. The company served in Linn and Miami counties. It was mustered into U.S. service July 24.[24]

The flight of loyal men—and families—from Missouri continued. Jennison determined to restore the balance of power as best he could. He left Mound City on July 4 with only thirteen men. By the time he crossed into Missouri the following evening, his command had grown to forty-five men, apparently mostly Missouri refugees. The men held an election and chose Isaac Morris, a Missourian from Vernon County, as captain. The next day "Captain" Benjamin Rice arrived with 150 Kansas and Missouri men. Jennison sent Morris and Rice on a scout down Drywood Creek for a few days, during which some secesh were chased; there were no casualties on either side, but horses, provisions, and an ox train were captured. By July 12 Jennison and Rice were back in Mound City; it is unclear whether the Missouri refugees remained behind to reclaim their homes.[25]

Prince sent a strong letter to Jennison regarding the capture of the ox train, which Prince stated was traveling under a safeguard from Major Samuel Sturgis of the regular army. He ordered Jennison to return the train to a Mr. Meyers, its owner, who was being accompanied by an officer for this purpose. He suggested that perhaps Jennison's men were not aware of the criminality of their actions, which Prince likened to pirateering. Prince also expressed his "deepest mortification" that the personal baggage of Captain William Steele, formerly of the U.S. Army, and "my *personal* and *warm friend*" had been molested. As Steele had resigned his commission to join the Confederate army, Prince's claim to warm friendship was unlikely to endear him to the men of Kansas.[26]

At Fort Leavenworth, James Williams's cavalry company was mustered in on July 12 and ordered to overtake and escort a wagon train en route to Fort Scott. Among other items, the wagons contained full rations for twenty-five hundred men for thirty days. On July 17 Prince countermanded this, ordering Williams to instead take the train to Camp Union at Kansas City.[27]

In Missouri, Major Robert T. Van Horn of the U.S. Reserve Corps in Kansas City had taken two companies to the relief of Major Abner H. Deane of the Cass County Home Guards, who was in trouble at Austin. Near Harrisonville on July 18, Van Horn found himself facing superior numbers and nearly surrounded; he sent messengers to Deane and to Fort Leavenworth, asking for reinforcements. Jennison learned of Van Horn's plight and on his own initiative rode out from Mound City. Weer also responded, taking the cavalry companies of Williams and John Ritchie, then at Kansas City, departing on July 20. However, Van Horn had evacuated his position in the midst of a heavy storm around 2:00 A.M. on July 19 and retreated to Camp Prince. Williams reached Van Horn the evening of July 22; Jennison arrived about the same time, and Weer took command of the entire force. Along his way Jennison had captured Morristown on July 22; while there Marshal Cleveland of Jennison's command shot a Mr. White, who had murdered one of John Brown's sons in 1856. Once in Van Horn's camp, Jennison distributed the proceeds of his foraging. According to one of Williams's men, "Capt. Jennison brought in about $2,000 worth of goods which was distributed through the camp. . . . This paper that I am now writing upon was presented to me by Capt. Jennison and came from Morristown. I also got two hats, a necktie, drawers, a bridle bit, soap, paper, pencils, blank books and, being company hospital steward, a supply of drugs and medicines, all contraband."[28]

Williams's company left Van Horn's camp on July 23, marching for Harrisonville. Jennison was headed there as well, but it is unclear if he was cooperating with Williams. The following day eight of Williams's men were sent ahead as scouts, and about eight miles from Crescent Hill they encountered a party of thirty horsemen who they assumed were Jennison's men. The scouts approached the larger party, then hesitated, now unsure of whom they were meeting. Sergeant William H. Hill moved forward, but when within ten yards of the strangers he was shot from the saddle; the scouts returned the fire. When First Corporal Robert Coleman dismounted to fire, his horse broke away from him. Contemporary accounts report he was shot and killed when the rest of the scouts broke and ran, or in the alternative he was taken prisoner and killed. Neither was true. While Coleman *may* have been separated from his comrades, he survived and would continue serving with his company. Hill's was the first battle death in the brigade.[29]

Williams's company reached Crescent Hill and while there had another skirmish with rebel irregulars. Williams sent out thirty men to attack a smaller party four or five miles south of town. The rebels were chased some eight miles to their camp, where another two hundred secesh were found. Outnumbered, Williams made a slow retreat to a ridge a mile away, where he prepared to make a stand, but his men urged him to avoid such a lopsided battle. The retreat continued until reinforcements were met, at which time Williams turned and went after the rebels, the effort coming to naught as the enemy had already withdrawn.[30]

Williams continued on to Harrisonville. Three miles outside of town he encountered a party of three hundred men and, together with Jennison's company, boldly charged them. The supposed secessionists fled into the woods, and no shots were fired. When the party reached the ground formerly occupied by the rebels, Harrisonville was within view; however, there was no indication of any alarm within the town. Harrisonville was situated in a small valley bordered on the north, south, and west by timber. Williams's men advanced through the timber to reach open ground on the east side of town. Apparently in no great hurry, they dismounted at a farmhouse and procured all the milk they could drink, as well as bread and cheese. "After refreshments the bugle sounded the assembly and the men fell 'into two rows, like the regulars' with unusual alacrity." Leaving guards behind, Williams with thirty men and Jennison with fourteen marched through a cornfield and along a stone wall until spying some two hundred mounted men drawn up in line. One of Williams's men wrote: "Our men with one accord rose and gave them the contents of their Sharp's [rifles,] and then came the fun. Such a stampede was never witnessed before! We think from their actions that they enjoyed it too, for they would throw up their arms and scream and yell, and those on the ground would draw up their legs and then straighten them out with a jerk."[31]

The secesh tried to reform but were scattered by another attack. Again assuming casual airs, the jayhawkers formed into squads and marched back to camp, singing "Happy Land of Canaan." Along the way they spotted three men sitting on a fence a half mile away. Believing they were secesh, and without further provocation, the rear squad was faced about and ordered to fire; their targets "immediately jumped from the fence—*backwards, and head first.*" One correspondent reported the skirmishes had resulted in twenty-three enemies killed or wounded, but a careful inquiry by another soldier the next day discovered the actual enemy losses were seven killed and three wounded. Upon arriving at camp, the men discovered that Weer and the rest of the force had arrived.[32]

Instead of taking immediate possession of Harrisonville, the force camped overnight. Weer issued orders for Van Horn to command the force entering Harrisonville; the force was to consist of Van Horn's men, forty of Williams's, and thirty-five of Ritchie's. Ritchie's men were to proceed on foot as the advance guard, and Williams's the rear guard. Weer also ordered the town's printing press would be used to print three hundred copies of a proclamation Weer had prepared. On July 26 the troops entered Harrisonville, Jennison now taking the lead, followed by Williams, Ritchie, and

Companies A and B of Van Horn's battalion.³³ The next morning the jayhawkers marched into town and were greeted by the few patriotic men and women who still remained. The companies were formed into a square around the courthouse, then the Stars and Stripes were hoisted amid cheers. According to a trooper of the Third: "Then Capt. W. very kindly gave his men permission to break ranks and go into the shade. . . . The Jay Hawkers had a rich harvest in Harrisonville that day.³⁴

The rich harvest was interrupted by the call of the bugle to rally. The commanding officer in Kansas City, fearing an attack there, had sent a messenger recalling Williams's and Ritchie's companies. They returned to Kansas City July 27, where they were honored with a ceremonial thirteen-gun salute, cheers, and waving of flags.³⁵ Captain Prince, acting a little too late, on July 24 telegraphed the commanding officer at Kansas City to order Weer to disperse the rebels at Harrisonville and return to Kansas City. The jayhawkers' triumphant return on July 27 alerted him that the deed was done, so he issued new orders to Weer, instructing him to have the commands of Williams, Ritchie, and Deane escort a wagon train to Fort Scott.³⁶

Weer did not dispatch the companies listed by Prince but instead sent five companies of the Fourth as escorts. Two companies, those under Josiah E. Hayes and Matthew Quigg, halted at the crossing of the Military Road on the Little Osage River about twelve miles north of Fort Scott and began erecting fortifications. This became what Lane christened Fort Lincoln. The other three companies encamped about a mile south. (As can be seen in a watercolor drawn by a Wisconsin soldier in March 1862, Fort Lincoln consisted of earthen breastworks enclosing a two-story building and a stable. It was later abandoned, then resurrected temporarily to house rebel prisoners.)³⁷ This march was followed by a huge wagon train from Kansas City formed to take supplies to Lyon near Springfield. It was escorted to Fort Scott by Ritchie's and Williams's companies, under the personal command of Weer.³⁸

As these movements took place, the slow work of filling up the regiments continued in Kansas. In Mound City, John Foreman's infantry company practiced at parade and drill but without weapons or uniforms. No uniforms would be issued for some time, so the men wore civilian garb. Recruiting was slowed because many men delayed enlisting in order to harvest crops already planted; in other instances the men were enlisted but then given a furlough to go home and attend to their crops. The boys who remained in camp at Mound City were "bored by all the annoyances of camp life. Drilling, eating, talking, loafing, &c., in fact almost anything to waste time" was occasionally accompanied by the martial music of a fife and drum. Neither whisky nor lager was to be found in town, which some men found to be a curse, while others considered it a blessing. All, however, appeared "eager for a fray, and exceedingly anxious to 'wipe out' somebody" and to be "let loose" upon the "red eyed rebels." All manner of rumors were flying about of threats of raids by Missourians. One recruit worried about the defenseless condition of southeast Kansas and that there were not enough weapons at Mound City to arm three hundred men. "Fill up your companies and come on," he urged Kansas men in a letter to a Leavenworth newspaper His description of "a 'right smart sprinkling' of pretty girls" in town was an encouragement to do so. Another soldier noted that many of the young ladies were "actually putting on city airs, and coquettishly attracting the attention of the young officers and soldiers connected with the regiment."[39]

By July 17 seven companies of the Third were at Mound City. Among these were the companies of Captains John Foreman, John E. Stewart, Henry C. Seaman, Eli Snyder, James M. Williams, and Charles P. Twiss. Within a few days Stewart and Seaman's cavalry departed for Leavenworth to escort a wagon train from there. Thomas Bickerton recruited men for an artillery battery despite possessing no cannon. In 1855 Lane had asked Bickerton to form an artillery company, although Bickerton had absolutely no military experience. Bickerton took charge of a cannon and drilled his men in its use, but he had no opportunity to use it; the cannon was subsequently surrendered to territorial authorities. As a foot soldier Bickerton later participated in the 1856 assault on pro-slavery forces at Franklin, where a six-pound cannon was captured. At the ensuing assault on and capture of Fort Titus, Bickerton would have his only experience with the firing of a cannon.[40]

William R. Allen's company of Ohioans did not reach Mound City until the end of July. Joseph K. Hudson of this company wrote a letter to his father, instructing that if he were killed to give all his property to his beloved, Miss Mary Smith. (Hudson would marry Miss Smith at Wyandotte, Kansas, on April 5, 1863, and survive the war, rising to the rank of major in the Sixty-second United States Colored Troops.) From Allen's store at Jefferson, Ohio, John Brown, Jr., son of the martyred John Brown, penned a letter July 9 to George Luther Stearns, asking whether, if Brown joined Montgomery's regiment, could he expect any financial assistance for his family; Stearns's response is unknown. Brown's wife, ironically named "Wealthy," wrote a few days thereafter to Stearns, reporting that her husband had gone off to war, and she had no funds available for support other than to draw upon money in Stearns's possession; she then requested he forward her a draft for $50. Brown was spied in Mound City on July 29 as the first lieutenant of Allen's company. However, Brown was not mustered in with the company the following day; Barclay Coppoc took his place as first lieutenant. Brown returned to Ohio to raise a company for the Third, but the company he raised, and one he would command, went into the regiment Jennison would raise.[41]

Among the more interesting members of the Third was Casimir Zulavsky. He had traveled from Boston on the assumption he would be commissioned an officer in Stewart's company. He arrived at Leavenworth on July 21 and traveled to Mound City where he met with Stewart. Stewart informed him he was under the impression Zulavsky was not coming and had made other arrangements for officers. Zulavsky went to Montgomery and offered to enlist as a private; Montgomery made him regimental adjutant instead. Zulavsky wrote he was glad he had not ended up in Stewart's company, as most of its members were horse thieves who took the livestock of Union men because there was nothing left to take from rebels: "Their being in Missouri is reason sufficient for their taking their horses." Zulavsky was curiously described as a "Polish refugee." Actually he was a Hungarian refugee and a nephew of the revolutionary Lajos Kossuth. Kossuth and the four Zulavsky brothers had fought in the unsuccessful revolt of 1848–49.[42]

John E. Stewart was one of the Kansas men who had taken up arms in defense of the Free State cause. A pioneer woman commented after meeting him in 1856, "Mr. Stewart I have since learned is a New England Minister—but I gathered from his conversation that he thinks that here in *the Territory* 'moral suasion' will be a little better for having something like a Sharpe's rifle to stand on." Shortly after this was written, Stewart was with the Free State men who used "moral suasion"—and rifles and cannon—to attack and rout a pro-slave party at Middle Creek and capture pro-slavery posts at Franklin and Fort Titus in September 1856. Also known as the "Fighting Preacher," Stewart was later an officer charged with enforcing the orders of the Free State squatter's court. While pursuing a fugitive from this court, he was apprehended by the U.S. marshal and imprisoned at Fort Scott for ten days. Stewart raised cattle on his farm in Douglas County, using this cover during forays into Missouri to liberate slaves. One of his tactics was to drive his wagon into Missouri under the pretext of buying goods, and while there he would engage slaves in conversation. If he found one who wanted freedom, he arranged to meet the slave at some secret point and then hide the escapee in the bed of the wagon. Writing to Thaddeus Hyatt in December 1859, Stewart reported that since September he had "brought away from Mo fourteen [slaves], including one unbroken family." That night he would be heading to a place of safety for two of his "black brethren" that he had delivered "from the land of bondage." Stewart's abolitionist activities extended to being one of ten men who in 1859 freed from the St. Joseph, Missouri, jail a Kansas man who had been convicted of spiriting slaves out of Missouri. Among the ten rescuers was Joseph Gardener, who would serve as a private in Allen's company.[43]

Stewart also went by the alias of "Levi Plum," and it was probably under this name that he followed another cause of his, that of horse and cattle stealing. On one occasion while being sought by a posse near Lawrence, he used hair dye to mask the appearance of a stolen horse. Stewart developed a wary relationship with the young ne'er-do-well William Clarke Quantrill, who hung around the neighborhood looking to make a quick buck. Quantrill delivered stolen

Missouri livestock to Stewart's fortified home, from where the animals were sold or sent elsewhere in Kansas—Stewart no doubt receiving some share. Unable to lure Stewart into Missouri where there was a reward for him, Quantrill helped arrange an assault on Stewart's "fort" to recapture escaped slaves held there. The assault failed. Stewart, unaware of Quantrill's complicity, asked him and another man to assassinate Allen Pinks, a free black man who had taken to helping slave catchers. The two men botched the job and Pinks escaped.[44]

The War Department on July 10 had ordered the mustering into U.S. service of the understrength "skeleton" companies of the brigade, the intention being that additional recruits would bring them up to full strength. By the end of the month, the Third was an organized, albeit understrength, regiment. Five companies of infantry were mustered in under Captains Foreman, John F. Broadhead, Snyder, Twiss, and Allen, along with three cavalry companies under Captains Williams, Seaman, and Stewart, plus Bickerton's cannonless battery. Williams's company had been mustered into U.S. service July 12; the others on July 24 and 25. Allen's was mustered July 30, and Samuel Stephenson's late-arriving infantry company would be mustered in August 2. On August 3 Prince dispatched an officer to muster in three companies for Weer's regiment at Quincy, Illinois, and five companies for Johnson's regiment at Chillicothe, Missouri.[45]

When finally organized, the Third, Fourth, and Fifth regiments reflected the haphazard nature of their recruitment. The Fourth contained seven companies of infantry, one of cavalry, and Thomas Moonlight's artillery battery. The Fifth, a cavalry regiment, initially possessed two infantry companies.

Similarly, the weapons issued to the three regiments were an odd lot. Records regarding this are limited, so the matter is subject to considerable speculation. Chaplain Hugh Fisher wrote that following a rebel incursion near Fort Scott on September 1, he broke open cases of Springfield rifles and handed them out to civilians. One assumes civilians were so armed only had Lane's infantry been fully equipped; Prince believed that Montgomery was so flush with long arms that Montgomery could fulfill the Fort Scott home guards' need for muskets. In early 1862 James Harvey's infantry company of the Fourth possessed fifty .58 caliber rifles and eight .69 caliber Prussian rifles. Letters from men in Ritchie's and Williams's cavalry companies told they were equipped with Sharps carbines or rifles. As it is unlikely the Federal government would have issued such prized weapons to western volunteers, the men must have equipped themselves with the Sharps. A likely source of such weapons were the shipments of Sharps rifles sent by New England supporters to Free State men during the territorial struggle. At the beginning of September the cavalry companies of the Fifth were armed only with revolvers, except for Ritchie's company. Later that month the arsenal at Fort Leavenworth issued to the Fifth 189 .69 caliber smoothbore muskets, 100 .58 caliber rifles, 361 .36 caliber Colt Navy revolvers, and 244 sabers and swords. The arsenal also issued 20,000 rounds of .54 caliber rifle ammunition to the Third. As late as March 1862 it was noted that the Fifth and Sixth had old smoothbore muskets, most of them pistols (their private property) but no swords. David P. Bond of the Fifth noted in May 1862 that he possessed a Sharps, but some in his company were without rifles and had instead drawn sabers, or "cheese knives," as the men called them.[46]

The number of men in the brigade waxed and waned. Recruiting brought in more men, while disease, accidents, casualties, and desertion accounted for the loss of others. The greatest loss of men was from disease. To give some idea of the strength of the brigade, the "Tri-monthly Report of Kansas Volunteers for the 10th day of January, 1862" gave the following regimental strengths: Third, 42 officers and 702 enlisted men; Fourth, 33 officers and 516 enlisted men; Fifth, 31 officers and 729 enlisted men; and the Sixth, 36 officers and 681 enlisted men. Effective strength would be less, as the rolls included men unfit for duty.[47]

In an election for regimental officers of the Third, held July 24, Montgomery was the unanimous choice for colonel; James Gilpatrick Blunt was elected lieutenant colonel.[48] Blunt, who had since been promoted, was described by a man writing from Fort Scott in late 1862:

Gen. Blunt is now about forty-five years of age. He is about five feet eight or nine inches in height, and possesses a remarkably stalwart frame. Broad-shouldered, deep-chested sturdy-limbed, his physique is that of an athlete. His head is large, with enormous perceptives, and deep-set eyes of hazel gray, overhung by pent-house brows. He reminds one of a mastiff, sturdy, wide-awake, surly when occasion seems to require, quick to bite, not over ready to bark, eager to fight when quarrels present themselves, and with a thorough pertinacity and stick-to-it when aroused. Gen. Blunt has a bushy head of dark brown hair, and a thick, full beard of the same color.[49]

Around age fourteen Blunt had left the family farm in Maine to serve on a ship. How long or how often he was at sea is questionable, as the evidence also indicates that in his teenage years he studied at the Ellsworth Military Academy in Ellsworth, Maine. He emigrated to Ohio in 1845, where he studied medicine at Sterling Medical College in Columbus, graduating in 1849. One of his instructors was his uncle, Rufus Gilpatrick. The year following his graduation, Blunt married fourteen-year-old Nancy G. Putnam; Rufus Gilpatrick had married Nancy's sister Elizabeth. Gilpatrick became Lane's brigade surgeon; he was killed by Confederate troops April 25, 1863, while tending to a wounded rebel soldier. Blunt practiced medicine in Ohio until, again following in Uncle Rufus's footsteps, he moved to Anderson County, Kansas, in 1856; Rufus had moved there the previous year, quickly allying himself with the Free State faction. After moving to Kansas. Blunt became one of the founders of the town of Mount Gilead in 1857. Then, during the troubles in southeast Kansas in December 1857, he led an armed party of fifteen men to defend the squatters' court at "Fort Bayne." The pro-slavery posse that subsequently arrived was chased off after a brief skirmish; it is not known if Blunt participated in this. He served on Lane's militia staff when Lane sent troops to southeastern Kansas in 1858. After John Brown made his December 1858 raid into Missouri, Blunt and Rufus Gilpatrick hid the freed slaves for a week.[50]

Four days after the election for regimental officers was held, the companies of Seaman and Stewart escorted into Mound City a train of eight or ten wagons from Fort Leavenworth. Any objections the officers of these companies had to missing the election were not made public.[51]

CHAPTER 4

"We Could Play Hell with Missouri"

Mound City was the scene of intense traffic the first week of August as Lane's war machine began to take shape. Montgomery had taken Stewart's and Seaman's cavalry companies and Thomas Bickerton's aspiring artillerists to Fort Leavenworth to draw weapons. Williams arrived in Mound City ahead of his company, which was several days away escorting the supply train from Fort Leavenworth. John F. Broadhead's infantry company was at the Marmaton River near Fort Scott, and the infantry companies of Snyder and Twiss were off in Missouri hunting secessionists (a mission ill-suited for infantry.) Only two companies of the Third were left in town, plus Jennison's company; Jennison himself was temporarily out of the state. Forty-five of Jennison's men, in two parties, were on their way into Missouri to wreak more mischief. Also absent was "Colonel" Nathan Bray, a Union man who had been driven out of Barton County, Missouri, and taken refuge in Mound City. Bray led an irregular company of 150 men, most of them fellow refugees, and was reported to be "operating on Dry Wood [Creek] in Barton county, Mo., with good success."[1]

Wiley Britton, a Missouri resident who later served in the Sixth, encountered Bray's camp as Britton was leading a party of Unionist refugees to Kansas. He described Bray's men as "Unionists from

Lawrence, Barton and Vernon counties, Missouri, and Neutral Lands, Kansas, who had collected there under Colonel Nathan Bray, a prominent lawyer of Mt. Vernon, Missouri, for purposes of defense and protection against attacks of independent bands of secessionists." Although Britton characterized these men as being "excellent, honest Union men," he also recorded that they "soon commenced committing depredations on the secessionist citizens, which were not a credit to our cause." According to Britton, Bray probably observed the men drifting into excesses, which he could not control, and after his company left Missouri, the men disbanded, most of them enlisting in the Sixth Kansas Volunteers.[2]

At Leavenworth, Bickerton published an advertisement for recruits for his battery, which he claimed would consist of four six-pound guns and two twelve-pound howitzers. Montgomery gave a speech at Leavenworth's Stockton's Hall. He told his audience he was a radical, that *all* men were entitled to freedom, that slavery had caused the war, and that he wished the war would not end until slavery was exterminated. Some time after his speech, Montgomery should have received from Captain William E. Prince, commander of Fort Leavenworth, the order from General Frémont to join General Lyon's command at Springfield, Missouri. Montgomery's response, if any, is unrecorded, but it does not appear he attempted to comply with the directive. Then on August 10, Prince ordered Josiah Hayes to take five infantry companies of the Fourth, and George W. Veale's cavalry company, to break up a rebel camp near Santa Fe, Missouri. The record is deficient as to whether this expedition came off and, if so, what the results were.[3]

Governor Robinson tried to impress upon Secretary of War Simon Cameron that Kansas needed a regiment of home guards and recommended Jennison as the man to organize and command this regiment. About the same time, Jennison left Kansas for Washington to seek authority to raise a mounted regiment. On August 10 Frémont, commander of the department that encompassed Kansas, authorized Jennison to raise a regiment—not a home guard regiment but one of U.S. volunteers. Jennison then published a recruiting advertisement for his "Independent Mounted Rangers," which stated that he had been authorized to raise a regiment of mounted men for independent service, and it was to be attached to Lane's Brigade. Jennison returned to Leavenworth on August 20 a colonel, carrying the commission he had just received from Frémont. Frémont then authorized Robinson on August 21 to raise three regiments of infantry, one as a home guard and two for service in New Mexico.[4]

Across the border a small Federal army under Lyon was driving toward Springfield in southwest Missouri, intent on destroying the remnants of the secessionist Missouri State Guard. In Washington the special session of the 37th Congress was adjourning, which meant the return of "General" Lane from Washington. Lane sent in advance a motley staff he had assembled in Washington—Captain Luigi Navoni, Lieutenant Giuseppe Laiguanite, Lieutenant Achille de Vecchi, Lieutenant Luigi Marini, and Lieutenant James M. Pomeroy. The first four were Italians who had been in the country for less than two months, while Pomeroy was the cousin of Senator Samuel C. Pomeroy.[5]

Despite the increased military presence in Kansas, many civilians along the border were terrified. At Olathe the fear of an invasion from Missouri had the citizens in "the utmost confusion and alarm," their thoughts "almost entirely absorbed by the fear of marauding parties in the state." These marauding parties included a band of local Kansas men who had organized ostensibly to operate against those who were reputedly "lukewarm on the Union question" but set out to "really rob every man of property." Seven of them had been arrested by the sheriff but released upon giving bail. To strengthen local defenses, the state delivered twenty muskets for the Olathe posse, with militia companies at Aubry and Gardner each receiving fifteen. Abraham Ellis of Miami County (formerly Lykins County) reported people sleeping in the fields at night, fearing an attack on their homes "by the prowling bands of Secessionists. If you call at a house, a little child or woman is sent to the door; the head of the family is not 'at home,' unless the caller is known to be a friend. Men watch by daylight with glasses for the approach of the enemy, and by night pickets are sent as far as possible towards the

Missouri line. Almost every house in the vicinity has Union refugees from Missouri. There are rumors of an attack every day."[6]

From the Cherokee Neutral Lands south of Miami County came stories of settlers being driven out by a force of five hundred secessionists and Cherokee, commanded by John Mathews, "hanging and shooting some sixteen of [the settlers], besides taking everything from them that he possibly could." Sixty families were said to have taken refuge in Humboldt and LeRoy; Mathews reportedly threatened to burn Humboldt and the Osage Mission. The only good news was that Father John Shoemaker at the Osage Mission had persuaded the Osage not to join Mathews. Another Kansas man disputed that matters were so dire in the Neutral Lands. He wrote that the only killings by Mathews's men were in retaliation for the murder of a Mr. Seymour and the looting of his store: "All who were not engaged in [the murder] escaped at Lightning Creek, and were not materially interfered with, while those who were of the expedition [against Seymour] suffered the penalty."[7]

A few days earlier, Prince had sent Colonel William Weer a dispatch advising him that a wagon train would be leaving from Fort Leavenworth under the command of Montgomery. Prince wanted Weer to return to Kansas City to complete the mustering in of his regiment; once this was done and Weer had returned to Fort Scott, he was to take overall command there—an arrangement Montgomery would probably ignore. Weer neither returned to Kansas City nor attempted to rule Montgomery. The wagon train, escorted by two cavalry companies, reached Fort Scott on August 11. The following day a seventy-five-wagon ox train, loaded with supplies for Montgomery and Lyon, left Fort Leavenworth, escorted by the companies of Stewart, Seaman, Bickerton, and Allen. A Leavenworth paper exclaimed, "All the drivers were negroes! The wagon-master, even, was a negro! Nearly all were 'contraband,' having left their 'comfortable homes' within the past ten days and made for the Fort and Montgomery. Two or three [negroes] a day have been coming in." Lieutenant Joseph Trego of Seaman's company commented, "The Irish who have hitherto been employed [as teamsters] are excusable for indulging in rather bitter and sometimes personal remarks as they are much interested in what may be the custom for the future."[8]

The situation changed dramatically in the days following August 10. On that day Lyon was killed in battle at Wilson's Creek after attacking a larger combined force of the Missouri State Guard and Confederate troops. The attack failed, and the army was compelled to retreat northeastward toward the railhead at Rolla. This left possession of southwest Missouri in rebel hands; from Springfield north to the Missouri River, and west to the Kansas border, there was no significant Federal force. Sterling Price wished to exploit this situation and drive north, but Major General Ben McCulloch, commanding the Confederate forces, refused to join him. Not dissuaded by this lack of cooperation, Price advanced with only his Missouri State Guard, picking up recruits along the way.

In southeast Kansas the citizens feared an invasion by the rebel army. The supply train being escorted by Williams's company reached Fort Scott on August 14, much to the relief of the town's citizens; prior to this the town's defense depended upon the three infantry companies of Judson's home guards, which were mustered into U.S. service on August 15. Williams did not remain idle; on August 17 he took fifty men into Missouri to visit a Mr. Karnes who was believed to be raising a secesh company. Karnes was not found, but plenty of food was. The Kansas men ate well, first at Karnes's house, and then at the homes of three of his supposedly secesh neighbors.[9]

Williams continued on to Nevada City where another secesh company was rumored to be. While passing a house along the way, "one of the boys discovered a saddle which suited his fancy, and he stopped to get it. The woman came out and began to cry, saying it was one her poor, dead husband used to ride, and begged him not to take it. At the same time one of the scouts saw the 'poor, dead husband,' making tracks through the bushes and sent a ball after him to encourage him along."[10]

The command arrived at Nevada City around six o'clock that evening and discovered a company of sixty men in formation in the center of town. Williams gave the order "Forward—on the gallop!" a quarter mile from town (another account says the order was given as they turned up Main Street.) The secesh fled, one of them pausing to take a shot at his pursuers. The result was one Federal horse wounded and one secesh dead. Another rebel took a shot at Lieutenant Ansel D. Brown and was close enough to swing his weapon at Brown's head; this tally was one Federal hat knocked to the ground and one secesh riddled with bullets from eleven Sharps rifles. The total rebel loss was estimated at five to seven dead and eight or nine horses captured; two Federal horses were killed. One secesh was captured and subsequently imprisoned at Fort Scott.[11]

Williams returned to Fort Scott, where an expedition was being organized to go to Ball's Mill in Missouri; three hundred armed secesh were believed to be in Ball's Mill. There was also a rumor of fifteen thousand men under Price within two days' march. In such circumstances making raids into Missouri and weakening the defenses of Kansas towns would seem folly, yet that is what was being done.

Kansas now witnessed an act of bravado that could be carried off by no one but Jim Lane. After having publicly declared in Congress that he was *not* a general, he arrived in Leavenworth on August 15 to personally take command of U.S. troops! True, he had in hand authority from the president to raise two regiments of soldiers, as well as directions from the War Department that these troops be supplied by the government, but Lane possessed no authority to command troops. Then again, no one else had been designated to command the troops in Kansas, and the highest-ranking Federal officer in Kansas was Captain Prince at Fort Leavenworth; Lane had found a niche not occupied by anyone else. Southeast Kansas was a remote theater of the war, connected with the rest of the Union by neither railroad nor telegraph. Given the need for someone to protect Kansas following Lyon's defeat, no one was quibbling over whether Lane was a general or not. However, that he continued to be treated as a legitimate commander by Federal authorities for nearly three months more is inexplicable. In his Stockton's Hall speech in Leavenworth two months later, Lane crowed, "I didn't accept the appointment, and haven't yet; but I have been playing big on them all the time—betting high on small cards."[12]

The evening Lane arrived in Leavenworth, he spoke to a packed crowd at the Mansion House, where he was introduced by his old friend Mark Delahay. The speech was masterful, if not altogether honest. Lane claimed the forces of secession were hovering on the border of Kansas, and he had arrived to raise an army for its defense—the unstated implication being that he alone could save Kansas. The two regiments raised by the governor, which had fought at Wilson's Creek, were in full retreat in Missouri. Lane said he had sent men to Quincy, Illinois, to procure one thousand cavalry mounts; all the weapons and uniforms his brigade needed were already on hand or on their way. Although Lane knew he only had the authority to raise two regiments, he informed his audience he would raise four. He exaggerated his authority even more, claiming he was empowered to raise an additional four regiments of home guards to be paid and armed by the Federal government. Ten days later he would write to Prince at Fort Leavenworth, stating that when his brigade was fully formed, it would consist of four regiments of infantry, two of cavalry, two batteries of artillery, and the home guard regiment at Fort Scott.[13]

Although Lane said he was in Kansas to provide for its defense, he talked about marching into the South. Repeating the theme he had voiced in the Senate, he said he would not march into Missouri or Arkansas for the purpose of destroying slavery, but neither would he be a slave catcher for traitors. The institution of slavery would perish with the march of a Union army, he asserted, and a Union army would march in while an army of slaves marched out. Such antipathy toward slavery did not necessarily translate into a love for blacks. He stated an ocean should separate blacks and whites. "No two people[s] can live advantageously together without intermarriage," the *Leavenworth Daily Conservative* quoted Lane as saying, but he didn't propose intermarriage. Ending his speech on an ominous note, Lane claimed when his brigade marched, the enemy "will know the avenger is at hand," and he would be tempted to flog any of his men who were compassionate enough to take a traitor prisoner.[14]

Lane's authority to command troops in Kansas was generally unquestioned, although Captain Prince on August 17 requested that Lane provide him a copy of the president's "instructions . . . to act without special reference to the routine of the service," a request with which Lane could not comply, for he had no such special dispensation. Weer naturally followed Lane, but so too did Montgomery and Johnson, neither of whom had raised their regiments under any authority of Lane's (although Johnson would be given his commission from Lane). Prince advised Lane that in light of Lyon's defeat, Weer's regiment then organizing at Fort Leavenworth should proceed by forced marches to Fort Scott. Lane agreed that Federal forces should concentrate at Fort Scott and, exhibiting the boundless energy for which he was known, immediately set out organizing and equipping his troops and issuing movement orders. He suggested that Napoleon Blanton's company, which had just drawn arms at Fort Leavenworth, should move to Humboldt and fortify that town. Lane wrote he would "direct an engineer to both points to mark out and superintend the fortification." He advised Frémont of his move to Fort Scott but complained his men were without "arms or equipments" and "uniforms, blankets, or shoes." He asked for artillery, small arms, and horse equipments, among other supplies. Kansas was destitute, he wrote. Horses were the only item in abundance. On August 17 Lane announced that the Third was making a forced march to Fort Scott, while the Fourth and Fifth, together with Lane and his staff, would leave Leavenworth that evening. The entire force numbered about two thousand men and two artillery pieces—a six-pound howitzer and a twelve-pound mountain howitzer.[15]

The ox train that had departed Fort Leavenworth on August 12 took two days to cross the Kansas River at Lawrence on August 15 and 16. At Lawrence, Seaman butted heads with local authorities. A black man named Bill Martin, suspected of horse theft, was stopped by a deputy marshal. Martin asked if the deputy had any arrest warrant, the constable said no but that he wanted Martin to go with him anyway. When Martin learned the destination was to be jail, he declined to go. The deputy tried to take him by force, but Martin grabbed a post and cried out for help; the deputy as well called for help. Seaman came up, inquired as to what was going on, and, deciding the deputy lacked proper authority, ordered his men to load their rifles. There were differences of opinion as to whether the guns were then aimed at the deputy, the justice of the peace Erastus Ladd, and the county attorney, Samuel Riggs. Riggs told Seaman the deputy was making an arrest upon a warrant issued by Riggs, but Seaman replied that he knew the facts regarding the horse theft and that Martin was innocent. Seaman then had his men escort Martin out of town."[16]

Lane, with some staff officers, reached Lawrence on the morning of August 17. He spent a few hours in town with his family and then left in the afternoon. He appeared briefly at Fort Scott the night of August 19 and explained his war plans to his officers. Five companies of Montgomery's regiment arrived the next day, and Lane moved north to the Little Osage River, where Fort Lincoln was being constructed on the north bank, and established his headquarters. A soldier there commented on Lane's Italians: "They are fine looking men, and if they could speak our language no doubt they would be very efficient officers." The Italians apparently departed soon after, for this was the last mention of them with the brigade. Montgomery remained at Fort Scott, from where Stewart and Seaman mounted yet another scout in Missouri. Ritchie took his cavalry company out on August 22 to destroy a fortification at Ball's Mill. Ritchie surprised the secessionists, killing one and taking twenty men prisoner. The prisoners were forced to destroy the fortification and were then released. (No accounts survive as to what the fortification consisted of; it was perhaps something left over from when part of the "Southwest Battalion" had been stationed there the previous winter.) Ritchie returned to Fort Scott triumphant, along with plunder of gunpowder, lead, eight horses, a safe, and a "receipt" for how to counterfeit money. Foreshadowing what was to become a flood of refugees of a new hue, two resourceful slaves followed Ritchie's track to Fort Scott and freedom.[17]

In one of the columns that passed through Lawrence was Daniel L. Chandler, hospital steward for the Fourth. Although the need for celerity should have been clear after the Wilson's Creek battle, Chandler complained that the two-day forced march from Lawrence to Fort Scott was unnecessary and done only so some colonel could claim to have won the race. He alleged "the men complained bitterly" about being so abused: many of them had dropped from exhaustion and had to be transported by ambulance; many then were hospitalized as a result of the march. In an interesting insight into the independent mind of the volunteer soldier—at least as it existed in the early months of the war—Chandler observed that the men "cannot forget that they are citizens and have rights that they have never surrendered." Or, as it was put by historian Bruce Catton, "It never entered the heads of most of these volunteers that a free American citizen surrendered any appreciable part of his freedom just by joining the army." Despite Chandler's warning, the men of Lane's Brigade never evidenced any great resentment over their treatment by their officers, perhaps because the nature of the campaign did not regularly call for strict discipline.[18]

Five companies, those of John J. Boyd, James H. Harris, James M. Harvey, Greenville Watson, and Thomas Moonlight, together with two artillery pieces in charge of now-Captain de Vecchi, did not leave Leavenworth until August 20. They left behind six companies that had been mustered into Johnson's Fifth cavalry regiment. Johnson had just returned from Iowa with three hundred volunteers, 175 of whom were already mounted. Another company for Johnson's regiment was at Liberty, Missouri. Captain Prince instructed Johnson to proceed with his command to Fort Scott, adding the admonition that Johnson was not to be delayed or interfered with by Colonel Weer, also en route to that post. Why Prince would suspect Weer of any such thing is unknown, but two days later he forwarded to "the general commanding Lane's Brigade" unspecified charges against Weer that characterized him as being "of a serious character." There is no evidence Lane gave these charges any notice. Two or three of Johnson's companies, after receiving saddles and bridles for their horses, started for Fort Scott on August 21.[19]

From Fort Lincoln, Lane wrote to Prince on August 25 detailing the disposition of his troops and his plans: At Fort Scott were 1,200 men, half of them cavalry; 230 Missouri troops of the Cass County Home Guards had departed the day before to return to Bates County; on Fish Creek were forty men; another one hundred were entrenching at Barnesville; Mound City was held by militia, also fortifying. Prince had written to Lane two days previous, suggesting that if necessary Lane should remove the forces and military stores from Fort Scott to Fort Lincoln. Lane had anticipated this and had already withdrawn most military stores from Fort Scott. At Fort Lincoln he had one hundred men in two companies busy digging entrenchments. Lane explained to Prince, "Fort Leavenworth and Kansas should be defended from this point." In actual practice, Lane would apply the stratagem that the best way to shield Kansas from the ravages of war was to fight on Missouri soil. In a hint of this, Lane asked Prince for reinforcements: "With it, we could play hell with Missouri in a few days."[20]

Another expedition left Fort Scott August 22 or 23. It consisted of the cavalry companies of Williams, Seaman, and Stewart of Montgomery's regiment; Lewis R. Jewell's newly recruited company of home guards; and an unidentified company under one Larnard—in all, approximately 140 men. The line of march was southeast through Vernon and Barton counties in Missouri, and part of the Cherokee Neutral Land in Kansas. Along the route of the "desolate looking country" were "deserted homes with closed doors, broken windows, stock and fowls roaming unrestrained over the yards and gardens." In Barton County, near the town of Medoc, a squad visited a rebel soldier named Wood who was home on leave. Two contemporary accounts differ on what happened next. According to one trooper, Wood attempted to flee into the brush and ignored calls to surrender; a ball through his heart from a Sharps rifle dropped him. Lieutenant Trego claimed the man was shot in the act of loading his rifle. Moving on, the expedition took possession of Lamar without any opposition, and finding little of interest there, returned to Fort Scott, administering the loyalty oath to several "wavering men" along the way. The expedition had started out with only two days' provisions in hard bread and salt. One soldier initially was puzzled as to what the salt was for and what the men would do for other provisions. "This mystery was solved, and the salt answered a good purpose; well, I'll tell you what we didn't do with it—we didn't eat it with dry crackers, and you may guess the rest." Lieutenant Trego recorded one morning some potatoes were dug up and roasted for breakfast. "Some of the boys had broiled chicken. I tried the hind leg of a hen that was pulled off of about twenty eggs that were nearly ready to hatch. It didn't eat very well because it wasn't warmed quite thro. . . . We had all the peaches and apples we wanted."[21]

No sooner had the expedition returned than Williams led another scout into Missouri, this time to Ball's Mill, which had so recently been visited by Ritchie. It was rumored the secesh were using the mill to grind flour for the rebel army. This scout consisted of the cavalry companies of Williams, Seaman, and Stewart, of Montgomery's regiment, and Moonlight's battery of one twelve-pound howitzer from Weer's regiment.[22] Moonlight's battery had originally consisted of the howitzer and a six-pound gun. Lane ordered Moonlight to turn his cannon over to Bickerton's battery of the Third, which was without any artillery. Moonlight refused; a compromise was reached by which the six-pounder was loaned to Bickerton for his men to train on.[23]

Ball's Mill, also known as Balltown and Little Osage, was a small settlement and trading post on the Osage River. The grist and saw mill on the west side of the Osage was owned by R. W. McNeil (Mr. Ball having passed away). Across the river via a fine covered bridge was McNeil's store, a few houses, and Dodge's "doggery."[24]

The jayhawkers captured a man who warned them there were 380 or 400 enemy on the near side of the river. Williams went forward with the prisoner to scout the best approach to town, when he encountered seven or eight mounted men. Williams assumed they were part of his advance guard, and not until they had come close did Williams suspect they might be otherwise. He ordered the horsemen to halt. They asked Williams, "Who are you?" "I am of the U.S. Army," came the reply. "Well, sir, we are after you." "And I," said Williams, "am after you." Immediately both parties drew their guns and fired. The rebels' fire knocked Williams's horse down, but Williams sprang to his feet with revolver in hand. With their muskets empty, the rebels retreated to town.[25]

At Ball's Mill, Colonel Thomas Cummins of the Missouri State Guard was using McNeil's mill to grind grain for Price's army. He had been reinforced by two Missouri State Guard companies just before Williams arrived, thus bringing his total force to around 150 men. Being warned of the approach of the jayhawkers, Cummins marched north of town to meet the enemy. The jayhawkers, spotting the cloud of dust raised by Cummins's men, advanced to meet him.[26] Williams formed his men in a line of battle along a strip of timber that separated him from Cummins. Cummins advanced into a cornfield about six hundred yards in front of Williams. Sharps rifle fire drove back a rebel flanking movement. Cummins attempted to make a stand in the center of the cornfield, but fire from Moonlight's cannon scattered Cummins's men in all directions. "Then commenced a running fight," one soldier wrote, "the different commands taking them in all directions and very soon the whole country was hid from view by a vast cloud of dust with an occasional Sharp's rifle crack and the boom of cannon . . . the chase . . . continued for an hour or more, during which time we had travelled four miles and killed fifteen seceshers not including those reported by the prisoners to have been killed by the shells. We took ten prisoners."[27]

With the pursuit over, the jayhawkers went around the neighborhood, collecting slaves and stowing them in wagons. One detachment rode to the home of the widowed Mrs. Ball and "returned with five niggers as contraband, with the masters overseer at their heels, a prisoner. Singular to say, the cattle, sheep and horses followed the master and servants to camp."[28]

Moonlight's howitzer was turned on the house of Judge Davis, supposedly because enemy soldiers were thought to be contained there; the house burned. The bridge and McNeil's mill received similar treatment. McNeil pleaded he was a loyal man and asked that his property be protected; his store had already been looted by the rebels. Williams replied, "We don't load cannons for nothing; that mill has ground its last grist for the rebels—fire into her, boys!" Moonlight sent three shells into the mill, the first one breaking the shaft and the other two passing clean through. Before leaving the next day, the jayhawkers burned the mill and the covered bridge over the Osage.[29]

One Kansas man subsequently defended the loyalty of McNeil. He reported that McNeil was an Ohio man who had purchased four slaves in Missouri yet told the slaves they were free to leave whenever they chose. Further, the man said that McNeil had wanted to send word of the rebels' presence to Fort Scott but was too closely watched. If this was true, and McNeil was a loyal Union man, destroying the mill might still have been necessary to prevent its use by the enemy. However, one gets the impression Lane's men were quick to condemn as secessionist anyone who did not actively oppose the rebels.[30]

Lieutenant Trego wrote: "There was no more property taken after leaving Ball's Mill by authority of the commander, tho' there was some Jay Hawking done. LaCount's barn was fired because it has been a good quarters for rebel troops. Fail's store and surrounding buildings were burned." William B. Fail, according to the *History of Vernon County, Missouri*, died in 1859, after having "established a store on the Kansas line, just in the edge of the Osage bottom, in about 1856. It was a huge log building—a fortress as well as a storehouse. Fails' customers were from both sides. Kansas jayhawkers and Missouri border ruffians met here on neutral ground and bought their supplies, all in a friendly way, without collision, and without collusion either."[31]

At Fort Scott on August 28, word was received that Williams had had a fight, destroyed the mill and the town, and was on his way back with three hundred head of cattle, seven contrabands, and "other spoils of war." On the assumption a rebel force would follow Williams, the troops in Fort Scott were issued forty cartridges apiece and ordered to remain in quarters. Despite the apparent excitement, Montgomery was "calm and serious," and "Gen. Lane was quietly gliding about as usual." That night Ritchie, returning from a separate scout, brought in around two hundred cattle he had liberated from their servitude in Missouri.[32]

Fort Scott was visited the next day by a large party of Osage Indians in full war costume, who came "to offer their services to their Father, at Washington." They rode around the plaza several times, singing their war song, all the while being followed by numerous curious soldiers. In the evening they held a war dance in the plaza, which was witnessed by many soldiers and citizens. The Osage offered their services "on condition that they be furnished with 'wabusca' (flour) and 'pacheney' (whisky.)" The kind offer was declined.[33]

Williams's command returned to Fort Scott August 30, along with twenty-five contrabands, two hundred cattle, fifty horses, and thirty-five to forty sheep. Immediately Lane made plans for another scout into Missouri, despite rumors that Brigadier General James S. Rains of the Missouri State Guard was marching on Fort Scott with three thousand men. Marching back into Missouri was a risky thing, for as far as anyone knew, the rest of the Missouri State Guard was following Rains, as well as McCulloch's Confederate troops. In fact, McCulloch had retreated into Arkansas with his Confederate troops. However, such a scout by Lane was consistent with his strategy that the best place to defend Kansas was within Missouri. One soldier observed, "Gen. Lane says they must whip us at Ball's Mills before they fight us at Fort Scott," and "Gen. Lane seems to think himself strong enough now to act entirely on the aggressive, and that is to be his policy from this forward." Perhaps Lane had second thoughts, for this scout never came off.[34]

That night a soldier was found asleep on guard duty. When court-martialed the following day, he pled that he had been drunk. Some men from his company went that night to the saloon where their companion had procured the liquor and forced their way in. The proprietor escaped out a window and went for help, only to be arrested and thrown into the guardhouse. At the saloon the men were pouring his liquid stock into the street when the owner's German wife rushed out, crying, "But you are not going to be after spaling my laker I hope." However, her plea failed, and her lager beer went into the ground as well.[35]

The "spaling" appears to have been motivated by more than merely exacting revenge upon a saloon keeper who helped a soldier get drunk. A few days before, at religious services, "Col. Montgomery made a forcible exhortation," at the close of which many regimental officers signed a temperance pledge. Moreover, the chaplain had told the men about General Benjamin Butler, who at Fortress Monroe had poured out the sutler's stocks of liquor. "The boys had got an idea that the late Congress passed a law imposing a fine of twenty-five dollars upon any one who should sell liquor to a soldier."[36]

Besides proscriptions against liquor, many of the captains issued orders banning profanity in their camps. One such officer, himself previously known for profanity, caught a man swearing and reprimanded him: "Joe, now hush up there. You know I have forbidden profanity in this camp. I've had to reprove you two or three times before, and now, I'll be d—d if this . . ." The captain was unable to finish his sentence, yet the reprimand was effective, at least for a little while.[37]

CHAPTER 5

Drywood and Osceola

Governor Robinson complained to General Frémont on September 1: "We are in no danger of invasion, provided the Government stores at Fort Scott are sent back to Leavenworth and the Lane Brigade is removed from the border . . . what we have to fear, and do fear, is that Lane's brigade will get up war by going over the line, committing depredations, and then returning into our State. . . . If you will remove the supplies at Fort Scott to the interior, and relieve us of the Lane Brigade, I will guarantee Kansas from invasion from Missouri." Robinson's tender concern for Missouri's sovereignty was a recent development. In a June letter he had written, "Missouri must be taught a lesson & I should be glad of an opportunity to give it." Robinson did not receive a positive reply from Frémont, only that the general would consider the governor's suggestions.[1]

Coincidentally, September 1 is when Lane issued a General Order relative to the taking of property:

> 1st. The rights, persons and property of the people of Kansas must be sacredly observed—not an article of property however trifling must be taken without payment in ready money for the same, or a receipt given by an authorized officer.

2nd. The rights, persons and property of the loyal citizens of other States must be sacredly observed, and every assistance and protection extended to them.

3rd. Such property of those in arms against the Government as can be made useful in the army, may be seized, but when so seized, must at the very earliest moment be turned over to the Quartermaster or Commissary's Departments, the Heads of such Departments giving receipts therefor. He who fails in this, and appropriates or attempts to appropriate any portion of the enemy's property so seized to his own use, is a base robber and shall be punished as such.[2]

Although constant rumors circulated of a Confederate attack upon Fort Scott, and Missouri bushwhackers roamed the border, there had been no movement toward Kansas. The jayhawker raids into Missouri seemed to succeed in keeping the enemy off balance, and out of Kansas. A resident of Fort Scott wrote, "Our people felt more secure. The military had somewhat relaxed their vigilance."[3]

Sunday morning, September 1, men of the Third repaired to a grove to hear Chaplain H. H. Moore give a sermon inspired by I Corinthians 16:13: "Watch ye, stand fast in faith, quit you like men, be strong." The rest of the Sabbath was one of relaxation, until about 4:00 P.M., when Weer was advised the enemy had raided his mule herd, killed a herdsmen, and made off with the mules.[4]

Sterling Price had sent a force of more than seven hundred mounted men under Brigadier General A. E. Steen toward Fort Scott. An advance party of seventy-five men struck the mule herd of Weer's regiment. The herd was guarded only by three teamsters, one of whom was killed and the other two taken prisoner. The entire herd of sixty mules was then driven off toward Missouri. Weer sent Veale's cavalry company in pursuit; as they closed on the retreating rebels, a body of dismounted cavalry rose up from the tall grass and fired a volley. Veale's men halted to return fire but were then charged by rebel cavalry. The jayhawkers turned tail and raced for town, the enemy in hot pursuit. Williams's company, riding out to join what was supposed to be a chase of a few raiders, formed into line and turned their Sharps rifles on the rebels. Now it was the rebels' turn to run, which they did while being pressed by Williams and Veale. Johnson's cavalry rode out to join the fight, while Lane formed the infantry and artillery into line of battle to the rear, Montgomery taking command of the cavalry. The rebels were thought to have made a stand in some timber two miles away. After some indecision, Johnson's cavalry was sent out to flank the enemy. Steen, faced with superior numbers that now included infantry and artillery, remounted his troops and fell back to another position. With nothing being heard from Johnson, Montgomery ordered an advance and soon encountered Johnson, who was retreating. Johnson reported that his men had had a fight, but because they were armed only with sabers and Colt Navy pistols—except for the Sharps rifles in Ritchie's company—the fight was inconclusive. Nightfall made further pursuit impossible, and the entire command returned to Fort Scott. Rebel casualties for the day were but three men slightly wounded.[5]

Lane dispatched a rider to Jennison with orders to bring forward his men from Barnesville, Kansas. Jennison arrived Monday morning; all the available cavalry from the regiments of Montgomery, Weer, and Johnson were already out in pursuit of the raiders, together with Moonlight's howitzer and Harris Greeno's company of home guards. The rebels were overtaken inside Missouri at Drywood Creek. Five or six of the enemy pickets were surprised by Greeno's men and taken prisoner. The others fell back through some timber to the main body, closely followed by the jayhawkers. Moonlight's howitzer was unlimbered on the open ground beyond. Williams's and Ritchie's rifle companies deployed to the right. To the left were Veale's and Stewart's companies, with the remaining companies in reserve.

The cavalry of both sides fought dismounted, which produced a curious result. Because the prairie grass grew as tall as a man's head, the opposing sides could see little of each other, and for the most part their shots went high. This was most fortunate for the jayhawkers, for it quickly became evident they were badly outnumbered, both in men and artillery—to Moonlight's one gun the rebels had five or six in action. After an initial exchange of rifle fire, the rebels fell back, and the battle was mostly conducted by artillery at long range (three hundred yards, according to Moonlight). That the jayhawkers were not quickly routed was due to several factors: They stood their ground and fought back fiercely, giving the appearance of greater numbers than they possessed; the tall grass concealed how few they were, making them poor targets; and Moonlight's one howitzer was extremely effective. His second shell burst among a rebel cannon, putting it out of action. During the fight, Moonlight changed position five times, yet he fired only eighteen shells.[6]

A company of rebel cavalry trying to go around the jayhawker right flank was met by a charge from John R. Clark's company, which drove them back. A similar move on the jayhawkers' left flank was met by Garrett Gibson's company and repulsed. The fight continued for an hour and a half, until Montgomery decided the time had come to retreat. To conceal this from the enemy, Montgomery went along the line giving the command instead of sounding retreat on the bugle; the ensuing retreat was largely obscured by the tall grass. Some of the men, who had so far stood their ground under artillery fire, nearly panicked while falling back. Veale's company in particular was affected, retreating well ahead of the main body and encountering Jennison's command heading for the battlefield. According to one account, Veale told Jennison his men "were badly whipped—all cut to pieces." Veale then assured Jennison that "nearly all of Richey's and Williams' command had been killed, and that Montgomery's retreat was undoubtedly cut off." Jennison urged Veale to turn his men around, but Veale claimed he could not control them. Veale then mistook Montgomery's retreating force for the enemy, and his company ran away. Jennison ignored Veale and rode on to assist Montgomery's rear guard.[7]

With the exception of Veale's company, the retreat was made in good order. The companies of Williams, Ritchie, and Jennison, plus ten men from Stewart's, formed the rear guard. The rebels belatedly realized the jayhawkers were retreating. A slight effort at pursuit was checked when Greeno's home guards, concealed in a cornfield, fired a volley into the rebels, cutting down their flag bearer. The Confederates abandoned further efforts at pursuit once the jayhawkers recrossed Drywood Creek. Jayhawker losses were five killed and six wounded; rebel losses were two to four killed and sixteen to twenty-three wounded. Among the rebels wounded were two cavalrymen whose mules foundered in a deep mud hole and were trampled by their own cavalry.[8]

Lane ordered Fort Scott evacuated of both military and civilians. Taking the infantry and artillery, he departed for Fort Lincoln at 2:00 A.M., along with the military stores from Fort Scott. Because Weer had lost his mules, civilian teams were pressed into service for the move. The march occurred during a thunderstorm that swelled the creeks waist-high to the infantry fording them. Only the cavalry companies, about 450 men, remained at Fort Scott; these were soon supplemented by militia, bringing the number of defenders to around eight hundred. Although Lane lacked the authority to do so, he called for the Kansas militia to take the field. Colonel Orlin Thurston's Seventh Regiment Kansas State Militia, from Allen and Woodson counties, responded. On Tuesday, Montgomery made a reconnaissance toward the rebel camp on the Drywood about ten miles from town. What the men saw was impressive. The rebel strength was estimated at six thousand to eight thousand men. "Their tents stretch out for a long distance, and their encampment looks like a city of tents." Realizing he was greatly outnumbered, Montgomery countermarched to town. Anticipating a successful rebel attack on Fort Scott, Lane ordered preparations made to burn the town to deny it to the enemy. "Fagots are piled in every house," wrote a soldier, "& will be fired if our men are compelled to retreat." The supposed rationale for burning the town was manifold: It was impossible to defend; its capture would be a disgrace; if captured, it would be too difficult to drive the enemy out; and the rebels would certainly burn the town if they had to evacuate it.[9]

The cavalry commandeered the empty homes for temporary quarters. Lieutenant Trego wrote in a letter: "Col. Montgomery, Adjt Zulasky, Chaplain Moore, Capts Jewel & Seaman, Lieuts Trego & Morse (I forgot to mention Capt Flint) with four soldiers as servants and a contraband wench for cook are occupying the house where Mr Williams was living. The parlor and one bed room are richly furnished, fine paintings & engravings on the walls, spring bottom sofa, divan, chairs & c. A good piano which Zoulasky in now amusing himself with. Preserves & jellies, magazines & book[s] and everything we want are here, so you see we are living high at present."[10] Trego was unrepentant about using a few of the luxuries of those who had "always been the enemies of Anti-slavery men," Other soldiers took more than minor liberties with the temporary absence of supposedly pro-slavery men by vandalizing and stealing from the vacated buildings. To rationalize such acts, Chaplain Moore explained that some of the men believed the town was to be burned anyway.[11]

For the next several days the cavalry at Fort Scott awaited the approach of the enemy. Barnesville was garrisoned with 250 militia. At Fort Lincoln the infantry, reinforced by about five hundred militia redirected from Fort Scott, were busy improving the fortifications and digging rifle pits under Moonlight's supervision. A hospital was set up at Fort Lincoln to care for the patients transferred from Fort Scott. The patients were under the care of Andrew J. Huntoon, a Topeka physician who had aspirations to be the assistant surgeon of the Fifth but was serving as a private. Huntoon had fifty-three patients, thirty-six of them from the Third. He noted the chief maladies were "Fever, Ague, Diarrhoea, Billious Fever, Colds with sore throat & cough." Among his patients were casualties from the Drywood fight. Hospital steward Daniel Chandler of the Fourth identified three of the wounded: one man who had his knee torn to pieces, another who had been hit in the groin, and the third whose arm was broken above the elbow. Huntoon considered two of the wounds for amputations—one an arm and the other a leg—but decided to hold off. This must have been the right decision, for a week later Huntoon was still caring for these men without any mention of amputation. One man for whom amputation did not present a dilemma was Thomas Easley of Zacheus Gower's company at Fort Lincoln, whose left arm was shot off by the accidental discharge of a musket while on duty September 11.[12]

Price never had any intention of invading Kansas. He had dispatched only a small portion of his army to clear the counties bordering Kansas "of the marauding and murdering bands that infested that section of the State." The retreat of the jayhawkers following the battle and the near-abandonment of Fort Scott convinced Price to keep his army within Missouri. Even had Price wanted to pursue Lane, the heavy downpour the night of September 2–3 had thoroughly soaked that part of his army facing Lane, extinguishing campfires and wetting the gunpowder in the guns. Price's decision was supported by Colonel John T. Hughes of the Missouri State Guard, who wrote on September 4: "A large army had just as well pursue a lot of 'Arabs' as these Kansas jayhawkers. They will hide in the grass, and shoot and run; no one can catch them. They are just like the Camanches—steal, kill suddenly and then run— there is no true bravery in them. It will not pay to waste time with them.—Hence, Gen. Price simply chastised them, and then resumed his line of march." Hughes's report was soon reprinted in the Northern press, and Lane's subsequent claims that the Drywood fight had saved Kansas from invasion should have met with skepticism.[13]

The day after the Drywood battle, the brigade suffered another fatal casualty, but not in open battle. The victim was First Lieutenant Barclay Coppoc of William Allen's company. Coppoc had traveled to Ohio to recruit more men and was returning by civilian rail with five recruits. As the train neared Leavenworth that night, it crossed the bridge over the Platte River in Missouri—or rather it would have had the bridge not been burned down by rebel guerrillas or sympathizers. The train plunged forty feet into a sandbar:

> Ghastly forms were strewn about the wreck, and groans, curses, prayers and appeals came from the heaps of ruins. Every seat in the cars had been wrenched from its socket, broken into splinters and hurled among the mass of crushed and bleeding humanity. . . . It was seven or eight hours before all the injured could be dragged from their frightful position. Twice the cars took fire, and the panic and terrible cries of the unreleased persons were beyond the power of description, but the fires were easily extinguished. Around twenty persons were killed and seventy injured, most of them civilians.[14]

Coppoc suffered a severe head wound and lived twenty-four hours. He and C. Fording, a recruit from Ohio, were given elaborate military funerals at Leavenworth. Private William H. H. Dickinson wrote in his diary that since hearing of Barclay's death, "we have been thirsting for blood: blood: blood."[15]

Coppoc had come to Kansas in 1856 when only seventeen years old. One account claimed that in December 1860 a cousin of his was one of three abolitionists who, while attempting to free slaves in Missouri, were ambushed and killed in what became known as the Morgan Walker raid. One survivor of the raid, Albert Southwick, enlisted in Allen's company in July 1861. In Kansas, Barclay and his older brother, Edwin, became associates of John Brown and traveled east to participate in Brown's raid on Harpers Ferry. While the rest of the raiders invaded the town, Barclay, Owen Brown, and Francis Merriam were detailed to remain behind at a farm in Maryland that was being used as a base of operations. This saved Barclay from sharing the fate of his brother, who was captured and hung. Coppoc and four other raiders set out on foot to escape Virginia. For the next two weeks they trudged over mountains toward safety in Pennsylvania, subsisting on corn and potatoes found in fields, wading frigid streams, and sleeping on the bare ground. Near Chambersburg, Pennsylvania, their hunger became so great, they took risks to obtain food. John Cook was chosen to go out and buy provisions, as he could "wield the glibbest tongue." The second time Cook went out, he never came back. Unknown to his compatriots, he had been captured and was returned to Virginia for a reward; he too died on the gallows. After this misadventure, the going became easier for the remaining fugitives who eventually found refuge among friends. Coppoc left Pennsylvania by rail, reaching his mother's home in Springdale, Iowa, around December 17, 1859.[16]

An arrest warrant was issued in Virginia for Coppoc along with a reward for his capture. The citizens of Springdale and the surrounding country made well-organized plans to resist any attempt to arrest him. In February 1860 Governor Henry Wise of Virginia asked Governor Samuel Kirkwood of Iowa for the extradition of Coppoc, which Kirkwood refused to honor because it allegedly contained technical defects. Immediately thereafter, a messenger was dispatched to Springdale to warn Coppoc of what was transpiring. Kirkwood was accused of having caused this. When a second extradition request, with the technical defects corrected, reached him, Kirkwood was compelled to issue an arrest warrant. Forewarned, Coppoc fled to Chicago, then to Detroit, and eventually went into hiding near Salem, Ohio, until joining Owen Brown in Dorset, Ohio. One of the men who helped Coppoc escape, Thaddeus Maxson, would join Captain John Foreman's company of the Third in October.[17]

Coppoc's role in bringing the "irrepressible conflict" to fruition has been overlooked until the recent scholarship of Lieutenant Colonel D. Jonathan White. According to White, "The refusal of northern Republican State Governors to extradite those wanted for murder and other crimes associated with the abortive Harpers Ferry insurrection figured prominently in precipitating secession." White discovered that Southern newspapers widely repeated Northern praise for John Brown's actions, recounting the notorious refusal of two Northern governors to extradite the fugitives, and editorialized that Northerners had endorsed anti-slavery radicalism. As stated by the Asheville *News:* "Now, we see what the irrepressible conflict Seward means. . . . We see the feast of blood to which [Republicans] will invite the South." The refusal to extradite the fugitives was raised again in the secession debates. "In Georgia," noted White, "when the legislature was deliberating on whether or not to form a State Convention, the issue figured prominently in the debate. Three Southern States, South Carolina, Georgia, and Texas, took the issue seriously enough to mention it in their declarations stating why they had seceded. In Virginia, the issue of extradition was mentioned in State convention while that body considered secession."[18]

On September 3 Lane sent a dire dispatch to Captain Prince at Leavenworth, explaining he had had a fight with 6,000 to 10,000 of the enemy and felt compelled to make a stand at Fort Lincoln or give up Kansas to disgrace and destruction. "If you do not hear from me again, you can understand that I am surrounded by a superior force. . . . Send me re-enforcements," Lane wrote. A day later Lane advised Prince of his efforts to protect the border. Lane reported he had 800 cavalry, "regular and irregular," at Fort Scott; 250 militia in log buildings at Barnesville; and 1,200 volunteers and 400 to 600 militia at Fort Lincoln. Again, Lane asked for reinforcements, especially artillery: "In twelve hours after being re-enforced I can be upon them, give peace to Kansas, confuse the enemy, and advance the cause of the Union." Prince received the first dispatch at 1:30 A.M. on September 5. He responded by instructing Colonel Everett Peabody, then at Lexington with his battalion of the U.S. Reserve Corps, to ensure that reinforcements reached Lane at the earliest possible moment. Prince stated he was assuming that reinforcements from Jefferson City had already reached Lexington, thereby implying that if they had not arrived, then Peabody could disregard Prince's instructions. A copy of Prince's dispatch was sent to Lane, thus giving him reason to believe Peabody was coming to join him. Affirming such a belief in Lane's mind was that Prince also sent him a copy of a dispatch from Prince to Frémont, also dated September 5, in which Prince recommended that Lane be reinforced with 3,000 men "to be detached at once from Jefferson City," with orders to unite with Lane on the Osage."[19]

It is unlikely Lane had received Prince's two dispatches when he again wrote to Prince on September 5, advising him that Price had broken camp and was moving northward. Although a deserter from Price's army reported that the rebel army was marching for Lexington, Lane discounted this, believing instead the rebels were moving to attack Barnesville, Fort Lincoln, and Fort Scott. "If the move is upon Lexington," Lane wrote, "I will annoy them as far as my forces and the protection of Kansas will admit of." Two days later Lane informed Prince of his plan "to pursue far enough to threaten their rear and confuse them. . . . The object of the pursuit is a hope that we will be able to cut off their train and recover the mules they have stolen from us." Prince approved Lane's plans, writing on September 9 that Lane should concentrate his men for an attack on the enemy's rear and find out where Peabody was.[20]

Lane dispatched three hundred cavalry under Johnson and Jennison with orders to keep between Price and Kansas. The cavalry left Fort Scott and marched to Ball's Mill, where it was learned Price had moved beyond Nevada toward Lexington. The command proceeded toward Papinsville, capturing along the way a woman of secessionist tendencies who was considerably upset until she was misled into believing her captors were rebels. This deception was aided by the fact that few of Lane's men had yet to be issued uniforms. The woman claimed that not one Union man lived in her part of the state, and she asserted it was well known the Kansas jayhawkers hanged innocent men, women, and children.[21]

Lane's men also engaged in pilfering, including "stopping . . . to pay their respects to the peach and apple orchards laden with an abundance of fruit which was declared 'contraband,' and treated accordingly." The loot included a wagon loaded with various items said to belong to a rebel captain, cattle (variously reported at from 40 to 289 head) alleged to belong to a secessionist and on their way to the rebel army, and as many as forty-five horses. Nine slaves were also taken, although it was claimed they had appropriated two wagons and teams on their own accord and, seeking freedom, joined the jayhawker column.[22]

Prince sent Lane a letter that, while couched in diplomatic terms, was nonetheless accusatory; this perhaps was what initiated Lane's growing antipathy toward Prince:

> I hope you will adopt early and active measures to crush out this marauding which is being enacted in Captain Jennison's name as also yours by a band of men representing themselves as belonging to your command. Captain Wilder will be able to give the details of their conduct at Leavenworth City, and doubtless their atrocities in other localities have been already represented to you. Please have a formal examination into the plundering of private and public buildings which has recently taken place as I am informed at Fort Scott. It will be necessary for representation to higher authority and for the adjustment of the accounts of disbursing officers.[23]

Lane apparently ignored the request.

When Johnson and Jennison drew close to Papinsville, a scouting party under Jennison went forward and spotted a small group of secesh in the timber on the far side of a clearing. As the main body of his command waited under cover, Jennison sought to entice the rebels out of their position, but only a few skirmishers came out. Jennison's men fired, prompting the rebels to retreat into the timber, only to reappear a short time later. This time one of them made the mistake of advancing into the range of the Sharps rifles and paid with his life. At this, all of the rebels retreated out of sight. Because night was now falling, and not knowing how close Price's troops were or in what strength, they thought it prudent to march back into Kansas.[24]

Lane's attention was drawn back to Kansas by another rebel raid. On September 8 John Mathews, acting in concert with the Missouri bushwhacker Tom Livingston, occupied Humboldt, Kansas, which was left defenseless with the militia being away at Fort Lincoln. The rebel raiders did little mischief in the town other than to rob a few stores and houses, but the very notion that they would strike in force this deep into Kansas caused great alarm. Word of the raid was carried to Blunt at Fort Scott and to Lane at Mine Creek; Lane ordered the capture of Mathews and put a $1,000 reward on his head.[25]

Blunt was given the task of punishing Mathews. He organized a force of 125 mounted men from the Fort Scott home guard companies of Greeno, John Rogers, and Henry Dobyns—all three cavalry companies being recent additions to the original three home guard companies. The expedition, encumbered by four or five wagons, got under way around five o'clock on September 14. They were joined at Lightning Creek by another 125 civilians and militia from Humboldt, commanded by a Captain Ford. The united command continued the hunt down the Neosho River to Mathews's home and trading post, but Mathews had gone south. On the evening of September 16 Blunt's force approached a house on the river just inside the Indian Territory, in which Mathews was thought to be spending the night. Dobyns was left to guard the wagon train (now doubled in size), and Greeno was detailed to surround the homes of two other secesh men. Blunt, and Lieutenant Colonel Lewis Jewell of the home guards, went forward in the dark and surrounded the house. Barking dogs alerted the occupants to Blunt's men, who then ran from the house, most of them escaping into the brush. One man was taken prisoner, and Mathews was shot and killed as he ran. On Mathews's body an order was found from Confederate Major General Ben McCulloch dated July 12, authorizing him "to raise a force of Osages and Cherokees, or other men," for his protection.[26]

A few more shots were exchanged that night as the jayhawkers scoured the neighborhood, resulting in the death of one secesh and the wounding of another. Blunt marched the command back to Mathews's trading post, where, among other things, horses, colts, jacks, jennets, mules, and wolf skins were discovered, which were mostly confiscated and turned over to the quartermaster. Five men found there were arrested. Blunt decided to try them by military commission. The prisoners were interrogated, but to their good fortune they were not found guilty of anything. After setting fire to Mathews's buildings, the expedition returned to Fort Scott September 20 with ten prisoners and the confiscated property.[27]

The raid on Humboldt terrorized a number of citizens into leaving for other parts of the state while some moved into the town itself. Most of those who remained in the rural parts of the county slept outdoors so as not to be caught asleep in their homes. In response to this raid, two companies of militia, one of infantry under Dr. George A. Miller and one of cavalry under Henry Dudley, were raised for self-defense. The infantry were kept on duty in Humboldt, while the cavalry picketed the approaches from the Indian Territory and built a fortification around O'Brien's mill.[28]

Around this time Judson's home guards at Fort Scott had increased to eight companies, so it was decided to form them into a regiment (the Sixth). In an election of regimental officers held September 9, Judson was elected colonel, Jewell made lieutenant colonel, and William T. Campbell made major. This regiment too was indifferently armed. Wiley Britton, who would join the Sixth in 1862, later remembered, "Some of the companies were furnished with Austrian carbines, a weapon soon found to be utterly worthless.

They were calibre 70, and the soldiers declared that when loaded and slung with the muzzles pointing downward the balls fell out of their own weight."[29]

Lane's military position was exceptionally ambiguous. He had guerillas operating in his rear, and Price's army to his front. He did not know whether Price was headed for Lexington or Kansas, and protecting Kansas was Lane's primary concern. Although Prince had supposedly sent Peabody to reinforce Lane, Peabody's whereabouts were unknown. Peabody's location was somewhat clarified when on September 9 Prince sent Lane another message, enclosing a telegram to Prince from a Major M. P. Berry at Kansas City. Berry explained that Peabody had marched from Lexington on September 8, heading for Warrensburg. Peabody assumed that Lane was retreating toward Kansas City, and Peabody intended to form a junction with him somewhere south of Kansas City. Prince recommended that Lane form a strong column and march at once upon the enemy's rear. Prince also directed Lane to determine Peabody's location."[30]

Without acknowledging whether he had received Prince's September 9 dispatch, Lane wrote to Prince on September 10 from Barnesville. He stated he was entering Missouri with 1,200 infantry, 800 cavalry, and two pieces of artillery. He proposed marching to Papinsville, "clearing out the valley of the Osage." From there, Lane wrote, he would turn north, "clearing out the valley of the Marais-des-Cygnes, Butler, Harrisonville, Osceola, and Clinton," and continue in that direction until hearing from the column under Peabody. To garrison Kansas, Lane left behind militia and some of his brigade troops—200 cavalry at Fort Scott, 300 infantry and cavalry at Fort Lincoln, and 200 infantry and cavalry at "Fort Lane" near Barnesville. Within two days Lane had modified his plans somewhat. He informed Prince he still had heard nothing of Peabody and had decided to pitch into Butler, Harrisonville, and Papinsville, so as to disturb the rear of the advancing column of the enemy. Lane's strategy was militarily sound, given the disparity in numbers of his brigade and Price's army. The raid on Humboldt prompted Lane to increase the garrison left in Kansas; now there were 800 troops at Fort Scott, 300 at Fort Lincoln, and 150 at Barnesville. In addition he ordered the construction of six stockades: on Turkey Creek in the Cherokee Neutral Lands; on the Verdigris, Fall, and Walnut rivers; and at Humboldt and LeRoy. This repositioning of forces left Lane a mobile force of 700 cavalry, 700 infantry, and two guns.[31]

Johnson's and Jennison's cavalry had already gone ahead; Lane followed on September 10 with Montgomery's and Weer's regiments. Two days later Lane camped northeast of Trading Post where he joined Johnson and Jennison. The following day a detachment went to Butler and "relieved" all the stores and a hotel stable of items the army needed. Seaman's company's share of the loot was a wagon, horses, and a harness taken from a hotel stable. From Butler the detachment marched for West Point. Along the way the jayhawkers branched out to scour the country of horses and mules. Trego accompanied a party that brought in twenty-nine mules and about twenty horses.[32]

During this pause in action, the Fifth held an election to fill the offices of lieutenant colonel and major. James H. Summers was elected major, and John Ritchie was elected as lieutenant colonel. William Creitz assumed command of Ritchie's cavalry company.[33]

Price continued on toward Lexington, arriving on September 12 and driving in the pickets of the two Union regiments there, one of which was that of Peabody's. His numbers swollen by new recruits, Price soon had the Federals trapped against the Missouri River and under siege. Frémont had been warned by Prince at Fort Leavenworth, and by Colonel Jefferson Davis at Jefferson City, that Price was moving north to the Missouri River; both commanders recommended that countermoves be taken. Frémont neglected to take their counsel. Instead, his attention was drawn to northeast Missouri, where Colonel Martin E. Green of the Missouri State Guard had assembled nearly three thousand recruits and was causing all sorts of mischief, including attacking Shelbina and chasing away two Union regiments on September 4. Green also captured Lieutenant William Woodruff of a company of Illinois men that was organizing at Quincy, Illinois, and preparing to joining Lane's Brigade. A correspondent at Quincy reported that "Mart" Green's men had held a mock court-martial, found Woodruff guilty "of several sins," and sentenced him to be shot, though they thought it unwise to carry out the sentence. The correspondent wrote: "The prisoner is a Kansas man, and was an active Free State man in '56. He is roughly treated on that account." Woodruff was not shot, and was released and returned to his company.[34]

Frémont sent Brigadier General John Pope (with the First Kansas and Twenty-third Indiana) and Brigadier General Samuel Sturgis (with the Twenty-seventh and Thirty-ninth Ohio) after Green, along with a complement of cavalry and artillery. Pope and Sturgis failed to corner Green, who crossed his force to the south bank of the Missouri River and then joined Price at Lexington. It was only after Lexington was invested that Frémont, from his headquarters in St. Louis, tried to organize a relief of the besieged Union forces.[35]

At 1:00 A.M. on September 13 Lane's Brigade broke camp at Trading Post and headed for West Point. Five miles out, rain turned the roads into slippery mud. The brigade reached West Point at 5:00 A.M.; whispered orders were passed for the men to load their weapons as quietly as possible. The town was quietly occupied, and the men were instructed to occupy houses and get out of the rain. At 5:00 that evening the drum beat out the call to arms and the men formed in line of battle. Rebels were seen retreating two miles off. Three more times that night the drum called the men into battle formation, but no fighting ensued. Around 3:00 A.M. this waiting to be attacked ended—the men were again formed, but this time they marched out five miles; whatever rebels there were in the neighborhood had disappeared. The men in Allen's company then visited a nearby house and helped themselves to peaches, chickens, turkeys, and pigs before the brigade returned to West Point at sundown.[36]

Operating out of West Point, scouting parties swept up three hundred horses and mules, "any amount" of cattle, and about fifty former slaves. The men feasted on apples and peaches; there was enough surplus fruit for Ritchie to send two dozen peaches and two dozen pears to Dr. Huntoon at the hospital in Mapleton, Kansas. Lane was ignorant as to the events unfolding at Lexington. As late as September 14, he inquired as to Peabody's whereabouts and suggested the enemy was maneuvering to prevent a junction of him and Peabody. Rumors abounded: Peabody was marching to form a junction with Lane; Peabody was falling back upon Lexington; Union troops were marching from Sedalia to get in Price's rear. By September 16 Lane had concluded it was most likely Peabody had been driven back. He implored Prince at Kansas City to start a column to meet up with him at Harrisonville to "make a diversion in favor of Peabody." Prince was equally in the dark as to where Peabody was. His only information came from newspapers that reported that Peabody was slowly retreating from Warrensburg.[37]

Perhaps to bring some order to the foraging of his troops, and perhaps in reaction to the apparently wanton destruction of a small printing press found in town, Lane on September 17 issued special instructions to all subordinate commanders, and a General Order no. 4. The commanders were admonished that the taking and destruction of private property had become intolerable, demoralizing, and affecting the troops' reputation. Officers were to be held responsible for the actions of their men, and General Order no. 4 was to be read to everyone. Dickinson noted the order in his diary: "Every man that breaks a safety guard shall suffer death & no Jay-hawking shall be allowed from a Union man & all the property taken from a rebel however small, must be given over to the Quarter Master or commisaries apartment [*sic*]."[38]

Lane had ordered another raid into Missouri. This force left West Point September 16 and camped near Morristown, a small town of about two hundred souls, the evening of September 17. A plan was devised whereby the next morning Johnson would move on the town from one direction while Montgomery, with about one hundred infantry and his cavalry, circled around and came from another direction. As the day dawned, Johnson further divided his command, leaving Ritchie and most of the regiment at a point north of town, while Johnson with Creitz's company and Moonlight's howitzer took a position on the road leading into town from the east. In Morristown was Colonel William Ervin of the Missouri State Guard with about 125 recruits. At the approach of Johnson's party, the rebel recruits ran from their camp and took up positions in a ravine and behind a stone wall in the southern part of town. Two weeks earlier at Drywood, Johnson had wanted to charge the enemy but had been held back by Montgomery; this time Montgomery was not around to restrain him. Without waiting for Montgomery to get in position, Johnson ordered a charge and dashed forward at the head of Creitz's company. Johnson's men had gone but fifty yards before being met by a volley from a concealed body of rebels. Johnson and Private James M. Copeland fell dead. Six men were wounded, several had their horses shot from under them, and a number of other horses were wounded. Still under fire, and unable to see the enemy, Creitz's men rode on through the center of Morristown and halted in the north portion of town. There, First Sergeant Chauncey L. Terrill spotted a civilian named Guthrie who had been loading a commissary wagon for the rebels. When Terrill loudly announced he had a prisoner, Guthrie ran, getting a bullet in the back from Terrill's pistol, yet he hobbled on. Terrill called on his men to shoot, but Guthrie made it into a house before more bullets found their mark. Supposedly Terrill's bullet inflicted a mortal wound.[39]

Creitz now found his company isolated, and the poor light made it difficult to distinguish friend from foe. He marched his company north and out of town. Moonlight had his gun in action and was lobbing shells at the enemy. What was designed as a concerted attack upon rebels was now in shambles, allowing the outnumbered and nearly surrounded enemy to successfully withdraw eastward to Harrisonville. The town was then occupied, and the looting began. "We took about 100 head of horses," recalled First Sergeant Terrill, plus "one dozen tents (which come in play now), a great quantity of camp equippage, saddles, bridles, drugs, merchandise, two or three stores, wagons, &c., &c., besides ten prisoners." A drum-head court-martial was held for the prisoners, and upon being convicted of some unspecified crime, five of them—privates and probably new recruits of the Tenth Cavalry Regiment, Missouri State Guard—were executed. The greater part of the town was burned (apparently on orders from Montgomery), and there being no other outrage to commit, the raiders returned to West Point.[40]

The burning of towns and the execution of prisoners had not been unknown in "Bleeding Kansas." Missouri militia had burned

Osawatomie, Kansas, in 1856, and both John Brown and Charles Hamilton had captured and executed men. The preceding August, Confederate forces had burned Hampton, Virginia, to prevent it from being used as a Federal post. However, such cruelties had not heretofore been practiced by Lane's men. Perhaps the men sought revenge for both the sacking of Humboldt and the death of the popular Colonel Johnson. One soldier offered another explanation: "These five had been acting as scouts, and had taken six Union prisoners—shooting two of them and leaving their bodies on the prairie.—Not having heard of the rebel defeat at Morristown, they were bringing the remaining four into the village to hang them." Fifty years later Henry E. Palmer, formerly of the Fourth, wrote that the executions were in retaliation for the murder a few days earlier of seven men in his regiment. The *Roll of the Officers and Enlisted Men* fails to document any such killing. However, Dickinson claimed that two men of the Third had lived in Morristown, and when they slipped into town to visit their mother, they had been captured and executed. The *Roll of the Officers and Enlisted Men* reports no such loss. An unidentified officer of the brigade claimed that Lane "took nine men, who had sworn allegiance, organized a drum-head court-martial, and shot several of them without delay." This officer also claimed a rebel messenger later came to Lane's camp under a flag of truce, carrying a proposal to shoot no more Union men if Lane would desist from shooting secession men, to which Lane agreed.[41]

Command of the Fifth fell to Lieutenant Colonel (soon to be Colonel) John Ritchie. Ritchie had come to Kansas in 1855 and settled just outside of Topeka. His one-year-old son died that year; a five year-old son would die in 1864. Ritchie speculated in land in and around Topeka and built what was then an impressive three-story commercial building in Topeka, the Ritchie Block. Among his causes was that of temperance. In 1857 he led a mob that sacked several liquor-carrying saloons and stores; one shop owner contested Ritchie's entrance and felled him with a blow to the groin. Ritchie was also an active Free State man. When Lawrence was threatened in December 1855, he joined a company from Topeka that marched to its aid. When in the summer of 1856 pro-slavery forces imposed an embargo of sorts by shutting off supplies coming through Missouri, Ritchie led armed parties into pro-slavery towns, taking supplies from stores for redistribution in Topeka. He was with Lane at the Hickory Point fight in September 1856, and was among a number of Free State men arrested after that fight by the territorial government and imprisoned at Lecompton. His incarceration was short, as he escaped in November. He was Shawnee County's delegate to both the 1858 Leavenworth Constitutional Convention and the 1859 Wyandotte Constitutional Convention. At Wyandotte, Ritchie spoke against attempts to deny equal rights to blacks and in favor of female suffrage and prohibition. On all three counts he was in a distinct minority.[42]

The Leavenworth *Daily Times* identified several "prominent members" of the Wyandotte convention, Ritchie being among them. Characterizing Ritchie as the "Radical of Radicals," "an ultra Abolitionist, woman's rights man, teetotaller, and general advocate for reform," the newspaper claimed:

> Mr. Ritchey [*sic*] is a man of medium size, with light hair and eyes, head narrow, long and high, with a frank face and cordial manner, rather rough in his appearance, free and easy, with an unshakable good humor. Everybody knows him, and in spite of his peculiar views, everybody respects him. He is very nervous both mentally and physically, and is a little apt to go off "halfcocked" but takes a joke against himself good naturedly. He is often on the floor, his sharp, nasal "Mr. President" being heard on almost every question. Being a man of good sense on all points not requiring an expression of his radical views, he has rendered efficient aid in the convention.[43]

Ritchie's abolitionism extended to assisting runaway slaves from Missouri in their flight to freedom farther north. In November 1857 a slave owner, escorted by a deputy U.S. marshal Butcher and soldiers, went to Ritchie's house looking for escaped slaves. An attempt to break down Ritchie's door was halted by the sound of gun hammers being cocked within. The delay occasioned by the slave catcher's call for reinforcements gave the slaves in the house time to escape. John Brown passed through Topeka in January 1859 as he left Kansas in anticipation of his attack on Harpers Ferry. With Brown was one last load of freed slaves, those he had just taken in his Missouri raid; one of Brown's men stopped to rest with Ritchie. After leaving Topeka, Brown was cornered north of town by a federal posse; he sent a messenger to Topeka asking for help. Ritchie was one of the Topeka men who rode to his aid. The reinforcements joined Brown, who decided his now enlarged force would ride slowly and deliberately straight at the positions occupied by the posse. Although this seemed rash, it so unnerved the posse that they fled without firing a shot, thus providing the name to this bloodless engagement—the "Battle of the Spurs."[44]

Although the territorial government had not actively pursued Ritchie after his escape, and that government was now controlled by Free Staters, Deputy U.S. Marshal Leonard Arms, on April 20, 1861, decided to arrest Ritchie on some old charge. Arms went to Ritchie's home but was unable to produce a warrant. Ritchie ignored Arms and retreated into his house; Arms followed him inside. Both men drew their pistols, and Arms advanced on Ritchie. Ritchie killed him with one shot to the throat. A hastily convened inquest before the local justice of the peace, at which Lane was one of Ritchie's defense counsels, found the shooting justified. Acting Governor Hugh Walsh nonetheless issued a warrant for Ritchie's arrest. He was never prosecuted.[45]

Creitz was a bitter critic of his former captain. He asserted that Ritchie had been elected captain only on the understanding that Ritchie would soon be promoted out of the company. Creitz ascribed Ritchie's ascent to lieutenant colonel to another conditional promotion, claiming that Colonel Johnson on September 10 had called a meeting of company officers and nominated Ritchie for the position. This, claimed Creitz, was "bitterly opposed by several company officers that were acquainted with his tyrannical disposition." The opposition relented "upon the express and only condition—that

Gen. Lane would appoint—and cause to be confirmed—Capt. E. E. Harvey of Co. 'E' of the 5th Kan. Cav. as United States paymaster—and Frank Clark of Co. 'B' as Lieut. on Lane's staff." These appointments never being made, the legitimacy of Ritchie's promotion was disputed.[46]

An acquaintance described Creitz as "a captain in the troubles of '56 and the prince of devils in a fight and of good fellows in a frolic, and as much of an abolitionist as Lovejoy or John Brown dare be." Like Ritchie, Creitz had been at the Battle of the Spurs. Although in his Free State fervor he had much in common with Ritchie, Creitz disliked the man. This feeling may have had its roots in resentment caused by Ritchie getting command of the cavalry company. In the summer of 1861 Creitz had recruited men for a company he wanted to command, but he attracted too few volunteers and had to consolidate his with the company being raised by Ritchie. Ritchie was elected captain of the combined companies, and Creitz was elected first lieutenant. At a public meeting in Topeka in late December 1861, both men would take the stage. Ritchie proudly stated he had obtained his commission from Lane and that Governor Robinson "should not black paper with his dirty hand in signing a commission for him." Creitz alleged Ritchie accused him of being a "Robinson man," merely because he had followed instructions from the War Department and obtained his commission from the governor. Creitz also claimed Ritchie had falsely accused him of cowardice.[47]

Creitz complained that Ritchie ignored the regular army drills for cavalry and instead "conceived a system of drills and evolutions entirely his own—so extremely ridiculous—that after he attained to the command of the regiment he not unfrequently rendered it the laughing stock of others by his curious and unsanctioned maneuvers." There is no doubt that Ritchie was a colorful character. David P. Bond of the Fifth noted that whereas other officers in a fight exhorted their men to give the enemy hell, Ritchie, when the bullets were flying all around, urged his men on by crying, "Give it to them boys. Remember your sweethearts." Bond concluded that Ritchie had a soft spot for sweethearts, recalling that when he asked for a furlough, Ritchie said he would deny it if Bond's purpose was to attend to business, but he would grant the furlough if Bond was going to see his sweetheart. Bond's honesty cost him the furlough.[48]

Lane appointed Ritchie as colonel of the Fifth on September 17. It is debatable whether Lane's authority to raise regiments extended to commissioning colonels. Lane apparently did not feel he had this authority, when on August 16 he requested Prince to muster Weer in as colonel of the Fourth.[49]

At West Point on September 19 Lane took the occasion to draft a proclamation "To the People of Western Missouri, Now Occupied by the Kansas Brigade." In it he assured the citizens that his brigade came not to steal from them, but only to put down rebellion. If they remained loyal, Lane would give them protection, and property taken for military use would be paid for. But, Lane warned, should they disregard his advice, "the stern visitations of war" would be "meted out to the rebels and their allies." Lane also set out rules of conduct for his own men. In a speech to them that same day, he cried: "The thieves of this command have had their day. This is the last appeal that I shall make to you. After this I shall visit upon you the severest penalty of the law." To emphasize his point, Lane read from an earlier brigade order prohibiting the taking of private property. "You sneaking thieves," Lane continued, "what did you think of yourselves when you were invading the premises of that widow in the north part of town, and stealing her night-dress, her skillets, and her chickens? Were you acting the part of soldiers then? Did you think we were at war with widows? Do you think we were at war with chickens or skillets?" Lane also read the brigade order drafted two days earlier, which emphasized that private property was to be left alone and prohibited men from wandering off from camp or while on the march.[50]

A trooper of Williams's company said that when Montgomery welcomed the unit into his regiment, he then addressed the company as to their duties as soldiers. "They had enlisted to support the laws and constitution of their country," Montgomery told them. "They should be the last ones to break the law by either taking or destroying private property; . . . we must set our enemy a good example, by showing them that we were there to protect their property and enforce the laws of our country." The same trooper described Montgomery as "at all times on the march instructing the officers and men that they must not take private property or disturb the homes of women and children."[51]

But now, jayhawking evidently had grown to a degree even Lane could not ignore. Only a week earlier Lieutenant Trego had written in his diary about two officers of the company: "These men who have heretofore been so violently opposed to Jay Hawking are as a general rule if not more, the most unscrupulous of all Jay Hawkers when they can have a share of the profits." Lane was probably willing to wink at his soldiers lining their pockets a little at the expense of secessionists, but excessive jayhawking could tarnish his reputation. If nothing else, Lane's speech to his men and his written brigade order put him on record as opposing theft.[52]

Lane's men were by no means the only or the first Union troops to be guilty of taking civilian property. Men of the First and Second Kansas Infantry regiments had, during General Lyon's Wilson's Creek campaign, supplemented their rations by foraging (stealing, if you prefer) from civilians. When in July some of these men were caught in the act, Samuel Sturgis, then a regular army major, had the Kansans horsewhipped. This did not sit well with Montgomery's recruits. One of them expressed their sentiment: "Whilst we deem it a duty and a sacred obligation to abstain from molesting everything belonging to Union men, we also consider it equally binding upon us to make the enemy furnish chickens, vegetables, fruits &c. In fact, to make them furnish the dessert for us, as the Government has to furnish the substantials." A contrary view was taken by Chaplain H. H. Moore of the Third, who felt "it right to cripple the enemy" by stripping him of whatever means could be used against the Union. "But every farthing's worth of property taken should be seized in the name and for the benefit of the Government. The soldier who appropriates any part thereof to himself, forfeits his character as a soldier, and becomes a thief, and is a burning disgrace to the army. Such is the view taken of the matter by Gen. Lane," Moore wrote. On the theory that actions speak louder than words, it would appear the majority of Lane's Brigade disagreed with

Moore. Lane apparently held to the middle ground, believing almost any action that weakened the rebels was appropriate.[53]

Lane intended for his brigade to live off the enemy. One of his officers reported that Lane had organized and fitted his supply train with little expense to Uncle Sam; as for meat and forage, he had an abundance—seized as contraband of war. Although this policy is understandable, in practice its application in occupied territory would prove difficult, as it was not always easy to distinguish the loyal man from the rebel.[54]

Not only did the brigade as an organization live off the enemy, but to some degree so did the men as individuals. Having yet to receive any pay, their temptation to appropriate property from traitors would have been considerable. A more honorable way of making a profit was to buy from the brigade quartermaster, at bargain prices, property that had been seized from secesh. In a letter home, Lieutenant Trego wrote of procuring "some contraband property taken at Morristown," which he and "the Captain . . . drew after the appraisement. I sent up a better buggy than the one Lyman got, for which I pay Gov[ernment] $35. I send to-day a lot of Merinos, velvet, barred muslins, calicos, shoes & c most of which is to be distributed among those who are unable to buy. There are about a dozen plaid shawls of various sizes." While the nature of many of these items suggests they could have been stolen from women, it is more likely they were looted from stores. Trego instructed his family to distribute this property "among those . . . unable to buy." Less than two months later he would make no pretense of succoring the poor, instead sending directly to his wife and another woman a white dress apiece, several yards of velvet for sacks, plenty of black silk thread, more than one hundred skeins, and some cheap ear bobs."[55]

A regular army officer later complained of how some of the mounted men—when they finally drew pay—inflated what they received: "Horses in great quantities and at extravagant prices had been purchased under irregular orders and paid for by the United States; these horses being then turned over to men and officers who were then drawing 40 cents extra per day for them as private property." A number of these horses certainly were "contraband" livestock appropriated in Missouri.[56]

Lane finally learned there would be no junction with Peabody, who was trapped at Lexington. Prince wrote Lane, hoping he would see the importance of an immediate concentration of his command upon Kansas City. Frémont, in St. Louis, sent Lane a message explaining his plan to send troops from Jefferson City to attack Price. The message commanded Lane to march with his forces to Kansas City, communicate immediately with Brigadier General Sturgis, and cooperate with him to defeat the enemy. While the term "cooperate" left it unclear whether Lane was to be subordinate to Sturgis in such a move, this apparently was the intent, for Frémont also advised Lane that if the rebels advanced on Kansas City, then Sturgis was to cooperate with Lane. In a message to Sturgis, whom he wrongly believed was at Lexington, Frémont stated that Lane was to put himself immediately in communication with Sturgis "with a view of co-operating" in an attack upon Price's forces surrounding Lexington. This was at best a confusing command structure. If Lane was believed to be a brigadier general, his date of rank should have been senior to that of Sturgis, thus giving him command in the absence of some other arrangement. If, on the other hand, it was believed Lane had command but no commission, orders to him could have been advisory only. In both of Frémont's communications just mentioned, he addressed Lane as "General," and Sturgis as "Brigadier-General."[57]

At Lexington the Federal troops were in dire straits. No relief had come, and the rebels had captured their source of fresh water. On September 20 the encircling lines drew perilously closer when the rebels adopted the tactic of advancing on the Union entrenchments while sheltered behind large hemp bales that were slowly rolled forward. Colonel James Mulligan, the Federal commander, seeing the situation was hopeless, surrendered September 21.

Frémont was poorly informed of the true situation at Lexington. On September 20 he dictated an order for Lane to "harass the enemy as much as possible by sudden attacks upon his flank and rear" to bring some relief to the besieged troops. Lane, equally ignorant of the surrender at Lexington, had already plotted a raid on Osceola. Osceola should have been an inconsequential target—the 1860 census listed only 265 residents, but it was a commercial landing on the Osage River, and now it was rumored to be a depot for Price's army. This expedition would take the brigade deeper into Missouri than before. In preparation, Lane called on the Kansas militia for ten days' service and to take up positions to protect southeast Kansas in the absence of the brigade. Remaining on the border would be the Sixth at Fort Scott, Jennison at West Point, and the militia under Blunt, which had been pursuing Mathews. Montgomery, in charge of the raiding column, left camp on September 19 with Ritchie and six companies of cavalry, Moonlight's battery, and 160 infantry under Weer. Their first destination was Papinsville, where several hundred secesh were reported gathering. After a night march Montgomery reached the town the following morning, but no enemies were found. The infantry, riding in wagons, rendezvoused with Montgomery and the march was resumed. Opportunities for jayhawking were limited, as most farms along the way were deserted; orchards, however, were literally ripe for picking. Chaplain Moore was pleased to write that the men left the orchards alone, except where "farms were found deserted, and fruit was just going to destruction, the boys were permitted to help themselves, but cautioned against breaking limbs, or in any way injuring the trees." Yet at Papinsville Private Dickinson had gone into a store to increase the inventory of his mess, taking vinegar and two Dutch ovens, and for himself he secured, among other things, a silver penholder and a powder horn. Lane's exhortation against taking property for personal use seemed to have little lasting effect.[58]

The brigade was guided to Osceola by a company of Missouri Unionist home guards commanded by Obediah Smith—possibly also assisted by George Washington Barnes, a private in Snyder's company, and a former Osceola resident. A small skirmish occurred the night of September 21 as the column crossed the Osage four miles from Osceola, with five prisoners being taken. The outskirts of the town were reached around 2:00 A.M. on September 22, with

Weer's infantry and Hunt's cavalry company forming the advance. The descent upon Osceola was too sudden for secessionist Captain John M. Weidemeyer to organize his company of home guards or the two companies of recruits gathered there. Weidemeyer could assemble only about twenty men, who fired a volley into Weer's infantry. This inflicted no casualties and was promptly returned, driving Weidemeyer's men off, two of whom were wounded, one mortally. Some other secesh opened fire from a nearby log houses and were driven out when shells from Moonlight's howitzer set the house on fire. These skirmishes resulted in two jayhawkers wounded and fourteen rebels killed and wounded. Rather than advancing into town in the darkness, the brigade made camp for the night. The next morning the jayhawkers crept into town, wary of ambushes at every corner. None came, as the town had been almost completely abandoned by its male population. Osceola was ransacked—everything that might benefit the enemy and could not be transported by the troops was destroyed, "including about two thousand barrels of liquors, thousands of bushels of salt, fifty hogsheads of sugar and molasses, large quantities of bacon, clothing &c." Even the records from the courthouse were carried off for some inexplicable reason (but not destroyed). The warning provided by the previous night's skirmish had allowed some valuables to be successfully hidden from the jayhawkers, most notably the contents of the Merchant's Bank. Moreover, the slaves of the town and neighborhood had been sent to hide in the woods."[59]

Osceola was the home of U.S. Senator Waldo P. Johnson, a Southern sympathizer who had absented himself from the Senate and who would soon be expelled from that body. Johnson's son told the story that they had a loyal slave named Aunt Cin, or Lucinda, who was looking after the Johnson household while the family was in Virginia. Aunt Cin, hearing of the approach of the jayhawkers, buried Mrs. Johnson's silverware and informed a neighbor what she had done. "Aunt Cin and the other negroes owned by my father were forced to go with the troops . . . and we never saw them again," Johnson's son noted in his memoir. The Osceola resident who appears to have suffered the worst monetary loss was merchant

John M. Weidemeyer, who in the 1860 St. Clair County census was identified as possessing more than $100,000 in personal property.[60]

Not every jayhawker sought to line his pockets. As the bank was about to be set afire, a jayhawker second lieutenant was approached by a woman who informed him there was money hidden therein, and she offered him half of it. The lieutenant replied, "Madam, I am not a robber. I don't approve what is being done here, but I can't prevent it. I will get your money for you if I can."[61] True to his word, he recovered the money and delivered it to the woman.

Besides being looted of its records, the courthouse suffered the insult of being the subject of casual target practice. Moonlight and Weer got into a discussion of the merits of artillery, when Moonlight bragged he could land a round from his howitzer between two windows of the courthouse. Weer expressed some doubt as to Moonlight's skill, so Moonlight fired a round and proved his point. Weer claimed this was pure luck, so Moonlight pointed out two more windows, and again hit his mark.[62]

Among the more outrageous and unreliable accounts is that of J. H. Mills of Chicago, who claimed to be with the brigade that day. According to him, Montgomery's men had been fired upon by two cannons that were subsequently captured, and another fight took place when the townspeople fired on the jayhawkers, killing two Kansas men and wounding three, while the secesh suffered seventeen killed and twenty-seven wounded. Another outrageous account, one that has been casually repeated by various historians, originated with Henry E. Palmer fifty years after the fact. Palmer, a soldier in the brigade, claimed many of the men got drunk and that nearly three hundred had to be hauled from town in wagons and carriages. One Osceola resident recalled only that some "soldiers seized on the whisky first, and soon became so ungovernable that the officers ordered the destruction of what remained of that article." Casting doubt on Palmer's story is the recollection of one of Williams's men that "the first thing Montgomery did was to have all the liquor destroyed, to prevent the troops becoming intoxicated." A trooper in Hunt's company wrote that Montgomery, "finding the boys filling their canteens with wildfire, ordered the same to be spilled." While it is not improbable that a few of the men partook of the liquor they were destroying, there is no evidence this was widespread. As there is no other source for Palmer's claim, and it is unlikely enough wagons would have been found to haul both three hundred drunks as well as appropriated property, Palmer's story is not credible.[63]

A correspondent for the *New York Times*, writing from Bolivar, Missouri, the following month, provided this apparently exaggerated account:

> At Osceola was a family named Vaughn—a man and his wife—wealthy, young, educated, refined, respectable. Vaughn took up arms for the South, received a commission as captain, but gave himself up to Lane and was released on parole. When Lane passed through Osceola, he burned the beautiful residence of Vaughn to the ground, then followed the family to a log house in the country where they had fled, and there, upon the information of a slave, dug up $8,000, which they had buried, sacked the house, taking seven silk dresses and all the valuables belonging to Mrs. Vaughn, and then left.[64]

The difficulty with this claim is that a review of the 1860 census for St. Clair County fails to suggest that there was any resident of Osceola named Vaughn who likely would have possessed that much cash.[65]

Modern historians have done their part to exaggerate what happened that day. Albert Castel repeated the story of the drunken soldiers and added that Lane's personal share of the loot included a piano and a quantity of silk dresses. The two sources cited by Castel fail to support this conclusion. One was merely an editorial comment to the effect that "we are credibly informed" that about the time Lane gave a speech in Lawrence around November 20, 1861, a quantity of silk dresses arrived in town and were distributed among Lane's "special friends." Even if one is willing to convict Lane of theft at Osceola, the accusation that he made off with a piano is ludicrous. Lane had been outspoken in charging his men that no thieving take place; had he an inclination toward larceny, his takings would have been small enough to conceal from his men, thus at least maintaining the outward appearance of honesty. Thomas Goodrich also repeated the drunken soldier tale, claiming "hundreds of shouting Jayhawkers ran through the streets," despite no contemporary sources documenting such wild behavior. He wrote that "reportedly" Lane's share of the loot "included silk dresses, a piano, and $13,000 snatched from the hands of a widow." Regarding Hugh Fisher, chaplain of the Fifth, Goodrich alleged he "looted Osceola churches to furnish his own back in Lawrence." Again, there is no contemporary documentation of such theft. But most damning is that Fisher was not at Osceola. He was in Leavenworth when word arrived of Colonel Johnson's death at Morristown. He remained in town awaiting the arrival of Johnson's body, and on the morning of September 20 conducted the funeral services. Edward Leslie repeated most of the legends, including that of the drunk soldiers, and regarding Lane, "His personal share of the plunder included a piano, $1,000 in gold, a quantity of silk dresses, and a handsome carriage." Leslie also claimed "the bank was robbed, the take said to have been $8,000." Using the phrase "said to have been" allowed Leslie to report a juicy story without personally vouching for its believability. As noted previously, the funds of the Merchant's Bank had been hidden before the jayhawkers entered the town. The common theme throughout all of these historians' accusations is the lack of credible sources.[66]

Within the town the jayhawkers discovered lead, gunpowder, cartridge paper, and a place where musket cartridges had been made. An Osceola resident conceded that a Colonel Snyder, of the state army, had operated a cartridge factory in the suburbs. "When Gen. Price moved up from Springfield to Lexington, a part of the ammunition was sent to Osceola for safe keeping until called for. All these things were well known to Lane and Montgomery, as we afterward discovered that the latter was in constant correspondence with a woman in our midst, a Yankee, it is true, but one whom we had considered a lady."[67]

The colonels held a conference as to whether to burn not just the cartridge factory but the entire town. Weer opposed this, but

Montgomery and Ritchie favored it. The arguments advanced in favor of burning were "that it was traitorous to the core; that the enemy intended to make of it, during the winter, a military post; that it was a strong position, and could be easily fortified; that we could not leave a force there; and that the Government could not afford to make weekly expeditions to disperse the rebels." With the exception of Morristown earlier that month, at no time previous in this war had the combatants burned enemy towns. The occupants of Osceola had every reason to believe that although there might be some thievery visited upon them, and even perhaps selected buildings destroyed, the persons and homes of the general population would be spared. Their shock must have been awful as they learned the decision had been made to burn the town. Yet not everything was to be burned. "Col. Montgomery ordered a tannery to be spared," wrote Chaplain Moore, "and all the private residences situated in the outskirts of the place, that the women and children might have a place of refuge till further provisions could be made for them." In one instance Montgomery personally intervened to prevent a soldier from burning a home. Not spared was Senator Johnson's residence.[68]

The burning of the Osceola was horrible, yet the extent of this has been greatly exaggerated. Goodrich wrote that the torching of "Osceola, the metropolis of southwest Missouri," left three thousand people homeless. Leslie claimed that more than one hundred houses were burned. The 1860 census of St. Clair County calls these assertions into question. In June 1860 only 267 white persons lived in Osceola, which included two men in the jail. These residents resided in only forty households and boarding houses.[69]

Although wagons and teams were appropriated to carry off the loot, not enough were found to carry everything. Some of the infantry had to give up their seats in the wagons so that more swag could be taken back to Kansas. In addition, scores of Union families joined the march out of Missouri. Captain Weidemeyer returned to Osceola on the heels of the departing brigade. He assembled twenty men and trailed the jayhawkers, hoping to net some careless stragglers. Only one straggler was caught—and presumably killed;

Weidemeyer appropriated the man's Sharps rifle. Weidemeyer next decided to pursue Obediah Smith, the Missourian who had guided the brigade to Osceola, and who had left town with his share of loot and was returning to his haunt along the Spring River. Being warned that Smith with sixty men was waiting in ambush, Weidemeyer called off the pursuit and returned to Osceola.[70]

On their return trip the jayhawkers took Charles Harris prisoner. Harris admitted he was a secessionist and had been a quartermaster in Price's army. Harris's fourteen-year-old son came into the brigade camp and offered to exchange himself for his father so the father could care for his sick mother; the offer was declined. Although they spoke well of their master, about twenty-five of Harris's slaves were in the process of emancipating themselves; they had appropriated horses and wagons loaded with provisions from Harris and were ready to join the jayhawker column. Chaplain Moore asked each of them if they wanted to leave and were ready to face the hardship of providing for themselves as free men and women. They all wanted freedom. The jayhawkers explained to Harris that they were merely giving practical application to Frémont's emancipation proclamation. Several weeks before, Frémont had shocked both Missouri and the Lincoln administration by declaring martial law throughout Missouri, authorizing the execution of certain prisoners and ordering the confiscation of the slaves of active secessionists. What was perhaps the most disturbing about this proclamation was that the confiscated slaves were declared *free*. Lincoln, concerned with the effect this emancipation proclamation might have on the loyal, and slaveholding, border states, asked Frémont to modify his order to conform with the recently passed Confiscation Act, which allowed for the confiscation of slaves without giving them their freedom. Frémont responded that he could not voluntarily modify the order and requested that if it had to be done for Lincoln to order him to do it. Lincoln did so.[71]

The brigade's column halted at Butler for the night. Dickinson noted Butler was "a nice place" of about four hundred people. A grist mill was to be burned, but Dickinson could not see the sense in the flour there going to waste. He salvaged what he could and donated it to a local lady and her mother. This generosity served him well when he visited the town after the war; he was saved from being lynched when it was discovered that one of his captors was the husband of the lady to whom Dickinson had given the flour.[72]

Just before the brigade arrived in Butler, Lane learned that a notorious rebel named Locke had been carried from town upon his sick bed; Lane had offered a $1,000 reward for him. Ritchie took about seventy men to find Locke, who was staying at a log house about five miles away. The house was surrounded and Locke was called for. A woman came out and indicated there were no men present. Ritchie then ordered the house burned. After a few minutes the woman asked permission to enter the burning house and retrieve some clothing. Thomas Stanfield of Hunt's company volunteered to assist her, but as he stepped through the door he was shot, and another soldier standing guard at the window was wounded. Stanfield's wound proved fatal, and his attacker, presumed to be Locke, somehow escaped. The following morning Locke was found in a cornfield and shot. The man at whose house Locke was staying was also killed. A separate party under Foreman went out to capture another "notorious" rebel, this one named Raney. Raney was not at home, but at least one of his slaves was. An old black man, perfectly blind, came to the door, and with his cane commenced feeling for the steps. In the darkness of the night this cane was taken for a gun (by one of Foreman's men), and at once he leveled his Sharp's rifle upon the old fellow, and snapped twice before he discovered his mistake. Without waiting for any apology or explanation, the old man said: "Massa, hab you any 'bacca? It seems as if in dese 'citing times cullud pussons couldn't git nuff 'bacca."[73]

After the brigade left Butler, a detachment was sent back to bring out three Union families who wished to escape their secessionist neighbors. As the soldiers and refugees made their way back to the brigade column, they were joined by other fleeing Unionists. Finally the expedition returned to West Point. Lieutenant Trego, who had been left at West Point, noted the jayhawkers came back with twenty wagonloads of valuables, fifty horses, and twenty-seven "darkies."[74]

Hospital steward Daniel Chandler wrote on September 28, "It seems barbarous and cruel to sack and burn towns, but I cannot tell how the rebels can be subdued by any other process." Wiley Britton, who served in the Sixth Kansas, but was not then in the brigade, writing after the war, thought otherwise: "In destroying [Osceola] General Lane seemed to be unconscious of the fact that his conduct would be just excuse for retaliation, and that it might possibly come with interest. And he did not seem to realize that he was making a name for his command that should not attach to troops engaged in honorable war." The problem with Britton's condemnation of Lane is that Lane was never at Osceola, and the ultimate decision to burn came from Montgomery, the senior colonel. Lane had not been in the van with Montgomery but had followed with other troops. Dickinson noted in his diary on September 22: "We came in sight of a large smoke, that Gen Lane said was the town of Oceola. We took a long rest in a dense wood. . . . At 3 we could see the burning of Oceola that had been fired by order of Col Montgomery. A messenger arrived and told us that Montgomery had entered the town." A trooper in Hunt's company wrote that on the retreat from Osceola, they encountered Lane about eight miles from Osceola, bringing up reinforcements. Lane may, however, be accused of culpable neglect. Less than two weeks earlier he had proposed to "pitch into" and "clear out" towns in Missouri. Certainly his subordinates knew of this sentiment, but the exact meaning of his words may have been left to their imaginations. This, coupled with the apparent lack of any rebuke for the arson at Morristown, could have led Montgomery into assuming he had license to burn whatever he wanted.[75]

Lane's initial reaction to the arson was to provide Frémont with two arguably contradictory reports, both dated September 24. In one Lane claimed the rebels had taken up positions in the town's buildings and that his men were compelled to shell them out; in doing so the place was burned to ashes. This implied the burning was accidental. In his other report, implying the destruction was intentional, Lane wrote that Osceola was the "depot of the traitors" for southwestern Missouri and trusted Frémont would approve the march on the town and its destruction. Similarly, Frémont's aide B. Rush Plumly gave conflicting analyses of reports received in St.

Louis. In a message to the assistant secretary of war on October 3, Plumly stated that when Lane burned Osceola, every house exploded with concealed powder. In a second message later that day he explained: "Lane chased Rains into Osceola, and was compelled to shell the place to dislodge the rebels. In doing so he burned the town and destroyed large stores of the rebels, of which the town was the depot."[76]

Montgomery's burning of Osceola put Lane in a difficult position. It would not take long for what had been done to be made public, and he could expect to be condemned for it. As a practical matter he could not lay the sole blame on Montgomery and discipline him without risking losing the loyalty of the Third, if not the whole brigade. As a matter of law, and of which Lane was acutely aware, he had no authority as a civilian to impose any discipline upon an officer of the U.S. Army. Lane's only option was to accept there was nothing to be done about what had happened at Osceola, create excuses to justify and condone the deed, and to embrace the new tactic of creating terror in Missourians who would think of resisting him. A superb example of this approach was displayed when in the following month Sturgis introduced Lane to a correspondent for the *New York Times*. The two generals were engaged in a heated discussion, Sturgis claiming that the government's policy was to make itself felt to its foes, conciliate the wavering, and reward its friends—but not to steal indiscriminately.

> This was agreed to by Gen. Lane—but with a smooth sophistry he combated the other's arguments, while he seemingly agreed with him, and alluded, with a humorous twinkle in his eye and a pleasant laugh at the fun of the thing, to reminiscences of negroes stolen, houses burned, citizens robbed, and prisoners shot, after being compelled to dig their own graves. He asserted that he had forbidden, under penalty of death, stealing on the part of his troops.
>
> "Yes, exactly, but didn't your men steal $8,000 from Mrs. Vaughn at Osceola?" queried Gen. Sturgis, "and didn't they take even the clothes of old —'s grandchild?" Gen. Lane's

eyes twinkled with fun as these interesting memories were called to his mind, and with a "I grant you my fellows have done some wrongs!" and a laugh of infinite gusto, he changed the subject and smilingly proceeded to discuss another part of the matter in question.[77]

Lane the politician certainly knew this interview might appear in the national press. His words were pure propaganda; with them Lane admitted nothing while implicitly admitting everything. What Lane did was little different from William Tecumseh Sherman's later use of propaganda as elaborated by Professor Phillip Shaw Paludan. Sherman made dramatic threats in writings, which he knew would be read by the enemy. At one time he wrote that to keep navigation open on the Mississippi, he would slay millions. On that point, he professed he was not only insane but mad. "For every bullet shot at a steamboat, I would shoot a thousand 30-pound Parrots into even helpless towns," Sherman wrote. But as noted by Paludan, "Sherman was barking, not biting." Lane, like Sherman after him, knew a threat could subdue the population as well as the torch. It worked. The *Times* correspondent noted in late October that a deadly terror toward Lane and Montgomery existed throughout western Missouri."[78]

CHAPTER 6

Frémont's Grand Army

Lane did not receive Frémont's order directing him to Kansas City until after the Osceola raid. He wrote to Frémont on September 24 from his camp at West Point (now called Camp Montgomery): "Although Lexington has fallen since your order of September 18, I propose to move on Kansas City, there to form a junction with General Sturgis. I will be able to move with about 700 cavalry, 500 infantry, 100 artillery[men], with a battery of two 6-pounder howitzers and two 12-pounder mountain howitzers. I will leave here Friday morning, September 27, at 5 o'clock A.M., and will reach Kansas City Sunday, 29th." From where the additional two cannons were acquired is unknown.[1]

As Lane wrote this, he probably had already received Prince's communication dated the previous day, directing him to form a junction at Kansas City with Sturgis. Lane recognized neither Prince nor Sturgis as his superior, and by his message to Frémont he could maintain that his movement to Kansas City was by his own volition. Prince's missive went beyond merely giving instructions to Lane; he saw fit to add commentary, obviously meant as an insult. It was regrettable, Prince wrote, that this movement had not been done earlier, as originally suggested, and had it been done, the enemy might have been frustrated. Sturgis added to this his endorsement that the order be complied with promptly and for Lane to march by the shortest possible route. An original of this document contains the handwritten note from Prince, "This letter made Lane my enemy." Another note from Prince two weeks later would do nothing to curry any favor with Lane. In it Prince wrote he would not comply with any orders from Lane until such time as Lane showed him he had such authority, yet he advised Lane he would at all times cooperate with him for the advancement of the public interest.[2]

The brigade, together with Jennison's men, reached Kansas City on September 30 and was joined there by five of Jennison's newly recruited (and unmounted) companies from Fort Leavenworth. Before entering town, the men changed into their dress uniforms and marched in behind a band. Lane himself gave little appearance of the conquering hero; he "was habilitated in an old straw hat, cowhide boots, blue blouse which had been thrown away by a private in Montgomery's regiment, some sort of an apology for pantaloons, and a butternut brown woolen shirt, with beard, hair, face, &c., to correspond." By the following morning, however, his dress had improved: "He had donned the new rig made expressly for him in Boston—blue coat and pants, buff vest, black chapeau, and feather as long as a war-leader in the Times, and such boots as would make Gen. Losee, or any other fast-horse man, stick his eyes out far enough for Sam Stinson's thanksgiving turkey to roost upon." Thus dressed, Lane received visitors in his tent while "seated upon an old split-bottom chair, one leg thrown across the other, intently engaged in caressing, with thumb and finger of right hand, a beard, if not remarkably luxurious, yet splendidly variegated in color."[3]

The brigade camp was in a section of Kansas City known as McGee's Addition, where the soldiers' tents covered several acres. Jennison's men were set up nicely "in good brick stores & dwellings." Lieutenant Colonel Daniel R. Anthony of Jennison's regiment was appointed provost marshal. Historian Stephen Starr noted that one of Anthony's first official acts was to issue an order prohibiting the sale of liquor to any soldier; the act also instructed all stores, eating establishments, and saloons to close at 6 P.M., and imposed a 9 P.M. curfew on all citizens. One soldier reported that Anthony attended to his duty faithfully and acted promptly to protect the property of civilians.[4]

Additional clothing was distributed to the men on October 2. Lieutenant Trego wrote of receiving cavalry hats for the company "with the yellow cords and tassells, eagles for the sides, ostrich feather &c which makes a splendid uniform. Lane is having his whole Brigade rigged out in as good style as any soldiers that I have seen since this war begun, the Regulars at Fort Leavenworth not excepted." William H. H. Dickinson wrote that his company received "new hats ornamented with an eagle & bugle & feather & scales for the shoulders." Dr. Huntoon, at the hospital in Mapleton, received letters from the men at Kansas City. He wrote to his wife recounting what he had thus learned: "Our entire army have plenty of Pork & Beef, Flour, Beans, Rice, sugar & coffee, candles & soap, also plenty of socks, drawers, under & over shirts, pants & coats & overcoats & good tents." There was such a supply of goods, he wrote, that they could trade those items for vegetables, butter, and chickens. He added that the soldiers in Kansas City lived "much better in camp than at the hospital." Jennison's men received plumed cavalry hats, their first suggestion of a uniform.[5]

On October 2, in what was to become a commonly repeated scene during the brigade's stay in Kansas City, Stewart brought in twenty-five slaves. For good measure he had also liberated five Union men who had been imprisoned in the jail at Independence. Twelve more slaves came into the brigade camp on October 4, but it was not recorded whether this was a result of brigade action or slaves liberating themselves.[6] Again a man from the brigade struck out from camp to lead slaves to freedom, but this time it was not a soldier but Edward Hill, a teamster for Allen's company. Private Dickinson noted in his diary on October 5, "Hill our Colored Teamster brought in 5 colored brother that were slave." Hill had joined Allen's company the previous summer as it passed though Lima, Ohio. The next day Hill, accompanied by some cavalry, went out again to bring in slaves. The results of that expedition are not known, but on October 9 Hill rescued another two score slaves. Hill's activities had become known to the authorities, and unknown to him a warrant had been issued for his arrest, as well as for other black men who assisted slaves in escaping. Captain Seaman, Dickinson, and others rode out to warn Hill. Dickinson encountered Lieutenant Trego, who informed him that he had warned Hill and redirected him and the slaves into Kansas.[7]

Soon a rumor began circulating in camp that Sturgis was going to return escaped slaves to their owners. Dickinson noted in his diary on October 8 that Lane's Brigade sent thirty-three slaves south into Kansas but that Sturgis would never find them. "I am afraid Gen Sturgis may lose his health if he sleeps with this brigade," he wrote. Dickinson's pre-war involvement with the shadowy Liberty League in Salem, Ohio, must have continued, for he also wrote, "Reports to Liberty Leigue shows that we have fried [*freed*] 126 slaves," among them one woman he was certain was "pure caucasian," "really beautiful and intelligent."[8]

During their stay in Kansas City, the men of Stewart's company found a strange attraction to nearby Independence, which they visited often. The day after their October 2 raid on the jail, Stewart's men invaded the building housing the Soldier's Relief Society—thought to be a secessionist organization—and the jayhawkers made off with the society's constitution, by-laws, and, most notably, a list of persons who had contributed money to the society. A Leavenworth paper warned that it was now known who in Leavenworth had contributed, and advised that they had better "go slow."[9]

Lieutenant John Bowles of Stewart's company went to Independence and compelled the release of a man who had been jailed there for two years on the charge of aiding runaway slaves. It is unclear exactly when this occurred; it may have happened during the October 2 trip. On his return trip, Bowles helped twenty-two slaves escape; they were last seen in Kansas, riding in government wagons. For this, Bowles was arrested October 7 and tried before a court-martial. The court tried other soldiers for various offenses, mostly for horse stealing. Philip Hobo of Stewart's company was drummed out of camp on October 3 for having committed some crime. Lieutenant Trego, who had been detailed as a member of the court, claimed Weer was determined to break up the court by throwing every obstacle in front of Montgomery, who presumably had instituted the proceedings. In Lane's absence Weer reportedly refused to obey Montgomery's orders, claiming he outranked Montgomery. For this Montgomery threatened to arrest Weer. With the exception of the appropriately named Hobo, the results of the trial are unknown.[10]

The cavalry companies of Williams, Creitz, and Seaman made a reconnaissance to Hickman Mills on October 2, but finding no secesh there, they went on to Lone Jack and Pleasant Hill before returning on October 4. Williams reported to Lane that Price was moving south, his strength was greatly exaggerated, his men were not well armed, half of them were barefooted, and there was discord in the rebel camp. It was argued that Price's army would melt away as he continued his retreat southward. This report was entirely true. Price knew he lacked the resources to maintain his position at Lexington and was retreating southward.[11]

Lane ordered Lieutenant Colonel Blunt, at Fort Scott, to move with most of his force to West Point and then in the direction of Harrisonville. Lane sent a message to Frémont informing him of his intention to move together with Sturgis to West Point and form a junction with Blunt. Apparently Lane had not consulted with Sturgis on this, for the move did not come off. Instead, a quarrel ensued over rank and who commanded whom. In a letter to Sturgis dated October 3, Lane wrote, "In answer to your note of this day I have this to say, that I don't care a fig about rank; I have enough of the glittering tinsel to satisfy me."[12]

Sturgis also complained about Lane's policy toward slavery. Lane responded, "My brigade is not here for the purpose of interfering in any wise with the institution of slavery. They shall not become negro thieves, nor shall they be prostituted into negro catchers. The institution of slavery must take care of itself. . . . In my opinion the institution [will] perish with the march of the Federal armies." Sturgis knew what it meant if a slave made it into Lane's camp. One woman complained to him her slave had walked off and into Lane's camp. Sturgis replied, "Madam, if I had your nigger, I should feel it my duty to return him, and would cheerfully do so; but if he has got into Lane's Brigade, all hell couldn't get him." Yet Lieutenant Trego would write in his diary on October 16 that Lane began returning slaves and property taken from secessionists who proved they were Union men.[13]

Another reason Lane's march to West Point did not come off may have been because of an unsettling communication from Frémont. Several days earlier Frémont had penned an order from Jefferson City directing Sturgis to fall back to Fort Leavenworth and destroy any government stores he could not move to prevent their capture. Frémont did not know Lane was in Kansas City. Sturgis did not immediately obey the order but asked Lane for his opinion of it. Lane replied he thought the order was predicated upon the false belief the enemy had crossed the river in force; if the order were acted upon, he warned, their forces would "present the singular spectacle of retreating from an army" that was itself retreating. Lane insisted, "Not until a battle is fought and a defeat suffered should Kansas City be given up to the enemy." Lane then sent Blunt, who had just arrived, toward Lone Jack with four hundred cavalry to ascertain Price's location and strength. Trego wrote that on the march, Blunt ordered that no property, whether secesh or Union, be disturbed, except by his permission, which would be given only if his men were fired upon or had "knowledge of any man being on the way or about to start with his effects—including negroes—for the Southern army." This order frustrated the men when they traveled through Independence, which they felt to be a secessionist town; they wished that somebody would fire upon them and thus create a justification for retribution. Yet Blunt's scout failed to disclose any rebel threat. Learning this, Lane and Sturgis ignored Frémont's order to fall back to Leavenworth. In fact, Price was beginning to retreat from his exposed and untenable position on the Missouri River.[14]

Being now better advised, and having finally assembled an army to challenge Price, Frémont on October 6 ordered both Lane and Sturgis to move in concert with Sturgis's command to Warrensburg, then on to Clinton, with the aim of proceeding toward Warsaw, where they would join Frémont's advance guard of ten thousand strong. Again, the command relationship between Lane and Sturgis was left undefined.[15]

Frémont's order did not prevent a military ball scheduled for October 8 in Kansas City from taking place. A brigade soldier sourly predicted that "gentlemen soldiers" would be in attendance to receive the attentions of "secession belles," while the "rough-coated, but brave Kansas boys, who go to war for the purpose of fighting the enemy and not courting it," would remain in camp.[16]

Lane missed the ball, having departed for Leavenworth the previous day. While there he made a fiery speech at Stockton's Hall on October 8, repeating his assertion that slavery could not survive the march of the Federal army—that there would be an army of one color marching into the slave states and an army of another color marching out. Regarding confiscating the property of secessionists, he claimed that any property confiscated by his brigade was turned over to the government. "Now if—oh! the dirty puppy—if that creature Prince, or that still dirtier creature, Robinson, can find an instance of a violation of this rule in my command, the guilty man shall be hung." And explaining his philosophy of how the war must be fought, he told his audience: "This war will never be successfully carried out so long as an army marches through slave States as a boat goes through a flock of ducks. They fly up on its approach and nestle down as soon as it has passed. The boat is safe and so are the ducks. When you march through a state you must destroy the property of the men in arms against the Government—destroy, devastate, desolate. This is a war. Take the Union man by the hand, but lay waste the property of traitors."[17]

A few days later Chaplain Fisher of the Fifth read Lane's speech to the regiment, which was drawn up in a hollow square. Despite the inherent difficulty of a whole regiment being able to hear an entire speech, even shouted out, it was nonetheless reported that cheers went up throughout the reading. Fisher repeated his performance for the Third regiment, with the same results.[18]

Governor Robinson drafted a public reply to Lane's speech, which was printed in the newspapers on October 13. Robinson condemned the conduct of Lane's men, "such as laying waste the whole country through which they pass, whether settled by Union men or Secessionists, sacking Fort Scott, burning towns, stealing horses, mules and beef cattle, and selling them to the Quartermaster of the army, &c., &c.... If our towns and settlements are laid waste by fire and sword, in my judgment, we will have Gen. Lane to thank for it.... The thieves are protected in, and are a part and parcel of, the Lane army." Robinson's remarks prompted a vicious response signed by fifty-four officers of the brigade, which they published in the *Leavenworth Daily Conservative*, accusing Robinson of being "a base slanderer, a traitor, and a coward." Among the signatories were Colonel John Ritchie, Lieutenant Colonel James Blunt, Lieutenant Colonel John Burris, Major Henry H. Williams, and Chaplain Hugh Fisher.[19]

Immediately following his Stockton's Hall speech, Lane wrote to Lincoln, accusing Robinson and Prince of conspiring to dissolve his brigade. He claimed Prince had refused to both recognize his authority as commander and ignored his requisitions for articles and supplies necessary to the brigade. To rectify this condition, Lane proposed the establishment of a new military department, to be composed of Kansas, the Indian country, much of Arkansas, and the territories. "If this can be done," Lane wrote, "and I can have the command of the department, I will cheerfully accept it, resign my seat in the Senate, and devote all my thoughts and energies to the prosecution of the war."[20]

Robinson penned a letter to Lincoln too and enclosed a newspaper clipping of Lane's speech. He complained:

> These are grave charges against the Executive of the State, and the officer in charge of Fort Leavenworth, which I pronounce to be false and malicious; and I ... demand the appointment of an impartial commission to investigate these charges, and the whole conduct of Gen Lane, and if it be found that his charges are false and his conduct otherwise improper and unworthy of an officer, I demand he be removed from the command of the volunteer militia of

this State—Many reports of the misconduct of Gen Lane's command such as plundering the inhabitants, stealing horses and cattle, and selling them to the Quartermaster, sacking and burning towns, and other like conduct—have hitherto reached me, and are now prevalent in this community, much to the discredit of the service.[21]

Lane's associates William G. Coffin and Mark Delahay also wrote to Lincoln, appealing for the creation of a new military department that would comprise Kansas, Arkansas, and the Indian Territory. They argued, with some merit, that the far reaches of the Department of the West could not be effectively managed from St. Louis. After making their case, the two men then suggested that—surprise!—Lane should be given command of the new department with the rank of major general. Coffin and Delahay accused Robinson and Prince of "doing all in their power to degrade and injure Genl. Lane, and, what is worse, to cripple and thwart the efforts of his army in the field," finally concluding their missive with charges of incompetence against the regular army officers at Fort Leavenworth.[22]

Lincoln, having more important crises to attend to, declined to involve himself in the spat between Lane and Robinson. Neither did he immediately respond to the suggestion of a new military department.

Lane and his supporters had another card to play against Robinson. They argued that the state constitution would require Robinson's term to end that November. The Republican State Central Committee, friendly to Lane, formed a ticket with George A. Crawford nominated as governor. Crawford was "elected" in legislative elections held in November despite receiving few votes, as no one else ran for governor. Crawford's claim to office was not recognized by the state election board, and the dispute went before the Kansas Supreme Court. The following January, in a decision written by Chief Justice Thomas Ewing, Jr., the court ruled against Crawford. That same month Robinson faced another attempt to evict him from office. Lane's supporters in the legislature engineered an investigation of Robinson's role in the sale of state bonds. Robinson was impeached in February, but an overwhelming lack of evidence resulted in an anticlimactic one-day trial and acquittal in June.[23]

The haphazard mustering in of the companies of the brigade was finally completed by October 10. Lieutenant R. H. Offley, the regular army mustering officer, reported that the Fourth comprised the companies of Hayes, Harris, Moonlight, Blanton, Boyd, Quigg, Ransom, William T. Campbell, James Harvey, and Veale; the Fifth comprised the companies of Graham, Rose, Leander Wilson, Ritchie, Williams, Elijah E. Harvey, Gibson, James S. Hunt, Clark, and Greenville Watson. Offley did not list the companies of the Third. The companies of Ransom and Campbell, credited to the Fourth, were actually two of the Fort Scott home guard companies raised by authority of Lyon and never were properly part of the Fourth. It is probable these two companies were claimed by the Fourth to give the appearance of being, if not a full-strength regiment, at least one that had a full complement of ten companies. Similarly, the Fifth was credited with ten companies, when at the time it had eight at the most. Although Ritchie was commanding the Fifth, Offley listed him as a company commander instead of William Creitz, who had assumed command of Company A.[24]

To crush Price, Frémont had organized a "Grand Army" of some forty thousand men in six separate columns. Lane and Sturgis were ordered to march from Kansas City, Major General David Hunter from Versailles, acting Major General John Pope from Boonville, acting Major General Franz Sigel from Sedalia, acting Major General Alexander Asboth from Tipton, and acting Major General Justus McKinstry from Syracuse. Lane certainly realized that his days as an independent freebooter were coming to an end. Up to now he had been able to deflect the efforts of Prince and Sturgis to command him, and Frémont, commanding from afar, exerted little influence. Now, however, he was no longer the ruler of a little army in some remote corner of Kansas but only the commander of a few regiments in a much larger army. He therefore began laying the groundwork for another way to obtain a major military command.[25]

Lane returned from Leavenworth in time to join the brigade as it marched south on October 12 to meet up with Sturgis at Warrensburg. Also marching with the brigade was Oliver P. Bayne's independent company from Kansas. Jennison's regiment remained at Kansas City, while the companies of Ransom and Campbell of the Sixth returned to Fort Scott. From Warrensburg the combined forces of Lane and Sturgis were to march to Clinton for a rendezvous with Frémont. The Sabbath on October 13 was observed by assembling the entire brigade and having the three chaplains address the men, followed by a speech from Lane in which he explained "that the fate of Treason and Slavery must be one and the same," recounted Chaplain Moore. "Our army could not be engaged in crushing the Rebellion and supporting Slavery at the same time. [Lane] earnestly exhorted his men not to interfere with a slave, or with any kind of property, only as they receive orders to do so."[26]

Lane's message was a mixed one: slavery must be destroyed, but don't free any slaves without specific orders. In practice the men would heed the former invocation. The evening following Lane's speech a scouting party returned to camp "accompanied by a drove of niggers with their teams and wagons, buggies, kitchen [equipment] & bedding."[27]

Creitz claimed that Lane also pretended to have a holy horror for anything savoring of what was commonly known as "jayhawking," but at the same time his "debased lickspittles" would under his direction steal every form of property that could possibly be removed to a secure place. During the pursuit of Price, some men in the brigade did prey on civilians. One soldier tried to explain away the abuses:

> I say that there is almost a sufficient excuse for any undue excesses that may have been committed by this brigade. There is hardly a house that we have come to, but is known by at least one of the brigade, as the habitation of an individual who figured largely in the Kansas troubles, at whose hands violence, either directly or indirectly, had been received, it is then not to be wondered at if some things are

done that ought not to be done; we are all mortal, and revenge is sweet even to a soldier. I am convinced, when we leave this neighborhood, as we are now doing, (en route for the secession army,) that such conduct will stop.[28]

Such conduct apparently did not completely stop. In a letter written a week later, Chaplain Moore complained that there were, indeed "a few professional thieves" in the brigade, "and . . . I have no doubt it would add to the happiness of their dying hours if they could steal the lumber of which their coffins would be made, and the spade that might be used in digging their graves." Moore attributed much of the thievery to camp followers who he felt should be shot or expelled from the camp. Yet despite the known presence of professional thieves and larcenous camp followers, there is no evidence any effort was made to punish such men.[29]

A somewhat contrary view was voiced by Judge Advocate H. Miles Moore who gloated, "Our Boys *press* what we need for transportation Mules Horses Waggons &c., confiscating Secesh property & paying *Union men* for theirs. A great many negroes slaves are nightly running away from their masters & joining the Brigade." Lane, through Ritchie, directed Moore on October 17 to take twenty men back on the Lone Jack road and sweep up transport for the brigade—anything he found was fair game, as Moore was told everyone along that road was secesh. Moore took a detachment from Gibson's company and returned with twelve mules, six to eight horses, two double wagons, and some harness.[30]

When the Fifth camped at one secesh farm, the men grazed their mounts in the cornfield and took rails from the owner's fences to build campfires. The secessionist's nearby store, known as Hughes' Store, was raided by the jayhawkers. In an odd twist to what heretofore appeared to be uncontrolled confiscation of secesh property, Ritchie appointed officers to appraise the property taken from the store, and the goods were turned over to the quartermaster. Two days later Ritchie and Judge Advocate H. Miles Moore butted heads when Ritchie directed Moore to distribute confiscated clothing to the contrabands who were following the brigade. Moore refused because the previous owner of the clothing was a Mason; he requested the task be given to someone else. Ritchie was furious, said some derogatory remarks about Masons, and gave Moore a direct order. Moore diplomatically resolved the dilemma by not personally distributing the clothing but merely letting the contrabands help themselves.[31]

Although the brigade was given the most notoriety for assaults on civilian property, the other columns of the Grand Army were hardly guilt-free. In response to reports of "depredations by individuals of the United States troops now marching southward," Frémont issued a formal order prohibiting, and calling a crime, the taking of civilian property unless needed for use by the army. Property could be taken only "by the proper officers, under orders only from the commanding general or generals of divisions," and would be "receipted for and the owners in due time paid."[32]

Lane's column was joined on October 15 by a band of fifty-four Delaware Indians commanded by Captain Fall Leaf, a Delaware chief. Fall Leaf's Delaware name was Panipakuxwe: "He who walks when leaves fall." He had served as a scout for pre-war army expeditions under Frémont, Edwin V. Sumner, and John Sedgwick. Frémont again sought out the Delaware to serve as scouts; Fall Leaf's company was mustered in at Fort Leavenworth on October 4. In addition to the Delaware, twenty Wyandot Indians were attached to George W. Veale's company of the Fourth. One correspondent noted the Indian scouts scoured the forests before the army marched through, and quick death was the punishment of all rebels who waited to shoot down Union soldiers. A civilian correspondent interviewed John Johnnycake of the Delaware, who informed him "that there were 54 of his tribe in the field; that they were armed with tomahawks, scalping-knives and rifles; that their principal business was scouting; and that almost all of the crowd had good horses, and had accompanied Gen. Frémont once before, in some of his expeditions across the plains and over the mountains."[33]

When the brigade reached Pleasant Hill on October 16, Lane noticed the town was lacking a Union flag. He ordered one made, as well as a flag pole. The flag was raised before an assemblage of citizens (whose presence for the ceremony was coerced) and accompanied by a three-gun salute by Moonlight's battery. Lane then made a little speech to the citizenry:

> This is the second time that a Union army has marched through this county, and this is the second Union flag that has been flung to the breeze by that army, and when I return, as most assuredly I will, if that flag is not still there, I will visit you with a terrible visitation, not a vestige of you will remain, you will be completely blotted out from the book of remembrance as men void of all principle, having been twice tried and found wanting; the fault lies with yourselves and not with me; leave that flag to float proudly over your town, your homes and yourselves, and you are my friends—tear it down, and by heaven I will do what I have said; utter destruction must and shall befall you, if you persist in plotting treason against the best Government that ever the sun shone on.[34]

A similar ceremony was repeated the following day ten miles away at Kingsville. A man visiting Pleasant Hill shortly thereafter saw the Stars and Stripes flying over the town, and he commented to a citizen that it must be a Union town. The citizen denied the charge, and when asked what the flying of the flag meant, he was told, "It means that Jim Lane raised it, and gave notice he would burn the town if it was disturbed."[35]

The brigade camped on the prairie about fifteen miles beyond Kingsville. The pause certainly came as a relief to Lieutenant Trego, who had been without sleep for sixty hours. "I might have slept some to-day but was not wanting to be snoozing while others were looking *up prizes,*" Trego wrote in his diary. That night the men were joined by Captains Moonlight and Quigg, who had made a dangerous ride unescorted from West Point to join their companies. The brigade then moved through Clinton and on to the crossing of the Osage River, which was reached October 21. The first troops to reach the crossing were the Delaware, who plunged their horses into the river and captured the ferry boat. The cavalry was able to ride across, and although the water was only three and a half feet deep, the current was too strong to allow the infantry to wade across. The ferrying of the infantry, wagons, and artillery took all night and until noon the following day.[36]

A lady of Osceola recalled that the precipitous crossing of the river by the Delaware, led by a Lieutenant Johnson, barely gave the gentlemen of the household time to leap the fences and run into the brush. Johnson's "band of whooping Indians" found a few guns, about sixty kegs of gunpowder hidden in the carriage house, and $10,000 in buried coins. This Southern widow alleged that Johnson, by threatening two of her slaves with death, coerced them into revealing the location of such animals, flour, furniture, clothing, and jewelry that had been saved from the previous raid: "The goods they distributed among their Union friends. The flour and clothing they bestowed on a train of negroes sent off in haste to Kansas. The furniture was broken up, the ladies bonnets, laces, jewelry, etc., stolen or wantonly destroyed." If this were not enough, she feared for her son in the rebel army: "We were kept in constant terror, however, by threats against our absent sons, brothers, and friends. Several of the officers told me that Lane has sent the Indians out, with orders to shoot them down wherever they were found. I went to his head-quarters with my son's wife, who was almost frantic, to learn the truth. He calmly told me it was so, and advised me to send him word to give himself up, spicing his remarks and advice with oaths and curses against the rebels." Lane's instructing Southern men to return to their homes was consistent with the reporting of a correspondent for the Cincinnati *Commercial,* who compared the positions of Lane and Sturgis: "Gen. Sturgis *invites* rebels to come to their homes and take care of their families. Gen. Lane says, gentlemen, *go* home, I have left your families helpless, and your presence is positively demanded or they will perish. He takes their horses, cattle, and does not run the niggers out of camp as [Sturgis] invariably does."[37]

Two of the Indians seized an Osceola man, who claimed ignorance of any hidden contraband. Not being convinced, the scouts each took hold of one of the man's arms and began dancing with him between them; every few steps in their dance they let out a blood-curdling war hoop that soon got the fellow's tongue working. The terrified man revealed the location of thirty kegs of gunpowder, plus lead and tobacco.[38]

Osceola still bore the ugly scars of Lane's previous visit. Among the rubble, Chaplain Moore noted shattered, burnt buildings, lonely chimney stacks, blackened foundations, rubbish piles, half-blackened sacks of salt, seared shade trees—general desolation. Moore, nonetheless, wrote that until his visit, he was not fully satisfied that the arson had been "righteous and a necessity." One of the things that had changed his mind was learning from the townspeople (the few who remained) that the destruction of the town was a great relief to the loyal citizens of that section of Missouri. Judge Advocate Moore, who only a few days before had heartily approved taking secesh draft animals, wagons, and slaves, now had a soldier from Williams's company arrested at Osceola for robbing a poor widow's house. "I hope to God he will be hung," he wrote in his diary.[39]

As the brigade prepared to leave Osceola, the Union men in the surrounding country were invited to come in and help themselves to salt and stores. Before the Union men could do so, Sturgis arrived and placed guards over the property. Lieutenant Trego complained that Sturgis, "instead of living on the rebels" as his brigade had done, "he purchased all his supplies of forage, beef &c from known rebels when he could have bought of Union men just as well. Such a course is regarded as traitorous because he is giving aid to the enemy by so doing." Trego's letter describing the invitation to Union men to "help themselves to salt and stores" appears to be at odds with his diary entry. There he wrote that Lane wanted the rebels to feel that his brigade had passed through their country and that it was not good for men to leave their homes to join a rebellious army. "Every man who is at *home attending* to his business and has not been in the Southern army is treated the same as though he was an avowed Union man," he wrote. A consistent policy would not permit the locals to help themselves to the salt and stores unless the owners were secessionists who had fled.[40]

The lady who was so offended by the Delaware in her house recalled that when Sturgis arrived, he vehemently denounced Lane. "But before he left we discovered the source of his indignation . . . that he had been awakened to the knowledge that Lane was the more successful and profitable rogue." Comparing the conduct of the troops of the two commanders, the lady acknowledged, "I must do the Jayhawkers the justice to say that some of their officers were respectful and kind to us, which is better than my experience of the 'gentlemanly Sturgis' and his lawless troops, who came just after." Sturgis's soldiers "were much more insulting than Lane's, and spared us neither curses or threats of evil. May God grant that I may never be placed in such brutal company again, where woman's purity and dignity were unrespected, and where, for the first time, my cheek burned with shame that I had ever been a citizen under their disgraced banner." She added, "Some of Lane's officer's deemed it their duty to protect the citizens who wished for it, by placing a guard around their houses. Terrified by the conduct of the soldiers under Sturgis, I rose from a sick bed to go and ask for a similar safeguard." Although promised such a guard, it was never sent.[41]

The correspondent for the Cincinnati *Commercial*, writing from Osceola, commented on Lane's reputation:

> There is great complaint in this country against Gen. Lane. When I stop at houses, as I travel along, and listen to the pathetic stories of the women—how Lane has taken everything they had—I have pitied them from my heart, and could say no Buckeye could do as he does. The next Union man I met who knew the man Lane had so despoiled, would say—"Lane served him right." Yesterday I stopped at a farm house where the post-office was kept; the poor woman, who was sick, informed me that Lane took her clothing, and shoes from her children's feet. I resolved that Lane was a scoundrel, and had no soul; but I met a Union man a mile or two off, who told me Lane did so because Johnson, the proprietor of said house, was the most notorious leader of secesh forces in this country. He had killed one Union man with his own hands, and had robbed a host of families.[42]

Two months later Lane delighted a Boston audience illustrating how much slaveholders valued their slaves. He said that during the march, a distraught Missouri woman came to him: "She was a big brawny woman, fat and over forty, and was crying. I asked her what the matter was. She said, 'My two sons have joined the Confederate army, and now your soldiers have taken my two niggers.' Said I, 'My good woman, that is not the worst thing that could have happened to you. I am on the track of your sons, and I shall probably catch them in a day or two and hang them.' She threw her arms about my neck and said: "Gen. Lane you may do what you want with my sons, if you'll only return the niggers."[43]

Not everyone in Lane's Brigade was overjoyed at the notion of contrabands coming into camp. Judge Advocate Moore, who was temporarily attached to the Fifth, noted in his diary on October 18 that there was considerable excitement in camp about so many blacks being present: "Some companies will not have one of them about them," Moore wrote. The brigade left Osceola at noon on October 23. As it did so, approximately 150 contrabands, with a good supply train, were sent toward Kansas under the protection of Bayne's independent company of scouts.[44]

Bayne had been an active Free State man during the territorial period. Like Stewart, Bayne had been one of the "officers" charged with enforcing the decisions of the squatters' courts, as was Dr. Rufus Gilpatrick, the brigade surgeon. A U.S. marshal's posse in December 1857 cornered Bayne and his followers at his home, dubbed "Fort Bayne." A skirmish resulted in the wounding of one man on each side and the retreat of the deputies. Companies led by him and Montgomery in 1858 were blessed by Lane, as major general of the Kansas territorial militia, to protect Free State men in southeast Kansas. Thereafter, Bayne and Montgomery, acting on their own authority, twice invaded and cowed Fort Scott by force of arms. Bayne and Montgomery so defied the authorities that in December 1858, Federal judge J. J. Williams issued arrest warrants for both, as well as for Jennison, Snyder, and Seaman; none were caught. Bayne's independent company had no official existence, never having been mustered into state or U.S. service, and it maintained but a tenuous connection to the brigade. After Bayne returned to Kansas, he refused to take orders from Colonel Judson and claimed to be responsible to no one but Lane.⁴⁵

Harris, the rebel quartermaster who had been captured during the previous month's raid on Osceola, had been released on October 15—William H. H. Dickinson believed this was only because he was a Free Mason—and now for some reason Harris reappeared in the brigade's camp on October 24. Chaplain Moore wrote, "He gave us a good name in all this section. I think we are indebted to him for much of the confidence and good-will which the army is receiving from the people. . . . Harris was hardly believed by his neighbors and friends when he told them that he was never treated more gentlemanly than by the Kansas Brigade, and a more orderly set of men he never saw."⁴⁶

The brigade took a parallel route to that of the main army, Lane having been given permission to make a westerly detour to Montevallo, Missouri, to get rid of the stores destined for Fort Lincoln. This permission presumably would not have been given had the authorities known the stores to be disposed of were contrabands destined for resettlement in Kansas. A correspondent of the *New York Times* witnessed the brigade send one hundred contrabands to Kansas on October 25 and another hundred "ebony chattels" on October 27. At Paola on October 27, A. T. Ward noted the appearance of "a flock of negros" who related that Lane "had sent over three hundred in the gang they came in." The companies of Hunt and Creitz of the Fifth were detached to take possession of Howard's Mill (also known as Ritchey's Mills) on the Sac River in Cedar County to obtain flour for the brigade. In the few days there, the mill was kept running day and night with twenty thousand pounds of flour ground from "contraband" wheat seized in the neighborhood. "Union" wheat had been swept up the week previous by the rebels. One hundred bushels of contraband grain hidden in a thicket was found with the aid of a local guide.⁴⁷

Moving south through Missouri, the brigade encamped at Humansville, about eighteen miles south of Osceola, where it was joined by Sturgis's column. Blunt, who had been given command of the brigade's cavalry, later commented that the march was nothing very remarkable except that their trail was marked by the feathers of secesh poultry and the remains of disloyal beehives.[48]

Price's retreat halted at Neosho on October 20, where the minority of Missouri legislators loyal to Governor Jackson passed an extralegal ordinance of secession; a month later the Confederate Congress voted to accept Missouri into the Confederacy. While the secessionist legislators debated, Frémont's cavalry occupied Springfield on October 25. Frémont, instead of continuing to pursue Price, halted his columns in and around Springfield.

A correspondent of the *New York Times* interviewed Montgomery at Humansville; he found Montgomery in civilian clothing but wearing "a black Kossuth hat, fastened up at one side with a red, white and blue rosette":

> I presented my credentials, shook an emaciated hand, which he cordially extended, and then dropped down on a pile of tents to have a chat. . . . At length some remark introduced the question of Slavery and the instant after a pair of cavernous dark eyes were turned full upon me as he waxed eloquent upon the emancipation of the negro and his hope of a millennium at hand, in which they would gain a political and social equality with the white man. He is a medium sized man, dark complexion, black whiskers and moustache, a tolerably full, white forehead, and an indescribable pair of black eyes, which now wander furtively to the ground, and the next moment are tuned full upon you, their depths all ablaze with enthusiasm. He is very thin, coughs incessantly, and, as I believe, has but a short time left in which to arrange his earthly affairs. . . .
>
> He gave his views at length upon the war. I will give only one of his remarks. "If our boys thought that this war had any other object than to give freedom to the slave, they would every one go home to-morrow." He informed me that he was a clergyman of the Christian, and not of the Methodist, persuasion, as is frequently said of him; and then,

with a shake of his cold, wasted hand, and with the fire of enthusiasm fast dying out in his melancholy eyes, I left him.[49]

In an unusual move, Lane on October 28 ordered all the contrabands in camp arrested. The officers for whom these people acted as servants were required to "enter into an obligation for their good behavior in [the] future." Judge Advocate Moore was absent from camp when this occurred, but Stephen R. Harrington, adjutant of the Fifth, obligated himself on Moore's behalf regarding Moore's servant, Aleck Mason, an escaped slave. Moore had hired Aleck in Kansas City; his wages were to be $10 a month and presumably all the army food he could eat. Aleck had arrived in Kansas City with a horse, probably taken from his former master, and which Moore then purchased from him.[50]

Weer had been absent from the brigade on its march south but rejoined it at Humansville. He procured an appointment with Major General David Hunter, Frémont's aide, to request assistance in getting his men paid. Hunter had some acquaintance with Lane; the previous April he was the officer who had assigned Lane's Frontier Guards to guard the executive mansion. Hunter told Weer he must provide the original muster rolls of the companies; Weer duly wrote to Prince at Fort Leavenworth, asking if he could obtain the rolls for the companies of Harris, Hayes, Quigg, Moonlight, Ritchie, Boyd, Veale, Harvey, Blanton, and Rose. Weer added that, based upon his conversations with Hunter, he believed all further plundering would be prohibited.[51]

Dickinson recalled a story about Weer told to him by Montgomery. Weer was believed to be pro-slavery and to have been complaining in Washington about the brigade liberating slaves. Seaman concocted a scheme to silence him. Seaman got Weer "warmed up" with some liquor and then got him to go out and help bring in some slaves. Weer apparently kept quiet from then on.[52]

Frémont received information that Price was marching upon Springfield and on October 30 ordered his subordinate commanders to join him at Springfield. Major William Dorsheimer of Frémont's staff noted the arrival of Lane's men in Springfield. Lane was at the head of his brigade. It was a motley procession consisting of the desperate fighters of the Kansas borders and about two hundred contrabands mounted and armed, who "rode through the streets rolling about in their saddles with their shiny faces on a broad grin." The scare of an attack by Price proved to be a false alarm.[53]

Lane was gaining fame in the national press. The *New York Times* correspondent who accompanied Frémont reported that everywhere Lane had been, he carried a torch and knife with him, leaving "a track marked with charred ruins and blood." The correspondent wrote: "An old man told me . . . with composure . . . that they had taken his horses, mules, grain, his wife's dresses, and then fired the log shanty that afforded his gray hairs shelter from the pelting rain and the nipping frosts. He told all this in detail with a firm voice, but when he added: 'They even stole the clothes of my little dead grandson[,]' [h]is lip trembled convulsively a moment, and then the hot tears gushed from his eyes and found ready channels down his time-furrowed cheeks."[54]

The national press generally painted a more favorable picture of Lane. The *Chicago Tribune* editorialized: "But for the brave brigade that has fought the cause of our Constitution in eight victorious battles—which has been the terror of secession wherever it has appeared in Western Missouri or Kansas . . . and the scourge of traitors, it is but just that the villainous lies invented in Kansas, remouthed by the Missouri *Republican,* and picked up and garbled by the Chicago *Times,* should be denied as base fabrications. Gen. Lane is upheld by all Union people of Kansas, and will be upheld by his Government." The correspondent of the Cincinnati *Gazette* reported that Lane confiscated secession property and often gave it to poor Union families who had been robbed by rebels. "Lane has done more, and is doing more, to put down this rebellion, in a way that it will *stay* down, than all the other armies together, in this State. He conquers as he goes," the *Gazette* correspondent wrote. The *New York Tribune* also lauded Lane's tactics: "We who have witnessed the contest in Missouri are glad to see the men who have inaugurated and aided the rebellion taught that it costs something to be a traitor."

His fame would not be diminished when his grizzled visage graced the November 23, 1861, cover of *Harper's Weekly*.[55]

In his public calls for war and the liberation of slaves of traitors, Lane enjoyed considerable popular support, and his tactics would be championed in newspapers across the country. The *New York Times* reprinted, with apparent approval, a letter from a Leavenworth man who, although prejudiced against Lane and Jennison, disagreed with those who entered upon "the wholesale condemnation of such officers as Col. Jennison and Brig. Gen. James H. Lane on charges of 'jay-hawking,' oppression and so forth.... My experience leads me to believe that [they] are fit and proper leaders for the kind of war we are obliged to wage here, and it is rare to hear any thoroughgoing, intelligent and earnest Union man condemn their proceedings." The *Tipton* (Iowa) *Advertiser* of January 16, 1862 editorialized, "We are not special admirers of Gen. Lane, but we do admire his manner of conducting this war. He conducts it so the rebels *feel* it. He does not spend his time in returning runaway negroes, but puts the rebels out of the way, and lets the slaves look out for themselves."[56]

While Lane was thus occupied in Missouri, life had not been quiet in Kansas. Peter Bryant of Holton, Kansas, had been a member of the company raised by Creitz. Being too poor to afford a horse, Bryant was excluded when that company mustered in as cavalry. Procuring a horse somehow, he briefly marched with Jennison. Writing to his brother on October 13, Bryant explained the difference between himself and Creitz:

> I mustered about 50 men and went into Missouri.... He jayhawked under cover of Uncle Sam and I under a lieutenancy from Governor R. I marched when I d—d please; he, when he was told to. I kept my plunder (if I chose); he didn't. I took my pay as I went along; he, when he could get it. I have disbanded my squad; he has got to stick her till war is over. I tell you Missouri has a d—d desolate look.... I never ran but once. Then I was scouting with 25 men and

ran into an ambush of 200 Texans. Then spurs came into play. Four of my men went under and seven or eight were wounded but got away.[57]

A. T. Ward decried the Kansans who crossed over into Missouri to rob, the Missourians who did the same in Kansas, and Kansans who didn't even bother to leave the state to commit their thievery. He noted revenge could be taken upon a neighbor just by accusing the man of being disloyal, an allegation not too closely investigated by men prone to theft. Ward wrote they were in constant fear of being robbed by jayhawkers and routinely hid their valuables. Many men of Southern sympathies had been driven into Missouri, just as Unionists had been driven from that state. Paola, Ward observed, was full of refugees from Missouri, who begged for food to stay alive.[58]

Probably in response to the jayhawking raids, Humboldt was sacked again on October 14, this time by three hundred or four hundred rebels under the command of one Colonel Talbot of the Confederate Army, assisted by the bushwhacker Tom Livingston. The town's militia cavalry pickets had just that day reported there were no rebels about. With their guard down, the militiamen were easily captured. One citizen was shot and killed; one story held he was trying to escape on a mule, another that he was trying to save his mules. Most of the houses were robbed and then set on fire; perhaps a dozen buildings out of fifty were saved from the flames. After setting the fires, the raiders retired southward, robbing such houses as they encountered on the way. This time there was no pursuit. Following this second raid on Humboldt, many settlers in the neighborhood abandoned their homes and fled north and east. The village of Gardner in Johnson County was raided by about twenty rebel irregulars under Dick Yeager the evening of October 22. The local militia was completely surprised, their sixteen muskets being safely locked up in a makeshift armory. In addition to taking the muskets, the raiders made off with goods looted from two stores, plus horses and wagons. Although the affair was frightening to the citizens, not a gun was fired and no one in town was hurt. However, when a posse was sent in pursuit, one of the men suffered a fatal head wound in an accidental discharge of his weapon.[59]

Judson's Sixth Kansas was strengthened by the addition of Captain Charles F. Clarke's company, which Clarke had recruited from Riley County. After being mustered at Kansas City, the company was sent to Fort Riley where it remained several months, thus being unavailable for service on the border. From Fort Scott, Greeno's company made a raid into Missouri on October 24, its object being a rebel band in Medoc. The town was surrounded and captured the following day. Although the secesh ringleaders were gone, about fifty men were arrested, most of whom were paroled, with a few kept for imprisonment in the Fort Scott jail. Greeno pressed on to Montevallo and eventually made his way back to Fort Scott after a six-day sojourn. He brought with him six prisoners, thirteen horses, two mules, and one carriage, all of which was properly turned over to the government. Not all of the men of the Sixth favored such excursions. Some of them in the original home guard companies protested against going into Missouri on the theory that as home guards they were required to serve only within Kansas. When the Sixth was raised to regimental strength, the home guard companies were remustered—but without any mention of their being only home guards. How the men failed to notice they were not being remustered in the limited role as home guards is a bit of a mystery.[60]

In early November Judson received word of hostile Cherokees camped on the Spring River. One column set out from the vicinity of Humboldt on November 5 to scour the Cherokee Neutral Lands, while the following day forces from Fort Scott and Fort Lincoln, numbering around three hundred men under the command of Judson, headed south on the old military road. To the east, operating along the Missouri border, was a Union force of unknown origin under a Captain Boyce with 140 men. The direction of Judson's force was changed on November 7 when a scout reported four hundred Indians near Shoal Creek and the guerilla Tom Livingston and twenty-five of his men at his trading post in Missouri. The Indians were forgotten for the moment, and a forced march was made that night to get Livingston. The column neared the target around 1:00 A.M.; Judson took a hundred men, surrounded the building, and rushed it. No bushwhackers were found, but the jayhawkers discovered rifles and shotguns, a keg of powder, buffalo robes, fifteen horses, two oxen, and other goods from Humboldt. Also found were three black men, one of whom was said to have been taken from Humboldt and who had been a free man for fifteen years. The pursuit of the Indians also proved fruitless, as they had either melted away or existed in rumor only.[61]

As noted previously, Lane had established posts at Fort Scott, Fort Lincoln, and Fort Lane (near Barnesville), and ordered the construction of six stockades in other locations. In addition to these posts there was the general hospital at Mapleton. In the month of October, 103 men were treated there and only two died, one from pneumonia. The hospital had a steady patient load of from thirty-five to fifty men. To assist in their care, four male nurses were assigned to the hospital. Dr. Huntoon, still a private, was the physician in charge until Dr. Gilpatrick arrived October 31. Aside from treating disease, Huntoon cared for an accidental gunshot wound that broke a leg bone, amputated a boy's fingers that had been smashed in a cane mill, amputated two fingers injured in another accidental shooting, and treated a gunshot wound to the shoulder. Dr. Gilpatrick's arrival heralded the move of the hospital back to Fort Scott, which was accomplished within a few days.[62]

Senator James H. Lane. Courtesy Library of Congress.

THE BATTLE OF BOONEVILLE, OR THE GREAT MISSOURI "LYON" HUNT.

Missouri governor Claiborne Fox and Missouri State Guard major general Sterling Price (holding his bowels) being pursued by Brigadier General Nathaniel Lyon. *"Let out! General, let out! he's getting close to us."* *"Oh Govner Jackson I'm trying all I can to hold in."* Courtesy Library of Congress.

Major General Sterling Price, Missouri State Guard. Courtesy Library of Congress.

James Montgomery, Third Kansas. From Cutler's *History of the State of Kansas.*

Fort Lincoln, looking east, showing gate, earthen breastworks, two-story blockhouse, and stables. Courtesy Kansas State Historical Society.

Thomas Moonlight, Fourth Kansas. Courtesy Library of Congress.

James G. Blunt, Third Kansas. Courtesy Library of Congress.

John Ritchie, Fifth Kansas. Massachusetts MOLLUS photo collection, U.S. Army Military History Institute, Carlisle Barracks, Pennsylvania.

Brigadier General Samuel D. Sturgis. Courtesy Library of Congress.

"General" Lane's image graced the cover of *Harper's Weekly*, November 23, 1861, along with depictions of the brigade camp at Humansville, Missouri, and Delaware scouts. Courtesy Harold Lane, Topeka, Kansas.

Major General Henry Wager Halleck. Courtesy Library of Congress.

Captain David Hunter, April 1861. Courtesy Library of Congress.

CHAPTER 7

Lane the Liberator

Even before he reached Springfield, Frémont had fallen out of Lincoln's favor. His administration had been tainted by purchasing irregularities, and then came the uproar ignited by his martial law proclamation. In some circles, Frémont was blamed for failing to relieve the siege of Lexington, and now he was pursuing Price at what appeared to be a snail's pace. Rumors had circulated for some time in the press that Frémont was to be replaced. Frémont knew the rumors had substance. He had been visited by Secretary of War Cameron around October 10, who showed him an order removing him from command. Frémont argued that to recall him at that point would not only destroy him "but render his whole expenditure useless." Frémont was granted a temporary reprieve; Cameron agreed to withhold the order until he returned to Washington. Lincoln decided Frémont must be replaced, but only if the timing was right. Orders were drawn up for Major General David Hunter to replace Frémont, but Brigadier General Samuel Curtis, the bearer of the order, was not to deliver it if Frémont was engaged in a battle or "in the immediate presence of the enemy in expectation of a battle."[1]

Curtis correctly assumed Frémont had heard the rumors and would try to frustrate the delivery of any order replacing him. In the meantime Frémont was seeking the battlefield victory that would restore his celebrity and make it inexpedient to remove him. When Major Generals Asboth and Sigel reported an advance of Price's forces, Frémont began drawing up battle plans. Lane issued written instructions to the officers of the brigade on November 2 to prepare for a fight the following day. They were told to examine every man's weapon and make sure each had forty rounds of ammunition, food in his haversack, and "good water" in his canteen. Lane exhorted his officers: "This Brigade is to fight to the last. We cannot surrender better [to] die upon the field than be murdered as we will be if taken prisoners. Let every man understand that his business is to kill as many of the enemy as possible and that he is to preserve perfect silence in the ranks so that orders may be heard."[2]

As Frémont's battle plans were being polished, the order removing him arrived on November 2. Curtis had arranged for an officer, dressed as a common farmer, to carry the order to Frémont's camp and seek an audience. This subterfuge was successful. Frémont unsuspectingly took the order and read it. It instructed Frémont to call Hunter forward to relieve him; Hunter did not wait for Frémont to do this but was hurrying on to Springfield. In Hunter's absence, Frémont still was in command, and he continued with preparations for the battle with which he might yet salvage his command.[3]

On November 3 acting Major General Justus McKinstry received permission from Adjutant General Joseph H. Eaton to reconnoiter the enemy's positions. Although Eaton assumed McKinstry intended a scout involving perhaps five hundred men, McKinstry took liberty with this and expanded his operation into a reconnaissance in force involving twelve thousand men, including Lane's and Sturgis's commands, and twenty-six pieces of artillery. When Eaton discovered what was afoot, he ordered McKinstry to hold fast, then obtained from Frémont an order sending McKinstry back to camp. Eaton then rode to the Kansas camp and found the brigade preparing to march. Eaton was told by a Kansas soldier that the brigade was on its way to Wilson's Creek to attack Price. A distraught Eaton cried, "There is something wrong here; this is all wrong! Who gave the order?" Eaton informed Lane that McKinstry's reconnaissance plan had been rejected by Frémont. The reconnaissance was thus called off and the army remained idle.[4]

Unfortunately for Frémont, he was as dilatory in attacking Price as he had been in chasing him. He dithered long enough for Hunter to appear at his headquarters on the evening of November 3. Frémont peacefully relinquished command to Hunter and departed with his bodyguard and the Delaware scouts. Under Hunter the Grand Army would pursue Price no farther.[5]

The reaction of the men of the brigade to Frémont's departure is not well reported. In early October, in response to a rumored sacking of Frémont, William H. H. Dickinson wrote, "[The men's] indignation waxed warm & if he was removed on account of his Anti Slavery views we wished ourselves at home." Presumably Dickinson was writing only of the reaction within his company, and presumably his company was equally indignant when Frémont was relieved of command. As Allen's company was more stridently abolitionist than many other companies in the brigade, it cannot be presumed this indignation was equally shared.[6]

In the following week the only activity of note within the brigade came on November 5, when Ritchie took the companies of Creitz and Hunt with two cannons and marched eighteen miles in the direction of Cassville to take possession of Linden Mills. Upon reaching that point, Ritchie's men procured several hundred bushels of wheat, which they seized from both secesh and Union farms.[7]

The evening of November 7 was a leisurely one for Chaplain Moore. First he was serenaded by a squad "singing the sweet songs of Zion." Next the Twenty-fourth Indiana Regiment and band performed at Lane's headquarters, enticing out of their tents the men of the brigade. The Indianans then called for "Lane! Gen. Lane! Lane the Liberator!" Moore claimed, "The Kansas boys, who would rather hear the General make a speech than eat a roast turkey, even after a day's march, joined most lustily in the call." Lane's appearance was greeted with cheers and huzzas.[8]

After paying a tribute to Indiana for the benefit of his Hoosier audience, Lane moved on to the main points of his speech. He reiterated his creed: "Let slavery take care of itself. . . . I do not propose to make war upon slavery, but upon rebels, and in the mean time to let slaves and slavery take care of themselves.... This war is *for* slavery—let us make it the mighty engine for slavery's destruction, and the rebels will soon cry, enough.... Let us be bold—inscribe 'Freedom to all' on our banners—and appear what we are, the opponents of slavery." Lane proposed that Congress direct Lincoln to issue a proclamation to the rebel states to end the rebellion within thirty or sixty days "or in default thereof, declare all men free throughout their domains." Loyal men who had their slaves thus freed would be compensated by the government. Lane voiced his hope that the rebels would decline any such offer, thereby enabling his men to "invade them and strike the shackles from every limb."[9]

As to the freed slaves, Lane suggested that many could be resettled in Haiti, Central and South America, and Liberia, but a mass resettlement to Liberia was not practical. And although North America was big enough to accommodate both races, the good of both races required their separation: "Ages of oppression, ignorance and wrong, have made the African a being inferior in intellect, and racial attainments to the Caucasian, and whilst together, we shall always have low, cringing servility on the one hand, and lordly domination on the other. It is better for both parties that each enjoy the honors and responsibilities of a nationality of his own. In such an event, our common humanity would make a vast stride towards perfection."[10]

Lane's speech met with resounding cheers. Although he and his men were zealots when it came to freeing slaves, this did not necessarily translate into a willingness to have blacks as neighbors. In a speech the following month Lane suggested the government could:

> adopt the policy pursued by our fathers toward the Indians. We need not furnish them with blacksmiths. We would not have to teach them to farm. After educating them let us obtain a country contiguous to us—say South America or South Carolina—and there let them live apart. Let there be a home of the white men, the home of freedom, and the

home of the black man, a home of freedom. It would be well if an eternal ocean could roll between the two races. While together a distinction will be made. Our prejudices are incurable. The two races can't live together without intermarriage, which [I am] opposed to.[11]

This was entirely consistent with his position stated in the Senate back on July 18; he had then proposed to form a plan to colonize outside of the Union those slaves who had liberated themselves by fleeing their masters. "I want to see, so soon as it can be done constitutionally these two races separated, an ocean rolling between; that—South America—the Elysium of the colored man; this the Elysium of the white."[12]

Whites in Kansas were noting that the sight of black people among them was becoming a more frequent occurrence. A man writing from Fort Lincoln on November 3 observed there were not less than one thousand Missouri refugees in Linn County, all of whom might otherwise "have been enjoying the sweets of slavery, had General Lane marched through the rebel country with an eye single to the 'compromises of the Constitution.'" A Leavenworth man claimed that since the war began, three hundred contrabands had passed through that city.[13]

White Kansans in general had mixed feelings about blacks. According to historian Albert Castel, most Kansans were opposed to slavery not for moralistic reasons but because they feared its social and economic effects on white farmers. In fact, Kansans "were almost as much anti-Negro as they were antislavery. . . . By keeping slavery out of Kansas they also kept out the Negro." Such attitudes only mirrored those prevalent in the Northern midwestern states from which most Kansas settlers came.[14] The most liberal Kansans, a small minority, appear to have considered blacks as full equals; among these could probably be counted Montgomery, Jennison, and Ritchie. At a time when black children did not go to school with white children, Jennison established a school for freed slaves of all ages at Osawatomie, and he contributed financially to a similar school in Lawrence.[15]

Napoleon Blanton, commander of a company in the Fourth, entertained an unsympathetic view of blacks before the war. In an 1855 letter to the Lawrence *Kansas Free State,* he argued, "This Territory will be better off without a State Constitution, than to have one that will admit free negroes and runaway slaves. . . . If there is to be negroes in Kansas, let them be slaves, and have masters to be responsible for their mean conduct." Whether the intervening years had softened his view is unknown. During the 1858 constitutional convention, Hamilton Johnson, future commander of the Fifth, and then a delegate from Leavenworth, moved to limit suffrage to whites.[16]

When Kansans next met in 1859 to frame a constitution, racism was prominent. Among the delegates were three future brigade officers, Blunt, Ritchie, and John Burris. William McDowell, a delegate from Leavenworth, proclaimed: "We stand upon the record as believing that God Almighty, for some purpose, has established this inferiority of the black race, and stamped an indelible mark upon them. Between the two races there is an unfathomable gulf that cannot be bridged." A proposal to establish a committee to study excluding blacks from the state was narrowly tabled, as were proposals to establish a constitutional bar to teaching black children alongside whites. Blunt, Ritchie, and Burris voted against the latter. An amendment that would allow blacks to serve in the militia was soundly defeated by a vote of 42 to 6; Ritchie voted for the amendment, while Blunt and Burris voted against it. When Ritchie proposed to give blacks the right to vote, it was voted down 37 to 3, Blunt voting to deny suffrage. But as to slavery, Blunt declared it violated the principles of Christian humanity and the laws of God.[17]

Chaplain Fisher, writing in 1861 to the *Leavenworth Daily Conservative* about the influx of blacks into Kansas, noted there was a need for their labor in the state, and such labor should be welcomed, at least until Haiti and South America were full of resettled blacks. However, Fisher assured his readers, "[our] land is broad, and the races will be separated in due time." It is unclear whether Fisher personally held such beliefs or whether he intended to allay the fears of white Kansans who may have been less than thrilled to have blacks as neighbors. The Leavenworth *Daily Times* agreed that colonization of the freed slaves was a good idea, but in the meantime, it argued, the slaves were still the property of rebel masters, and it behooved Kansans to ensure that they did not suffer.[18]

There were concerns the freed slaves lacked the skills to live on their own and would become a burden to support. One Leavenworth man wrote to the *New York Times*: "The people of this State are poor, and have but little either to give for charity, or to pay for labor. The Winter is coming on and a large majority [of contrabands] are destitute." The writer noted the freed blacks "must shift for themselves." Two months later another Leavenworth man commented on the apparent lack of planning among the fugitives. He found them "promenading around town in all the glory of their new found freedom without a thought of what was to become of them on the morrow." When one was asked where he was going, he responded, "Goin' wid de wagin, massa—we's free folks now."[19]

A Lawrence man worried that large numbers of fugitives were fleeing from Missouri into Kansas and especially Lawrence. He noted that blacks who had found employment with farmers would soon be unemployed come winter and would drift into town and live upon the charity of the townspeople. "There is not an intelligent slave in Mo," he wrote, "but knows where Lawrence is and we shall have them here by thousands, and unless our friends from the east assist there will be starvation and death among them." The Lawrence *Republican* reported that the influx of freed slaves startled the townspeople, who were unprepared to deal with them. The Leavenworth *Daily Times* of December 21 reported similar concerns of handling the arrival of 105 contrabands "in every stage of destitution and want."[20]

Chaplain Moore acknowledged the concerns of whites. "The impression is general," he wrote, "that if the shackles were stricken from the limbs of the slave, he must be turned loose upon community, and become a dependent, worthless thing. At the thought of this, visions of theft, plunder, rape and all sorts of horrors rise up before the ignorant or diseased imagination." However, Moore argued that those concerns were unfounded, and he cleverly appealed to the self-interests of whites: "The Africans are needed as laborers," Moore wrote. "It is always perilous for a country to part with its firm sinews and strong muscles. Labor is more valuable and important than capital, and should be parted with only in obedience to the laws of necessity."[21]

A similar conflict among the views of Kansans was still evident a few months later. On January 14, 1862, Colonel George W. Deitzler, commanding the First Kansas Infantry at Lexington, promulgated an order that, following the dictates of Major General Henry Halleck, prohibited slaves from being within the camp of the First. Some of the soldiers published an unofficial regimental newspaper, *The Kansas First*, which praised the order, and denied that they were engaged in an abolition crusade. The soldiers complained that in Kansas, people were already threatened with oppression and crushing taxation "in support of alms-houses, infirmaries, jails and penitentiaries, for these miserable, unfortunate, half-starved, poorly-clad trophies of war. . . . Our prairies, rich in promised wealth, have already been converted from a living green, into a sickly ebony hue, from which we see no escape, save in the expulsion of the offensive and blighting cause. The people there have their *gorge* of contrabands and will have no more of them."[22] The Lawrence *Republican*, which reprinted this excerpt, denied that the contrabands presented a curse upon Kansas:

> In Lawrence, are more "contrabands" than in any other locality in Kansas; and, whatever may happen in the future, no such inconveniences have yet arisen from the presence of the colored people amongst us. We doubt whether an un[en]lightened people ever conducted themselves with so much propriety as the manumitted slaves now in Kansas, and we know that more crime has been committed in many white communities than the freed slaves commit here. We hope that "these miserable, unfortunate, half-starved, poorly clad trophies of war," will continue to flee from oppression, and become even as respectable as those around Lawrence, and we are willing to take our share of the burthens.[23]

For the moment, nominal goodwill toward blacks in Kansas would be easy to maintain as long as there were few of them around, and as long as their emancipation was seen as a thumb in the eye of rebels. The Leavenworth *Daily Times* sneered that Southerners began the war to perpetuate the institution of slavery, but after six months Missouri was "niggerless."[24]

When Lincoln decided the previous month to sack Frémont, he also drafted advice to be delivered to the new commander of the Department of the West. Lincoln offered the suggestion that if Price had retreated into northwest Arkansas, the Federal commander should not maintain a lengthy supply line, but instead retreat and establish two observation corps, one in Sedalia and the other in Rolla, with Lane guarding the Kansas border. This was a reasonable suggestion, considering the difficulty of maintaining a large force far from any railhead. As Price had retreated to the Arkansas border, Hunter took Lincoln's advice and fell back. Thus occurred what Lane had argued against in Kansas City—retreating from an army that was itself retreating.[25]

The retreat of the Federal army came as a bitter betrayal to the loyal citizens of Springfield and its environs who had welcomed the return of Union forces. Rather than be left to the tender mercies of the rebels, many citizens chose to flee. Late that month about 240 wagons were escorted north by the cavalry of Major Clark Wright, a Missouri home guard unit. Loyal citizens from southwest Missouri petitioned Major General Halleck with a resolution asserting that rebel forces were "laying waste the whole country and subjecting women and children to destitution and starvation." The resolution further stated: "The retrograde movement of our army from Springfield has been the cause of from 3,000 to 5,000 men, women, and children leaving their homes, without money and many in a suffering condition." Halleck was requested to send in fifteen thousand troops to drive the rebels out. In the wake of the Federal withdrawal, Price, who had retreated yet farther south to Pineville, near the Arkansas border, turned about and marched north, eventually going into camp near Osceola, while McCulloch temporarily reoccupied Springfield.[26]

Lane's Brigade, together with John W. Rabb's Second Indiana Battery and Andrew Newgent's regiment of Cass County Home Guards, left Springfield on November 9. While the brigade was in and around Springfield, it had acted as a magnet to slaves seeking freedom. Chaplain Moore wrote of one boy who came in after hearing his master speak of slaves escaping to the army, and of another instance where a former slave, acting as a teamster for the brigade, freed his brother and sister when the brigade approached his former residence at Springfield. Moore also noted: "Our colored teamsters and servants act as so many missionaries among their brethren, and induce a great many to come into camp. It cannot be denied that some of our officers and soldiers take great delight in this work, and that by personal effort and otherwise, they do much towards carrying it on." Now accompanying the brigade away from Springfield was a wagon train of contrabands, some five hundred men, women, and children dressed in butternut-colored jeans and other homemade goods, much worn and patched. Rickety furniture, chickens, ducks, and an occasional pig filled their decrepit wagons, which were pulled by oxen, lame mules, and old horses, with harnesses mostly made of hemp rope.[27]

As the brigade neared Kansas, Lane believed the many contrabands had become an excessive burden. Accordingly, on November 12 he ordered Chaplains Fisher, Moore, and Reeder Fish to take charge of the contrabands, escort them to Fort Scott, and then "superintend the entire business of seeing them located, and their property secured to their possession before leaving them." Moving with great speed, the chaplains organized their "Black Brigade" of 218 refugees by the afternoon of November 12. The wagon train, a mile in length, included twenty-five wagons and twenty mounted men. The large amount of furniture being hauled no doubt came mostly from the property of their former masters, as had been the wagons and teams. No soldiers were detailed as escorts for the trip of some thirty miles through dangerous country, but Colonel Newgent provided a number of old muskets. Although there was no ammunition for the weapons, it was hoped the sight of the men shouldering muskets would deter any bushwhackers from attacking.[28]

Seventeen miles were made that first evening, a halt being called at 3:00 A.M. The following day the train passed into Kansas, whereupon Fisher gave the contrabands a speech and proclaimed them forever free. The ensuing "cheers and shouts, which extended along the whole line, beggar description. They must have equaled the shouts of Israel after the passage of the Red Sea. They then gave three hearty cheers for Gen. Lane, the Liberator." The Black Brigade camped south of Fort Scott that night. The following morning there came out from town both the curious and those citizens

> desirous to relieve us of a portion of our command. One wanted a little girl to dress & bring up like her own—one wanted a boy—another a family to occupy a vacant house, &c. In parting with any of our charge, we took their name, age, the name of their old master, and a written pledge from the Guardian, that they should be treated kindly and honestly. But as few negroes have any name except "Jack," "Bill," "Tom," &c., we had to supply the deficiency. I asked a little fellow his name, and he answered in a low, grum voice, "Abe." "Abraham, I suppose." "Yase," he replied. "Your name shall be Abraham Lincoln." Another large, powerful and very black fellow, came up, and in reply to my question, said his name was "Dan." "Daniel, I suppose, sir." "Yes." "Your sir name." "Bonham." "Was that your master's name?" "Yes." "Well, sir, your name shall not be Dan. Bonham, but "Daniel Webster." I complimented my friend Fisher by giving a family his name. This part of our business created much amusement.[29]

The chaplains found homes for about fifty of their charges and moved to Fort Lincoln on November 13, where the process of finding homes began again; another forty or fifty refugees found homes. Then it was on to Mound City, where another thirty or forty were found "good homes, with 'plenty of work.'" The remaining refugees were marched to Dutch Henry's Crossing, where arrangements were made to send detachments to Ohio City and Topeka. Baldwin

City was reached on Sunday, where speeches were made by Moore and others, recounting the tale of the refugees, "and with one voice [the audience] consented to and invited the settlement of such families in their neighborhood."[30]

As Lane's Brigade neared the Kansas border, the men in Allen's company were met on November 14 by their former lieutenant, John Brown, Jr., who advised that Captain Allen was camped ahead on Drywood Creek. Three days earlier rebels had tried to disrupt the march of the brigade by firing the prairie grass. Although the men countered by setting a backfire, the flames came perilously close to the ammunition wagons. The rebels tried once again, but again the tactic was unsuccessful. As the men of Allen's company were putting out the fire, they were greeted by Edward Hill, their teamster, who had last been seen a month earlier spiriting freed slaves out of Kansas City. Accompanying Hill was another black man, Richard White of Salem, Ohio. Hill advised the company that a number of recruits were waiting for them at Drywood Creek; these were the men recruited by Allen in Ohio.[31]

Lane and the brigade marched into Fort Scott on the evening of November 14 and into the morning of November 15. The married men were given leaves of absence. The adjutant of the Fifth announced that the U.S. paymaster had finally arrived with the men's long-overdue pay. However, it soon became apparent this was not the case. Captain Creitz obtained a meeting with Lane at his hotel to inquire about the pay. Lane advised Creitz he was going to leave immediately for Fort Leavenworth, where the paymaster awaited his orders to pay the men. Creitz wrote that Lane "himself would bring him down to Ft. Scott and that 'By God' the men *should* have their pay forthwith. This was the last I saw of Gen. Lane. . . . No effort was made by him to have us paid off." To everyone else, the official story being circulated was that Lane was leaving for Washington to be appointed a major general. Lane probably had learned he did not get command of the separate department he had urged upon Lincoln the previous month. He was among those surprised by the War Department's November 9 announcement of the creation of "The Department of Kansas, to include the State of

Kansas, the Indian Territory west of Arkansas, and the territories of Nebraska, Colorado, and Dakota, to be commanded by Major General Hunter, headquarters at Fort Leavenworth." At the same time, Halleck was made commander of the Department of the Missouri, which included Missouri and Arkansas. Halleck formally took command of the Department of the Missouri on November 19; the following day Hunter took command of the Department of Kansas, arriving in Leavenworth November 25.[32]

Lane's first stop as he left Kansas was Weston, Missouri. Although Lane traveled incognito, his presence was discovered, and soon he was surrounded by a crowd calling for a speech. Lane gladly complied, following which his entourage moved on to St. Joseph, where a similar scene was reenacted, but with the addition of a band to serenade the senator. Lane proclaimed the war was initiated by the slave power, but the war was ending because the cause of it was on the move. To illustrate what he meant by the cause of it being on the move, he gave the example of the slaves his brigade had freed as it marched from Springfield. One observer noted: "The General was most vociferously cheered," noted an observer, "but some musty, whiskified seeds, shook their vacant heads and muttered. Others stood aghast at the expression of such sentiments *unrebuked* on the 'sacred soil' of Missouri." Continuing his triumphal return to Washington, Lane was received by adoring crowds at Cleveland, Boston, and New York along the way.[33]

With Lane's departure, the overall command devolved upon Montgomery who was the ranking colonel; he named his command the "Army of the Western Border." In his military duties he would be distracted by a personal matter. "Squint-eye Veatch has run away with Col. Montgomery's daughter," noted Lieutenant Trego, "and the Col. is just boiling about it." As events would reveal, Lane's departure heralded the gradual decline of the brigade, largely due to neglect by the Federal government.[34]

The previous month Secretary of War Cameron had authorized the six guns of Captain John Gibbon's Battery B, Fourth U.S. Artillery, to be transferred to Lane. Moonlight was dispatched in early October to St. Joseph to retrieve the guns but was rebuked by Gibbon who was under orders to proceed to Washington. Then, at Springfield, Hunter promised Moonlight he would receive rifled Parrott guns for his battery. After the brigade returned to Fort Scott, Moonlight and Rabb left for St. Louis to draw the guns, only to be refused these by Halleck. On Moonlight's return from St. Louis, his train was stopped at Weston on November 28 by Si Gordon's guerilla band. Moonlight was taken prisoner along with Rabb and a Lieutenant White; the prisoners were taken by ambulance to the guerila camp near Platte City. Along the way, in order to conceal his identity as one of Lane's men, Moonlight swallowed several documents identifying him as such and hid those he was unable to eat. Fortunately for Moonlight he was wearing a new uniform and not the well-worn threads of a brigade man. He lied to his captors, claiming to be an Eastern soldier coming straight from West Point Military Academy to report to Hunter at Leavenworth. "I played my cards very fine," recalled Moonlight, "denouncing Kansas and her nigger-loving population; pelting democratic rocks at Jim Lane, Jennison & others until I *almost* made myself believe them, they were damned scoundrels." In another stroke of luck, Gordon—who would have recognized Moonlight—had remained behind at Weston and not yet examined his captive.[35]

The guerillas wanted the release of several of their men held prisoner by the Federals. Moonlight offered to negotiate an exchange; this was agreed to, and he was delivered to St. Joseph, where he met with Colonel Robert Smith. Smith refused to negotiate with guerilas. Moonlight was then honor-bound to return himself to captivity. However, he learned that Gordon had since found out his true identity, had sent men to recapture him, and had made threats to kill him. Concluding that this violated the terms of his release, Moonlight decided to stay put and wrote a letter to his captors explaining why the deal was off. Shortly thereafter, the guerillas took Rabb and White to Lexington and paroled them, but with no exchange made, the officers were not allowed to return to duty. On Halleck's order, Captain Rabb was exchanged later that summer for one of Price's captains; whether White was ever exchanged is unknown.[36]

Within a week of Moonlight's capture, Hunter issued a proclamation "To the Trustees of Platte City, Platte County, Mo," giving the citizens there ten days to either deliver up Gordon or drive him away. Hunter threatened that if they failed to do so, he would send a force to their city "with orders to reduce it to ashes, and to burn the house of every Secessionist . . . and to carry away every negro." Three companies were sent across the river into Platte County after Gordon; although Gordon was neither captured nor forced out of the county, Hunter did not make good on his threat.[37]

Bushwhackers and jayhawkers were active in southeast Kansas as well, especially while the brigade was occupied in Missouri. On October 29 two parties of Missourians entered Kansas near Mine Creek in Linn County. One group, commanded by a man named Locke, invaded the northern portion of the county; at the village of Brooklyn they murdered one man and made off with four wagons and twenty-two horses. The other party of forty men commanded by Sheriff Clem of Bates County murdered Richard Manning and William Upton and swept up cattle and horses in the neighborhood. In response fourteen citizens set out in pursuit and set up an ambush. In the ensuing fight two of the Missourians were killed; one Union man, Joseph Speakes, was killed and another one or two wounded. The same day, another band of Missourians entered Miami County, stole livestock, burned homes, and reportedly murdered two men. Linn County was raided again on November 12 by thirty Missourians who took cattle, killed a refugee from Missouri (James Sage), and wounded two other men. Sam Reader in Topeka had a conversation with a refugee from southern Kansas, who informed him "that bands of Mo. miscreants were almost continually making inroads into K[ansas] in his neighborhood plundering the defenceless inhabitants and in many instances shooting the Union men down like dogs."[38]

Such cross-border raids were not one-sided affairs. Sam Reader noted the refugee he conversed with claimed "these [Missouri] ruffians were incited in these deeds to retaliate the plundering of Seceshers by some of the K[ansas] guerrilla parties who were stealing 'on their own hook.'" In early November seven Missouri men, who had been driven out of their homes and into Johnson County, Kansas, went back into Missouri to procure livestock. Accompanied by two Kansas men, they got their livestock but were then attacked by "about thirty drunken rebels" while encamped at the Big Creek bridge in Cass County. Although that attack was repulsed, the rebels came at them again the next day; in a half hour fight, the rebels suffered two killed and six wounded; the invaders lost one man killed and one wounded, plus all their booty. Lieutenant Trego commented: "The Missourians have been into Kansas at several points retaking some of the property that was taken from them by those fellows who would not join the army because they could do better at Jayhawking on their own hook. Several of them were killed. Three on Mine Cr[eek] one of them was in our company last summer."[39]

In late November jayhawking civilians from Linn County raided into Bates County, sweeping up "a large amount of stock and other property, at some locality beyond Butler. While returning, they were attacked by a large body of rebels, completely stripped of their plunder and badly cut up." In reporting this, the *Osawatomie Herald* said of the jayhawkers: "Verdict, served them right." The newspaper's verdict was not prompted by a disapproval of jayhawking but because Missouri traitors were left alive "to wreak vengeance upon some innocent Kansas man." In what may be this same incident, other accounts described a raid by seventy civilian jayhawkers who rode out of Mound City and into Missouri to get their share of plunder. A citizen of Mound City accused the party of partaking in jayhawking even before they entered Missouri. About nine miles east of Butler the civilian band encountered what was described as a rebel band of jayhawkers," 150 to 200 men strong, who attacked the Kansans. All of the jayhawkers ran except for thirteen who made a fighting retreat. Five or six of these did not make it out and were presumed killed. The missing men were said to have left wives and families in destitute circumstances.[40]

Soon after returning to Fort Scott, Ritchie took the cavalry of the Fifth on a six-day scout into Missouri, passing through Lamar, Carthage, and Preston, returning on November 28; Montgomery congratulated Ritchie on his "brilliant sweep." Creitz, however, complained the march accomplished nothing, except that horses died by the dozens and the men were fatigued to such an extent that when the regiment finally reached Osawatomie on December 1, only one-third of the men could be mustered; the rest were exhausted and encumbered by lame and worn-out horses scattered for twenty miles along the route."[41]

The same day that Ritchie began his scout into Missouri, Montgomery received a report that Price was again marching northward toward the Missouri River and possibly into Kansas. Montgomery dispatched a messenger to recall Ritchie—the messenger apparently never caught up with Ritchie—while taking it upon himself to send a protective force to Shawnee. The first units to move were the Third and Fourth regiments, which passed through Mound City on November 29. They were followed the next day by Oliver P. Bayne's independent company and a day later by the two infantry companies of the Fifth.[42]

In truth Price was in no shape to mount a campaign, especially a winter campaign with his poorly clothed soldiers. Although his taking of Lexington had brought forward recruits that swelled his strength to more than sixteen thousand men, this was only temporary. Thousands deserted because, according to Price, "feeling that they had been betrayed and abandoned by the Confederate Government, [they] returned to their homes discontented and disheartened." Price was weakened further when, on his advance to the Osage River following the Federal retreat from Springfield, the enlistments of three-fourths of his men expired. Price consented to their leaving the army to procure winter clothing and take care of their families, as most of them had left their homes months earlier, without an hour's notice, and not one of them had ever been paid for their service. Some of these losses were replaced when at the end of November, Price sent a thousand men on a quick march to Lexington and back, which brought in twenty-five hundred recruits.[43]

Price on November 26 issued a "Proclamation to the People of Central and North Missouri" calling for fifty thousand volunteers. This was a very badly worded invitation. Price asked: "Are Missourians no longer true to themselves? Are they a timid, time-serving, craven race, fit only for subjection to a despot? . . . Do you stay at home to secure terms with the enemy?" Although Price added he would not attribute such motives to his countrymen, this proclamation was nevertheless an implied insult to the honor of the men who had not yet responded to the Southern cause. It invited volunteers to endure extreme hardships. Price wrote of his men having "dared the dangers of the battle-field . . . the scorching suns of summer, the frosts of winter, the malaria of the swamps . . . fatigue, and hunger, and thirst, often without blankets, without shoes, with insufficient clothing, with the cold, wet earth for a bed, the sky for a covering, and a stone for a pillow." If this was not enough to deter a young man from volunteering, Price also enumerated his soldiers who had been killed in battle or taken by disease. If the would-be volunteer were concerned about the safety of the farm and family he was to leave behind, Price cavalierly admonished him to leave his property to take care of itself and entrust his home to the protection of God. A noble sentiment, no doubt, but to outward appearances God was forsaking much of secessionist Missouri at that time. Even the proclamation itself claimed, "The country bleeds, and our people groan under the inflictions of a foe marked with all the characteristics of barbarian warfare." If none of this had yet dissuaded a man from volunteering, he must have harbored some trepidation at joining an army so impoverished. The proclamation's instructions for recruits read: "Come with your guns of any description that can be made to bring down a foe. If you have no arms, come without them, and we will supply you as far as that is possible. Bring cooking utensils and rations for a few weeks. Bring blankets and heavy shoes, and extra bed-clothing if you have them." As a recruiting tool, Price's proclamation had little to commend it and produced few recruits.[44]

CHAPTER 8

Visitations of Mercy

Montgomery's northward movement to Shawnee halted when it became clear the threat of an attack by Price was a false alarm. The Third and the two infantry companies of the Fifth camped at Osawatomie; the Fourth encamped further north at Wyandotte. First Sergeant Luther Thrasher noted that Osawatomie showed little evidence of having recovered from being burned by Missourians in 1856, and it was "now nominally inhabited by darkies." A resident of Osawatomie noted the soldiers had not been paid for many months: "They begin to talk pretty loud, and if they do not get some [pay] soon I think there will be trouble in the camp. I visited the camp on Saturday morning. The men are in good spirits—have plenty to eat, and speak well of their officers. They feel anxious to see Price and his command. All is right except the pay. There is quite a number sick with the measles. Almost all the men seem to have a little money." Fortunately for the men, the weather in early December was practically balmy.[1]

Captain Elijah E. Harvey, in command of the two infantry companies of the Fifth, directed a plea to Montgomery on December 1. Harvey related that even before the march began, a number of his men were sick and unfit for duty; now twelve of them were laid up in a temporary hospital and another six or eight were sick in camp.

Measles was the prevalent disease, with a few cases of pneumonia. He complained the regiment had no surgeon, and he was using a private physician he had employed through a verbal agreement. His men suffered from an "utter destitution" of tents, blankets, and clothing; his own company possessed only seven small tents and had drawn only four pair of blankets. "We ask for relief," pleaded Harvey. Ritchie and the Fifth's cavalry companies arrived that same day and went into camp on Pottawatomie Creek.[2]

Captain William R. Allen of the Third was again absent, having set off on a recruiting trip back to Ohio. He was also escorting Colonel Montgomery's wife, who was traveling east. On the evening of December 3, Allen, Mrs. Montgomery, and a Lieutenant Ellenwood were riding in a carriage when they were captured by guerillas at Winthrop, Missouri, just east of Atchison, Kansas. Allen later wrote that he was taken to Lexington and then to the headquarters of Brigadier General A. E. Steen of the Missouri State Guard, located ten miles below Osceola; he made no mention of what fate befell Lieutenant Ellenwood. At Osceola he was released by Price and provided with a written safeguard to obtain a concomitant release of a Missouri State Guard officer. However, Allen had gone only a dozen miles before being captured by a band of guerillas who refused to honor Price's safeguard and was taken to their camp. That night the guerillas began passing around the whiskey jug; Allen shared the jug and feigned passing out. As the guerillas prepared to sleep, Allen heard one of them remark that it wasn't worthwhile to watch him as he was too drunk to get away. Around midnight he made his escape. Allen made his way to a house, procured some old clothing as a disguise, and began trekking northward. Allen wrote about his experiences on the way:

> I met several parties going to Price's army. I always hailed them first and asked them where they were going. Talked knowingly of the army. Told them the Federals were trying to catch us, and soon passed on without being suspected. Where I staid nights we discussed the cause of the war and the chances of success. We always felt confident that if the

federals would let our niggers alone, and not confiscate our property, that we could whip them easy. But we generally came to the conclusion that they would steal our niggers so that we should not be able to raise any crops next summer, and that we would be forced to leave the State. I arrived at Smithton on the Pacific R. R. on the 23d of Dec. from whence I made my way home [in Ohio] by the way of St. Louis.[3]

Hunter gave Brigadier General James W. Denver command of the "Troops in Kansas" on December 2. Hunter assigned him the task of inspecting the troops and reporting on their condition; he also canceled all leaves of absence. When Denver inquired as to what troops were in Kansas and where they were located, Hunter replied, "I don't know anything about them; you must find them the best way you can." While serving as a territorial governor, Denver had challenged the legality of Lane's command of the militia. Lane had responded by publishing the charge "I do arraign one G. [*sic*] W. Denver before the country, and denounce him as a calumniator, perjurer and tyrant" and alleging that Denver came to Kansas "a professed duelist—his hands reeking with the untimely shed blood of his fellow man." Denver had been no fan of Lane or the Free Staters. In private letters to his wife while serving as territorial governor, he accused Lane of murdering Gaius Jenkins, and of the Free Staters he claimed: "Some outrageous acts have been perpetrated. At one place they took three respectable women, stripped them naked, and paraded around the yard for their amusement. This was done in the name of the Free State party, and by men claiming to act under orders from Jim Lane." Neither did Denver hold a high opinion of Montgomery, who was now his subordinate. While territorial governor, he complained that Montgomery and his band had managed to keep some people quiet, while others were robbed of their property and driven out of the country. "Between 100 and 200 families have thus been plundered and driven away from Linn county alone. . . . That Montgomery and his band have committed crimes meriting the most severe punishment known to our laws is true," Denver wrote. Hunter's selection of Denver was not a popular one: "This appointment has roused strong feelings of indignation.... Denver, as Kansas governors go, was endurable, but there are many things which rankle bitterly in relation to his career." Another man wrote that Denver was "one of the Pro-Slavery Governors" and that "the officers and soldiers do not like the appointment." Montgomery was reported as threatening to resign "rather than serve under the man who hitherto denounced him as a robber and murderer, and who . . . never retracted these charges." An article in the *New York Times* characterized Denver's relationship with the Kansas troops as antagonistic, but the Leavenworth *Daily Times* disputed this and asserted that as territorial governor, Denver "was just, impartial and resolute in administering the duties of his office, and his brief administration was satisfactory to our people and honorable to himself." Denver departed Leavenworth on December 12 to establish his headquarters at Fort Scott; he was not there long, returning to Leavenworth December 26.[4]

The Fourth was ordered to Kansas City on December 5, which it reached on December 7. Weer immediately issued a general order announcing he was in command of the troops in the vicinity of Kansas City, that he was there "to relieve, with his regiment, Col. Jennison, 1st Kansas Cavalry, in the occupation of Kansas City," and to protect the people "against rebels, and marauding parties from Kansas or elsewhere." To maintain proper discipline, he appointed Captain James Harvey as provost marshal, with instructions for him to visit drinking saloons, public resorts, and houses of ill repute, should there be such. Soldiers were prohibited to be out of camp without passes, and a regular program of daily drill, parade, and roll calls was instituted.[5]

Montgomery then received orders from Denver to move the Fourth to Wyandotte. Jennison's regiment and Rabb's battery were ordered to Leavenworth. Newgent's regiment of Cass County Home Guards was to remain at Paola, and the Third and Fifth were ordered back to Fort Scott. The Third would reach Mound City on December 11, but intervening events changed the plans to send the regiment to Fort Scott. Weer on December 20 wrote from St. Louis to Captain Harvey, advising him Hunter had ordered the Fourth to

Wyandotte and that Weer had been ordered to Washington. Weer informed Harvey he wanted the move to Wyandotte rushed and that Harvey was to ensure that proper hospital arrangements were made for the sick. Weer also wanted Harvey to communicate to the men that while Weer was in Washington, he would be looking after the interests of the regiment, including getting them their pay and whatever equipment they needed. It is unclear why Weer was writing to Harvey instead of Lieutenant Colonel John Burris. The Fourth moved to Wyandotte December 24.[6]

While the Fifth was at Osawatomie, the men received word that the regiment had never properly been organized and that no report of the regiment's condition had been made to the proper authorities, as required; consequently, the War Department had no knowledge of the Fifth's existence. Hearing that the regiment therefore might be disbanded, the company officers met to effect a proper organization and elect the field officers; Ritchie was not among those then elected. Ritchie accused the officers of a conspiracy but agreed to submit the matter to an election by the entire regiment, to include the enlisted men. Ritchie conspired with Montgomery to attach the independent companies of John H. Vansickle and Oliver P. Bayne to the Fifth just before the election, believing these men would favor Ritchie. However, the men of these companies objected to the scheme, and Montgomery revoked the transfer. In the ensuing election Ritchie received only two votes out of 475. James H. Summers was elected colonel, Elijah E. Harvey as lieutenant colonel, and Thomas Scudder was elected major. Ritchie refused to recognize the results of the vote, and Governor Robinson did not validate the result by issuing commissions to the men so elected.[7]

The contest over the colonelcy was continued at Fort Lincoln, and again Ritchie agreed to put the matter to a vote of the whole regiment, the enlisted men again included. This time Ritchie received six votes. Thoroughly humiliated, he soon left the regiment. Ritchie later claimed he had agreed to a proposal by which he and the major would both resign and an election would follow—and that he had duly resigned but the major reneged and took command. Denver granted Ritchie a twenty-day furlough on December 17, at the end of which Ritchie was to report to Denver at Fort Leavenworth; Ritchie declined to so report. Summers secured a meeting with Denver and reported the regiment had no colonel and produced Ritchie's written resignation. Denver decided to investigate the matter personally. Denver reported he rode into camp without being halted once, although they were within several miles of the Missouri border. "There was not a sentinel out. The Lieutenant-Colonel [Ritchie] was absent. . . . I suppose he had gone home; at any rate he was not there. The Major [Summers] was up at Fort Leavenworth. I put the senior Captain [James S. Hunt] in command. . . . Colonel Ritchie denied that this was a bona fide resignation; that it was gotten from him under a false pretense." Hunt was subsequently superseded by Summers, formerly a first lieutenant in Gibson's company. Creitz described Summers as "a liar—a drunkard and a libertine. A swindler and a hypocrite & a scoundrel of the blackest dye. . . . His imbecility—ignorance & total depravity soon gained for him an unenviable reputation. . . . Without exaggerating—this weakminded Major Summers—was the embodiment of everything that was vile, low lifed & detestable."[8]

The company of John H. Vansickle possessed an interesting pedigree. Vansickle, a merchant from Xenia in Bourbon County, had enlisted most of his men at Fort Lincoln; fifty-nine men were enrolled by October 18, most of them joining in that last week, with another thirty-one enrolled over the next several months. It is unclear whether the men enlisted as only local militia or intended to be in the U.S. service. The unit was known as Vansickle's Company of Independent Scouts; at some point it was, without proper authority, designated as Company L, and then Company K, of the Third.[9]

In addition to the normal threats to Kansas posed by guerrillas and bushwhackers, there arose a new class of enemy. According to a soldier in the Third, marauders had deserted Price and had taken up the "business of plundering and assassination." The marauders also included discharged rebel soldiers who had returned to their homes, only to carry on the "single-handed war of the assassin upon

Union men." Fortunately for Kansans this war of retribution mostly happened within Missouri.[10]

Just the previous month a *New York Times* correspondent, writing from Springfield, had with remarkable prescience foretold of this new threat:

> It is beginning to be understood that a ragged fellow in the brush, with a double-barreled shot-gun, in which are twenty-six buckshot, is nearly as formidable as a Federal on a prancing steed, dressed in costly blue and armed with heavy sabre, with pistol and carbine of improved pattern. It is also beginning to be generally thought that a thousand ragged, dirty fellows, mounted on sorry steeds, and skulking from timber to timber, always avoiding a direct fight, laying ambuscades where they can do the greatest damage with the least danger—always missing when sought, and found when least wanted—are foemen much to be feared, and little to be contemned.[11]

The threat presented by Missouri bushwhackers would be acknowledged by William Tecumseh Sherman in January 1862: "These local secessionists are really more dangerous than if assembled in one or more bodies, for they could be traced out & found whereas now they are scattered on farms and are very peaceable, but when a Bridge is to be burned they are about."[12]

Constant scouting along and across the border was necessary to suppress both those bands of ex-rebel soldiers and the few men who remained with Price as an organized army. On one such scout in early December, twelve men of the Sixth under Lieutenant Reese Lewis of Greeno's company went through Vernon County, spending the night at a house near Shanghai. Lewis had taken a prisoner that day who advised him that there were large numbers of secesh about, so Lewis sent one man back to Fort Scott for reinforcements. About dawn the next morning, while it was still dark, the young son of the homeowner announced that many men were approaching the house. The troopers grabbed their guns, but Private Lewis H. Mylins, thinking these might be the reinforcements from Fort Scott, stepped onto the porch to inquire who they were. "They" were seventeen Vernon County men who called on Mylins to surrender. Mylins replied he had not come into Missouri to surrender and dashed for the door. The rebels opened fire, wounding six men including Mylins, who got five buckshot in his shoulder. The troopers returned fire and drove off their attackers, killing one horse and wounding one or two of the attackers. Upon Lieutenant Lewis's return to Fort Scott, Colonel William Judson dispatched Greeno with eighty men to Shanghai and Montevallo, "with instructions to deal out his accustomed justice to the returned rebels." The guerilla captain James M. Gatewood assembled forty to fifty men and shadowed Greeno's movements, looking for an opportunity for an ambush. It was questionable who was chasing whom. Greeno sent word back to Fort Scott that he was pursuing the enemy and asked to be reinforced with fifty men. Wyllis Ransom was sent with sixty infantry and cavalry. In the end neither side caught the other, and Greeno returned after two days.[13]

During Greeno's scout, four of his men left the command and stopped at the house of a Mr. Wallace at Clear Creek so that three of them could tend to, and presumably provide a guard over, the fourth trooper who was ill. They were surprised by Gatewood and taken prisoner, eventually being delivered to Price's headquarters at Osceola. Judson sent a message to Price that he had at least two hundred prisoners, including several officers who he had released, some unconditionally and some on parole for exchange. Judson proposed to exchange one rebel officer for each one of his enlisted men. This request went unheeded, and on December 23 Judson followed this with another request for an exchange. Judson's men had already been paroled on December 20 at Bear Creek when Price broke camp and retreated southward. The paroled men returned to Fort Scott and, in an apparent contravention of the rules regarding paroles, returned to duty.[14]

Montgomery was greatly worried by the rebel threat. Writing from Osawatomie on December 8, he told Lane: "Everything is going wrong here. What you and I feared at Springfield is coming to pass. The enemy is advancing. He disbanded his three months' men about the 20th of November, and moved north with his regulars, some 10,000 strong. . . . The disbanded men have carried their arms home with them and engaged in guerilla operations. The country swarms with guerillas, and this makes it difficult to procure information." Moreover, Montgomery overestimated the strength of Price's army at ten thousand men with twenty pieces of artillery. As to his own strength, Montgomery reported: "I am in no condition to fight if the enemy comes in force. The measles are still raging in our camps, and our regiments are reduced to mere skeletons. One mountain howitzer and an 8-pounder gun, with 6-pounder ammunition, constitute my show for artillery." When he tried to alert Denver of the threat, Montgomery expressed being "cooly snubbed" with the information that Price's advance was "all stuff," that Price had no army—that his army had disbanded."[15]

As Montgomery was writing to Lane, southeast Kansas was again awash with rumors of secesh entering Kansas. A Captain Miller in the vicinity of Barnesville took his company of scouts out looking for the invaders. Miller reported that the enemy numbered around 150; instead of forcing a fight, he obtained twenty reinforcements. Apparently no fight resulted. New rumors soon circulated that the rebels were the advance of a force of three thousand headed for Fort Lincoln and another two thousand headed for Fort Scott. Messengers were sent to Montgomery at Osawatomie, asking for reinforcement. Montgomery did not hesitate and marched for Fort Lincoln on December 9. However, the following day patrols sent out from the Fifth reported that the enemy—if there ever had been any—had retreated. Montgomery returned to Osawatamie, while for the moment the Fifth set up camp near Fort Lincoln.[16]

Where only days previous Denver had "cooly snubbed" Montgomery's warnings, on December 10 he ordered Montgomery to concentrate the troops under his command to the vicinity of Fort Scott with instructions to defend that post, and if he could not so defend, he was to retreat to West Point where was located Jennison's regiment and the Eighth Kansas Infantry. Denver gave Montgomery a fair amount of discretion, writing that Montgomery's judgment would dictate what was most conducive to the public interest. In fact, there was no threat from organized rebel troops. Major General Ben McCulloch had once again retreated into Arkansas with his Confederate troops, and Price, finding his position near Osceola too exposed, fell back with the Missouri State Guard to winter quarters at Springfield.[17]

Irregular forces of Missourians and Kansans kept tensions high by engaging in cross-border raids. On December 6 fourteen civilians, thirteen of them refugees from Missouri, left Olathe to reclaim their livestock. Just across the border they were attacked by thirty or forty secessionists and driven back into Kansas. The Kansas party gathered 150 to 200 men and went back into Missouri the next day, where they again met the secessionists, who had themselves been reinforced. The ensuing skirmishing lasted all day, with two Kansas men wounded and allegedly three secessionists killed and another five mortally wounded. The loyal men recovered their property. Later that month Dr. Huntoon described a fight that took place fifteen miles southeast of Fort Scott between twelve Union men and twenty-five secesh. Supposedly the secesh suffered three or four killed and three wounded before retreating. The Union loss was six wounded.[18]

An Osawatomie resident wrote there were not more than twenty or thirty able-bodied white men in town, among whom were "six first-rate Jay Hawkers," who frequently went down on the line to see the secesh. In Linn County, Henry Fitzpatrick, a deserter from Stewart's company, "had been 'running the machine' on his own account a few weeks." He was apprehended by Captain Dobyns. When captured, Fitzpatrick had with him a fine horse and buggy, a revolver, and other items that he said he took from a man he had encountered on the road. It was assumed by Fitzpatrick's captors that the previous owner had been murdered. Fitzpatrick then joined the ranks of men shot while allegedly attempting to escape.[19]

A civilian in Leavenworth wrote in *The New York Times* that the country was plagued by bands of men calling themselves jayhawkers who were implementing a system of general plunder under the pretense of driving away the secesh. Among these was Marshall Cleveland, late captain in Jennison's regiment, who had a gang in Doniphan County; incongruously, the writer noted Cleveland surely was one of the finest-looking men he had ever seen. Another writer in Leavenworth claimed the irregular levies on both sides were using the war merely as a "pretext for the retaliation of personal injuries and the indulgence of private revenge—with a good share of plunder and horse-stealing not by any means omitted."[20]

In his January 1862 *Annual Message to the Kansas Legislature,* Robinson claimed the state had become "overrun with thieves and highway robbers." So numerous had these criminals become that in some localities they had the community under complete control. "Citizens of property and influence have been cowed into silence," he claimed, "lest they should become the next victims of the spoilers. . . . Some affect to justify the stealing of their neighbor's property on the ground that it has been forfeited, by the disloyalty of its owner, to the Government, while much the larger class steal from mere wantonness or purposes of gain."[21]

While most of these skirmishes were between private parties, one compelled a response from the Federals. On December 12 a large party of bushwhackers, believed to be commanded by Sheriff John Clem of Bates County, raided homes around Potosi in Linn County and looted J. E. Hill's store. At the home of seventy-two-year-old Joseph Searight, the raiders represented themselves as Texas Rangers. The house was thoroughly looted. Searight's daughter remembered that as the men mounted to leave, one threw his gun over his saddle, pointed at her father, and shot him, killing him almost instantly. After he did this, she recalled, "he mounted and as he was riding away a man came rushing back, asking angrily, 'Why in hell did you do that?—didn't I order you not to shoot?'" The house of Josiah Sykes was among those looted, but Sykes was able to slip away on foot and make his way to Montgomery's headquarters at Mound City. Three companies of cavalry under Major Henry Williams, and several infantry companies under acting Major John Foreman went in pursuit.[22]

With the infantry riding in mule wagons, the column reached Potosi in the early evening of December 12. Their guide was a Mr.

Lupton, formerly of Papinsville, and the father of one of the men in Foreman's company. Marching all night, the men reached Papinsville mid-morning the following day. Finding no rebels, they took their breakfast, supplementing their rations with meat from pigs and turkeys they shot, as well as eggs and honey taken out of a beehive. The bees provided the only resistance met that day, stinging the robbing soldier.[23]

The destruction that happened next is unexplainable, but it was apparently preplanned. Vansickle's wife, writing on December 15, advised a friend that her husband was gone with his company "to burn Papinsville and Butler to ashes," as they were both secesh towns. Perhaps the officers believed that Papinsville had some involvement with Clem's raid, or perhaps incensed at "learning that no Union man had or could live in the place for the past few months, applied the torch." Luther Thrasher wrote that only twenty uninhabited houses were consigned to the torch, but not before the jayhawkers were allowed to take what they needed from inside. He claimed the inhabited houses were spared. However, Chaplain Moore recalled that "after looking after and providing for the sick, the women and the children of the place, the rest of the town went up in smoke and flame."[24]

Papinsville had been the Bates County seat until 1856 when Butler assumed that honor. The courthouse in Papinsville, constructed in 1855, and now used as a business building, was also burned. The men built a fire in the interior of the courthouse and then closed the building up except for the cupola. Soon flames leapt skyward through the cupola. A trooper described it as being "grand in the extreme . . . when all at once a report much like the heaviest artillery was heard, and the building flew into a thousand atoms, filling the very heavens with brands and lurid flames of fire."[25]

As part of this expedition Stewart's cavalry was sent to Butler, where he burned the business portion of the town. Major Williams, passing nearby after his sacking of Papinsville, ordered forward Lieutenant Frederick A. Smalley with five men to make contact with Stewart. However, Stewart had already departed, and Smalley instead ran into a party of rebels, who, "after a little parleying, opened fire."

Corporal William M. Durno of Snyder's company and Private Jasper Wright, of Vansickle's company, were killed—either in the firefight or executed after being taken prisoner. Official records list both as having been killed in action.[26]

The destruction continued after the men left Papinsville. Homes, barns, and mills, were burned. "We marched home by the light of the bonfires of Rebel houses," recalled Luther Thrasher. Chaplain Moore attempted to explain such actions: "As they passed through the country it was ascertained that loyal families had been very recently robbed and plundered of all they possessed. This sharpened up the wrath of our boys . . . and full atonement made. If women and children were not the innocent victims of this fratricidal strife, we might look upon it with more complacency."[27] In Moore's opinion, "Gen. Lane's expeditions in comparison with this were visitations of mercy." Lieutenant Trego commented, "It was a hard case as families had to be set out of doors, not however without every thing that belonged to them except their buildings. This was done to stop, if possible, the persecution of Union men in Missouri, who have since the federal troops left, been robbed and driven from their homes, more than at any former time." Reportedly, cattle and horses stolen in Kansas were found in this raid, which Foreman turned over to civilians who had accompanied the jayhawkers. The expedition returned to camp at Mound City December 15 with "two prisoners, seventy-five head of cattle, five horses, two yoke of oxen, one wagon, and a large quantity of hogs . . . a large train of Union refugees, many of whom had tried to get out of that place for weeks back but were prevented by Jackman and his gang."[28]

Chaplain Moore reported that following this expedition, the homes of all Union men in southern Bates County were burned in retribution, "and a fresh stampede" of persecuted loyalists in Missouri headed into Kansas. "A few have succeeded in getting away their stock and household furniture," Moore wrote, "but many come stripped of all their earthly possessions. These sights of homeless, half-naked and hungry women and children, wandering about and going no one knows whither, is enough to excite one's indignation, mingled with pity to their utmost extreme." In an interesting example of circular reasoning, Moore claimed the raids on Papinsville and Butler were conducted only in retaliation for the Potosi raid. The chastising that followed, he argued, was given reluctantly, though it was necessary to teach the rebels they could not invade Kansas with impunity. Of course, the Potosi raid was in retaliation for earlier jayhawker raids, which had of course only been prompted by secesh outrages, and so the circle of violence continued and would do so until the war ended.[29]

By mid-December a number of forces rendezvoused at Mound City. These were the Third and Fifth regiments, Bayne's independent company of scouts, General Denver and his staff, and Vansickle's independent company of scouts that had been attached to the Third as Company K. On December 17 the Third made a short march to Mine Creek, where it went into winter quarters, the same being christened "Camp Defiance." The Fifth moved into winter quarters at Barnesville. Summers, who had been elected colonel of the Fifth, needed to obtain his commission as such from Robinson. He sent Creitz and Gibson to Lawrence to meet with the governor and procure his papers. They returned on December 30 with commissions from Robinson for the captains and lieutenants of the regiment but none for the field officers. Robinson sought to influence the selection of officers by writing to Denver on December 28, requesting that he muster Powell Clayton as lieutenant colonel of the Fifth and O. B. Gunn as major of the Fourth. Had Clayton been elected by the officers of the Fifth, such a request by Robinson would have been a pure ministerial act, but no such election had taken place. Nonetheless, Clayton was mustered in as lieutenant colonel on December 28. Clayton formerly was captain of Company E, First Kansas Infantry, and a veteran of the bloody battle of Wilson's Creek. The men of the Fifth had no objection to Clayton as a soldier, but they grumbled that the appointment should have come from an officer already within the regiment. The concurrent promotions of Quartermaster M. H. Insley and Commissary A. C. Wilder from captains to majors, however, were well received. Clayton would not arrive in camp until February.[30]

Jennison's regiment was at Morristown, along with two companies of the Seventh Missouri, two of the Eighth Iowa, and two of the Eighth Kansas. The Eighth subsequently moved to West Point, where it met Colonel Newgent's regiment of the Cass County Home Guards. West Point had been a flourishing trading post of about a hundred frame and log buildings, which were now "in all stages of dilapidation, and everywhere presenting a picture of woe and desolation. But one family resides in the town." Newgent's men had "made stables of the best buildings and broken out the few remaining windows that were left when they arrived."[31]

At other locations in southeast Kansas, the Federal government was providing subsistence to irregular troops not mustered into the U.S. service. These were the four hundred men of Major Charles S. Clarke's battalion at Iola and the company of state representative Prince Gorum Davis Morton at Chelsea in Butler County. Morton was sometimes referred to as "Pegleg," in honor of his wooden appendage. The main accomplishment of his company was the capture in November of a stolen thirty-wagon ox train and the construction that winter of a crude breastwork fort that it occupied. Clarke's command was variously known as the "Iola Battalion," "Neosho Battalion," "Independent Battalion Cavalry," and the "First Battalion Kansas Cavalry." It contained the companies of Captains Charles F. Coleman, Henry Flesher, Thomas P. Killen, Willoughby Doudna, and Benjamin F. Goss. Elsewhere, a company of eighty mounted men, raised by John R. Row after Humboldt was sacked, was at "Fort Row" on the Verdigris River in Wilson County. In late December, Hunter announced he was cutting off the rations to irregular troops unless mustered into the U.S. service. Clarke's battalion was incorporated into the Ninth Kansas Cavalry, while Morton's and Row's companies dissolved in the spring of 1862, with two dozen of Morton's men going into Company L of the Ninth Kansas Cavalry.[32]

Late in December Bayne's independent company was disbanded, something that should have occurred much earlier, according to Chaplain Moore. Another soldier attributed this to some irregularity in the mustering process, and therefore Bayne's men had received no pay. About Bayne, the soldier wrote: "[He] has been jayhawking the Secesh in order to get his pay," and two companies of cavalry had been sent out to capture him and his company. It was rumored the pursuit would be halfhearted, as many of those in pursuit sympathized with Bayne and his men.[33]

Weer was again absent, having gone to Washington to present evidence in support of Lane's defense of his Senate seat. In Weer's absence, command of the Fourth fell to Lieutenant Colonel Burris. Burris issued an order dated December 25 announcing that he had assumed command of the Fourth due to Weer's absence and had moved with his command to Wyandotte under a special order from Major General Hunter. Burris took steps to improve the efficiency of the regiment, which apparently he felt had declined under the command of, or in the absence of, Weer. His order required the acting surgeon to procure a suitable hospital building and for the company commanders to "labor to restrain their men from excesses of every kind, and encourage sobriety, temperance, and regularity in their modes of living." Officers would be granted leaves of absence to recruit men. Detailed instructions were given as to when company drill and dress parade were to be held, as well as for reveille and tattoo. Guards were ordered to arrest anyone outside of camp without a pass or intoxicated and to suppress the selling of liquor to soldiers. Burris's order also prohibited soldiers from carrying arms except when on duty. It read: "The rights of person and property must be held sacred. Any infringements upon either will be punished with the greatest severity." Burris concluded his order with the admonition, "Soldiers! We are on the soil of our own Loyal State! Let us so act to advance the interests of our Country and the great cause in which we are engaged, be a benefit to the city and county of Wyandotte, and a credit to ourselves."[34]

Just a few days earlier, Burris had received a report of rebels recruiting at Independence. The infantry companies of Hayes and Quigg were sent there, along with Moonlight's command (with a six-pound gun) and detachments from Boyd's company. The force left Kansas City at 1:00 A.M. on December 17, arriving at Independence before daylight. The town was surrounded. When all was ready, an artillery shell was fired over the town, exploding in the air. The explosion surely evoked an especial terror in the inhabitants of Independence, for only a month earlier the town had been suddenly occupied by Jennison's regiment on November 14. On that day the men of the city had been herded into the town square and examined as to their loyalty—all of whom earnestly proclaimed they were Union men. Jennison made a speech claiming he had the names of everyone with secessionist sympathies and that the citizens had the duty to keep rebels out of the town and to prevent government property from being molested. If they did not comply, Jennison would return and the town would be made to suffer, which would include his leveling it to the ground. Following this, several stores allegedly owned by secesh were looted, the home of one store owner was burned, and the regiment left, its number swollen by eighty-eight slaves on their way to freedom, together with confiscated wagons and teams necessary for their conveyance.[35]

The townspeople offered no resistance to Burris's troops. Even though these were not Jennison's men, their being Lane's men promised no better treatment. Like Jennison before him, Burris established a "Court of Inquiry" to determine who was secesh and who was loyal, and like Jennison no one could be found who claimed to be a secessionist. Twelve men were taken prisoner on the grounds that they had either taken up arms against the government or had aided rebels. The townspeople could only dread what was to happen next. Would the town be leveled, or merely looted? But in an anticlimax, oaths of allegiance were administered to the remaining corralled citizens and Burris's command left peacefully.[36]

The brigade now celebrated its first Christmas in uniform. The boys of the Third spent Christmas Day as best they could while encamped on the prairie and without money. Lieutenant J. K. Hudson of Allen's company gave William H. H. Dickinson's mess twelve chickens and six cans of peaches; two cans were eaten for Christmas, along with four rabbits. That afternoon, Dickinson wryly noted, "6 more chickens flew into our mess its strange why they will do it." Allen's company spent the day "reading writing singing playing cardds &c." Judge Advocate Moore noted that the men in the regiment feasted on fruit and oysters. In the evening Moore, with James Blunt, John Broadhead, Lieutenant John Bowles, and a Lieutenant Jones, and piled into a wagon and rode to Mound City where there was a dance at the hotel; tickets to the dance were $1.50. "A gay time we had," noted Moore in his diary. They danced all night until about five o'clock the following morning, not arriving back in camp until about six. Moore slept only a couple of hours—he wrote the next evening, "Have felt dull & stupid all day."[37]

Little is known as to how the Fourth and Fifth spent Christmas. Dr. Huntoon noted there was some drunkenness in the camp of the Fifth. Jennison's regiment at West Point celebrated Christmas by departing for another raid into Missouri while the four companies of the Eighth Kansas and Newgent's regiment remained behind.[38]

Three days after Christmas a detachment from Seaman's company rode twenty miles into Missouri "to attend a secesh ball." Having arrived too late for the dance, the detachment scoured the neighborhood and took some prisoners, one of whom was a Southern army officer who had come home for a while. The men took with them several teams loaded with bacon, dried fruit, apples, lard, butter, and honey. The captured officer was Second Lieutenant Elias Coe of Marchbanks's company, Rains's division, Missouri State Guard. Coe was tucked away in the guardhouse, but a month later he was paroled and held in camp pending his exchange for a captured Federal officer.[39]

On Monday, December 30, Burris took 150 men on a scout into Jackson County. Their first stop was Morgan Walker's farm, which reportedly was being used as a headquarters by William Clarke Quantrill. Arriving at 2:00 A.M. but not finding guerillas, they had to be satisfied with helping themselves to breakfast. As the troops left, they took with them twenty mules, five or six horses, and four thousand pounds of bacon. Continuing on to a house owned by a Mr. Dixon, the men helped themselves to dinner and confiscated thirty-six cattle. On the way back to Kansas, the jayhawkers met "a little darkey about 15 years old," who "hailed them and wanted to know if he could go to Kansas with them—said he had heard that colored folks were free in Kansas." The soldiers invited the boy along. The boy revealed where his master had hidden his horses, which the jayhawkers then confiscated. The expedition returned to Kansas January 1; the confiscated livestock were to be sold at auction the following week.[40]

Lane bragged in a December 7 speech that he had never seen one of his men intoxicated in the three months he was with them. If this had been true once, it was not so much now. The men's self-discipline seemed to erode as they spent less time in the field and more time in camp with the greater availability of liquor and fewer duties to keep them busy. On November 30 a Fifth regiment trooper wounded another in a Mound City saloon. This—together with saloon keeper By Hildreth's ill-timed arrival with a load of liquor from Leavenworth—appears to have prompted a saloon smashing that same day. Mrs. Height of Mound City recruited eight like-minded women from nearby Moneka for the assault. The ladies took axes in hand, stormed the saloon of Hildreth and Eli Bradley, and destroyed their entire stock of liquor. Mound City suddenly becoming dry, four or five soldiers of the Fifth traveled to Mapleton on December 11, where "they secured some liquor and made free use of it." On the way back, one of the intoxicated soldiers waved his pistol about, when it accidentally discharged, "the ball taking effect near the left breast and coming out on the left shoulder." The wounded man was sent to the post hospital at Fort Scott. A few days later "mortification" set in, necessitating an amputation by surgeon John W. Scott of the Fourth. This may be the same accident described by August Bondi. He wrote that J. A. Parker and Oliver G. Triplett of the Fifth headed for Fort Scott, each with a flask of whiskey. Parker soon returned, bringing Triplett with him, who had a pistol wound to the left shoulder. Triplett said they had been firing their pistols—at what was not mentioned—when Parker's horse stumbled and Parker shot himself. Parker was taken to the hospital at Fort Scott where gangrene set in, and the arm was amputated at the shoulder. Despite such a grievous wound, Parker remained with his company as a bugler for almost three years![41]

A court-martial was convened at Camp Defiance in the last days of December, with H. Miles Moore serving as the judge advocate.

Among the defendants were men who had "had their hands deep into dry goods boxes" and had "spirited away fine horses to Lawrence, Leavenworth and other places.... Many of them were never connected with the army, only as hangers-on and camp-followers." Others remained in Kansas and took charge of the property that had been sent to them. The stealing of horses and their transfer to the interior of the state seemed to be of primary concern to the court. An anonymous soldier reported that nearly half the commissioned officers of the Third regiment were under arrest, on various charges. He noted further, "We expect a thorough cleaning out in the company officers; then we propose to commence on the field officers." Due to difficulties with assembling court members, the trials did not commence until January 2.[42]

On December 3 the War Department issued instructions to consolidate and reorganize the Kansas regiments; the execution of it was left to Robinson. Upon learning of this, Lane's associate Mark Delahay telegraphed Lane in Washington requesting that Robinson's authority in the matter be transferred to Hunter and Denver. If Lane tried to do this, he failed.[43] By the end of the month Robinson had reorganized the Brigade's regiments:

THIRD REGIMENT (all infantry except as noted):
Company A, Captain John Foreman
Company B, Captain James Williams (cavalry)
Company C, Captain William Allen
Company D, Captain John Broadhead
Company E, Captain Henry Seaman (cavalry)
Company F, Captain Charles Twiss
Company G, Captain Eli Snyder
Company H, Captain Samuel Stevenson
Company I, Captain John E. Stewart (cavalry)
Company K, Captain John Vansickle (cavalry)
Bickerton's battery was to be attached to the Third.

FOURTH REGIMENT (all infantry):
Company A, Captain James Harris

Company B, Captain Matthew Quigg
Company C, Captain Josiah Hayes
Company D, Captain Zacheus Gower, formerly of the Sixth
Company E, Captain S. Bird [John Boyd?]
Company F, Captain Napoleon Blanton
Company G, Captain James Harvey
Company H, Captain William Rose
Moonlight's battery was to be attached to the Fourth.
Veale's cavalry company was transferred to the Sixth.

FIFTH REGIMENT (all cavalry except the companies
   of Harvey and Watson):
Company A, Captain William Creitz
Company B, Captain John B. Clark
Company C, Captain Garrett Gibson
Company D, Captain Elijah E. Harvey
Company E, Captain James Hunt
Company F, Captain Greenville Watson
Company G, Captain Wilton Jenkins
Company H, Captain Samuel Thompson
Company I, Captain John Lockhart
Company K, Captain Adoniram Miller

SIXTH REGIMENT (all cavalry except as noted):
Company A, Captain W. C. Ransom (infantry)
Company B, Captain Gordon (infantry)
Company C, Captain George Veale, transferred
   from the Fourth
Company D, Captain John Rogers
Company E, Captain H. S. Greeno
Company F, Captain J. W. Orahood
Company G, Captain John Laing
Company H, Captain H. M. Dobyns
Company I, Captain Charles F. Clarke
Captain A.W. J. Brown's company of the Sixth was transferred
   to the Eighth Kansas infantry.[44]

Adoniram Miller's company was a new addition to the Fifth. It had been formed in mid-December by combining Miller's independent company of scouts and a detachment of new recruits under William E. McGinnis. Among those recruits was August Bondi, a Jew who had fled the Austro-Hungarian empire after the failed revolts of 1848. He settled in St. Louis and then emigrated to Kansas in 1856, where he soon became an ally of John Brown. He fought alongside Brown in the defeat at Osawatomie in 1856 (two other men who fought with Brown that day also served in the brigade— Luke Parsons enlisted in Clarke's company of the Sixth and W. W. Updegraff served as brigade paymaster). Miller's men already had muskets, and the recruits were issued similar weapons. Miller's men had found a bayonet on a longarm musket to be a useless appendage for a cavalryman and had been using the bayonets as picket pins. To adapt the muskets for cavalry use, the men "filed off a foot or more of the musket-barrels, and so turned the muskets into musketoons." Although they were issued tents and cooking utensils at Camp Denver, blankets and uniforms were not to be had. Until more equipment was issued, the men had to carry cartridges in their pants pockets while out on scouts. The lack of blankets was mitigated somewhat by filling the tents with two feet of hay into which the men burrowed for warmth.[45]

Zacheus Gower's infantry, transferred to the Fourth, departed Fort Scott on January 11, making a leisurely march to Wyandotte; after ten days the men had gotten only as far as Mound City. A wag there described them as "a portion of the Home Guard who nestle around Fort Scott, and whose principal object of organization is to eat government beans."[46]

And what of Lane? Lane did his best to inform eager Eastern audiences of the accomplishments of his brigade, and especially his humble role therein. In Washington on December 2, he was serenaded by a band at Willard's Hotel, after which he and Owen Lovejoy gave speeches arguing that emancipation was necessary to undermine the rebellion.[47]

He gave another speech in New York on December 3. In it he distinguished the conduct of his brigade from that of Lyon's army, which he said paid secessionists for the provisions the Federal army took, and the money so paid maintained the farm while the men fought in the rebel army. By comparison, Lane said his brigade "took horses, mules, corn, and in three or four days, the slaves came to them. At one time the brigade of 1,200 men had 500 slaves within its lines." Lane asserted they were fighting not for slavery but for freedom. He argued that the rebellion was supported by the labor of four million slaves: "Remove them, and the rebellion would be at an end." When asked what was to be done with the freed slaves, Lane suggested they be educated and then settled in "a country contiguous to us—say South America or South Carolina—and there let them live apart. Let there be a home of the white men, the home of freedom, and the home of the black man, a home of freedom." Prejudice against black people was too strong, Lane acknowledged. Yet if the two races lived together, intermarriage would inevitably result, a thing he was opposed to.[48]

The next day, still in New York, Lane was serenaded by the band of the Nineteenth Indiana, giving him another opportunity for a speech. Lane proclaimed that the rebels in arms, by the Constitution and the laws of God and man, had forfeited their rights to property of every kind, even to the heads on their shoulders. He conceded that confiscating the slaves of rebels implied emancipating them, but before emancipating the slaves, preparations should be made to colonize them. He suggested it would be permissible to enlist blacks into the army, but he softened this radical idea by saying to do so would be inexpedient while thousands of white men would be fighting but for a lack of arms. Further, to arm the slaves would be a confession of weakness, he claimed. Winding up his speech, he said there should be no compromise with rebels that did "not give to the leading rebels a felon's death," and "he hoped the time would soon come when the black and smoking ruins of Charleston would be the monument of its stupendous crime." The reporter covering the speech wrote it was "exceedingly eloquent, and frequently interrupted by loud cheers."[49]

A few days later Lane spoke at Tremont Temple in Boston. He repeated his theme that it was impossible for the army to both crush treason and protect the institution of slavery. Addressing the charges that his brigade had taken the clothing of women and children, "he observed that a number of slave women and children took into their heads in a certain instance, to be free, and they furnished themselves with a portion of the clothing of their former owners. All the Kansas troops did was to see that the whites did not deprive the blacks of all the clothing which had thus come into their possession."[50]

Lane then returned to Washington for the second session of Congress, where Frederick Stanton's challenge to Lane's Senate seat, which had been deferred from the first session, was again taken up. The issue was debated off and on over the next month. Documents were produced showing that on June 20, before a justice of the peace in Washington, Lane had taken an oath of allegiance to the United States. The document stated he had been "appointed brigadier general in the Army of the United States." Lane explained to the Judiciary Committee that after he had been appointed, he had gotten wind that to accept would vacate his seat in the Senate. He then sought a meeting with Brevet Lieutenant General Winfield Scott, who advised him on June 22 that he could not hold both offices. Lane advised Scott he therefore could not accept and then visited both Lincoln and Secretary of War Cameron the same day and told them he could not accept. Senator Samuel C. Pomeroy volunteered that he was present when Lane advised Cameron and Lincoln he would decline the brigadiership if it meant vacating his seat.[51]

Lane also suggested that the appointment was conditional upon the brigade being recruited to full strength and the men then electing him as their commander. He claimed a document in Weer's possession would prove this, but he had been unable to obtain it. Several months earlier, the Leavenworth *Daily Times* reported Lane had received a state commission from Governor Morton of Indiana that he might take command of his Kansas brigade without resigning his Senate seat. Lane now claimed that following the special session of Congress, and while passing through Indianapolis, the Indiana governor had presented him with a commission as a brigadier general. This was true to an extent—Lane had been commissioned by Governor Morton on July 22 as a brigadier general in the Indiana Legion, the state's militia.[52] The Judiciary Committee, probably tired of the whole matter, resolved the issue in Lane's favor on January 16, 1862.

CHAPTER 9

Monotony and Mutiny

The new year was welcomed at Camp Defiance with the ragged celebratory firing of hundreds of muskets into the air, which continued off and on for more than an hour. Montgomery ordered the firing to cease, but the men ignored him. Finally, "he issued [an order] to shoot every man who would not obey the order, & that stopped it."[1]

South of Camp Defiance, instead of celebration a human tragedy was unfolding. A stream of ragged refugees was straggling into Kansas, led by Opothleyahola, a Creek chief. In the months following the Federal evacuation of the Indian Territory the preceding year, the Confederacy had negotiated treaties with all of the major tribes, which, like the Southern states, embraced slavery. Yet Opothleyahola, as leader of the full-blood Creeks, had resisted Confederate entreaties and sought to remain, if not actively loyal to the Federal government, at least neutral. Opotheleyahola was not the only such dissident. Emissaries from the Creek, Chickasaw, and Seminole nations met in November with Federal Indian agents at LeRoy, Kansas, in what proved to be an unsuccessful bid for military assistance. About the same time, the Confederates and their new Indian allies decided to obtain Opothleyahola's obedience by force. Word of this reached Opothleyahola, who decided to flee the territory with his people.[2]

The exodus began in early November. Around five thousand men, women, and children were involved, together with their personal belongings and horse herds. The Creeks made up most of the refugees; the Seminoles were the next largest group, constituting perhaps a fifth of the total number. Amazingly, the flight of so many people came as a surprise to the rebels, who hastily organized columns of Confederate troops and Indians to bring back the escapees. This proved easier said than done, as the fleeing Indians fought a series of successful rear-guard battles. Although each fight was tactically a success, each one cost Opothleyahola warriors and forced the refugees to hurry their pace, losing precious camp equipage in the process. The march in the dead of winter without adequate shelter or food began to take a horrible toll on the Indians. "During their progress they were reduced to such extremity as to be obliged to feed upon their ponies and dogs," wrote George W. Collamore. "Many of the ponies died from starvation. The women and children suffered severely from frozen limbs, as did also the men. Women gave birth to their offspring upon the naked snow without shelter or covering, and in some cases the new-born infants died for want of clothing." The rebels finally achieved a clear-cut victory at Shoal Creek on December 26, but bad weather as well as the exhaustion of the rebels ended any further serious pursuit.[3]

The refugee Indians, thoroughly exhausted and disorganized, drifted into southern Kansas and sank into camps on the Verdigris, Fall, Cottonwood, and Walnut rivers. In late January, Dr. A. B. Campbell visited the camps on the Verdigris near Fort Row and reported:

> It is impossible for me to depict the wretchedness of their condition. Their only protection from the snow upon which they lie is prairie grass and from the wind and weather scraps and rags stretched upon switches. Some of them had some personal clothing; most had but shreds and rags which did not conceal their nakedness, and I saw seven varying in age from three to fifteen years without one thread upon their bodies. . . . Many have their toes frozen off; others have feet wounded by sharp ice or branches of trees lying on the

snow. But few have shoes or moccasins. They suffer with inflammatory diseases of the chest, throat and eyes.[4]

Opothleyahola and other chiefs met with Indian agents in Leavenworth and were assured "the Great Father" would march his troops into their country and that loyal Indians should be enlisted into units to help reclaim their land. For his part Opothleyahola claimed, "The rebel Indians are like a cross, bad slut. The best way to end their breed is to kill the slut."[5]

Other groups of refugees retreating from the Indian Territory joined their brethren in Kansas. Indian agents did their best to provide for them, and for a while Major General Hunter was able to supply food from army coffers, but to a large extent the Indians were on their own. Dr. George A. Cutler, agent of the Creeks, reported that in two months 240 Creek refugees died. W. G. Coffin, superintendent of Indian Affairs, later observed that upward of one hundred amputations of frosted limbs had taken place.[6]

Coffin inspected refugee camps near LeRoy in April. He reported that "measles, diptheria, rheumatism, and bone fever" were prevalent, and there were a few "cases of scrofula and syphilis." However, overall conditions had so improved that at least a hundred of the Indians felt up to participating—semi-nude—in a vigorous ball game. Coffin also documented a bathing ceremony. It began with the Indians drinking two pints of a boiled concoction of roots, which produced immediate and violent vomiting. Then, in a large circle around a campfire, they danced "a very laborious and ludicrous dance, keeping a song or kind of 'yahoo,' responded to or echoed by all the dancers," which numbered three hundred or four hundred. "They keep this up all night," Coffin wrote, "vomiting and dancing, and just at daylight they all run to the river and jump in, and remain some minutes in the water, no matter how cold; this, they think, makes them impervious to bullets or sickness."[7]

George Collamore, writing only nine days after Coffin, painted a different picture; perhaps he had visited a different camp. The shelters he saw "were made in the rudest manner, being composed of pieces of cloth, old quilts, handkerchiefs, aprons, &c., stretched upon sticks, and so limited were many of them in size that they were scarcely sufficient to cover the emaciated and dying forms beneath them." He also observed people so injured by the effects of frostbite that they were unable to move, including "a little Creek boy, about eight years old, with both feet taken off near the ankle."[8]

Eventually those loyal Indians who survived this ordeal would return to the Indian Territory, led by their own men who had been organized and armed by the Federal government into Indian Home Guard regiments. For the moment, however, their lot in life was to suffer.

The general courts-martial in the brigade, which had convened in December, finally got under way on January 2, with H. Miles Moore acting as the judge advocate. When he was ordered to report for duty at a regimental-level court-martial, Moore escaped this task by explaining that a regimental court was not entitled to a judge advocate. Although the activities of the court are not well documented, Moore's diary identifies several defendants, all of whom were from the Third. Where it is clear a conviction resulted, the accused's name is marked with an *:

Captain Eli Snyder*
Lieutenant Ansel D. Brown, Stewart's company
Michael Sawyer, company unknown
First Lieutenant John Bowles,* Stewart's company
Sergeant Elnathan Rhodes, Stewart's company
Corporal Argent K. Cansdell,* Stewart's company
Sergeant Thomas Riley,* Bickerton's battery

As of February 28, Snyder was still under arrest and awaiting sentence of a court-martial. Stewart also had charges of an unknown character levied against him. Brigade surgeon Rufus Gilpatrick wrote on January 8 that due to "indisposition," Stewart was incompetent to attend court. Gilpatrick did not state whether Stewart was to attend as a defendant or court member, but as Stewart's name was not on lists of those officers detailed as court members, it is obvious he was a defendant. In addition, the company's muster-out roll indicates he and Bowles had been under arrest since December 15.[9]

In only two of these trials is the nature of the charge known; both were for horse stealing, by Cansdell and Rhodes. The sentences are unknown as well. Moore noted in his diary that Snyder's sentence was "very severe of course," and Cansdell's was "much lighter" than that received by Rhodes, who was reduced in rank. That Rhodes was punished more heavily than Cansdell is understandable—he had the bad luck to have had stolen the black stallion of the judge advocate who was presiding over the hearings. Moore gave no indication that the judge advocate recused himself as a biased participant.[10]

Brigadier General James W. Denver did not approve the charges against Snyder, as they had not been signed by a commissioned officer, and Denver reduced the charges against Rhodes from grand larceny to theft. Charges against Captain Gower and Lieutenant Michael Tippie were held by Denver and not pursued. Also charged was John Hartman, a Missouri civilian accused of murdering or abetting the murder of a soldier. His prosecution was brought to a sudden conclusion when Hartman, in answering the call of nature one evening, slipped away from his guard and escaped.[11]

While the courts-martial plodded along, life in camp plodded alongside, with "nothing under God's heavens to designate one day from another" except the weather, recalled Lieutenant Colonel Blunt. "For the want of anything else to kill, we 'killed time,' in masticating government rations." The men devoured any reading material that came their way. Chaplain Moore asked citizens to forward newspapers to the camp after they had been read. Another shortage in camp was money. Amazingly, the men had yet to receive their pay after many months of service. This had been tolerated in the heady, early days of the war, especially as they were able to supply many of their needs from the larders of Missouri. But now jayhawking forays into Missouri had been curtailed, and the onset of harsh winter weather only highlighted their suffering. Chaplain Moore reported many of the men were unable to afford postage for a letter, and their families at home were destitute.[12]

Dr. Huntoon at Camp Denver wrote that he had not had a cent for six months and hardly remembered how money looked. Vansickle at Camp Defiance wrote that his men had been without pay during their three months of service. However, whatever dissatisfaction this may have caused did not keep his "bois" from disturbing his sleep with their gabbing, singing, and cutting up outside his tent. Judge Advocate Moore, also at Camp Defiance, noted in his diary on January 21, "There is a dark cloud of despondency settled over the camp on account of the prolonged absence of the Paymaster." A few days later Montgomery made a speech that appeased the men some about their pay. Montgomery granted twenty-day furloughs to a number of the privates who had been without pay for six months. In case the paymaster arrived while they were absent, these men left behind powers of attorney so others could draw their pay for them. Denver, who had been tasked by higher authority with assembling an expedition into the Indian Territory (which eventually failed to materialize), revoked all furloughs later that month.[13]

Camp life could be as dangerous as campaigning. A soldier of Williams's company was playing with his revolver on January 5 when it went off, hitting Private James Ryan who was sitting across from him. The ball entered Ryan's stomach and lodged near his spine. Ryan lived three days in agony before dying. Another soldier was injured when a tree fell on him in the night. A civilian wrote: "It is a great wonder more accidents of this latter kind do not occur in camp. It is quite a common occurrence for the soldiers of a cold day to take axe in hand and cut away at the nearest tree, for the mere sake of keeping warm or amusement. Their skill in this department of service is evinced in the close proximity to their tents or their horses tied around they can lay the falling timber. A close shave they make of it sometimes, amidst the applause of the surrounding auditors." George Flanders wrote from Camp Denver the following month that he would not want soldiers to camp near any timber he owned, for they would cut down every tree that could be dragged to camp by a team of horses. Logs as thick as two feet were used for common campfires.[14]

August Bondi contracted measles in early January and was sent to the regimental hospital tent. The tent was in a sorry state, Bondi recalled. "The old rotten canvas was full of holes. It was large enough to hold six beds, consisting of rails deeply covered with straw which was held in place by old staves driven into the ground. In the center of the tent was a hole in which, in extreme cold weather, a kettle with live coals in it was set. Three pieces of hard bread and three cups of smoke-tasting tea was my daily allowance. I took good care to keep my bowels open." During his approximately one-week stay, Bondi was cared for by Edward M. Rice, who had been detailed from Captain Garrett Gibson's company as a nurse, and Mrs. Andrew Frank, whose two sons were in the same tent. Two months later, after the Fifth had moved to a new camp, Rice "was caught bathing in the spring from which the cooking and drinking water was obtained, and was court-martialed and never after with company or regiment." Also occupying Bondi's tent were "negroes, officers and servants," all sick with measles. One of them died and his place taken by another patient who "was given the place of the dead without change even of the straw. The snow inside the hospital tent was about as deep as outside." Captain Samuel Stephenson of the Third died of measles in mid-January in the hospital at Mound City. A correspondent wrote, "Unfortunately he allowed it to gain too much headway before he would consent to undergo medical treatment. For some time after being attacked with this prevailing epidemic, he continued to occupy his old quarters at the encampment, and sleep in his tent during the late severe weather. The old story, a cold followed this imprudent exposure, and the consequence as stated. His family was with him in his last moments."[15]

Camp Defiance was enlivened somewhat by a confrontation between Montgomery and the infantry. The men wanted to build a sentinel fire at the commissary tent but Montgomery prevented it. The men were near mutiny when Major Williams intervened and sent them back to their tents. Judge Advocate Moore attributed the affair to enmity between the men and Adjutant Casimir Zulasky, whom Moore described as overbearing and tyrannical.[16]

Creitz noted that from December 19 to February 22, the Fifth remained comparatively inactive. Chaplain Fisher recounted the monotony of camp life and the men's wish that spring and Lane the "liberator" were there, and Lane would say, "Onward towards the sunny South!" According to Fisher, occasionally a contraband would come into camp asking, "'Where am massa Lane?' But they do not come as numerously as we could wish. O, for a horse rake, or seine, or a lot of grappling hooks to drag secession as the gay and festive Jennison does."[17]

The "gay and festive Jennison" was doing his part—as he saw it—to crush secession. In just the first month of the new year, Jennison's regiment had several skirmishes with the enemy, burned the Missouri towns of Dayton, Columbus, and Holden, seized dozens of horses and mules, freed a like number of slaves, and evacuated Union families from Missouri. No doubt, much of Missouri breathed a sigh of relief when this regiment was removed from the border. On February 2 the regiment reached Mound City on its way to its new station at Humboldt; within its ranks was John Brown, Jr., who had originally planned to serve under Montgomery. He had instead raised a cavalry company in Ohio and returned to Kansas as its captain to serve under Jennison.[18]

The departure of Ritchie and the monotony of camp life contributed to a decline in discipline in the Fifth. According to Bondi, the situation became unruly, as each man did what pleased him. "As the scouts went out, it generally took them half a day to get them ready. The [regimental] commissary lieutenant and sergeant stole by wholesale. . . . All the first lieutenants could do was to furnish enough for camp guard details. When a parade was ordered, the boys made it up not to turn out and there was no parade. Major Summers had two barrels of whiskey in his tent retailing at $1.00 per gallon."[19]

Creitz alleged that some men "were frequently in a state of open mutiny and insubordination," which he blamed on the "imbecility" of Major James H. Summers. He also wrote that an illegal organization known as "Company X" had emerged "to bid defiance to military law and order" and to manage the affairs of the regiment as it saw fit. Creitz thought Summers lacked the moral courage to suppress Company X, and the organization's influence was contained only by Creitz's company boldly opposing the "dangerous institution" at the outset."[20]

Daniel W. Boutwell was a private in Creitz's company. In a diatribe written nearly fifty years later, he railed against the secretary of war's new regulations that did not allow soldiers to elect their officers. Boutwell claimed that in early January six hundred soldiers assembled and chose him as their spokesman, following which the assembly marched to the regimental headquarters and accosted E. P. Sheldon, who had been mustered in as assistant surgeon on January 1. Sheldon was advised he would not be allowed to supersede Andrew Huntoon as surgeon (Huntoon had enlisted in Boutwell's company as a private and was later promoted to assistant surgeon). Sheldon left camp and Huntoon was mustered in as surgeon on January 5. Boutwell was placed under arrest, taken to Fort Scott, and charged with having organized his own company (Company X), with having opposed lawful commands, and with breeding discord among the soldiers.[21]

Huntoon's letters give a more objective account. When Sheldon reported for duty as the assistant surgeon, surgeon Johnson's reply to this unexpected visitor was he already had as good an assistant surgeon as he could wish for, and he had no use for Sheldon or any other outsider. Sheldon remained in camp, and on January 26 a delegation of men from each company visited Sheldon and informed him his services were no longer needed and that for his own health he should depart the next morning. "During the affair a little difficulty occurred between Mr. Boutwell & Lieutenant Scudder in which B. drew his revolver upon S. & was consequently arrested to await court-martial. The Dr. left on Monday morning as requested." When the regiment was mustered for pay on February 3–4, Huntoon was placed on the rolls as the assistant surgeon even though he still held no commission. Sheldon did eventually return to the regiment; in March, Huntoon returned from a furlough and found Sheldon in camp, whom he described as being the assistant surgeon and very sick. Huntoon sent him to Fort Scott. Sheldon, thinking he would die, sent for his wife. Sheldon died at Fort Scott on

April 3, 1862. Huntoon was eventually commissioned as regimental surgeon.[22]

Boutwell's saga did not end with his arrest. He was convicted of some charge but escaped from his guards while being escorted to supper. Rather than remain in hiding, he tracked down the Fifth at Carthage, Missouri, and reported for duty. He was allowed to report, but three men were detailed to take him back to Fort Scott. What happened next was recounted by fellow trooper George Flanders: "When they had proceeded about three miles he put spurs to his horse and left them; they fired the contents of their revolvers at him but he got away." Boutwell would eventually secure some measure of asylum with Ritchie, who was then commanding a regiment of Indian Home Guards in southwest Missouri. In September 1862 one of Ritchie's lieutenants alleged that Ritchie was giving the known deserter "a soldiers and a Lieutenants duty." Boutwell's subsequent military career is a bit of a curiosity. Flanders later noted Boutwell returned to the regiment at Helena, Arkansas, on April 28, 1863: "There will be nothing done with Boutwell; he is glad to get back and the boys are all glad to see him." Boutwell was wounded in battle at Pine Bluff, Arkansas, in October, 1863, and was mustered out of the Fifth on August 11, 1864. He subsequently served as a scout in the Kansas State Militia during the Price raid in the fall of 1864.[23]

The infantry officers of the Third held a meeting in Major Williams's tent on January 24 to discuss the impending reorganization of the regiment. They decided it would be left up to Williams to arrange the companies as he pleased. As there were only enough infantrymen to make up about three full companies, it was agreed that officers who were excess after Williams reorganized the companies would then resign. This agreement lasted only two days, when a number of officers reneged on their agreement, apparently upon finding they were the ones expected to resign.[24]

The paymaster in the person of Lieutenant C. S. Bowman finally arrived in Fort Scott at the end of the month. He also was under orders to remuster the Third, Fourth, Fifth, and Sixth regiments. Bowman did not immediately attend to business. Sergeant

Major Marcus deLafayette Tenney reported Bowman had been drunk ever since he arrived.[25]

Events that transpired within the Third and Fifth regiments are amply documented, Yet there is no mention of the Fourth's activities in their camp at Wyandotte. As far as leaving any written record, the Fourth just disappeared. Any letters from the soldiers were no longer published in the newspapers, and neither were any accounts of any regimental news. Lieutenant Colonel Burris must have infused such discipline that the men generated no controversy. In fact, the next documentation of anything substantial would not be found until the first week of April.

At the end of January, Lane returned to Kansas, not to resume command of the Kansas Brigade, as those troops were firmly under the jurisdiction of Hunter, but to try to wrest that jurisdiction away from Hunter. In this he was helped by the departure of Denver, who had been ordered by General-in-Chief George McClellan to report for duty in western Virginia. Robinson advised Denver that he had written to the secretary of war and to McClellan, requesting that Denver be retained in Kansas, and he asked Denver to delay leaving as long as possible. Robinson's effort failed. Lane's earlier attempt at the creation of, and command of, a new military department of Kansas had failed, but he had been busy with a new scheme, that of resigning his Senate seat if—and only if—he could get a commission as a major general and the command of a thirty-thousand-man army that would sweep out of Kansas and into the bowels of the western Confederacy.[26]

As was his custom—seemingly whenever he stopped moving—Lane made a speech. To a crowd at the Leavenworth Mercantile Association on January 27 he called for:

> war, perpetual war, until the North is conquered by the South, or the South is conquered by the North. . . . Who feeds this rebellion? four million slaves. Who clothes this rebellion? four million slaves. Take them from that side and put them on this side. If they were *mules* you would do it in

a minute. And yet I think a man is worth more to the enemy than a mule. . . . The true way to close this rebellion is to detach the four million slaves. A man says, "Lane, if you do that won't you make them *free*?" Great God! what a terrible calamity! Every slave within this Government is destined to be free. God has so determined.[27]

The idea that the best way to cripple the South was to take her slaves was a familiar theme of Lane's; his assertion that every slave would be freed was a new but not radical twist. However, he then laid a radical proposal before his Leavenworth audience: "It would not pain me to see the negro handling a gun, and I believe the negro may just as well become food for powder as my son. . . . I don't propose to punish the negro if he kills a traitor. . . . Give them a fair chance, put arms in their hands, and they will do the balance of the fighting in this war."[28]

The following day Lane's pursuit of command of a Southern expedition was abruptly crushed when Hunter on January 27 issued an order stating that he, Hunter, would personally command any such expedition.[29]

CHAPTER 10

Dissolution

Colder weather limited the active operations of the soldiers, but they were constrained further by Major General Halleck, who instructed Major General Hunter on February 2: "Keep the Kansas troops out of Missouri and I will keep the Missourians out of Kansas. They can't agree, and make infinite trouble. The only way is to keep them apart." This admonishment would come too late to stop at least one more incursion into Missouri.[1]

John I. Worthington, lawyer and loyal Unionist, had fled his home in Granby, Missouri, in January and now made his way to Fort Scott, where he enlisted in the Sixth Kansas as a private. Worthington was quickly promoted to regimental commissary sergeant and entrusted with managing the scouts. Around February 3 he led seven men, dressed as civilians, into Newton County, Missouri, using as a cover story that they were scouts for the Confederate colonel Stand Watie. On the fourth day they attacked a party of twelve guerrillas led by one Dr. Cummings, killing three and capturing seven horses. Wending his way through the county, by February 9 Worthington had been joined by twenty Union men who wished to flee and for whom he provided arms and horses. In the previous days he had captured fifty soldiers and other rebels, thirteen of whom he paroled while keeping the others prisoner; forty-three horses were captured as well. On February 9, while heading back to Fort Scott with his new accessions, Worthington encountered sixty guerillas. He intermixed his armed men with his prisoners to give the appearance of greater numbers than he had. This dissuaded the rebels from attempting a frontal attack. A flanking movement was tried, but a volley caused the rebels to fall back and then withdraw completely. Worthington returned to Fort Scott without further incident.[2]

The abuse of liquor continued to be an occasional problem within the brigade. In early February it led to the wounding of two soldiers of Allen's company, when Andy Moore of Jennison's regiment got drunk at Mound City and "took the town." Stanton Weaver was shot in the shoulder, a wound that led to his being discharged for disability in May; Charley Bonsall received a lesser wound in the hand. An intoxicated Private James Hurd of Stephenson's company (now commanded by Lieutenant James M. Arthur) got lost on the prairie and froze to death; the Kansas adjutant general's report charitably listed Hurd as having died from disease. Montgomery responded to this problem by issuing a proclamation putting all saloons in Linn County below the Marais des Cygnes River under martial law. The proclamation decreed that any person who sold liquor to soldiers would receive thirty-nine lashes for the first offense and would be shot upon a second offence. Two or three saloon keepers were arrested for selling liquor to soldiers. Judge Advocate H. Miles Moore and Major Henry H. Williams conducted an examination of one of these men, Eli Bradley of Mound City, and absolved him of any guilt in the death of Private Hurd. Although the liquor that contributed to Hurd's death had been purchased at Eli Bradley and By Hildreth's saloon, it had been sold to a private citizen who provided it to Hurd. Further, it was proven that Bradley had not sold any liquor to soldiers since Montgomery's declaration of martial law. Nonetheless, Montgomery was determined to have a public whipping. The regiment was formed into a hollow square, Bradley was tied to a cannon wheel, and ten lashes were laid on. The whole thing was a bit of a farce. Bradley was allowed to wear his vest and two shirts underneath, which provided a measure of padding; he never winced, but laughed when the whole thing was over. After his whipping, Bradley was drummed out of camp to the tune of the "Rogue's March."[3]

To keep the men of the Third busy, and to improve their efficiency and discipline, Lieutenant Colonel Blunt issued an order requiring company drill every morning, officer drill at 2 P.M., and dress parade at 5 P.M. This development was noted approvingly by Judge Advocate Moore: "This looks a little more military." A civilian visiting the camp in early March observed that all of the teamsters were blacks; the teamsters were paid $20 to $25 a month. Thirty or forty other blacks were employed by officers as cooks and servants, for which they received the same pay as enlisted men.[4]

At Barnesville the Fifth was mustered for pay and the payrolls were prepared on February 3–4, in time for the arrival of Lieutenant Bowman, the paymaster. The men were in good spirits knowing the money for their payment was forthcoming. Four companies were paid on February 8. The men were paid only for service through December 1861. Dr. Huntoon's back pay amounted to $616.28; he also received $85 for the use of his horse. The mounted men who claimed the fifty cents a day for the use of their horse were required to swear to the oath: "You do solemnly swear that the horse in your possession is your own, was not purchased with government money and is not confiscated property." Private Marcellia Pardia of Jenkins's company, who had been born in Mexico nineteen years before, was mustered out at the same time he received his pay because he could not understand English. Undaunted by this rejection, Pardia enlisted into the Sixth on May 20, 1863. Sadly, he died on September 18, 1864, "from injuries received by [a] government wagon."[5]

Bowman arrived at Camp Defiance on February 9 and at Camp Denver on February 10. He also served as mustering officer, courtesy of Hunter, who the previous month had issued orders for the reorganization of the Third, Fourth, Fifth, and Sixth regiments. These orders required understrength companies to be consolidated in order to meet the minimum strength, and officers in excess of those permitted to the reorganized companies would be mustered out.[6]

In the Third, William Allen's company was consolidated with John Foreman's, Allen being mustered out and Foreman taking command, and the company of the late Captain Stephenson was consolidated with Broadhead's, Broadhead commanding. As Snyder's company was without an officer—Captain Snyder being under arrest, First Lieutenant John Downing having resigned, and Second Lieutenant Frederick Smalley absent—Montgomery ordered Judge Advocate Moore to take command of the company.[7]

It was subsequently discovered that there was some irregularity in the muster of Judge Advocate Moore, and Bowman refused to pay him. Moore was the victim of sloppy paperwork. He initially had received a commission on October 1 as first lieutenant in Allen's company (without that company's knowledge) and immediately transferred to brigade staff as judge advocate. The paperwork for this came from Montgomery, who had several blank commission forms already signed by Robinson. Moore was then supposedly sworn into the U.S. service for three years by Moonlight on October 23 (officers did not enlist for a term of years). In an unsuccessful attempt to get Moore paid, his name was put onto the muster roll of Snyder's company, which Moore was temporarily commanding. In utter frustration, Moore wrote in his diary, "If I am not a Lieut. in this Regt, in the name of God where do I belong[?]" On February 16 he gave up and headed home to Leavenworth. It appears the irregularity of his appointment voided the convictions obtained in the previous month's general court-martials.[8]

Although Moore paid the penalty for having been irregularly mustered, the same fate did not then befall John Vansickle's independent company of scouts, who were paid off without being mustered out. Vansickle noted his monthly wage was $175. If the men had been improperly mustered, as they would discover, there is little evidence they knew it then. Everything about them suggested they were proper soldiers. They had been attached to the Third, the government had paid them, and provided rations. They had accompanied the Papinsville expedition, and only the month before, Vansickle was expecting to be ordered south. To cap it all, the men had been remustered on February 10, Vansickle subsequently identifying himself as being in Company K of the Third.[9]

The men of Allen's company bore some ill will toward being consolidated under Foreman's command. When Foreman ordered them to march to his company, First Sergeant Luther Thrasher gave the men the option of whether to obey. None did, and despite Foreman accusing them of disobeying orders, they then refused to turn out for roll call. They did turn out for dress parade under their own Lieutenant Clayton Kille, and there Thrasher was arrested. Kille was ordered by Adjutant Zulavsky to march the company over and attach it to Foreman's, but Kille declined. Zulavsky then tried to assume command. His orders addressing the men as Company A (Foreman's) were ignored; the men refused to move until he gave orders to Company C. The same farce was reenacted minutes later when Foreman tried issuing orders. "Compromised our differences & will get along," recalled William H. H. Dickinson.[10]

The remustering in the Fourth produced little change, although an examination of the rolls led to the discovery that Quartermaster Alfred Larzalere had never been mustered or commissioned. Accordingly he was ordered to immediately "cease to perform the functions of that office." Bowman made the following changes in the Third: "The Colonel to become Lieut. Colonel; the Lieut. Colonel to become Major; the Major [to be] Chaplain; Captains Tives [Eves?], Bickerton, Lieuts. Brown, Downing, Smalley, Arthur, McDonald and Brooks, to be mustered out. Privates Cooper, Aldeman, Besin, Gibson, and Mitchell, of Capt. Williams' Company, are also mustered out." In addition, Chaplain Moore and surgeon Albert Newman were also released. Lieutenant Colonel Blunt had no intention of becoming major and announced that he would contest Montgomery for the lieutenant colonel's position.[11]

Major Henry H. Williams was also mustered out, which he refused to accept, along with refusing to accept the pay due him upon being mustered out. Second Lieutenant Ansel Brown of James Williams's company circulated a petition that called for Blunt and Major Williams to be retained in their former positions; for this Montgomery ordered Brown put under arrest. Then, in an apparent temporary compromise of his dispute, Major Williams accepted his pay. Williams would eventually retain his rank and position.[12]

A few officers of the Fifth were mustered out when it was found their companies had less than the minimum number of men.

Lieutenant Colonel Powell Clayton finally arrived to take command of the regiment. August Bondi had been gone from camp when Clayton arrived and began putting things in order. "What a change in three days!" wrote Bondi. "Camp guards were posted around the camp about 100 yards apart. All were let in but no one permitted to go out. Regimental drill from 2 to 5 p.m. every day." Creitz appreciated the improvement brought by Clayton, who "by discreet management speedily created order out of chaos. . . . The regiment was almost constantly exercised in the Cavalry drill—men soon arrived at an astonishing degree of perfection." According to William Creitz, Clayton gave Major James H. Summers the option of either resigning or facing a court-martial; Summers chose to resign. Summers tendered his resignation to Hunter on February 18, claiming a great injustice has been done by Governor Robinson in refusing to commission Summers as colonel, and he wanted only to return to his home state of Iowa. Robinson commissioned Clayton as colonel and Edward Lynde as lieutenant colonel on March 7.[13]

No longer was southeast Kansas the exclusive province of Lane's Brigade, and the future of the brigade was uncertain. Fort Lincoln, a pet project of Lane, was being abandoned and its stores moved to Fort Scott. The Fifth was moved to a new site, christened Camp Hunter, twelve miles south of Fort Scott on the Drywood Creek in the Cherokee Neutral Lands, where the efficient Colonel Clayton "had the boys provided with proper uniforms and blankets; clothes and blankets were sorely needed." The Thirteenth Wisconsin Infantry arrived at Fort Scott to relieve the Sixth, which was sent to join the Fifth. The civilians of Fort Scott were pleased with the Thirteenth Wisconsin because of their orderly and soldierlike manner: "No more firing of guns and pistols at random in the thoroughfares, much to the annoyance and dread of decently behaved folks. The departed Sixth did these things for pastime." The provost marshal maintained a measure of law and order, and the secesh prisoners were made to work on the streets, "shovelling up the loose dirt, preparatory to carting it away." Colonel Charles Doubleday of the Second Ohio Cavalry was made acting brigadier general and given command of a brigade comprising the Second Ohio Cavalry, the

Ninth and Twelfth Wisconsin Infantry, and George S. Hollister's battery. Colonel George Deitzler of the First Kansas, also an acting brigadier general, traveled to Fort Scott to take command of a brigade encompassing the First, Fifth, and Sixth Kansas, Thirteenth Wisconsin Infantry, and Rabb's battery. Jennison as well had been made an acting brigadier, his brigade consisting only of his own regiment and Charles S. Clarke's independent cavalry battalion. The Third, Fourth, and Eighth Kansas regiments were not brigaded. Deitzler's brigade was intended to cooperate with Major General Samuel Curtis's campaign against Price, but Curtis's expedition went forward without the Kansas troops. He forced Price to evacuate Springfield on February 12 and then retreat into Arkansas; Curtis would go on to defeat Price and McCulloch in the battle of Pea Ridge on March 7–8.[14]

Hunter's General Orders no. 26, dated February 28, announced the further reorganization of several Kansas regiments, "pursuant to instructions from Head Quarters of the Army . . . and by and with the consent of His Excellency, the Governor of Kansas." The order left intact the First Kansas Infantry, Jennison's regiment, and Clarke's independent cavalry battalion. The regiments to be reorganized were the Third, Fourth, and Eighth Infantry, and the Fifth, Sixth, and Ninth Cavalry. To effect General Orders no. 26, "mustering officers were sent to re-muster the regiments of Lane's brigade and consolidate the companies to the minimum standing, mustering out the surplus officers and all who could prove they had been enlisted as Home Guards under General Lyon's call. These mustering officers found the companies ranged from 25 to 60 men each, but the average about 50, each having a captain and two lieutenants, and in some instances more."[15]

The reorganization of the regiments of the brigade, as set out in General Orders no. 26, was to be as follows:

THIRD REGIMENT:
Company A, Captain John Foreman
Company B, Captain John F. Broadhead
Company C, Captain Eli Snyder

Company D, Lieutenant Jones
Company E, Lieutenant Norman Allen, artillery, formerly Bickerton's battery
Company F, Captain Moonlight, artillery, formerly of the Fourth
Company G, Captain Wyllis C. Ransom, infantry, formerly of the Sixth
Company H, Captain Simeon B. Gordon, infantry, formerly of the Sixth
Company I, Lieutenant Kelly's and Robinson's detachments, First New Mexico Kansas Volunteers, consolidated
Company K, Lieutenant Elijah K. Fleming, formerly of Greenville Watson's company, Fifth Kansas (Captain John E. Stewart's company became Company M, Ninth Kansas Cavalry, headquartered at Quindaro; the Ninth was later redesignated the Second Kansas Cavalry.)

FOURTH REGIMENT: still being remustered

FIFTH REGIMENT:
Company A, Captain William F. Creitz
Company B, Captain John R. Clark
Company C, Captain James S. Hunt
Company D, Captain Wilton H. Jenkins
Company E, Captain Garrett Gibson
Company F, Lieutenant Samuel C. Thompson[16]
Company G, Lieutenant John Lockhart
Company H, Lieutenant Johnson
Company I, Captain Henry C. Seaman, formerly of the Third
Company K, Captain James M. Williams, formerly of the Third

SIXTH REGIMENT:
Company A, Captain George W. Veale, formerly of the Fourth
Company B, Captain John Rogers
Company C, Captain Harris S. Greeno
Company D, Captain John W. Orahood

Company E, Captain Henry M. Dobyns
Company F, Captain Charles F. Clarke
Company G, Lieutenant John M. Laing
Company H, Captain David Mefford
Company I, Captain Vansickle's scouts, formerly attached to the Third
Company K, Captain Elijah E. Harvey, formerly of the Fifth

Further reorganization was mandated when Halleck telegraphed Robinson on March 21 with instructions to consolidate the fragments of the regiments to their minimum strength as required by law. Any surplus officers were to be mustered out.[17]

Robinson and Hunter cooperated in issuing an order transferring Moonlight's artillery company to the Third to serve as infantrymen. When the mustering officer arrived to execute the transfer, Moonlight and his men refused; the company was ordered to proceed to Fort Leavenworth under arrest, where it was stripped of its artillery equipment. Prince again ordered the company to report to the Third as infantry, and again Moonlight refused. According to Moonlight, Robinson then ordered the men distributed among the First Kansas Infantry, but Moonlight appealed to the War Department and was "sustained." His battery was then consolidated with Bickerton's (now commanded by Lieutenant Allen) to become the First Kansas Battery. This left Moonlight temporarily adrift, without any command.[18]

Robinson argued that he ordered Moonlight's artillery and Veale's cavalry company transferred out of the Fourth because the War Department would not permit the mixing of different branches within a regiment. Consistent with this, the two infantry companies of the Fifth were transferred to other regiments: Elijah Harvey's to the Sixth and Watson's to the Third. Seaman's and Williams's cavalry companies of the Third were transferred to the Fifth. On March 13 the Fifth left its camp on the Drywood for Carthage and locales deeper in Missouri. This effectively terminated whatever connection it still had with the Kansas Brigade.[19]

Kansas was still being plagued by criminals, especially horse thieves, who took advantage of the disorder caused by the war. In early February a citizen arrived in the camp of the Fifth reporting that men he described as secesh had stolen his horses. A detachment was sent in pursuit, the thieves were found, and one was killed and another captured. On the dead man was found a book describing a number of horses and where they were; two of them had been stolen from the company. Hunter found it necessary to declare martial law throughout Kansas on February 8 due to "armed depredations and jayhawking." Those persons accused of such activities were to be tried by military commissions. Kansans generally welcomed the move.[20]

Hunter succeeded in halting most of the cross-border raids by Kansas and Missouri civilians. Although the amateurs were put in check, professional bushwhackers from Missouri stepped in to fill the void. On the morning of March 7, William Clarke Quantrill led forty guerrillas out of Missouri to the little town of Aubrey, Kansas, entering the town screaming and shooting. The town was quickly taken, yet three men were shot down as they tried to flee. Another was shot when Quantrill spied movement in an upstairs window and snapped off a shot from his pistol. The ball went through the window sash and square into the man's forehead. "He made a good shot," admitted Abraham Ellis, quartermaster of Lane's Brigade, who witnessed it. One of the captured town occupants was Lieutenant Reuben Randlett of Creitz's company, who had been on leave and was on his way to rejoin his company. Randlett was interrogated by Quantrill, and in the course of their conversation the men discovered both had been in the Drywood battle. Randlett mentioned he had been near Moonlight's gun when it disabled one of Price's guns; Quantrill revealed he had been stationed near that gun when Moonlight put it out of action and that after Lexington he left Price's army to form his own band.[21]

As Randlett and Quantrill were talking, they were interrupted by a bloody visitor. Quantrill recognized him as Abraham Ellis, who, as a county superintendent of public instruction, had several years before granted Quantrill a certificate to teach school in Lykins County, Kansas. Ellis was bleeding from a bullet wound to the forehead, the one given to him minutes earlier when the guerilla leader shot at the movement in the upstairs window. Quantrill had not known it was Ellis when he fired. According to historian William E. Connelley, Quantrill "sat him in a chair and called for a washcloth and water and personally washed his face, apologizing profusely." According to Connelley, Quantrill told Ellis he was "damned sorry" to have shot him and that Ellis was one of the Kansas men he did not want to hurt. Ellis recovered, but with a prominent indentation in the middle of his forehead; he was known afterward as "Bullet Hole" Ellis.[22]

The raiders looted the town and set one building on fire. In addition to stealing goods, they took Randlett and J. W. Miller with them when they left. Miller was quickly released, but Randlett was kept prisoner. From his refuge in Missouri, Quantrill sent letters to Fort Leavenworth proposing to exchange Randlett for one of Quantrill's men held prisoner. After eleven days, no response had come. Quantrill then delivered Randlett to an Independence hotel, and "gave Randlett a ten-day parole so that he might negotiate an exchange in person." Randlett felt it was his honorable duty to either negotiate an exchange or deliver himself back to Quantrill. The Federal authorities would not agree to an exchange, but Randlett, not knowing the location of Quantrill's camp, was unable to surrender; he had to satisfy himself with trying to get a note to Quantrill stating that his effort had failed. Randlett's survival was a near thing. The day after his release, Quantrill learned of Halleck's new order, which called for the hanging of captured guerillas. Thereafter, Quantrill would frequently kill his prisoners. Although Randlett was described by one of Quantrill's men as "a splendid fellow" that "we all became much attached to," this may not have been sufficient to save him from execution, had Quantrill then known of Halleck's order.[23]

The following week Major Charles G. Halpine, assistant adjutant general at Fort Leavenworth, noted that in response to reports of "jayhawkers murdering and pillaging in Jackson County [Missouri] and border," all six companies of the Fourth were sent to Independence and Westport, Missouri, to guard the state line.[24] Halpine detailed the disposition of such troops in Kansas, which as of March 14 he considered to be "in effective condition for active service." These were the First Kansas, Ninth, Twelfth, and Thirteenth Wisconsin, the Second Ohio Cavalry, Rabb's Second Indiana Battery, all at Fort Scott, Jennison's regiment at Humboldt, and the Eighth Kansas, whose companies were stationed at several locations in the state.[25]

Halpine did not consider the Third, Fourth, Fifth, and Sixth Kansas to be in effective condition. He wrote to Halleck:

> Nothing could exceed the demoralized condition in which General Hunter found the Third and Fourth Kansas Infantry and Fifth and Sixth Kansas Cavalry, formerly known as "Lane's brigade," on his arrival in this department. The regimental and company commanders knew nothing of their duties and apparently had never made returns or reports of any kind. The regiments appeared in worse condition than they could possibly have been in during the first week of their enlistment, their camps being little better than vast pig-pens, officers and men sleeping and messing together; furloughs in immense numbers being granted, or, where not granted, taken; drill having been abandoned almost wholly, and the men constituting a mere ragged, half-armed, diseased, and mutinous rabble, taking votes as to whether any troublesome or distasteful order should be obeyed or defied. . . . The few officers willing to do right, if they knew how, had to be instructed in nearly every branch of their duties, and this was the more difficult, as for the first two months the department was almost entirely destitute of blanks and has never had a proper supply.[26]

Upon what facts Halpine relied to make his assessment of the brigade is subject to speculation. There is no evidence either he or Hunter ever left the environs of Leavenworth, although Denver and Oscar E. Learnard had made their inspection tour in December.

First Sergeant Luther Thrasher's diary clearly shows that in December at least Company C of the Third was in good condition, being regularly drilled, taking target practice, and undergoing inspections. A great deal of Halpine's information probably came from complaining Missourians as well as Captain Prince at Fort Leavenworth. Yet it is clear there was much demoralization in the Fifth before Clayton took command in mid-February, a condition that Clayton quickly rectified (and which should have afforded Halpine no complaint when he wrote to Halleck).[27]

Halleck recommended the consolidation of the Departments of the Ohio and the Missouri; the Department of Kansas, being less connected to the ongoing operations, could be left alone. The commands of Hunter and Halleck, together with part of the command of Brigadier General Don Carlos Buell, were consolidated on March 11 into the Department of the Mississippi, with Halleck taking command. Hunter was transferred to South Carolina and to the command of the Department of the South; in his absence, acting Brigadier General Deitzler temporarily commanded the newly formed District of Kansas until replaced by Denver, who had been ordered back from western Virginia.[28]

Denver on March 19 was given command of the District of Kansas. Lane and Senator Pomeroy protested to Lincoln against Denver having this command. Lincoln directed Halleck on March 21 to "suspend the order sending General Denver to Kansas" until he heard from Secretary of War Edwin M. Stanton or himself, and then referred the matter to Stanton for his comments. At the same time, Halleck was informed by a citizen named E. A. Hitchcock that on the evening of March 22, he had had a conversation with Stanton about the matter. Stanton told Hitchcock that Lane claimed to have an order from Lincoln stating Denver would not be put in command, but instead Brigadier General Thomas A. Davies was to have it. Hitchcock reported that Stanton's "answer to Lane was a positive refusal to attend to any such order," and if attempts were made to enforce it, he would leave the office. Stanton's response to Lincoln, however, was only to write an endorsement that Halleck "should do as he thought best for the service," with a copy of this being mailed to Halleck. Evidently Stanton's intention was that Halleck, upon receipt of the mailed copy, would take this as permission to "do as he thought best for the service." The mail was slow in arriving. Halleck on March 26 telegraphed Stanton that Denver had already reported at St. Louis, and he asked, "What shall I do? There is no one in command in Kansas at the present time."[29]

Halleck wrote to Stanton again two days later. He complained of politicians in Washington dictating the selection of officers for specific duties within his department, and reiterated his preference for Denver: "I think General Denver would preserve peace on the border and enable me to send most of the Kansas troops into the field, where they might be of some use. As it now is they are really worse than useless, for they compel me to keep troops from other States on the Missouri border to prevent these Kansas troops from committing murders and robberies. . . . Nevertheless I shall comply with the President's wishes, and place some other officer in command in Kansas as soon as I can spare one for that purpose."[30]

Apparently Halleck then received Stanton's reply to Lincoln, for on the same day Halleck ordered Denver to proceed to Fort Leavenworth and take command of the District of Kansas. In Washington, Lincoln was being pushed to reverse the assignment. The president sent Halleck a note on April 4: "I am sorry to learn that, after all, Gen. Denver has gone to Kansas—Can not Gen. Davies go there—There is a hard pressure on me in this matter." Halleck complied on April 6, ordering Brigadier General Samuel Sturgis to proceed to Fort Leavenworth and take command of the district. He also instructed Denver to be sent with such forces as could be spared from Kansas to Fort Scott, "to take the immediate command in that vicinity, and particularly to take the general charge of the Indian tribes. Denver was to "observe the enemy's movements near the Arkansas frontier, and break up all insurgent and guerilla bands in the western counties of Missouri." Sturgis assumed command of the District of Kansas on April 10.[31]

In some last-minute lobbying Kansas attorney R. S. Stevens and Pomeroy asked Stanton to retain Denver at Fort Leavenworth, with Pomeroy telling Stanton that he and the people of Kansas wanted this. This was an odd turnabout by Pomeroy, who had lobbied against Denver having command; perhaps Denver was a less offensive choice than Sturgis, who may have been tainted by his horsewhipping of Kansas soldiers during the Wilson's Creek campaign. Stevens then telegraphed Halleck telling him that Stanton wanted Denver to remain at Fort Leavenworth and for Sturgis to be sent to New Mexico, if this would not prejudice the public service. This effort went for naught; Denver was not restored to command.[32]

The ongoing game of martial musical chairs in the brigade came to an end with the promulgation of orders to consolidate the Third and Fourth into a new regiment, the Tenth Kansas Infantry. The infantry companies of the Third were mustered for the purpose of consolidation on February 28; those of the Fourth on March 4. The remustered companies were marched to Paola, where the consolidation was effected on April 3. The mustering officer was instructed by Halpine that when the Fourth was remustered and consolidated, Weer was to be mustered down to lieutenant colonel. However, Weer was mustered out, not down. Among the other officers mustered out were Lieutenant Colonel Burris and Adjutant J. A. Phillips of the Fourth, and Montgomery and Blunt of the Third. Blunt expected to be mustered out of the service, but the day before his regiment was to march to Paola, he received the unexpected news he had been appointed a brigadier general, to be effective April 8.[33]

The Sixth was reorganized under an order dated March 27. The original three home guard companies of Ransom, Campbell, and Gower were mustered out. Brown's infantry company was transferred to the Eighth Kansas. The companies of George W. Veale (Fourth regiment) and Elijah E. Harvey (Fifth regiment) were transferred into the Sixth. A company commanded by Lieutenant John Rogers was assigned to the regiment, and a new company was organized under Lieutenant John M. Laing. Vansickle's independent company was also attached to the Sixth, but as this company had never been regularly mustered into the U.S. service, it was subsequently disbanded. This took some time. For a while the company was stationed with Elijah Harvey's company at Little Santa Fe, Missouri. In June part of the company was escorting a paymaster, and at that time Vansickle learned his regiment was moving south; by early July Vansickle was in the Cherokee Nation. The government finally concluded that his company had been "irregularly mustered" and that it allegedly "had been recruited for home defence." The company was mustered out about August 1, 1862.[34]

Although Weer had been mustered out, he did not fade away. Someone, presumably Lane, had been busy on his behalf. On April 12 the War Department issued this order: "Colonel William Weer, having been illegally deposed by the Governor of Kansas, is reinstated in his position of Colonel Fourth Regiment Kansas Volunteers. Any order that may have been given by the Governor of Kansas for the consolidation of the Fourth regiment with other Kansas troops are hereby revoked, and the regiment will preserve the organization it had prior to the issue of such order." This did not however result in those companies formerly belonging to the Fourth separating from the Tenth and a reconstitution of the Fourth.[35]

The following month Stanton instructed Blunt, now commanding the newly created Department of Kansas, to reinstate Weer, Lieutenant Colonel Burris, and Adjutant Phillips to their former positions. Blunt dispatched Moonlight, now his assistant adjutant general, to deliver this message to Robinson. Robinson refused to reinstate the officers. He instead protested to the War Department that Weer and Montgomery had been mustered out in accordance with Hunter's General Orders of January 17, as the remustering left the regiments with only five full companies each, too few to entitle the regiments to be commanded by a colonel. He claimed he had then been asked by Halleck to consolidate the fragmentary regiments, so therefore the ten full-strength infantry companies of the two regiments were consolidated into the Tenth. Robinson had chosen to appoint neither Weer nor Montgomery as colonel of the Tenth, but instead selected William F. Cloud, former major of the Second Kansas Infantry and a veteran of the Wilson's Creek battle.[36]

Weer advised the adjutant general's office that "great confusion" would result if the order reinstating the Fourth regiment was followed, thereby suggesting that he be made colonel of the new consolidated regiment. The Secretary of War ordered Blunt on May 30 to follow Weer's suggestion. Moreover, the secretary indicated that Weer, Burris, and Phillips be given positions in their own grade, and that any field or regimental staff officers displaced by them be reassigned to vacancies in their respective grades in other Kansas regiments. Weer took command of the Tenth; Cloud was given command of the newly formed Second Kansas Cavalry.[37]

As this last chapter in the story of Lane's Brigade was being played out, so too was Lane's maneuvering to obtain another military command.

CHAPTER 11

The Great Southern Expedition

In newspaper stories published in 1871, Daniel Horne told of a wartime plot to give Lane command of a new military department. According to Horne, the scheme was hatched not by Lane but by Horne as a means of making Topeka the state capital. When the war began, Kansas had just achieved statehood, but the permanent location of its capital had yet to be determined; the state constitution provided that the matter was to be resolved by popular vote. In June 1861 the legislature fixed the date for this vote as the November 5 general election. Although Leavenworth was the state's most populous city, the contest was clearly between Topeka and Lawrence.[1]

Horne wrote that the plan involved two key elements: "1st. To divide the military department and make a new department for Kansas with head-quarters at Fort Leavenworth, providing the city of Leavenworth would vote for Topeka for State Capital. 2d. Gen. Lane to resign his seat in the United States Senate and be promoted to a Major-Generalship and command the Kansas department."[2] Lane's command would then make a triumphal march through the Indian Territory, Arkansas, and Texas, ending the war and thereby making Lane a candidate for president in 1864. Apparently the selection of Leavenworth as departmental headquarters, and the military contracts to be issued therefrom, was the inducement for the bosses at Leavenworth to urge its citizens to cast their votes for Topeka.

As Horne's story goes, Lane was summoned to Topeka for a meeting with a committee of conspirators. Lane was highly pleased with the proposal, commenting that Missouri would provide all the horses needed for the expedition. It was agreed that a public meeting would then be held in Leavenworth; Lane's October 8 Stockton's Hall speech in Leavenworth did call for the establishment of a separate military department in Kansas. The timing of this speech is at odds with Lane having met with Horne shortly before. The Topeka *Kansas State Record* does not mention any appearance by Lane in Topeka the first week of October, which would have been the only opportunity for him to be there and meet Horne. His presence would have been difficult to hide; therefore, some doubt must be cast on whether Horne's story is accurate. However, that paper did announce on October 12 that Horne had been authorized by Lane to raise the Twelfth Regiment of Kansas Volunteers for Frémont's Grand Army, suggesting there could have been a meeting. Lane had issued an order on October 3 ordering "Captain" Horne to proceed to any state in the United States to recruit men for Colonel Daniel H. Horne's regiment, Kansas Brigade, and the document *requested* government officers to assist him. While not quite a grant of authority to do anything (Lane possessed no such authority), the document nonetheless *looked* official. Horne raised no troops, although he would enlist in the newly formed Eleventh Kansas that following August and served as its sergeant major. It is also possible that Horne and Lane met when Lane was in Topeka on May 10 and that Lane announced then he had been given authority to raise and command troops to recapture the Federal forts in Arkansas and the Indian Territory.[3]

Is Horne's story true? A review of Topeka newspapers at the time he made his claim in 1871 revealed neither rebuttals nor confirmations; contemporary Leavenworth and Lawrence papers were silent on the subject. Horne was a well-respected citizen who had been active in the Free State struggles and had a distinguished record of public service, both governmental and military. It would be unlikely he would publicize a claim that could be easily rebutted and hold him up to ridicule. Had Lane been so approached by Horne, such an expedition would have been in line with one espoused in May, which would have had Lane leading an army to recapture Federal forts in Arkansas and the Indian Territory.[4]

Lane's Stockton's Hall speech was consistent with Horne's story. In it Lane called for the establishment of a separate military department in Kansas, garrisoned by ten thousand troops, and he suggested these troops could retake the Indian Territory and lands south of it.[5] Horne recalled that Lane's speech in Stockton's Hall was well received. He also claimed that rounds were made among hundreds of rebel prisoners at Leavenworth regarding the Southern expedition: "All agreed to give up slavery, and meet us half way and divide the offices," Horne was quoted as saying "All that was asked of those in the rebellion was to surrender; give up slavery, and vote the Free State ticket [in the lands to be conquered]." While on its face this sounds unbelievable, it is consistent with Lane's speech in Chicago on January 22, 1862, in which he said he would establish free state governments as his expedition moved south.[6]

Horne wrote that Lane, Dr. James Fletcher, and "Commissary Cart. Wilder" went to Washington to put the plan before Lincoln, who "was pleased with the programme, and promised to aid the same, even to furnishing money from the contingent fund to aid the political plan. The department was divided, and Fort Leavenworth was made the headquarters of the Kansas department."[7]

Whether or not any of Horne's story can be proved, it is clear that several of Lane's supporters lobbied Lincoln for the creation of a new department and for Lane as a major general to command it. Superintendent of Indian Affairs William G. Coffin and attorney Mark Delahay wrote to Lincoln on October 21, suggesting that once in command Lane would retake the Indian Territory, which would give the troops an advantageous position for operating against the rebels of Arkansas, Texas, and Louisiana. They compared Lane, who "so far from acting on the defensive, carried the war into Africa" with regular army officers at Fort Leavenworth, who did little "except to gallop through the City of Leavenworth on fast horses, to visit drinking saloons, and other disreputable scenes of dissipation." While Coffin and Delahay acknowledged that "depredations and outrages" had likely been committed by some under Lane's command, the acts surely had not been authorized or sanctioned by him. Lane, they asserted, had adopted the most rigid rules to maintain the discipline of his brigade, including punishing the perpetrators of such offenses with death. Senators Zachariah Chandler and Benjamin F. Wade wrote Lincoln, suggesting that Lane, as a major general, should command a new district that would encompass Kansas, Arkansas, and the Indian Territory.[8]

Others counseled Lincoln against placing Lane in command. One was Governor Hamilton Gamble of Missouri who, having "received several communications in relation to the depredations committed by Lane's men," urged Lincoln that Lane not have command should a new department be established. Lieutenant Governor Willard Hall of Missouri advised Lincoln: "Genl Lane is exceedingly obnoxious to the people of this state, & they very generally believe that his appointment would lead to the invasion of this state by lawless men who would depredate upon our property without regard to the position or views of its owners."[9]

When Hunter was suggested as a commander of the new department, Secretary of the Treasury Salmon Chase counseled Lincoln against this. "The Colonels of the Kansas Regiments," he wrote, "to say nothing of General Lane, will be extremely dissatisfied, if they find themselves in a new Department under a Regular Army Officer who will wish to reduce the contest with the Rebels to a regular system and take out of it the largest part of its moral element by repressing all Anti-Slavery sentiment."[10]

As noted previously, Hunter did get command of the Kansas department, which Lane so desperately wanted. This was only a temporary setback for the tenacious Lane. Although he had fought hard to keep his Senate seat, he was willing to trade it for the office of a major general and its attendant perquisites, and in the Southern expedition Lane saw the opportunity to wear the stars of a major general. Someone, probably Lane, again pitched the idea of the expedition to Major General George McClellan, who endorsed it.

In fact, McClellan had proposed a similar expedition to Lincoln in August. Hunter was advised in a message dated November 26: "[McClellan] thinks an expedition might be made to advantage from your department west of Arkansas against northeastern Texas. He accordingly desires you to report at an early date what troops and means at your disposal you could bring to bear on that point." So far Lane was remaining in the background, pushing the expedition, but not yet nominating himself for command.[11] Hunter asserted in a December 9 letter to Senator Lyman Trumbull that if he had command of the expedition, he "would advance South, proclaiming the negro free and arming him" along the way. "The Great God of the Universe has determined that this is the only way in which this war is to be ended," he wrote.[12] Despite such bluster Hunter complained to McClellan he could not advance: "I think the expedition proposed by the general-in-chief altogether, impracticable. We have a hostile Indian force, estimated at 10,000, on the south, and Price's command, some 20,000, on our east and north. To cope with this force we have only about 3,000 effective men, scattered over an extended frontier." McClellan responded immediately, repeating his proposal and requesting that Hunter indicate what forces he needed for the expedition. McClellan explained that three regiments of Wisconsin infantry, plus a battery and two cavalry companies from Minnesota, had been ordered to report to Hunter. He assured Hunter that other troops would follow as rapidly as would be needed.[13]

Hunter complained to McClellan on December 19 that the instructions for the proposed expedition were extremely vague. He protested that this was his first intimation he was actually to formulate a plan of action and to state what men and supplies he would need. Now that he understood the question put to him, he decided first to complain about Generals Halleck, Buell, and Sherman getting commands that he thought should have been given him. His anger spent, Hunter concluded his letter: "Being now for the first time made aware of what is expected of this department, I shall lose no time in preparing and forwarding exact estimates of the force that will be necessary for the proposed expedition; and at present may say in rough that at least 20,000 men will be necessary, in addition to those already in and ordered to the Department; and as the nearest point in Northeastern Texas is 440 miles from this point and the route through a country entirely destitute of supplies, a large transportation train will be absolutely necessary."[14]

Hunter did not get a quick response from McClellan. According to historian Dean Trickett, McClellan had come down with typhoid fever before Christmas and was confined to his bed for several weeks. During McClellan's illness, Lincoln appeared to have taken over the direction of the expedition. Secretary of War Cameron was absent from Washington and knew nothing of the plans until much later.[15]

Behind the scenes, Lane was laying the groundwork to seize command of the expedition. Some of these machinations reached Brigadier General Denver via a letter from his friend R. S. Stevens in Washington: "Lane is here, making speeches and trying to play hell in general. His ultra ideas find far more favor with the people than with the administration. He is determined to be made a Maj. Gen., if possible—failing in that he wants a Brigadiership, if he can be assigned to Kansas. According to best information the President is just a little inclined to gratify him, but the Cabinet and advisors generally are so opposed to it, that Lane will hardly be sent to K., though he will very likely be offered a Brigadier's commission." A few days later in another letter, Stevens added that Lane was trying,

> with every power and influence he can command, to secure a Major Generalship & then to supersede Hunter. He professes great regard and respect for Hunter, and therefore is urging the president to put Hunter in Halleck's place, so that he (Lane) can be the head of the Kansas Division. . . . You know of old his unscrupulousness of character & that he would not hesitate to do or say anything to gratify his vaulting ambition. He hates you with more intensity than ever. When Governor you controlled and humbled him now [you] have secured the position he has coveted above all others, & are in his way.[16]

Stevens wrote to Denver again on December 21, warning him that Lane had already arranged his staff and was now involved in "manufacturing public opinion." Stevens included a clipping from the *National Republican* that—although purportedly a letter written by a Leavenworth man—Stevens accused Lane or his associates with having authored. The clipping commented on Denver being assigned to Kansas, and it complained that the War Department should have selected a Kansas man for promotion to general and to command in Kansas instead of someone (Denver) from California. Further, Denver's presence in the camp of the Kansas brigade would "go very far to disorganize and dispirit the men" and "disgust the officers of that gallant corps."[17]

A rumor was being circulated that Lane had, this time for real, been appointed a brigadier general. The prospect of this horrified Halleck. "I cannot conceive of a more injudicious appointment," he wrote to McClellan on December 19. "It will take 20,000 men to counteract its effect in [Missouri,] and, moreover, is offering a premium for rascality and robbing generally." The *Leavenworth Daily Conservative* of December 18, in a story captioned "James H. Lane a Major General," printed a telegram from Washington authored by T. J. Weed, stating that Lane would be appointed to command all Kansas troops.[18]

The rumor about Lane's commission was true—sort of. On December 16 Lincoln had written to Cameron stating his wish that Lane "be appointed a Brigadier General of Volunteers, to report to Gen. Hunter, and to be so assigned to duty as not to be under, over, or in immediate contact with Gen. Denver." Lane was so nominated, and he was confirmed by the Senate on December 18. The paperwork for the commission was prepared the following day, but as before, Lane did not accept it.[19]

News of a Southern expedition was soon being publicly circulated. The Leavenworth *Daily Times* reported twenty thousand troops were to be concentrated in Kansas for active service. A Leavenworth citizen reported that Hunter was organizing a force for a campaign into Arkansas and Texas. The *New York Times* of December 24 wrote that Hunter would recapture the Indian Territory, and "tickle the ribs of Arkansas itself; perhaps to trespass Texas; and may be, in certain events, to make a bold push southward even for the Gulf of Mexico." And in an indication the Lane propaganda machine was gearing up, both the citizen from Leavenworth and the *New York Times* repeated rumors that Lane would be replacing Hunter.[20]

Even as Hunter proceeded with preparations for the expedition, he continued to question it; in an end-run around McClellan, he wrote directly to Secretary of War Cameron. Although that letter has been lost, Cameron's reply indicates Hunter was wondering why his leadership was being questioned and why he had apparently been superseded in command.[21]

It was bad enough for Hunter that McClellan, from far-off Washington, without consulting Hunter, had imposed a risky military venture upon him. Now he discovered he was to have an unwanted partner. Hunter received a most unwelcome letter from Lane dated January 3: "It is the intention of the Government to order me to report to you for an active winter's campaign. They have ordered General Denver to another department." Lane also mentioned that eight cavalry regiments, three infantry regiments, and three artillery batteries had been ordered to report to Hunter. And Lane wrote of another burden being sprung on Hunter: that Hunter was to cooperate with the Indian Department to organize and arm four thousand Indians.[22]

Cameron finally responded to Hunter's December 19 letter on January 3, saying he had been unable to meet with McClellan because of the general's illness but had met with Lincoln, who expressed great confidence in Hunter's capability and experience. "I have never yet understood why you were superseded," he added, "as the change occurred while I was absent in New York." Cameron continued: "I have just had a conversation with General Lane, who, I understand, was authorized during my absence to make preparations to act in conjunction with yourself and with whom I have had no consultation until yesterday. He informs me that he is to go to Kansas to act entirely under your direction, and the Department has made preparations for sending him 30,000 troops. Authority was given yesterday (in pursuance of your wishes, as I understood) for the employment by you of 4,000 Indians." If Cameron had any intention to oppose the expedition, he did not express it to Hunter. Instead Cameron assured Hunter that whatever he needed for the expedition would be provided.[23]

The Eastern press began reporting stories of Lane's ascendancy over Hunter. Among them: Hunter being replaced by Lane in the command of the expedition; Colonel Wilson's regiment of Mechanic Fusileers ordered to report to Lane at Leavenworth; Lane making preparations for the campaign and the government furnishing the supplies; Lane having the support of the administration; Lincoln assigning Kansas, southwest Missouri, Arkansas, and the Indian Territory to Lane; and Lane to get thirty thousand men.[24]

Hunter was reading the same stories in the Kansas papers. The *Leavenworth Daily Conservative* reported the arrival of T. J. Weed from Washington who was proclaiming Lane would probably resign his Senate seat, take a commission as major general, and assume command of twelve thousand cavalry, six thousand infantry, four thousand Indians, and thirty artillery pieces. The Lawrence *Republican* of January 9 reported "The *National Republican*, the organ of the Republican party at Washington, says: 'The Administration *will co operate with Gen. Lane fully and heartily.* He will have such an army and such a command as he desires to have.... Gen. Lane's command is destined to the South, thro' the Indian country." In an appeal to the self-interest of Kansans, the Lawrence *Republican* claimed that such an enterprise would buy the surplus productions of the state: "Our farmers will realize better prices for their corn, hay, beef and other produce."[25]

A week later the *Lawrence Republican* reported that Lane's expedition would certainly not fall short of twenty-five thousand men. Lane would have full command to wage war in his own way and to "take all its responsibilities." The *Republican* quoted from the *Chicago Tribune* of January 8, which stated Lane had been authorized by Lincoln to command an army of thirty thousand men, with Leavenworth as his headquarters: "Lane's force will be chiefly mounted men. He expects to start with 15,000 cavalry, 10,000 infantry, 1,000 flying artillery, 1,200 fusiliers, 4,000 loyal Indians, and about 1,000 contrabands, now in Kansas, on the start; but the latter force is expected to increase as he proceeds South. He can employ 8,000 to 10,000 able bodied contrabands to great advantage as servants and laborers. . . . Gen. Lane claims that with the help of eight or ten thousand robust, loyal blacks, he can double the efficiency and striking power of his troops." Other endorsements of Lane as commander of the expedition came from such diverse sources as the *Tipton* (Iowa) *Advertiser* and an anonymous Jewish Union soldier writing to the New York *Jewish Messenger*.[26]

Such reports filtered south. The *Arkansas True Democrat* reported that "Lane at the head of 25,000 desperadoes" was preparing to march through the Indian Country and western Arkansas "fully authorized to . . . steal every negro and other property" he could lay his hands on, "burn every building and murder every white man" he could find. "He proclaims no quarter; he hoists the black flag and swears that his march shall be one of devastation. . . . These columns are to take very little baggage, but to depend upon subsistence by robbing the country as they pass. No white prisoners are to be taken, and all slaves who are willing to fight will be armed." The *Richmond Daily Dispatch* matter-of-factly reported Lane was to command such an expedition, but without the *Arkansas True Democrat's* lurid claims.[27]

Newspaper stories claimed Lane had obtained an audience with Lincoln, McClellan, and the secretary of war. Supposedly McClellan (recovering from his bout of typhoid) asked Lane what he would do should his expedition not encounter pro-Union sentiment. One newspaper alleged that Lane replied he intended to leave no rebel sentiment behind him. If Missouri, Arkansas, and the Indian Country refused to come peaceably under the laws of the government, Lane planned "to make them a wilderness" and would "give the traitors twenty-four hours to choose between exile and death. . . . If I can't do better I will kill off the white traitors and give their lands to the loyal black men!" This was said to have brought laughter from McClellan. Given McClellan's opposition to emancipation, or injection of the "negro question" into any discussion of the Union's war aims, it is unlikely he would have been so amused by Lane's proposal regarding blacks.[28]

The plot thickened as Lane continued maneuvering the expedition away from Hunter (who had never wanted it in the first place) and into his hands. McClellan wrote Hunter on January 24, informing him that seven regiments of cavalry, four of infantry, and three artillery batteries were being sent to Kansas to support Lane's Southern expedition and that Lane had been authorized to raise an additional eight thousand to ten thousand Kansas troops and four thousand Indians. Moreover, McClellan stated, that in obtaining such authority, Lane had represented that the outlines of this plan were stated by him to be consistent with Hunter's own views. "The General-in-Chief, in conveying to you this information, desires it to be understood that a command independent of you is not given to General Lane, but he is to operate to all proper extent under your supervision and control, and if you deem proper you may yourself command the expedition which may be undertaken."[29]

McClellan advised Major Absalom Baird he had no control over the expedition, "it having been determined upon by the President." Baird passed this information on to Hunter in a letter dated January 26, along with the report that Adjutant General Thomas told him Lane had persuaded Lincoln to back the expedition and that McClellan was disapproving Hunter's request for leave in order for Hunter to stay in Kansas and keep a watch on Lane.[30]

Lane left Washington with his family January 20. At Chicago on January 22 he reviewed the Mechanic Fusileer regiment and gave a speech to a packed crowd at the Tremont House. He told his audience the time was past to protect the institution of slavery: "The rebels must submit or be sent down forthwith to that hell already yawning to receive them." He claimed Lincoln had asked him how many black men he needed for his expedition, and he had responded he would have one contraband as a servant for every white soldier. If Lincoln had reacted to this, Lane did not recount it for his audience. When asked by a man in the crowd, "What are you going to do with the niggers?" Lane replied he would settle them along the Gulf, with a paternalistic government to supervise them.[31]

Lane arrived at Leavenworth on January 26. During the trip his youngest child, George, only thirteen months old, became sick with scarlet fever and remained at Quincy, Illinois, with his mother. The child did not recover and died January 30. His body was taken to Lawrence for burial.[32]

The day after his arrival, Lane made a speech to the Mercantile Library Association. Again he argued that the rebellion could be ended by taking away the four million slaves whose labor sustained it. "When I think who caused this war," he cried, "I feel like a fiend." After railing against secession traitors, he implied more drastic measures should be taken to win the war: "The only way to close this war is to fight, and to fight everything that stands in the way." Lane then described an incident during the Mexican War in which Comanches had butchered Mexican men, women, and children, and General Zachary Taylor allegedly responded, "The Comanches seem to be fighting on the same side we are. We won't interfere with them." Lane proposed arming black men and letting them "do the balance of the fighting in this war. . . . I care not whether the punishment is inflicted on the battle-field, on the gallows or from the brush by a negro."[33]

Finally moving on to discuss his expedition, Lane asserted Kansas could annex enough of the Indian Territory to make the state square in shape (versus its rectangular dimensions). He argued it was the business of Kansas *exclusively*, with the help of Wisconsin, Ohio, and other states, to free all slaves west of the Mississippi. "I am authorized by the Government to say to every officer and private that I will feed a slave for each one of you, and I don't care how soon you catch him," he said."[34]

Hunter did not wait to see what Lane's next move would be. In an order published the next day, he announced, "In the expedition about to go south from this department, called in the newspapers General Lane's Expedition, it is the intention of the major-general commanding the department to command in person, unless otherwise expressly ordered by the Government."[35] Lane immediately telegraphed a copy of Hunter's order to U.S. Representative John Covode, of the Joint Committee on the Conduct of the War, with the notation, "See the President, Secretary of War, and General McClellan, and answer what shall I do." Covode telegraphed his reply: "I have been with the [men] you name. Hunter will not get the money or men he requires. His command cannot go forward. Hold on. Don't resign your seat." A copy of this fell into Hunter's possession, which he would soon share with Halleck.[36]

Delahay then wrote to Lincoln from Leavenworth that there was a strong public sentiment in favor of Lane having command of the expedition. He assured Lincoln that Lane was "the man for the experiment" and requested that he be made a major general.[37]

To strengthen his hand, Lane secured the alliance of two prominent refugee chiefs of the Creek and Seminole nations, Opothleyaholo and Aluktustenuke. The chiefs approved a message to Lincoln requesting that Lane be put in charge of the expedition. "General Lane is our friend. His heart is big for the Indian.... Our people ... will follow him wherever he directs. They will sweep the rebels before them like a terrible fire on the dry prairie."[38]

Lane's allies in the Kansas legislature procured resolutions endorsing him. The Senate urged Lincoln to appoint Lane major general and give him command of the expedition south from Kansas. In the House, the proposed resolution was a statement that Lane was "pre-eminently worthy of a Major General's position," but this was watered down to state that the legislators had faith in "the skill, courage, patriotism and capacity of Gen. Lane to command the expedition which is supposed to be about to be led by himself south." The final version actually delivered to Lincoln gave an earnest recommendation that Lane receive the appointment of major general and that he immediately be assigned the command of the expedition.[39]

Lincoln was now in an awkward position. He held personal debts to Lane and Hunter. In October the previous year, Major Hunter had written Lincoln, warning him of a plot to assassinate him should he be elected. Hunter followed this with a similar warning after the election, with the suggestion that "Wide-Awake" men infiltrate Washington for the inauguration. Hunter was one of several army officers Lincoln chose to escort him from Illinois to the inauguration. The escort duty was unofficial and voluntary; Hunter performed it while on leave. While doing so, he suffered a dislocated collarbone in the crush of a crowd at Buffalo. As noted previously, Hunter was assigned to guard the president at the White House in April. In August, Lincoln had recommended then-Brigadier General Hunter for promotion to major general. When Lincoln became disenchanted with Frémont's service in Missouri and asked Hunter to serve as Frémont's chief of staff—a position to which Hunter could not be ordered because of his rank relative to Frémont's—Hunter acquiesced. Hunter felt himself on such intimate terms with Lincoln that he wrote directly to the president complaining about the inadequacy of his command in Kansas.[40]

Lincoln no doubt wanted to please both men, but he was forced to step in and set right a situation that appeared to be spiraling out of control. He advised Secretary of War Stanton on January 31: "It is my wish that the expedition commonly called the 'Lane Expedition' shall be as much as has been promised at the Adjutant-General's Office under the supervision of General McClellan *and not any more*. I have not intended and do not now intend that it shall be *a great, exhausting affair*, but a snug, sober column of 10,000 or 15,000. General Lane has been told by me many times that he is under the command of General Hunter, and assented to it as often as told."[41]

Stanton, who had replaced Cameron only two weeks before, professed ignorance as to the expedition. Writing to Charles A. Dana of the New York *Tribune*, he said, "What Lane's expedition has in view, how it came to be set on foot, and what is expected to be accomplished by it, I do not know and have tried in vain to find out. It seems to be a haphazard affair that no one will admit himself to be responsible for.... There will be serious trouble between Hunter and Lane. But believing that Lane has pluck, and is an earnest man, he *shall have fair play*."[42]

Lincoln's letter did not mollify Hunter, who poured out his frustration in a letter to Halleck dated February 8. He complained that neither Lane nor anyone in Washington had consulted him regarding the expedition, and that regiments and assorted officers were reporting to him for service under Lane. Lane's "great Southern expedition," he wrote, "was entertained and sanctioned by the President under misrepresentations made by somebody" to the effect that it was the design of both Lane and himself. He stated he had been informed that the apparent vote of confidence by the Kansas legislature to having Lane command the expedition was done only as an expedient way to remove Lane from the political arena.[43]

Hunter also claimed Lane, being disappointed in his quest for command, was determined to cause trouble and obstruct the expedition. "He is bestirring himself in a thousand little irritating processes, trying to make a quarrel or 'disagreement' with me his present pretext for backing out of an employment which he never intended to accept," Hunter asserted. As an example of this, he provided Halleck with a copy of Lane's correspondence with Representative Covode mentioned above.[44]

Hunter was also complaining to Stanton. He reported Lane did not want to accept a commission and serve under Hunter, and being frustrated in his plan, Lane was determined to make trouble. He requested that Lane be forced to accept the commission and report for duty, and if he did not do so within a specified time, the commission should be withdrawn. A few days later Hunter followed this up with a letter to Lincoln. He complained he first learned that Lane was to be involved in the Southern expedition from Adjutant General Thomas's letter of January 24, and Lane had never consulted with him regarding this expedition. He argued that Lane now had no intention of accepting the commission, as he had lost his chance to gain control of the department with the freedom to place members of his own staff and personal retinue in charge of the quartermaster and commissary departments at Leavenworth. "Now he is seeking to make 'disagreement' with me a pretext for the refusal of a commission which he never intended to accept," Hunter wrote. He quoted from Covode's telegram to Lane and asked Lincoln to require Lane to accept the commission or have it withdrawn.[45]

Even if he was to have fair play, Lane apparently sensed the demise of his plan. Abelard Guthrie, the delegate to Congress from Nebraska Territory, expressed in his diary on February 4 strong doubts about Lane's real desire to command the expedition to Texas. "But by *not* having his wishes complied with he enjoys the *eclat* of attempting to make a great sacrifice to save the country," Guthrie wrote. Guthrie was not such a confidant of Lane as to easily discern such an attitude of Lane. Instead it is more likely Lane was leaking information in order to put the best face on an impending defeat.[46]

Lane had not yet given up. Pomeroy introduced a resolution in the Senate on February 3 that called for the secretary of war to identify the forces and supplies that were to be provided to the Federal command in Kansas, whether such forces were to be commanded by General Lane or some other person, and whether Hunter's order taking command of the Southern expedition was in accord with instructions from the War Department. The resolution went nowhere and was tabled. Pomeroy, Representatives Martin Conway and Covode, and a Dr. Weed were to have a meeting with Lincoln on February 8 to plead Lane's case. The *New York Times* reported that if this meeting were unsuccessful, Lane would return to his seat in the Senate; the paper also stated that it appeared the expedition was the joint concoction of Lane and Cameron—without their consulting Lincoln or McClellan. Pomeroy was apparently sincere in his desire to help Lane. In a letter to Lane's son, Pomeroy explained he was trying to get Hunter "consigned" to Kentucky, "then your Pa will be given command of the Division. But old [Adjutant General] 'Thomas' is now in the way—and some 'Red Tape' must first be broken, " he wrote.[47]

Joseph Medill, editor of the *Chicago Tribune*, penned a letter to Lincoln on February 9, asking that he not let Lane's expedition fall through:

> The very mention of Lane as commander of the South Western expedition revived the drooping hopes of the people and sent a thrill of joy and confidence through the hearts of millions of good and true men, and you received the credit for it. . . . Lane's little army would perform wonders. In a few weeks he would have the whole Indian country restored to loyalty. He would sweep Western Arkansas from the rebels and establish a free state in Western Texas—

having the loyal Germans for the basis. His going forth would infuse new life into the people and spread terror and panic among the rebels. Suppose Slavery—the cause of this accursed rebellion, does get hurt, who cares?[48]

In a February 10 letter addressed to both men, Lincoln left no doubt as to the relationship that was to exist between Lane and Hunter: "My wish has been and is to avail the Government of the services of both General Hunter and General Lane, and . . . to personally oblige both. General Hunter is the senior officer and must command when they serve together; though in so far as he can, consistently with the public service and his own honor, oblige General Lane, he will also oblige me. If they cannot come to an amicable understanding, General Lane must report to General Hunter for duty, according to the rules, or decline the service."[49]

Hunter met with Lane on February 12, during which he informed Lane that because serious misunderstandings had occurred regarding what was said in previous interviews, he insisted that all their future official communication be in writing. Lane was evasive when Hunter pressed him as to whether he was accepting the commission. Following that meeting, Lane wrote to Hunter, repeating his position that he would not accept a military command in Hunter's department unless such command was agreeable to Hunter or unless the two could work harmoniously together. He asked Hunter whether he would be given the command of the Southern expedition with Hunter as his senior officer and commander when serving together. A copy of this note was separately sent to Lincoln by Lane.[50]

Hunter replied that from Lane's past behavior, as well as the telegram from Covode—which he now revealed he possessed—he did not believe Lane was interested in a commission: "In view of the several letters which you have written to me, with regard to my administration of the affairs of this Department,—I must frankly state that I do not think, without some change on your part, that there is any strong probability of our working 'harmoniously together.'" However, should Lane accept a commission, Hunter promised to assign Lane a command suitable to his rank.[51]

Hunter now wrote directly to Lincoln, indicating he had been unable to reach an accommodation with Lane, whose idea of cooperation meant that he was to command the expedition while Hunter remained at Fort Leavenworth approving of his requisitions on the quartermaster, commissariat, and ordnance departments, which were to be filled by officers of his own appointment.[52] McClellan finally woke up to Lane's machinations and took action. On February 12 and 13 he notified Halleck to send no more troops to Kansas and indicated that Lane had no authority to issue any orders. Halleck was to countermand all that did not come from the adjutant general and to use his discretion to suspend movement of any troops en route or under orders for Kansas.[53]

Halleck responded to Hunter's February 8 letter a few days later. He denied having ever been given any information regarding what he termed Lane's "great jayhawking expedition." He alleged the chain of command had been circumvented by orders being sent from Adjutant General Thomas directly to the regiments that were to form part of the expedition:

> To put a stop to these irregularities I issued General Orders, No. 8, and protested both to General Thomas and General McClellan against such an irregular and unmilitary proceeding. No reply. I stopped some of the troops on their way, and reported that they could not move till some order was sent to me. No reply. I am satisfied that there have been many of such orders issued directly by the President and Secretary Cameron without consulting General McClellan, and for that reason no reply could be given without exposing the plans of the great jayhawker and the imposition of himself and Cameron on the President. Perhaps this is the key to the silence of the authorities at Washington. I know nothing on the subject except what I see in the newspapers.[54]

The game was over, and Lane had lost. He telegraphed Lincoln on February 16: "All efforts to harmonize with Major General Hunter have failed. I am compelled to decline the brigadiership." In a letter sent to several members of the Kansas legislature, Lane then claimed he had returned to Kansas to "arrange matters" with Hunter and resign his seat in the Senate when offered a commission as brigadier general. He disingenuously claimed he "made every effort which self-respect would permit to effect this arrangement" with Hunter and that he could not have served under him without suffering humiliation. Lane denied having had any military ambition, wanting only to serve to end the rebellion: "Without fault on my part . . . I have been thwarted in this, the cherished hope of my life." In response, Senator Edward Lynde offered a sarcastic resolution that the Senate offer to Lane "its warmest sympathy and condolences, in this his hour of sadness, bereavement and disappointment, in thus being 'thwarted in the cherished hope of his life.'" The senators voted 16 to 7 to postpone any vote on the resolution.[55]

By March 9 Lane and family were back in Washington, where he found his influence waning. As recently as January 19 Nebraska territorial delegate Guthrie had noted: "Lane is a great lion here and his room is always filled with visitors, at this moment there is not a man more sought after." On January 30, "Lane is certainly acting very strangely if not insanely. Constantly beset by an army of sycophants who pander to his vanity and obey his behests he turns a cold shoulder to old and real friends." Circumstances had changed by the time Guthrie wrote on March 15, "Lane either is or affects to be deeply wounded by the explosion of his military projects he doubtless does feel the apparent and comparative neglect of the swarms of sycophants who clustered around him when he had offices to bestow and glory in prospect."[56]

Denver enjoyed but a short tenure as commander of the District of Kansas, being soon replaced by Sturgis. Lane and Pomeroy wrote to Lincoln, suggesting that six brigadier generals in Kansas were too many, that two should be retained, Denver and Sturgis, and the rest sent to other theaters. In a surprising move on May 5, Kansas was restored as a separate department, Sturgis was relieved of command, and newly promoted Brigadier General Blunt was installed in his place.[57]

According to historian Albert Castel, Blunt owed his promotion and his command of the Department of Kansas to Lane's influence:

"By making Blunt commander in Kansas, Lane finally solved the dilemma which had plagued him from the beginning of the war—how to be a Senator and a general simultaneously. Since he could not be both in person, from now on he would be both in essence. Henceforth, where military matters were concerned, Blunt was to all intents and purposes merely Lane in a different body and under a different name."[58] Army contracts emanated from Fort Leavenworth under the supervision of Blunt. Castel concluded that Lane got a cut from the profits in return for using his influence with Blunt and other officers to obtain contracts for the civilian contractors. Blunt also shared in the profits, as did many quartermaster and commissary officers appointed by Lane via Blunt or who were "amenable to Lane's bribes and other inducements."[59]

Lane, so ignominiously frustrated in his quest for command of the great Southern expedition, had gotten the last laugh.

Conclusion

Many wild tales have been told of Lane's Brigade, and professional historians have not been immune from spreading such stories. David McCullough wrote, "In Missouri [Lane] was known as a 'freedom' soldier, meaning he would free you of anything he could lay his hands on—food, forage, money, silk dresses, the family's silver, even a piano on occasion." While not literally true, this claim certainly reflected the belief of many Missourians.[1]

McCullough recounted the tale told by Harry Truman's grandmother, who said Lane's men had visited her farm twelve miles south of Independence and slaughtered four hundred of her hogs, taking only the hams and leaving the rest to rot. They also threw a noose around the neck of a fifteen-year-old boy and repeatedly lifted him into the air in an attempt to get information as to his father's whereabouts. "Hay barns were set ablaze," so the legend went. "Lane and the rest rode off, taking the hams, biscuits, feather beds, and the family silver." A compelling story, but one that is misleading at best. The only time troops under Lane's control were in the vicinity of Independence was the first two weeks of October 1861. I have found no evidence of such a raid; the number of men needed to make off with the hams of four hundred hogs as well as feather beds would not have been inconsiderable, and the event would be hard to hide. Further, the taking of beds by an army on the move would be nothing short of impractical. However, in January 1862—*after* Lane's departure—brigade troops did make a scout into Jackson County, and at Morgan Walker's farm they were said to have made off with four thousand pounds of bacon.[2]

McCullough noted that when Truman's grandmother filed a formal written claim in 1902, "Lane was accountable only for fifteen mules and thirteen horses." There was no mention of buildings having been burned, or four hundred hogs butchered, or family silver taken. It is possible Truman's grandmother, aware of the stories about Lane, ascribed any thievery by any soldier in blue to Lane's men. As McCullough implies, to many Missourians a historian's precision was secondary in importance to giving vent to the hatred held for all Union soldiers. McCullough related how in 1905, Truman, after joining the Missouri National Guard, came home wearing a new dress blue uniform, "expecting to impress his grandmother. But as he stepped through the door, she could think only of Union soldiers. He was never to wear it again in her presence, she said."[3]

Other historians have espoused similar views. Thomas Goodrich claimed the brigade "was little more than a mob of thieves and adventurers. Soon after crossing the border, the Kansans went on a looting and burning rampage." Albert Castel went Goodrich one better, asserting in his first book, "as soon as [Lane's Brigade] crossed the border his men began to plunder, burn, and perhaps murder and rape. Far from restraining them, Lane urged them on. 'Everything disloyal,' he cried, 'from a Durham cow to a Shanghai chicken must be cleaned out.' Even the chaplains shared in the loot." When Castel's next book came out ten years later, he dropped the suggestion of rape but came down hard on the charge of murder: "After Price had gone to Lexington, Lane had re-entered Missouri and proceeded to plunder, burn and kill indiscriminately."[4]

A review of the primary sources cited by Castel and Goodrich fails to support their allegations. The "everything disloyal from a Durham cow to a Shanghai chicken" quote comes from an 1870 magazine article by Verres Nicholas Smith writing under the name Jacob Stringfellow. Smith was a contemporary of Lane and had owned a half interest in the Lawrence *Republican* for three months in early 1861. However, no evidence has been found to suggest he had any firsthand knowledge of the activities of the brigade, and he failed to document the source of any of the stories he related in the article. His tales, while colorful, cannot be considered as reliable and should never have been repeated by historians. Smith is also the source of this gem: "Even the chaplain was seized with a pious zeal to complete his unfinished church at home from his spoils of ungodly altars." Again, Smith's account was unreliable; he did not identify the witness to any such act, and he neglected to identify which one of the three chaplains he was accusing.[5]

Smith was not the only contemporary to criticize Lane. Kansas governor Charles Robinson was another. Especially vocal was Major General Henry Halleck. In a January 6, 1862, letter to Lincoln, Halleck alleged: "The operations of Lane, Jennison & others have so enraged the people of Mo., that it is estimated that there is a majority of 80,000 against the government. We are virtually in an enemy's country." The accuracy of his assessment, at least as it applied to Lane and Jennison, was unwittingly contradicted by Halleck in a subsequent sentence: "This city [St. Louis] and most of the middle and northern counties are insurrectionary, burning bridges, destroying telegraph lines, &c., and can be kept down only by the presence of troops." The insurrection in St. Louis "and most of the middle and northern counties" could not be blamed on Lane and Jennison, who had never operated in those areas. If the hostility of the supposedly loyal civilian population of in western Missouri was simply a reaction to Lane's actions, there should be a corresponding explanation for the rebellion north of the Missouri River, where regular army officer Brigadier General John Pope was in command, or in St. Louis, where Halleck maintained his headquarters. Halleck looked for a simplistic answer and found an easy scapegoat in Lane and other volunteer officers.[6]

Halleck focused his ire upon Lane and Jennison without identifying the "& others [who] have so enraged the people of Mo." He could have mentioned Nathaniel Lyon, who had captured the Missouri State Guard camp at St. Louis, whose men fired upon civilians there, and who then attacked the Missouri government at Jefferson City. Or Halleck could have mentioned the acts of the troops under Frémont during the pursuit of Price in October. A correspondent of the *New York Tribune* reported: "[Frémont] realizes that we are in a condition of war, and in marching across Missouri, he has left a track behind which will long be remembered by the rebels. As the Israelites, in obeying the divine injunction, not only went out, but also spoiled the Egyptians, so he, in addition to protecting Union men, has freely taken possession of all the property of traitors, which could be of service to the Army, wherever he could find it." A correspondent of *Harper's Weekly*, also wrote of Frémont's troops: "The utmost license in the way of foraging is allowed to the troops, and thus the feeling of the secessionists is embittered while Union men are converted into enemies."[7]

Adding to this chorus, Charles Halpine, on the staff of Major General David Hunter during Frémont's pursuit of Price, wrote to his friend Thurlow Weed:

> From Tipton to Warsaw the march was one continuous devastation. . . . The cavalry galloped in all directions over the prairies lassoing mules and shooting oxen, pigs and sheep which they then chucked into their wagons and marched on, though literally weighed down with the burden of useless and unusable flesh. There is not a . . . whole looking glass or bit of crockery or unrifled bureau or blanket that has not been seized "for the public service." . . .
>
> I do not accuse Gens. Fremont, Asboth or Sigel of being deliberate organizers of this dreadful work, or even consciously permitting it. On the contrary both Asboth & Sigel appear rather fair, upright & able men.[8]

Halpine instead blamed, without explaining how they were responsible, "the irresponsible swarm of so-called Colonels, Lieut Colonels, Majors, Adlatuses, Directors &c, &c, &c, illegally appointed by Fremont." Halpine expressed his fear that if Frémont's army had to retreat through the area it had just devastated, no man would return to tell the story: "For we shall have left behind us a maddened, beggared, famishing, frenzied population, in which those who were Union men ten days ago are today our most bitter enemies."[9]

Although much of what is said of the brigade is wildly inaccurate, there is no dispute that the Union occupation did have a serious effect on western Missouri, both upon its population and its infrastructure. A trooper of Jennison's regiment in late December described the countryside from Harrisonville to West Point. Near Harrisonville some crops had been salvaged, but beyond that for a distance of twenty miles nothing had been harvested. Only six of more than forty houses in Bates County were still occupied, often by only women and children. Corn went ungathered and was eaten by wandering cattle. West Point was devoid of civilians except for one family. Colonel Newgent's men encamped there were using the vacant houses as stables and maliciously had broken out the remaining windows.[10]

The effect of the brigade upon slavery in western Missouri is difficult to assess. Lane claimed credit for his brigade having helped twenty-five hundred slaves to emigrate. While this number is exaggerated, obviously hundreds of slaves were spirited into Kansas by the direct actions of the brigade as well as those slaves who attached themselves to the unit as it marched out of Missouri. Other slaves, encouraged by the military incursions, saw Kansas as a beacon of freedom and took it upon themselves to flee. Some slave owners took or sold their slaves south to protect their property from the various Union forces operating in western Missouri. As early as June 1861, Margaret J. Hays of Cass County noted, "People is taken their Negros off in drooves to Texas." Even north of the Missouri River, where the brigade and Jennison never set foot, slaves escaped into Kansas; a Leavenworth man reported in November that 300 were there, and 150 in another Kansas town up the Missouri River. One modern writer has concluded that the number of slaves who fled Missouri in 1861 "was so small as to be almost insignificant," although this analysis considered the loss of slaves throughout the entire state and not in the western counties. The greatest slave losses in 1861 were in western and southwestern Missouri—the theater of operations of Lyon, Lane, Frémont, and Jennison. Margaret J. Hays wrote in late September 1861, "There is but few negros in the country now what the Jayhawkers has not stole, [or] people has taken south." Tax assessor records of 1862 for Bates County document a halving of the number of slaves that were in that county before the war. From a pre-war population of 627, the number of blacks in Kansas swelled to around 13,000 by 1865. The only source for such an influx was Missouri—which incidentally was from where Kansas would get the bulk of its recruits for the First and Second Kansas Colored infantry regiments.[11]

The operations of the brigade dissuaded some Missourians from joining the rebel cause and to remain obedient, if not loyal. It is also probable that such operations pushed some men into the ranks of the rebels. The degree to which this happened is much less certain, but some idea can be gleaned from an analysis of guerilla membership. Don R. Bowen examined the backgrounds of the men who became guerillas in western Missouri and concluded, "The young men who rose up against the Union Army between 1861–65 tended to be as a group the elder offspring of well-to-do, slave-holding farmers," whose "families constituted, in the main, a local rural elite." According to Bowen, "The military occupation represented a direct and immediate threat to the families of the guerillas—and more so to them than to the rest of the population." In other words, most guerillas were motivated less by vague principles such as "states rights" than by threats to their property, including the right to keep human chattel.[12]

Can Lane be blamed for either the onset of the guerila war or its barbarity? To some degree, yes, but in the main, no. Missourians themselves bore some blame for having set the stage by their antebellum assaults upon Kansas Territory. When the war began, and before there was any trespassing by Kansans, Missouri secessionists were persecuting their Unionist neighbors. Other Missourians, notably the Unionist home guards, contributed to the "brother against brother" nature of the guerila war. Margaret J. Hays wrote that the Cass County Home Guards were the worst jayhawkers:

"These men looks upon going to a Secessionist house with wagons and loading everthing they can find, negros and everthing else, as right. They don't think it is Stealing. Two of the Cass companeys has preachers for the Captains." And as to the theory that the brigade pushed peace-loving Missourians into taking up arms against the Federal government, to the extent that this ever occurred, the troops of Lyon, Frémont, Pope, Jennison, and the Missouri State Militia bear greater blame.[13]

In October Frémont and Price had entered into secret negotiations that culminated in the issuance of a joint proclamation on November 1. Among other provisions, the proclamation held that civilians would not be arrested "on account of political opinions, or for the merely private expression of the same," and that armed bodies "not legitimately connected with the armies in the field" were ordered to disband. However, as soon as Hunter replaced Frémont, he repudiated the agreement, thus throwing away an opportunity to maintain some semblance of civility; throw in Halleck's March 13, 1862, declaration that guerillas were to be treated as outlaws, and it was inevitable the guerilla war would be an unnecessarily cruel one.[14]

The impact of Lane and his brigade reached beyond the bounds of Missouri, primarily by demonstrating how the war had to be fought. Lane and the brigade had already achieved national prominence by what they did in Missouri, and in Congress Lane would continue to advocate his brand of war. On December 17, 1861, he railed against the "living burial" of the army "in the inglorious obscurity of winter quarters. . . . If Washington could march his barefooted soldiers over the frozen roads of New Jersey, their footsteps marked with blood, and, in the middle of winter, cross the Delaware river filled with floating ice, can we not, at the same season, move our well-clad legions toward the mild valleys of the South to re-establish that freedom which their sufferings secured?" Lane concluded his speech: "Cheat yourself no longer with the delusive idea that your camps are still schools of instruction; henceforward, your lessons must be taught in the field. Advance rapidly, and strike boldly. The [enemy's] country is favorable; the climate invites; the cause demands. Advance, and all is accomplished; the Government is saved, and freedom is triumphant."[15]

The *Chicago Tribune* of January 8, 1862, reported what was supposed to be Lane's plan for his Southern expedition: "He will take some provisions with him at the start, and trust to the resources of the country and to the enterprise of his boys to collect what they need." To this end it was reported that Lane had purchased "a patent horse-power saw mill" and "five hundred hand corn-mills, being about two to a company, to be run by the contrabands." The plan as stated was that when a regiment came to a secesh cornfield, the contrabands would "husk out the corn, shell it, dry it on pans, and grind it in the mills, and convert it into hoe-cake, pone and other forms of the article." Where the *Tribune* obtained this information about Lane's plan for supply is unclear, but if accurate it was nothing short of audacious. If true, Lane was planning to cut his army off from its base of supplies and advance deep into enemy territory. Such a tactic would be briefly utilized by Grant in his 1863 Vicksburg campaign and Sherman in his 1864 march to the sea, but to propose this in January 1862 was revolutionary.[16]

Lane was an early proponent of emancipating the South's slaves as a tool to end the war. In the Senate, Lane had offered an amendment that would allow the military to interfere with slavery if a military necessity existed in enforcing the laws and upholding the constitution. He had advocated that Lincoln issue a proclamation giving the rebel states thirty to sixty days to end the rebellion "or in default thereof, declare all men free throughout their domains." In his December 17 speech in the Senate, he argued that slavery supported the rebellion. The slaves were made "not only to feed and clothe their oppressors, but to build fortifications for their defence," he asserted. Liberate the slaves, and the rebellion would collapse, Lane maintained. The following June, in a speech at the Cooper Institute in New York, he proposed giving the rebel states thirty days to lay down their arms or have their slaves declared free. Three months later Lincoln did just that in his preliminary emancipation proclamation, justifying this due to "military necessity" (but differing from Lane in generously giving the rebel states slightly more than ninety days to decide). In addition, Lane was among the first proponents of putting weapons into the hands of black men.[17]

While others in the North were preaching conciliation, Lane argued for an aggressive war against the South. While others made speeches saying an aggressive war should be applied, Lane used his brigade to put into practice what he preached, and in doing so he showed the nation how to defeat the rebellion. And although Halleck professed disgust at the actions of Lane, it was not long before he, and the rest of the Federal army, were following Lane's lead and engaging in "total war" against civilians. Missouri was the first theater in which total war was practiced to any extent. As can be seen in the following examples, Federal commanders in Missouri in 1861 established official practices and policies where civilians were legitimate military targets, but which—for now—were less harsh in their application of this than was Lane's Brigade.

Lyon authorized the seizure of civilian property, for use by the army, in "cases of necessities of the service." The impact of this would be softened by his requirement that "the property either [be] paid for or a certificate of the seizure and a statement of the price due given." He later directed that persons and property of all law-abiding citizens should not be disturbed, but this order did not extend to persons who incited others into acts of rebellion and were themselves in arms against the government. Yet if any property was so seized, it could only be for the limited purpose of "disarming and depriving them individually of power for mischief." Frémont gave his officers limited liberty to seize or destroy civilian property; this could be done only "in cases of military necessity."[18]

Halleck assumed command of the Department of the Missouri in November. He authorized the taking of private property "where necessary for the subsistence or transportation of the troops or in cases of persons in arms against the United States or affording aid and assistance to the enemy." He also ordered that a "contribution" be assessed against "men known to be hostile to the Union," to support unionist refugees who had fled to St. Louis."[19]

To deal with the continuing sabotage of railroad and telegraph lines, Halleck ordered that where such damage was done, the slaves of all secessionists in the vicinity, and, if necessary, the secessionists themselves and their property, were to be used in repairing the damage. Further, the towns and counties in which such destruction occurred would be required to pay for all repairs, unless the citizens of such locales could not have prevented the damage.[20]

Pope commanded the state north of the Missouri River. To counter sabotage to the North Missouri Railroad, he issued a directive requiring civilians "to pay in full of property or money for any damage done in their vicinity."[21] That policy not being immediately effective, Pope promulgated a new policy requiring civilians to "furnish quarters, subsistence, and transportation" for Federal troops sent among them to preserve the peace.[22]

Brigadier General Ulysses S. Grant, operating in southeast Missouri, allowed for the "pressing" of wagon teams from active secessionists, yet he—at least initially—required an accounting of property so taken. He also authorized the seizure of property used to aid the rebel cause, even if not needed by the army, to deny the enemy of its use.[23] People, as well as property, were seized on Grant's orders. On at least three occasions he ordered that secessionists be arrested and held as hostages to ensure the behavior of the citizenry or the return of a captured Union man. In August, Grant ordered the arrest of the editor of the Booneville *Patriot* and the seizure of the printing equipment.[24]

In January 1862 Grant took an action that was harsher than anything previously done by Lyon, Frémont, or Halleck. In response to a report that four Federal pickets had been assassinated by civilians, Grant ordered Brigadier General E. A. Paine at Bird's Point, Missouri, to clear out the whole country for six miles around and give word that any citizens making an appearance within those limits were liable to be shot. The citizens so gathered up that winter were housed in tents at the Federal camp.[25]

In November Colonel Grenville Dodge, commanding the post at Rolla, ordered Colonel Nicholas Greusel into Texas County with the instruction "If the men who are away from home in the rebel army, or if their families cannot give a good account of themselves or their whereabouts, take their property, or that portion of it worth taking; also their slaves . . . take all they have got." Greusel returned with nine prisoners, five hundred cattle, forty horses, and mules—all allegedly property of armed rebels.[26]

The conduct of the Union commanders in Missouri was consistent with the accepted laws of war. Those laws allowed the making of war upon civilians, but Union commanders generally exercised great restraint in doing so. When Lane's men took livestock, food, and slaves from active secessionists, or destroyed industrial property, they were acting within the limits of contemporary law. The burning of private residences, however, was indefensible. Also indefensible was the taking of items of no military significance such as clothing and furniture, even when taken from abandoned homes; such thefts, however, appear to have resulted from the initiative of individual soldiers rather than being directed from above. Although such stealing apparently was condemned by most officers of Lane's Brigade, the evidence is less than compelling that rigorous steps were taken to squelch such thievery.[27]

The accomplishments of Lane's Brigade, as a military instrument, were relatively insignificant. Although not known by its citizens at the time, Kansas was never in danger of an invasion by Price's forces, and the brigade played but a supporting role in chasing Price out of Missouri. If nothing else, the presence of the brigade on the border gave comfort to Kansas civilians. Had the jayhawkers stayed on their side of the state line, secessionist irregulars were unlikely to have raided into Kansas. However, the actions of Missouri secessionists in persecuting and driving loyal men out of that state compelled Kansas men to go to the aid of their Unionist brethren. In the final analysis, the actual military accomplishments of the brigade were twofold. The lesser of these was that the brigade's incursions into Missouri broke up nascent rebel military companies. The greater, and lasting achievement, was the blooding of the brigade, the weeding out of the lesser officers, and the transformation of the men from recruits into veterans who would serve honorably and bravely for then next two years and beyond.

The Man He Killed
by Thomas Hardy

Had he and I but met
By some old ancient inn,
We should have sat us down to wet
Right many a nipperkin!

But ranged as infantry,
And staring face to face,
I shot at him as he at me,
And killed him in his place.

I shot him dead because—
Because he was my foe,
Just so: my foe of course he was:
That's clear enough; although

He thought he'd 'list, perhaps,
Off-hand like—just as I—
Was out of work—had sold his traps—
No other reason why.

Yes; quaint and curious war is!
You shoot a fellow down
You'd treat if met where any bar is,
Or help to half-a-crown.[28]

APPENDIX A

Necrology

The Regiments

The Tenth Kansas Infantry took to the field in June 1862 as part of the Indian Territory expedition. The expedition, commanded by William Weer, included two regiments raised from the Indian refugees. After capturing the Cherokee capital at Tahlequah and Principal Chief John Ross, Weer seemed gripped by indecision. His supplies were low, and the men suffered greatly from the heat and being on half rations. Colonel Frederick Salomon concluded that Weer "was either insane, premeditated treachery to his troops, or perhaps that his grossly intemperate habits long continued had produced idiocy or monomania." Salmon placed Weer under arrest and ordered a retreat.[1]

Neither Weer nor Salomon were punished for their actions, and Weer was placed back in command of the Tenth. The regiment went on to fight with great credit at Newtonia, Cane Hill, and Prairie Grove. In the spring of 1864 the Tenth assumed control of the military prison at Alton, Illinois. While there Weer was dismissed from the service, after which the Tenth continued its service under Lieutenant Colonel John Burris. Their term of service expiring, many of the men reenlisted as Veteran Volunteers in August 1864, but the regiment was in truth only at battalion strength; Major Henry H.

Williams commanded the diminished regiment. It participated in the battles of Franklin and Nashville, ending its wartime service by taking part in the April 1865 storming of Fort Blakely, Alabama. The regiment was mustered out in September 1865.[2]

The Fifth served in Missouri for several months, spending some time in Springfield. At that place, Captain John R. Clark, the Missourian who had raised Company B, suffered an undignified death on May 21, 1862. Although officer of the day, Clark got drunk and went to visit a house of "accommodating girls." However, the girls had moved out and were replaced by a family. Previous visitors were unaware of the change in occupancy and continued to call. This became so annoying to the family that a military guard had to be posted. The intoxicated Clark tried to force his way past the guard and was shot. "An old nut named Rice" who was in the company of Clark, fired a revolver at the guard and killed a young lady in the family. Her betrothed was present, and he in turn fired upon Rice, hitting him in the shoulder, inflicting a mortal wound.[3]

The Fifth marched to Helena, Arkansas, in the summer of 1862. Its duties there were consistent with those of other cavalry regiments in the west: scouting, escort duties, cavalry drill, anti-guerilla operations, foraging, and the occasional skirmish against Confederate cavalry. Pitched battles were rare. The Fifth participated in the captures of Helena and Little Rock, acting in a supporting role in both operations. The regiment moved to a post at Pine Bluff, Arkansas, in September 1863, where it fought a bitter battle October 25, when it was surprised in town by a superior Confederate cavalry force. Its next, and last, pitched battle came on April 25, 1864, at Marks' Mill, Arkansas. A detachment of the regiment was serving as part of the escort of a wagon train attacked by Confederate cavalry. The escort was routed and the train captured; a number of the men of the Fifth were taken prisoner and imprisoned in Camp Ford at Tyler, Texas.[4]

The Sixth would find most of its time consumed with the same ordinary duties performed by the Fifth, that is, scouting and escort duties. It partook in few battles of any size. The regiment formed part of Weer's expedition into the Indian Territory in the summer of 1862; a detachment participated in the capture of Talequah. In relatively quick succession, the Sixth fought battles at Newtonia, Missouri (September 30 and October 4, 1862), Cane Hill, Arkansas (November 28), and Prairie Grove (December 7). Lieutenant Colonel Lewis Jewell was killed in the charge at Cane Hill. Four companies of the regiment fought at Honey Springs in the Indian Territory the following July. The Sixth was moved to Fort Smith, Arkansas, in November 1863, from where it departed to participate in the Camden expedition. A week before the disaster to the Fifth at Marks' Mill, a similar experience befell a detachment of the Sixth serving as part of an escort of a wagon train at Poison Springs, Arkansas, but in this instance most of the detachment escaped. The slower wagon train and the foot soldiers of the First Kansas Colored Infantry were not so lucky; dozens of the black soldiers were murdered. Three months later a battalion of the Sixth was encamped outside of Fort Smith at Massard Prairie, when it was surprised and quickly overrun by a daring Confederate cavalry raid. Over one hundred men were captured and imprisoned in Camp Ford. Another rout occurred September 19 to two companies at Cabin Creek in the Indian Territory. Seven companies were mustered out in December 1864 as their terms of service ended; the remaining men were consolidated into a battalion that was moved to Little Rock. After the war the prisoners from Camp Ford joined the regiment at DuVall's Bluff, Arkansas, and were mustered out, the other men being mustered out the next month.[5]

The Commanders

James Blunt would have a distinguished, yet unappreciated military career. Among his first acts as commander of the Department of Kansas was to reverse Brigadier General Sturgis's ban against recruiting Indians. He proceeded with the raising of the First and Second Indian Home Guard regiments from the refugee Indians and followed this up with organizing the expedition into the Indian Territory in the summer of 1862. His command was constricted in September 1862 when the Department of Kansas was merged into the Department of the Missouri; Blunt retained command of the District of Kansas, which included Kansas, the Indian Territory, and western Arkansas, as well as command of some troops then operating within the Department of the Missouri. With these troops Blunt would fight at Newtonia, Missouri, Old Fort Wayne in the Indian Territory, and the battles of Cane Hill and Prairie Grove in Arkansas. In Arkansas, Blunt and Generals Herron and Schofield were advised by Major General Curtis of the reported arrival of Confederate reinforcements: "Do not venture too far at present. . . . If necessary, fall back toward Crane Creek." While Herron and Schofield stood fast, Blunt's reaction was to immediately organize an audacious raid some forty miles through the Ozark Mountains to Van Buren on the Arkansas River, hoping to catch the rebels in the act of crossing the river. This was no small affair; it numbered about eight thousand infantry, cavalry and artillery. On December 28 the Second Kansas Cavalry dashed into Van Buren, scattered its surprised defenders, and captured the town. Two days later Blunt led an orderly withdrawal back into northern Arkansas. Following this feat he went to Fort Leavenworth and would act more in the role of an administrator and less as a field commander. Blunt's command was compressed when the district was split into the District of the Border and the District of the Frontier. Blunt received command of the latter which included the Indian Territory, western Arkansas, and southern Kansas. With his reduced forces, Blunt won a victory at Honey Springs in the Indian Territory on July 17, 1863, and captured Fort Smith, Arkansas on September 1. He narrowly escaped death when on October 6 his escort was ambushed by William Clarke Quantrill in southeast Kansas near Baxter Springs. Eighty-seven men, including unarmed band members, were not so lucky. The following month Blunt was relieved of command while being retained in the service. During this time he organized the Eleventh United States Colored Troops at Fort Smith. Although the Federal high command did not appreciate Blunt's aggressive qualities, his enemies did. "Generals Blunt and Cloud are both good officers," wrote Confederate assistant adjutant general T. M. Scott in April 1864, "and have the necessary dash to make the attempt to penetrate Texas." Fortunately for the

Confederacy, in August 1864 Blunt was given command of the backwater District of the Upper Arkansas. From Fort Riley he launched a futile chase of Plains Indians—an "Indian hunt," as he described it.[6]

Blunt's exile ended in October, courtesy of Sterling Price, whose twelve thousand–man raid into Missouri was now angling westward toward Kansas. Major General Curtis organized two divisions for the defense of Kansas, one of militia and one of militia and volunteers; Blunt commanded the latter. Among his first acts was to relieve the brigadier general commanding the militia brigade in his division, and the colonel of one of its regiments. The militia colonel was replaced by James Montgomery, Blunt's old commander in Lane's Brigade. Blunt conducted a masterful fighting retreat until Price reached Curtis's defensive line on the Big Blue River. The battle of Westport on October 23 was a tactical draw but a strategic defeat for Price. Blunt pursued Price as he retreated southward, but his rash attack on Price at Newtonia on October 28 resulted in over one hundred Union casualties. The remainder of Blunt's wartime career was uneventful; he resigned his commission in June 1865.[7]

For a short time after the war, Blunt practiced medicine in Leavenworth. He was recruited briefly to lobby Washington on behalf of the Kansas and Neosho Valley Railroad, and at some time he was admitted to the bar of Kansas. In 1869 he relocated to Washington, D.C., and acted as a solicitor in presenting claims against the government. In 1873 he and others were charged civilly with conspiracy to defraud the government and a North Carolina Cherokee tribe. Evidence suggests a judgment in excess of $5,400 was obtained against him but subsequently dismissed. Another legal difficulty arose in 1879 when he was arrested for an incident involving his endorsement of a U.S. Treasury check. When he appeared in court, his mental condition was such that he was admitted to St. Elizabeth's Hospital for the insane in Washington. He died there July 26, 1881.[8]

After leaving Lane's Brigade, James Montgomery moved east and was commissioned in 1863 as colonel of the Second South Carolina Colored Volunteers. Among his more notable actions were to participate in the occupation of Jacksonville, Florida; the burning of Darien, Georgia, which so appalled Colonel Robert Gould Shaw;

and the command of a brigade at the battle of Olustee, Florida, on February 20, 1864. He resigned his commission in September 1864 and returned to Linn County in time to be given command of a militia regiment during the Price raid. As commander of this regiment he would fight his old nemesis Sterling Price at the battle of Westport. Returning thereafter to a quiet private life, he died December 6, 1871.[9]

Weer commanded the Tenth Kansas when in the spring of 1864 it assumed control of the military prison at Alton, Illinois. Again Weer came to the unfavorable attention of his superiors. A prison inspector found Weer "an intelligent but very intemperate man. He was drunk when I saw him, and in my opinion entirely unfit to hold any position in the military service of the United States. I cannot too strongly urge his removal from the command of this post." Another inspector wrote: "[Weer] is frequently so much under the influence of liquor as to be utterly unfit for duty. Charges have been preferred against him." Weer was dismissed from the service on August 20, 1864. According to the Tenth regiment's official history, the charges against Weer were set aside a year later.[10]

After his dismissal from the service, Weer returned to Kansas but hardly as a broken man. Like Montgomery he was again in the field commanding a militia regiment during the Price raid. His regiment, the Twenty-third Kansas State Militia, saw no combat. Weer served in the Kansas Senate in 1865–66, and was one of the founders of the Kansas City, Kansas, town company. He died at Wyandotte February 28, 1867.[11]

Colonel John Ritchie received authority in April 1862 to raise a regiment of Indians from the refugees in Kansas. He became colonel of the Second Indian Home Guard regiment; his brother Andrew was regimental surgeon. Ritchie's headstrong ways quickly got him into trouble. In early September 1862 Colonel William R. Judson delivered orders from Weer for the movement of a section of guns; Ritchie decided to disobey the order and personally dragged Judson from his horse and put him under arrest. Ritchie was in turn arrested by Colonel William B. Phillips. Weer released him from arrest with the brusque admonition that Ritchie could go back to his command or go to hell. Weer was dissatisfied with Ritchie as a commander. He complained in September 1862: "Colonel Ritchie utterly refuses to obey my orders. His camp is, from what I can learn, a motley assemblage. His presence in the army is nothing but embarrassment to the service, and I most urgently recommend his dismissal." The following month Blunt complained that nearly the entirety of six companies of Ritchie's regiment had deserted. "Had there been an officer over them, fit to command, it might have resulted differently," he wrote, "but their commander, Colonel Ritchey, was entirely incompetent as an officer. He is now under arrest and should be discharged from the service by order of the President." Ritchie was not dismissed, and while on leave in Topeka in early 1863 he was excommunicated by the Congregational Church on a charge of slandering a local deacon. Returning to the Indian Territory, his regiment participated in the battle of Cabin Creek in July 1863. At the time of Price's 1864 raid, Ritchie was again visiting Kansas and served as an aide on Curtis's staff. Once again he got himself arrested, this time for attempting to arrest officers whom he thought were interfering with orders regarding the custody of Confederate prisoners. He was soon released and managed to make it to the end of the war without further confinement. He was mustered out of the service May 31, 1865.[12]

In civilian life Ritchie continued advocating women's suffrage and temperance, both unpopular causes at the time. Before the war he had speculated in real estate, and he resumed doing so after the war. He became the first mayor of a town he created, South Topeka. He died August 31, 1887.[13]

Following his stint as a civilian general, Lane returned to being a U.S. senator. In 1862 he was appointed a recruiting commissioner, in which capacity he led the recruiting of the Eleventh, Twelfth, and Thirteenth Kansas regiments. In addition he raised another regiment for which he had no authority to do so—the First Kansas Colored Infantry. That the United States was not accepting black troops was of little consequence to Lane. He managed to get them clothed and armed by the government, and they fought a successful engagement against Missouri guerilla in October 1862, well before the regiment was accepted into U.S. service in January 1863.[14]

Lane narrowly escaped death on August 21, 1863, when guerillas under Quantrill made a daring raid on Lawrence. Lane was able to run and hide in the brush but his house was burned. Others were not so lucky; by the time Quantrill's men left over 150 men and boys had been murdered.[15]

Kansas become a two-party state—Lane, and anti-Lane. Generally the anti-Lane faction lost, although Lane's dominance in Kansas politics, and his seat in the Senate, were threatened in the 1864 election. Ironically his victory was guaranteed by Price's 1864 raid, which gave Lane an opportunity to very publicly take to the field as an aide to the victorious Union commander.[16]

Lane stumped for Lincoln in the 1864 presidential campaign. Lincoln's renomination was not a sure thing. A radical faction in his party made an attempt at the Union League meeting that June to derail the nomination. Lincoln the candidate was broadly attacked—and then Lane rose to speak. "Sentence by sentence, piece by piece, he began pulling apart the indictment against Lincoln" was how historian John Waugh described Lane. "No one rose in reply—the movement against Lincoln had lost all its momentum," wrote Waugh. "The radicals had launched their last preconvention shot, exhausted their ammunition, and been undercut by the senator from Kansas." Following Lane's speech, the Union League passed a resolution calling for Lincoln's renomination.[17]

Lane the war hero, Lane the ally of Lincoln, seemed to have a secure future. Lincoln's assassination changed that. Lane aligned himself with Andrew Johnson and abandoned the radicals' plan for reconstruction. His influence faded, as did his health. At Leavenworth on July 1, 1866, he placed a pistol in his mouth and sent a bullet into his brain. Ten days later, on July 11, he died.[18]

APPENDIX B

Brigade Staff

No independent list of the members of Lane's Brigade staff has been found, but several who served at various times have been identified:

Henry J. Adams, paymaster
Richard M. Ainsworth, post surgeon at Fort Lincoln (on contract)
T. J. Anderson, acting assistant adjutant general; lieutenant of engineers
William P. Chandler, assistant quartermaster
Abram Cutler, acting assistant adjutant general
Dr. James Davis, quartermaster
A. G. Ege, quartermaster and acting assistant quartermaster
Abraham Ellis, quartermaster
Rufus Gilpatrick, brigade surgeon
M. H. Insley, quartermaster
R. H. Kerr, lieutenant, position unknown
H. Gray Loring, military secretary
J. N. McCall, brigade wagon master
Henry Miles Moore, judge advocate
Marcus J. Parrott, assistant adjutant general

James M. Pomeroy, lieutenant, position unknown
W. W. Updegraff, brigade paymaster
George W. Weed, ordnance sergeant
Dr. T. J. Weed, acting assistant adjutant general
A. C. Wilder, assistant commissary of subsistence[1]

The four Italian staff officers were Captain Luigi Navoni, Lieutenant Giuseppe Laiguanite, Lieutenant Achille de Vecchi, and Lieutenant Luigi Marini.[2] I have been unable to find any further mention of the Italians' service with the brigade beyond their initial appearance at Fort Lincoln, although de Vecchi, noted in two articles as being either a captain or a major, was reported to be raising a battery at Leavenworth in November.[3]

APPENDIX C

Brigade Casualties

One hundred thirty brigade men (Third, Fourth, Fifth, and Sixth regiments) died from combat, disease, and accidents. Twenty died as a result of enemy action, including Barclay Coppoc, who was killed as a result of sabotage to a railroad bridge. Of these twenty, thirteen died in September.

During the war twice as many soldiers died from disease as died from combat. As noted by James McPherson, the three main killer diseases were diarrhea/dysentery, typhoid, and pneumonia. Close-in living conditions contributed to the spread of communicable diseases. The importance of sanitation in preventing the spread of disease was poorly understood, even among physicians. Neglect of basic sanitation could lead to supplies of fresh water becoming tainted by camp waste, as well as patients being exposed to infected bedding and other hospital supplies. Once a soldier became ill, the treatments available for infectious disease were as likely to harm the patient as to help.[1]

The following list shows the deaths within the brigade from July 25, 1861, through March 1862. "KIA" means killed in action. Not included are men who may have taken sick by then but succumbed later. The data is compiled from the *Roll of the Officers and Enlisted Men*, supplemented by the *Report of the Adjutant General* where indicated.

APPENDIX C

Date of Death	Name	Company	Cause, Location
1861			
Jul 25	William H. Hill	Williams	KIA near Butler, Mo.
Aug, none			
Sep 2	Joseph Emerick	Stewart	KIA Drywood, Mo.
Sep 2	Charles Gordon	Stewart	KIA Drywood, Mo.
Sep 2	William Henry	Stewart	KIA Drywood, Mo.
Sep 2	Simeon Pennington	Veale	KIA Drywood, Mo.[2]
Sep 3	Barclay Coppoc	Allen	Killed in fall of Platte River bridge
Sep 6	Hiram K. Loomis	Blanton	Disease, near Humboldt
Sep 9	Fernando A. Herrington	Greeno	Killed in skirmish, Mapleton
Sep 12	Samuel Schultz	Williams	Killed by enemy near Butler Mo.[3]
Sep 15	Francis Miller	Williams	KIA Bates County, Mo.
Sep 17	Hamilton P. Johnson	Staff, 5th	KIA Morristown, Mo.
Sep 17	James M. Copeland	Creitz	KIA Morristown, Mo.
Sep 18	William Vance	Foreman	Killed by guerrillas in Bates County, Mo.
Sep 24	Thomas Stanfield	Hunt	KIA West Point, Mo.
Sep 25	Paris R. Teater	E. Harvey	Disease, Mound City
Sep 25	Elliott Austin	Rogers	KIA Papinsville, Mo.
Sep 30	Augustus Newton	Rose	Disease
Oct 20	Jeremiah Allen	Stewart	Typhoid fever, Fort Scott
Oct 20	Cornelius Clancy	Rogers	"Debility," Fort Scott
Oct 20	William Grigsby	E. Harvey	Disease, Keokuk, Iowa
Oct 23	Maxwell P. Johnson	Greeno	Killed in skirmish, Cow Creek, Mo.
Oct 25	Richard Mann	Clark	Disease, Greenfield, Mo.
Oct 25	Peter Wylan	Stewart	Killed at Maple Creek, Mo.
Oct 26	James Britton	Greeno	Disease, Fort Scott
Oct 26	Isaac H. Gray	Rogers	Measles, Fort Scott[4]
Oct 28	William B. Davis	E. Harvey	Disease, Fort Scott
Oct 28	John B. Gibson	Gibson	Disease, while on march in Mo.
Oct 31	James M. Gowers	Snyder	Disease, Kansas City, Mo.
Oct —	William Griffin	Harris	"Probably murdered by rebel neighbors in Clay County, Mo."
Nov 1	Francis Gattliff	Gibson	Disease, while on march in Mo.
Nov 4	Robert R. Keith	Hunt	Disease, Fort Scott
Nov 11	Eugene B. Elliott	Foreman	Disease, near Lamar, Mo.
Nov 12	John Ireland	Greeno	KIA, Jasper County. Mo.
Nov 12	William Wallace	Greeno	KIA, Jasper County, Mo.
Nov 13	Harvey D. Duncan	Clark	Disease, Lamar, Mo.

Date of Death	Name	Company	Cause, Location
Dec 1	Thomas J. Phelps	Greeno	Disease, Barton County, Mo.
Dec 1	Edward C. Ross	Foreman	Disease, Fort Scott
Dec 5	William H. Sutton	Gibson	Disease, Fort Scott
Dec 7	Thomas W. Bryan	Clark	Disease, Fort Scott
Dec 8	James Coplin	Blanton	Disease, near Humboldt
Dec 10	Thomas H. Rote	Stewart	Disease, Osawatomie (pneumonia, per AGR)
Dec 11	John M. Snodgrass	Rogers	Congestive chill, Fort Scott
Dec 11	Andrew J. Chester	Greeno	Disease, Fort Scott
Dec 11	James R. McClelland	Twiss	Disease, Fort Scott
Dec 11	Job Crabtree	Dobyns	Disease, Fort Scott
Dec 12	John W Fender	Foreman	Disease, Fort Scott
Dec 12	John Curtis	Gibson	Disease, Fort Scott
Dec 13	Thomas Welch	Rose	Gunshot, Kansas City, Mo.
Dec 14	William M. Durno	Snyder	Killed while scouting near Butler, Mo.
Dec 14	Jasper Wright	Vansickle	KIA at Butler, Mo.
Dec 14	Henley B. Trotter	Gower	Gunshot received in an affray at home near Mapleton
Dec 14	Gideon D. Miller	Jenkins	Measles, Fort Scott
Dec 15	Jeremiah Allen	Stewart	Disease, Fort Scott[5]
Dec 15	James W. Curtis	Gibson	Disease, Fort Scott
Dec 15	Lycurgus Alexander	Harris	Died at Kansas City, Mo.
Dec 15	Addison R. Warner	Jas. Harvey	Disease, Fort Leavenworth
Dec 16	A. B. Defreese	Orahood	Disease, Fort Scott
Dec 19	James A. Quisenberry	Hunt	Disease, Osawatomie
Dec 20	Robert McGloughlin	Clark	Disease, Mercer County, Mo.
Dec 22	Leander Wilson	Stephenson	Disease, Osawatomie
Dec 22	Harman W. Vermillion	Gower	Disease, in hospital at Fort Scott
Dec 22	John U. Parsons	Jas. Harvey	Died at Lawrence
Dec 24	Joseph Alexander	Harris	Died at Kansas City, Mo.
Dec 25	James Knoop	Clark	Disease, Barnesville
Dec 25	John Walters	Twiss	Disease, Fort Scott
Dec 26	August Gloge	Clarke	Disease, Fort Leavenworth
Dec 27	Thomas G. Jones	Jas. Harvey	Disease, Kansas City
Dec 28	Chauncey J. Reynolds	Clark	Disease, Barnesville
Dec 28	Martin Long	Gower	Lung fever, Fort Scott
Dec 28	William Sebert	Creitz	Measles, Fort Scott
Dec 30	Joseph McCord	E. Harvey	Disease, Fort Scott

Date of Death	Name	Company	Cause, Location
Dec 31	John W. McGlasson	Twiss	Disease, Fort Scott
Dec 31	John C. Lawrence	Williams	Measles, Camp Denver
Dec 31	Curtis W. Alden	Thompson	Disease, Osawatomie
Dec —	Samuel Stephenson	Stephenson	Disease, Mound City
Dec —	Amos L. Dunkin	Stephenson	Disease, Osawatomie

1862

Date of Death	Name	Company	Cause, Location
Jan 1	William Yeager	Stewart	Disease, Mound City (pneumonia, per AGR)
Jan 1	William B. Lewis	Miller	Disease, Camp Denver
Jan 6	Moore Lumpkins	Jenkins	Measles, Camp Denver
Jan 7	Francis M. Woolsey	Hunt	Disease, Burlington
Jan 8	John C. Woodward	Blanton	Disease, Wyandotte
Jan 8	Henry C. Welch	Blanton	Disease, Wyandotte
Jan 8	Henry Reynolds	Jas. Harvey	Disease, Wyandotte
Jan 11	James Ryan	Williams	Accidental gunshot in Dec '61
Jan 14	John P. Rose	Dobyns	Measles, Fort Scott
Jan 15	James K. Farrow	Foreman	Disease, Fort Scott
Jan 17	Jacob F. M. Frank	Miller	Killed while foraging, Eminence, Mo.
Jan 17	James W. Pruitt	Miller	Disease, Camp Denver
Jan 18	Benjamin F. Nickel	Orahood	Disease, Fort Scott
Jan 21	Samuel F. Cash	Dobyns	Died on furlough
Jan 26	Nicholas Stewart	Gower	Typhoid fever, at home near Fort Scott
Jan —	James Hurd	Stephenson	Disease (got drunk and froze on prairie)
Feb 2	William Stockham	Gower	Lung fever, at home near Fort Scott
Feb 9	William Shackelford	Orahood	Disease, Fort Scott
Feb 11	Joseph C. Morton	Miller	Drowned in Osage River, Kans.
Feb 13	James B. Throgmorton	Gibson	Disease, Camp Denver
Feb 14	Daniel Sellers	Gibson	Disease, Camp Denver
Feb 14	James A. Hornback	Miller	Disease, Camp Denver
Feb 16	Lewis Denny	Rogers	Measles, Fort Scott
Feb 17	Sidney S. Smith	Quigg	Disease, Wyandotte
Feb 20	James A. Blakely	Lockhart	Disease
Feb 21	Isaac Miller	Miller	Disease, Camp Denver
Feb 23	Charles N. Everts	Gower	Typhoid fever, Wyandotte
Feb 24	John C. Nedrow	Orahood	Disease, at his home in Linn County

Date of Death	Name	Company	Cause, Location
Feb 25	Chauncey L. Terrill	Creitz	Pneumonia, Barnesville
Feb 26	William J. Freeman	Stephenson	Disease, Mound City
Feb 26	Samuel P. Parsons	Jas. Harvey	Disease, Wyandotte
Feb 27	Fielding Loe	Gibson	Disease, Barnesville
Feb 28	John Hageman	Orahood	Disease, Fort Scott
Feb 28	Mark Hageman	Orahood	Disease, Fort Scott
Feb 28	William H. Angela	Harris	Died at Wyandotte
Feb 29	Aaron O. Cox	Jenkins	Pneumonia, Camp Denver
Feb 29	Amasa Falkner	Thompson	"General debility," Barnesville
Feb 29	James Shutes	Miller	Disease
Feb —	James A. Ralston	Williams	Disease, Mound City
Mar 1	Jacob L. Vanwert	Stewart	Pneumonia, Mound City
Mar 1	William Empson	Miller	Disease, Fort Lincoln
Mar 2	Wyatt Brownlee	Lockhart	Disease, Fort Scott
Mar 3	Samuel T. Serber	Creitz	Pneumonia, Camp Hunter
Mar 3	Charles Coger	AWJ Brown	Pneumonia, Camp Halpine, Mo.
Mar 4	Reuben H. Gorton	Rogers	Measles, Fort Scott
Mar 7	Solomon J. Boots	Orahood	Disease, Camp Deitzler
Mar 8	Frederick Brown	Miller	Disease, Barnesville
Mar 8	John G. Moore	Clark	Disease, Barnesville
Mar 10	Noah McCollister	Seaman	Lung fever, Iola
Mar 15	Anson E. Reed	Orahood	Disease, Springfield, Mo.
Mar 17	Charles Miller	Miller	Disease, Camp Hunter
Mar 19	Brice A. Jackson	Stewart	Typhoid, Prairie City, Kans.
Mar 25	James H. Rolston	Williams	Measles, Mound City
Mar 29	John M. Dudley	Stephenson	Disease, Mound City
Mar 30	Malachi Tyler	Foreman	Disease, Fort Scott

Notes

Introduction

1. Halleck to McClellan, December 10, 1861, *The War of the Rebellion: A Compilation of the Official Records of the Union and Confederate Armies* (Washington, D.C.: Government Printing Office, 1880–1901), Series I, 8:818–19. Hereafter the *Official Records* are referenced as *OR*, and all citations are to Series I unless noted otherwise.

2. Halleck to Stanton, March 25, 1862, *OR* 8:641–42.

3. Addicott, "Operation Desert Storm," 122–23, 133. Mark E. Neely, Jr., argues, "The *essential* aspect of any definition of total war asserts that it breaks down the distinction between soldiers and civilians, combatants and noncombatants, which no one in the Civil War did systematically, including William T. Sherman." Neely, "Was the Civil War a Total War?" 27. It can be argued, however, that late in the war the Union made little distinction between military versus civilian *property*.

4. Brinsfield, "Military Ethics of General William T. Sherman," 39; Kent, *Commentaries*, 53, 88. The primary text for such instruction at West Point was Kent's *Commentaries*. Brinsfield wrote that *Commentaries* was William T. Sherman's favorite text of the chaplain's course at West Point. Henry Halleck's book *International Law; or, Rules Regulating the Intercourse of States in Peace and War* was published in 1861, but there is no reason to believe that in early 1861 it was widely read by the army or any other audience.

5. Jefferson to Colvin, September 20, 1810, in Ford, *The Works of Thomas Jefferson*, 146–49; Williams, "The Battle of Newtown," 9–10, 15; Remini, *Andrew Jackson*, 63–64, 68, 79–81, 133, 147, 153; Birtle, *U.S. Army Counterinsurgency and Contingency Operation Doctrine*, 17; Levinson, "Occupation and Stability Dilemmas."

In language that presaged Lincoln's defense of suspending the writ of habeas corpus, Jefferson argued to Colvin that "a strict observance of the written laws is doubtless *one* of the high duties of a good citizen, but it is not *the highest*. The laws of necessity, of self-preservation, of saving our country when in danger, are of higher obligation. To lose our country by a scrupulous adherance to written law, would be to lose the law itself, with life, liberty, property and all those who are enjoying them with us; and absurdly sacrificing the end to the means."

6. Kiper, *Major General John Alexander McClernand*, 38, 54.

7. General Orders no. 100, April 24, 1863, *OR* Series III, 3:148–64.

8. Sherman to John Sherman, September 22, 1862, in Simpson and Berlin, *Sherman's Civil War*, 301. A Confederate policy regarding the destruction of civilian property is found in the instruction from Secretary of War G. W. Randolph to Major General Mansfield Lovell in Louisiana: "I now instruct you to destroy cotton, tobacco, military and naval stores, or other property of any kind whatever which may aid the enemy in the prosecution of the war whenever and wherever in your judgment it is necessary to prevent such property from falling into the hands of the enemy." Randolph to Lovell, May 21, 1862, *OR* 15:741.

9. *Congressional Globe*, 37th Congress, 2d sess., 111. Halleck came to see liberating slaves—without necessarily emancipating them—as a tool for winning the war: "It is the policy of the Government to withdraw from the enemy as much productive labor as possible. . . . Every slave withdrawn from the enemy is equivalent to a white man put *hors de combat* . . . withdraw from the use of the enemy all the slaves you can, and to employ those so withdrawn to the best possible advantage against the enemy." Despite having described this as governmental policy, Halleck advised he was writing this as an "unofficial letter simply as a personal friend and as a matter of friendly advice." Halleck to Grant, March 31, 1862, *OR* 24, part 3:156–57.

10. Harney to Gantt, May 14, 1861, *OR* 3:373; General Orders no. 3, Headquarters Department of the Missouri, November 20, 1861, *OR* 8:370; Waring to Asboth, December 18, 1861, *OR* 8:451–52; Berlin et al., *Free at Last*, 12–29 ; *New York Tribune*, January 24, 1862.

11. Trego to My Dear Wife, October 28, 1861, in Langsdorf, "The Letters of Joseph H. Trego," 298; Joseph Trego diary, 1861–1863, entry of October 31, 1861. Hereafter these sources are cited as the "Trego Letters" and "Trego diary," respectively.

12. Lewis, "The Man the Historians Forgot," 89.

13. Richardson, *Beyond the Mississippi*, 44, 45.

14. Wilder, *The Annals of Kansas*, 318, quoting the *Leavenworth Daily Conservative* of May 12, 1861. Wilder identifies the author of the letter as J. J. Ingalls; the microfilm of this newspaper at the Kansas State Historical Society shows the letter was anonymous; the paragraph quoted above it is cut out and missing from the original.

15. Stephenson, *The Political Career of General James H. Lane*, 161; *Topeka Tribune*, March 23, 1861, quoted in Gaeddert, *The Birth of Kansas*, 102.

16. Stephenson, *The Political Career of General James H. Lane*, 161n8; Burlingame and Ettlinger, *Inside Lincoln's White House*, 9.

17. Phillips, *The Conquest of Kansas*, 139, 140.

18. Lewis, "The Man the Historians Forgot," 90.

19. Connelley, *The Provisional Government of Nebraska Territory*, 130–34, 142–49, 151–52. On May 8, 1862, the distraught Guthrie wrote of Lane: "Nothing but a heart as black as hell could impel a man to so much baseness as this man is guilty, meantime I am the victim. My whole soul is filled with anguish from the discouragements, ill treatment, and embarrassments that overwhelm; and but for my poor family I had far rather be in my grave than thus submit to these oppressions, and humiliations." The next day he again sought a favor from Lane.

20. Castel, *A Frontier State at War*, 83–85; Stephenson, *The Political Career of General James H. Lane*, 164; "A Fine Sight," Leavenworth *Daily Times*, August 16, 1863, quoting the Lawrence *Republican*.

21. James H. Lane probate estate; *Index to Deeds No. 2 —Grantor*, Douglas County, Kansas.

22. Lewis, "The Man the Historians Forgot," 92; "Gen. Jim Lane," *New York Times*, December 3, 1861, p. 2

23. Used with permission of the John Quincy Wolf Folklore Collection, Lyon College, Batesville, Arkansas. This song can be heard online at http://www.lyon.edu/wolfcollection/songs/jonesold1232.html, and another version, also recorded in 1952, at http://www.lyon.edu/wolfcollection/songs/detherowoldjim1236.html.

Chapter 1. Bleeding Kansas

1. Hoole to Dear Major, May 17, 1856, in Hoole, "A Southerner's Viewpoint of the Kansas Situation," 49.

2. Blackmar, *Kansas*, 2:354; Robley, *History of Bourbon County*, 153, 154–55.

3. Richmond, *Kansas*, 6–7, 27–28.

4. Oliva, *Fort Scott*, 57–58, 75–76.

5. Gates, *Fifty Million Acres*, 15–22.

6. Goodrich, *War to the Knife*, 28–43.

7. Letter from Galway, October 27, 1861, *New York Times*, November 9, 1861, p. 2.

8. Stephenson, *The Political Career of General James H. Lane*, 17–23, 26.

9. Ibid., 30–34, 37–38.

10. "Narrative of My Life," Doniphan *Kansas Crusader of Freedom*, February 3, 1858; "Jim Lane," *Lecompton Union*, August 30, 1856.

11. Stephenson, *The Political Career of General James H. Lane*, 43.

12. Ibid., 44–45; Speer, *Life of Gen. James H. Lane*, 37, 43.

13. Stephenson, *The Political Career of General James H. Lane*, 46–47, 50–52, 54.

14. Speer, *Life of Gen. James H. Lane*, 51–63; Stephenson, *The Political Career of General James H. Lane*, 55–56, 58.

15. Stephenson, *The Political Career of General James H. Lane*, 76–82; Speer, *Life of Gen. James H. Lane*, 116–18, 123–24.

16. Speer, *Life of Gen. James H. Lane*, 124, 135–36, 167–68; Stephenson, *The Political Career of General James H. Lane*, 89, 93; Welch, *Border Warfare*, 45.

17. R. G. Elliott to Dear Sister, May 8, 1857, in Berneking, "Letters from Robert Gaston Elliott," 284; Gates, *Fifty Million Acres*, 107–108, 133; Gower, "Gold Fever in Kansas Territory," 58–74. The inflow of people seeking riches would become known as the Pikes Peak Gold Rush in 1859.

18. "Remarried," White Cloud *Kansas Chief,* June 11, 1857; Stephenson, *The Political Career of General James H. Lane*, 96–97; "A Scrap of Kansas History," Arkansas City (Kansas) *Traveler*, April 3, 1878.

19. Stephenson, *The Political Career of General James H. Lane*, 98–99.

20. Welch, *Border Warfare*, 11, 27–30, 45–51; J. G. Anderson to Dear Brother, February 17, 1858, Richard Hinton collection, Box 1, Folder 8; Villard, *John Brown*, 681–82.

21. Connelley, *A Standard History of Kansas and Kansans*, 3:1, 232; Cutler, *History of the State of Kansas*, 1:302, 2:1,106; "Capt. Montgomery," Leavenworth *Daily Times*, December 6, 1860; Richardson, *Beyond the Mississippi*, 126; Dirck, "By the Hand of God," 106–107, 111–12.

22. Welch, *Border Warfare*, 46–47, 51, 56–58, 64, 72–73, 89. A Lawrence newspaper in June 1858 reprinted an alleged order of Lane dated February 18, 1858, which instructed Montgomery and Bayne to disband their companies. The newspaper suggested this was a postdated order and a trick by Lane. This was followed by a letter from Montgomery dated June 6, 1858, in which he said he had resigned his command as a militia officer before February 18 and instead had been operating on his own, being "identified with a popular movement in this section of the country, having for its object a redress of grievances." Ibid., 126–27.

23. Ibid., 97; Hougen, "The Marais des Cygnes Massacre," 74–94.

24. Welch, *Border Warfare*, 129, 158–63, 178, 181–83, 188–90.

25. Ibid., 150, 181–92, 196–97.

26. Ibid., 211, 214, 218, 222.

27. "An Earnest Appeal in Behalf of the Suffering and Destitute," September 14, 1860, Abraham Lincoln papers.

28. Cutler, *History of the State of Kansas*, 1:178.

29. Connelley, *A Standard History of Kansas*, 2:693–94; Cutler, *History of the State of Kansas*, 2:1070, 1106.

30. *History of Vernon County*, 262–65.

Chapter 2. The Blast of War

1. Connelley, *A Standard History of Kansas*, 2:710.

2. Lane to Speer and Smith, Topeka *Kansas State Record*, January 19, 1861, quoting the Lawrence *Republican*.

3. Robley, *History of Bourbon County*, 163–64.

4. Speer, *Life of Gen. James H. Lane*, 228, 230.

5. McPherson, *Battle Cry of Freedom*, 278–80.

6. Delahay to Lincoln, February 17, 1860, Abraham Lincoln papers; Lane et al. to Lincoln, January 1, 1861, ibid.; Lane to Lincoln, January 2, 1816, ibid.

7. J.K.B. to Dear Times, April 19, 1861, Leavenworth *Daily Times*, April 26, 1861.

8. Connelley, *A Standard History of Kansas*, 2:614–15; Talbot to Lane and Clay, April 24, 1861, *OR* 51, part 1:335; Langsdorf, "Jim Lane and the Frontier Guard," 13–25; Harris to Johnson et al., August 18, 1861, *OR* Series II, 2:1519–20; Miller, *Lincoln's Abolitionist General*, 55–57.

9. Stephenson, *The Political Career of General James H. Lane*, 105; Grant to Craig, April 21, 1861, *OR* 1:649; Farrar to Cameron, April 21, 1861, ibid., 649–50; Miles to Townsend, May 10, 1861, *OR* 3:369; Eldridge, *Recollections of Early Days in Kansas*, 167; Easton to Williams, May 4, 1861, *OR* 1:652; Stephenson, *The Political Career of General James H. Lane*, 105–106.

10. *OR* 1:661. Most of the information regarding the actions of Lyon comes from Phillips, *Damned Yankee*, 164–214.

11. Sherman to Thomas Ewing, Jr., May 11, 1861, in Simpson and Berlin, *Sherman's Civil War*, 79–80. Lyon's troops consisted of the regulars, the reserve corps, and home guards. The reserve corps and home guards were recruited largely from the ethnic German population of St. Louis. Henry Halleck observed: "There seems to have been some misapprehension at Washington in respect to the Reserve Corps and Home Guards. The former . . . are regularly mustered into service for three years, without any limitation as to their place of service. They are regularly-organized Missouri Volunteers, and entitled to pay and allowances the same as any other volunteers. They will be paid accordingly. The Home Guards are not a regular organization; some have been mustered in with the reservation of serving only in this State, while others, although long in service, have never been mustered at all." Halleck to Thomas, *OR* 8:434–35.

On April 30 the War Department gave Lyon permission to enlist up to ten thousand men as a reserve corps to serve within St. Louis to maintain the authority of the United States and to protect of the inhabitants of Missouri. Lyon circumvented Jackson's refusal to provide troops by obtaining authority from the Secretary of War to enlist troops to protect the public property and execute the laws. Prior to this in St. Louis, thousands of loyal men had offered their services to the Federal government, but Jackson would not commission their officers or muster them in as Missouri Volunteers. Lyon's predecessor in command, General William Harney, had declined to muster these same men into Federal service, as he had not been given authority to do so. Harney's lack of aggressive action infuriated many Union men, including Congressman Francis P. Blair, Jr., and Captain Lyon, who conspired successfully to have Harney replaced by Lyon.

12. Phillips, *Damned Yankee*, 214. Lyon has also been quoted as stating: "Rather than concede to the State of Missouri for one single instant, the right to dictate to my government in any manner however important, I would see you, you, and you, and every man, woman, and child in the state dead and buried. This means war. In one hour one of my officers will call and conduct you out of my lines." Price, *Nathaniel Lyon*, 29.

13. Jackson secretly sent a messenger to Confederate general Ben McCulloch in Arkansas, requesting that he advance his troops into Missouri and come to Jackson's aid. At the same time Sterling Price, commander of the Missouri State Guard, called the Missouri militia into active service and ordered the destruction of bridges and telegraph lines between St. Louis and Jefferson City. McCulloch to Walker, June 14, 1861, *OR* 3:594–95; Lyon to Thomas, June 13, 1861, ibid., 384; General Orders no. 11, Headquarters Missouri State Guard, June 12, 1861, *OR* 3:592–94.

14. Untitled article, Fort Scott *Democrat*, May 18, 1861; "Constitution, By-Laws and List of Officers and Members of the Frontier Guard, 3d Regiment, K.V.M.," ibid., May 25, 1861; untitled article, ibid., June 29, 1861.

15. Montgomery to Stearns, May 8, 1861, George Luther Stearns papers.

16. "Public Meeting," Fort Scott *Democrat*, May 25, 1861.

17. Goodrich, *War to the Knife*, 214–15; untitled article, Fort Scott *Democrat*, June 8, 1861; "Kansas and Missouri," ibid.; "News from Missouri," ibid., June 29, 1861; "Texas," Leavenworth *Daily Times*, October 20, 1860.

Chapter 3. A Fighting Brigade Is Born

1. Lincoln to Cameron, June 20, 1861, *OR* Series III, 1:280; Cameron to Lane, June 20, 1861, ibid., 282.

2. "Gen. Lane to Retake Fort Smith," *Leavenworth Daily Conservative*, May 11, 1861; Samuel Reader to My Dear Brother Frank, May 12, 1861, "Letters of Samuel James Reader," 30–31.

Newspaper accounts of Lane's May 10 speech in Topeka omitted any mention of a plan to recapture the forts, recounting instead only that Lane said he had returned to Kansas to assist in raising two regiments. "Gen. Jim Lane," *Topeka Tribune*, May 11, 1861; uncaptioned articles, Topeka *Daily State Record*, May 10, 1861, and *Topeka State Record*, May 18, 1861.

3. Lincoln to McClellan, April 9, 1862, in Basler, *The Collected Works of Abraham Lincoln*, 5:185; McPherson, *Battle Cry of Freedom*, 414, 464; Browne, *The Every-Day Life of Abraham Lincoln*, 418.

4. Leavenworth *Daily Times*, June 26, 1861; Leavenworth (weekly) *Conservative*, June 27, 1861; Lawrence *Republican*, June 27, 1861. News of Lane's appointment quickly spread south. "The Kansas Regiment" and "Jim Lane's Brigade," the latter quoting a New Orleans newspaper, both in the *Richmond* (Virginia) *Daily Dispatch*, July 1, 1861.

5. *Congressional Globe*, 37th Congress, 2d sess., 336. Stanton had been secretary of state for Kansas Territory and twice had served as acting governor.

6. *Congressional Globe*, 37th Congress, 1st sess., 82, 440; ibid., 2d sess., 363.

7. *Congressional Globe*, 37th Congress, 1st sess., 440; ibid., 2d sess., 293, 361.

8. Tidball, "The View from the Top of the Knoll," 188.

9. *Congressional Globe*, 37th Congress, 1st sess., 192, 265.

10. Ibid., 190. See also Lane's comments on p. 189.

11. Ibid., 187.

12. Stephenson, *The Political Career of General James H. Lane*, 78–79, 162; "Opinions of a Connecticut Paper," Richmond (Virginia) *Daily Dispatch,* July 9, 1861. Albert D. Richardson wrote that on his pre-war travels to "the remotest cabins of Missouri and Arkansas," he was asked, "Do you know that man Lane, up in Kansas? I reckon he must be a powerful fighter!" in Richardson, *Beyond the Mississippi.*

13. "The New Troubles in Kansas," Richmond (Virginia) *Daily Dispatch,* November 24, 1860; "The Montgomery Outrages in Kansas," ibid., December 4, 1860; "Montgomery," ibid., December 8, 1860; "The Abolition Raid on Texas," ibid., May 16, 1861; untitled article, Houston *Tri-Weekly Telegraph*, December 20, 1860, quoting the Dallas *Herald*; "Kansas Montgomery at Fort Ouachita," Paulding (Mississippi) *Eastern Clarion,* May 24, 1861, quoting the New Orleans *Picayune*; "Late and Interesting from Texas," ibid., May 27, 1861; "From the Macon Citizen: Late and Interesting from the Indian Territory," Augusta (Georgia) *Daily Constitutionalist,* June 22, 1861.

14. "Official Roster of Kansas," 658; James Montgomery commission dated June 24, 1861, James Montgomery collection. Robinson recognized Montgomery as the ranking officer in Kansas and denied that Lane, Weer, or Johnson had valid military commissions. Robinson to Blood, August 24, 1861, Charles and Sara Robinson papers, roll 1.

15. "Our Western Missouri Letter," *Chicago Tribune* (daily), January 5, 1862, p. 1; Speer, *Life of Gen. James H. Lane,* 85; "Record of Events," William Creitz diary; Johnson to Lincoln, February 24, 1860, Abraham Lincoln papers; advertisement, Leavenworth *Daily Times,* July 14, 1861; uncaptioned article, ibid., August 2, 1861.

16. *Biographical and Historical Record of Ringgold and Decatur Counties, Iowa,* 504; Holcombe, *History of Greene County, Missouri,* 416–17; Rogers and Rogers, *Souvenir History of Mercer County, Missouri,* 52.

17. Starr, *Jennison's Jayhawkers,* 68–69; Dickinson, "War Notes": Hunt, *History of Salem,* 44, 63, 111, 142, 145; Atherton, "Daniel Howell Hise, 349–52, 355n47; [U.S. Senate], *Select Committee on the Harpers Ferry Invasion,* 91–92, 94.

Elijah E. Harvey had served a year in one of Lane's Mexican War regiments. "Death of Capt. Harvey," *Douglass* (Kansas) *Tribune,* May 11, 1906. William R. Allen wanted to serve under Montgomery and inquired whether his company "will need to take arms or any thing else but our clothing." Allen to Stearns, June 28, 1861, George Luther Stearns papers.

18. Robley, *History of Bourbon County, Kansas*, 168; *Military History of Kansas Regiments*, 119; A. H. Campbell interview, Sixth Kansas Cavalry collection; Prince to Sir [Hollister], August 7, 1861, in "Fort Leavenworth Letters Sent."

19. Jennison to Miss, June 7, 1861, in the Lawrence *Republican,* June 13, 1861; Prince to Captain [Jennison], July 9, 1861, in "Fort Leavenworth Letters Sent."

20. Montgomery to Stearns, June 21, 1861, James Montgomery papers, "Montgomery 1861" folder.

21. Montgomery to Stearns, June 27, July 5, July 10, 1861, George Luther Stearns papers; Swingley to Most Worthy Friend Mollie, July 7, 1861, in John Stillman Brown Family papers; "From Southern Kansas," *Leavenworth Daily Conservative*, July 11, 1861.

22. Welch, *Border Warfare*, 100–101, 150–52, 162–63, 196–97, 201.

23. Leslie, *The Devil Knows How to Ride*, 79–81.

24. "News from South-Western Mo.," Leavenworth *Daily Times*, July 23, 1861; "Southern Kansas," *Leavenworth Daily Conservative*, July 9, 1861; "Muster Out Roll of Captain Eli Snyder's Infantry."

25. Letter from Jayhawker, July 10, 1861, *Leavenworth Daily Conservative*, July 17, 1861; letter from John, July 12, 1861, ibid., July 16, 1861.

26. Prince to Captain [Jennison], August 5, 1861, in "Fort Leavenworth Letters Sent."

27. Prince to Capt [Van Vliet], July 11, 1861; Prince to Captain [J. M. Williams], July 12, 1861; Prince to Capt J. M. Williams, July 17, 1861; Prince to General [Lyon], July 27, 1861; all in "Fort Leavenworth Letters Sent."

28. Letter from A.B.M., July 23, 1861, *Leavenworth Daily Conservative*, July 27, 1861; "Record of Events," William Creitz diary; Van Horn to Prince, August 3, 1861, *OR* 3:41–43. Van Horn stated Camp Prince was located "some 18 miles southwest of Harrisonville," near the state line; A.B.M. located it "Near Morristown, Pony Creek."

29. J.F.V. to Editor Times, July 27, 1861, Leavenworth *Daily Times*, July 30, 1861; letter from A.B.M., July 29, 1861, *Leavenworth Daily Conservative*, July 30, 1861.

30. Ibid.

31. Letter from A.B.M., July 29, 1861, *Leavenworth Daily Conservative*, July 30, 1861.

32. Ibid.; J.F.V. to Editor Times, July 27, 1861, Leavenworth *Daily Times*, July 30, 1861.

33. Special Orders no. 2, Headquarters, Camp at Harrisonville, July 26, 1861, Thomas Moonlight collection.

34. J.F.V. to Editor Times, July 27, 1861, Leavenworth *Daily Times*, July 30, 1861.

35. Ibid. "A.B.M." attributed the "rich harvest" at Harrisonville to Jennison's and Tucker's men. He also commented, "We don't know whether Capt. Tucker was under command of Col. Weer or not."

36. Prince to — Officer, Kansas City, July 24, 1861; Prince to Col. Weer, July 27, 1861, in "Fort Leavenworth Letters Sent."

37. Barnes, "An Editor Looks at Early-Day Kansas," 134–35. The diary of John Howard Kitts cited by Barnes describes the fort as having a log stockade, as does the memoirs of a Fort Scott civilian. Isely described the fort in May 1863 as a large square-hewn block house and stable surrounded by earthen breastworks. It appears the log stockade was a later addition. Isely to Mr. Henry Isely, May 4, 1863, in Christian Isely papers; Goodlander, *Memoirs*, 66.

38. "Record of Events," William Creitz diary.

39. Letter from John, July 12, 1861, *Leavenworth Daily Conservative*, July 16, 1861; letter from Sojer, July 20, 1861, ibid., July 25, 1861; John to Dear Journal, July 22, 1861, Lawrence *Kansas State Journal*, August 1, 1861; Kansas to Eds. Journal, July 15, 1861, ibid., July 18, 1861.

40. Letter from W.H.F., July 17, 1861, *Leavenworth Daily Conservative*, July 23, 1861; "Testimony of Capt. Thomas Bickerton," in Thaddeus Hyatt papers; Brewerton, *The War in Kansas*, 344.

41. J. K. Hudson to John Hudson, July 13, 1861, Joseph Kennedy Hudson papers, 1861–1898 folder; "Military Record of J. K. Hudson," ibid.; marriage certificate of J. K. Hudson and Mary Worrall Smith, Miscellaneous Material folder, ibid.; John Brown, Jr., to Stearns, July 9 and August 9, 1861, Wealthy C. Brown to Stearns, August 13, 1861, John Brown, Jr., to Stearns, October 5, 1861, George Luther Stearns papers; letter from Kansas, July 29, 1861, Lawrence *Kansas State Journal*, August 1, 1861. Hudson was born May 4, 1840, in Carrollton, Ohio. His family moved to Salem, where his father, John, was the printer for the *Anti-Slavery Bugle*. "Joseph Kennedy Hudson," typescript biography, Joseph Kennedy Hudson papers; Cutler, *History of the State of Kansas*, 1:566–67.

42. Montgomery to Stearns, July 26, 1861, Zulavsky to Stearns, July 26, 1861, George Luther Stearns papers; Descriptive Roll 10th Kansas Infantry, Field & Staff 3d Kansas Volunteers; Beszedits, "Notable Hungarians," http://suvcw.org/mollus/articles/htm, and "Prominent Hungarians," www.hccc.org/A2e/A20303b/shtml, both accessed August 21, 2006.

Zulavsky's name has been recorded as Zularsky and Zulaosky. The signature on the cited letter to Stearns looks like Zularsky, but two other letters in this collection show other spellings, such as E. A. Zulasky to Stearns, January 8, 1863, and L. L. Zulasky to Stearns, February 15, 1863.

43. Sarah Everett to Dear Cynthia, July 22, 1856, in "Letters of John and Sarah Everett," 26; Johnson, *The History of Anderson County, Kansas*, 51; Cutler, *History of the State of Kansas*, 2:1322, 1323; reminiscence of John E. Stewart, Thaddeus Hyatt papers, 14–18; Welch, *Border Warfare*, 39, 42–43, 64, 158–60; Morgan, *History of Wyandotte County, Kansas* 1:227–30; John E. Stewart to Thaddeus Hyatt, December 20, 1859, Thaddeus Hyatt papers; Blackmar, *Kansas*, 1:542–44.

44. Goodrich, *War to the Knife*, 220; Leslie, *The Devil Knows How to Ride*, 66–69; "Stop Thief!" broadside, in "Governor Denver's Administration," 540.

45. Prince to Sir [Weer], July 14, 1861, 1861; Prince to Sir, August 3, 1861; Prince to Col. [Weer], August 4, 1861, in "Fort Leavenworth Letters Sent"; *Congressional*

Globe, 37th Congress, 2d sess., 224, 361; Kansas to Editors State Journal, July 29, 1861, Lawrence *Kansas State Journal*, August 1, 1861. Bickerton had command of the Free State cannon in the assault on Fort Titus in 1856. Speer, *Life of Gen. James H. Lane*, 115. Allen's and Stephenson's companies were the most skeleton of the companies mustered, each numbering only about thirty men.

46. Fisher, *The Gun and the Gospel*, 161; "Inventory of Arms in Possession of Capt. James M. Harvey Comd'g Comp'y 'G' 10th Regt Kans Volunteers, November 18, 1862," James M. Harvey papers, Box 1, correspondence 1861–1865; Thaddeus Hyatt to Nat. Kansas Committee, September 12, 1856, and Hyatt to National Committee, September 14, 1856, Thaddeus Hyatt papers; "Invoice of Ordnance and Ordnance Stores turned over by Capt. J. L. Reno, Commanding Leavenworth Arsenal, to Col. H. P. Johnson," Fifth Kansas Cavalry collection, Box 2, Folder 17; Porter, "Personal Reminiscences"; invoice dated Leavenworth Arsenal, September 4, 1861, James Montgomery collection; Halpine to Halleck, March 14, 1862, *OR* 8:615–17; Bond to Old Boy, May 25, 1862, Rowland Mantor papers. Hyatt indicated 200 to 250 Sharps rifles were being sent from Boston via Chicago.

47. "Tri-monthly Report of Kansas Volunteers for the 10th day of January, 1862," *OR* Series III, 1:787.

48. Letter from Sojer, July 25, 1861, *Leavenworth Daily Conservative*, July 31, 1861. Henry H. Williams was elected major. Like many other officers of the Third, he appears to have been a radical. His pre-war activities are mentioned in Cutler, *History of the State of Kansas*, 2:888.

49. "The War in the Southwest," *New York Times*, December 31, 1862, p. 1.

50. Cutler, *History of the State of Kansas*, 1:302, 2:1322, 1323; "Deaths," Ellsworth (Maine) *Herald*, May 29, 1863; *OR* 22:314; Johnson, *The History of Anderson County, Kansas*, 50–52; Welch, *Border Warfare*, 47; Collins, *General James G. Blunt*, 15–20, 23; Hinton, *John Brown*, 221, 223. Fort Bayne was also known as Fort Bain. It was the fortified home of Oliver P. Bayne.

51. Letter from Kansas, July 29, 1861, Lawrence *Kansas State Journal*, August 1, 1861.

Chapter 4. "We Could Play Hell with Missouri"

1. Uncaptioned article, Leavenworth *Daily Times*, August 3, 1861; unsigned letter dated Mound City, August 7, 1861, *Leavenworth Daily Conservative*, August 10, 1861; letter from Maumee, August 18, 1861, ibid., August 22, 1861. In Quincy, Illinois, was Lane's brigade quartermaster, M. H. Insley, who had let a contract to purchase a thousand horses at $93 a head.

2. Britton, *Pioneer Life in Southwest Missouri*, 155–56.

3. "Recruits Wanted," Leavenworth *Daily Times*, August 9, 1861; "Col. James Montgomery," *Leavenworth Daily Conservative*, August 3, 1861; Kelton to Prince,

August 4, 1861, *OR* 3:425; Prince to Col. [Montgomery], August 7, 1861, in "Fort Leavenworth Letters Sent; Prince to Sir [Capt. Hayes], August 10, 1861, ibid.

4. "Home Guards for Kansas," *Leavenworth Daily Conservative*, August 6, 1861; "Jennison's Regiment," ibid., August 21, 1861; uncaptioned article, Leavenworth *Daily Times*, August 7, 1861; Frémont to Jennison, August 10, 1861, Charles S. Bowman papers, Box 1, "Recruiting Appointments January 1861–November 17, 1862"; letter from Maumee, August 18, 1861, *Leavenworth Daily Conservative*, August 22, 1861; Frémont to Robinson, August 21, 1861, Charles S. Bowman papers, Box 1, "Governor's Correspondence, August 1861–February 1862"; advertisement, *Leavenworth Daily Conservative*, September 10, 1861; uncaptioned article, Leavenworth *Daily Times*, August 21, 1861.

5. "Arrival of Military Officers," Leavenworth *Daily Times*, August 2, 1861; "Brigadier-General J. H. Lane," *Frank Leslie's Illustrated Newspaper*, August 17, 1861, p. 24.

Major de Vecchi resigned around November 1, allegedly because the brigade had an insufficient number of artillery pieces for him to superintend. In mid-November he reportedly organized the Kansas Battery of Light Artillery; he was unsuccessful in this. He subsequently organized the Ninth Battery, Massachusetts Volunteer Light Artillery. He so antagonized the men, they forced his resignation in January 1863. Untitled article, *Leavenworth Daily Conservative*, November 3, 1861; untitled article, Leavenworth *Daily Times*, November 15, 1861; Deane, *My Dear Wife*.

6. E. S. Lowman to Robinson, August 13, 1861, Charles and Sara Robinson papers; "The Border Conflict," *Leavenworth Daily Conservative*, August 4, 1861.

7. *Chicago Tribune* (daily), August 13, 1861, quoting the Leavenworth (weekly) *Conservative*, August 9, 1861; "Startling News from Southern Kansas!" Leavenworth *Daily Times*, August 9, 1861; letter dated August 20, 1861, *Leavenworth Daily Conservative*, August 24, 1861; Blackmar, *Kansas*, 2:354–55.

8. Creitz, "History of Company 'A' Fifth Kansas Cavalry Volunteers"; Trego to Dear Wife, August 13, 1861, in Trego Letters, 288; "Military Affairs," Lawrence *Republican*, August 22, 1861; Trego diary, entry of August 12, 1861.

9. Letter from A.B.M., August 18, 1861, *Leavenworth Daily Conservative*, August 22, 1861; J.F.V. to Editor Times, August 18, 1861, Leavenworth *Daily Times*, August 22, 1861; Hollister to Halpine, February 4, 1862, Charles S. Bowman papers, Box 1, "Muster Orders, June 1861–Sept 1862."

Captain Prince on August 12 authorized an additional five companies to be raised for Judson's home guards. However, these were mustered in for three years' service, unlike the original three companies for whom no term of service was specified. These additional companies were officered by Captains L. R. Jewell, H. S. Greeno, J. W. Orahood, H. M. Dobyns, and A. W. J. Brown. These were all cavalry, except for Brown's, which was infantry. *Military History of Kansas Regiments*, 119. Although Montgomery would vacate Mound City on August 17, the town was not devoid of troops; Jennison was there organizing his First Kansas Cavalry regiment. The town's population had grown considerably with the influx of Unionist refugees from Missouri, particularly after the Federal retreat from southwest Missouri. Kansas to Eds. State Journal, August 26, 1861, Lawrence *Kansas State Journal*, August 29, 1861.

10. Letter from A.B.M., August 18, 1861, *Leavenworth Daily Conservative*, August 22, 1861.

11. Ibid.; J.F.V. to Editor Times, August 18, 1861, Leavenworth *Daily Times*, August 22, 1861.

12. "Meeting at Stockton's Hall," Leavenworth *Daily Times*, October 9, 1861.

13. Lane to Prince, August 28, 1861, "James Henry Lane Letters."

14. "Reception of Col. Lane," *Leavenworth Daily Conservative*, August 16, 1861. Jennison and his wife were in Quincy. Letter from Maumee, August 18, 1861, *Leavenworth Daily Conservative*, August 22, 1861.

15. Prince to Lane, August 17, 1861, "Fort Leavenworth, Kansas Letter Book"; Prince to Lane, August 15, 1861, *OR* 3:446; Lane to Prince, August 15, 1861, *OR* 3:446; Lane to Frémont, August 16, 1861, *OR* 3:446; Lane to Frémont, August 17, 1861, ibid., 447. The Leavenworth *Daily Times* of August 17 stated Lane's staff had departed on August 16.

16. "Gen. Lane's Brigade," Lawrence *Republican*, August 22, 1861; Kansas to Eds. State Journal, August 26, 1861, Lawrence *Kansas State Journal*, August 29, 1861.

17. "Military Affairs," Lawrence *Republican*, August 22, 1861; untitled article, Fort Scott *Democrat*, August 24, 1861; M. to Friend Speer, August 24, 1861, Lawrence *Republican*, August 29, 1861; B. to Editor Olathe *Mirror*, August 26, 1861, Olathe *Mirror*, September 5, 1861. The Leavenworth *Daily Times* of August 20 reported Lane left Leavenworth Saturday night, August 17.

18. Chandler to Dear Friend Brown, September 1, 1861, in John Stillman Brown Family papers; Catton, *This Hallowed Ground*, 26.

19. "Southward," *Leavenworth Daily Conservative*, August 20, 1861; "More Troops," Leavenworth *Daily Times*, August 17, 1861; untitled article, *Leavenworth Daily Conservative*, August 20, 1861; Prince to Colonel, August 19, 1861, and "Endorsement," August 21, 1861, "Fort Leavenworth, Kansas Letter Book"; untitled article, Leavenworth *Daily Times*, August 22, 1861. "Southward" identified the five companies as all belonging to the Fourth; Watson's company would be assigned to the Fifth as Company F, later transferred to the Third, finally becoming Company K of the Tenth Kansas Volunteer Infantry.

20. Lane to Prince, August 25, 1861, *OR* 3:454–55; Lane to Prince, August 25, 1861, "James Henry Lane Letters"; Prince to Lane, August 23, 1861, "Fort Leavenworth, Kansas Letter Book."

21. M. to Friend Speer, August 24, 1861, Lawrence *Republican*, August 29, 1861; letter from B.J., August 27, 1861, *Leavenworth Daily Conservative*, August 31, 1861; Trego to My Dear Wife, September 5, 1861, in Langsdorf, "The Letters of Joseph H. Trego," 291–92.

22. Unsigned letter dated Fort Scott, August 28, 1861, Lawrence *Republican*, September 5, 1861; Trego to My Dear Wife, September 5, 1861, in Langsdorf, "The Letters of Joseph H. Trego," 291–92. Trego commanded his company, Captain Seaman being sick at Mound City.

23. Lindberg and Matthews, "'The Eagle of the 11th Kansas,'" 6.

24. *History of Vernon County, Missouri*, 264, 386–89.

25. Letter from Rover, August 30, 1861, *Leavenworth Daily Conservative*, September 5, 1861.

26. *History of Vernon County, Missouri*, 288, 390.

27. Letter from Rover, August 30, 1861, *Leavenworth Daily Conservative*, September 5, 1861.

28. Ibid.

29. Ibid.; *History of Vernon County, Missouri*, 288, 390–91.

30. Letter from Kansas, September 9, 1861, Lawrence *Kansas State Journal*, September 12, 1861.

31. Trego diary, entry of August 29, 1861; *History of Vernon County, Missouri*, 410.

32. Unsigned letter dated Fort Scott, August 28, 1861, Lawrence *Republican*, September 5, 1861; unsigned letter dated Fort Scott, August 29, 1861, ibid., September 5, 1861.

33. "Indians," Lawrence *Republican*, September 5, 1861, quoting the *Fort Scott Democrat*.

34. Letter from Rover, August 30, 1861, *Leavenworth Daily Conservative*, September 5, 1861.

35. Letter from M., September 1, 1861, Lawrence *Republican*, September 12, 1861.

36. Ibid.; Windsor to Messrs. Editors, September 2, 1861, Lawrence *Kansas State Journal*, September 5, 1861. "Windsor" claimed the liquor had been destroyed by the officer of the day: "Thank God we have temperance officers who will see the law prohibiting the sale of intoxicating liquors to soldiers, enforced at whatever hazard."

37. Letter dated Fort Scott, August 29, 1861, Lawrence *Republican*, September 5, 1861. About a month later a private in Allen's company wrote, "Tonight we organized a pledge among ourselves imposing a fine on any member that used profane language." Dickinson diary, entry of October 6, 1861.

Chapter 5. Drywood and Osceola

1. Robinson to Frémont, September 1, 1861, *OR* 3:468–69; Robinson to My Dear S., June 17, 1861, Charles and Sara Robinson papers; Howard to Robinson, September 18, 1861, "Governor's Office—Correspondence Files—Governor Robinson, Box 1.1, Folder 13, Military Affairs."

2. "Lane on Property," Leavenworth (weekly) *Conservative*, September 26, 1861.

3. Letter dated Fort Scott, September 4, 1861, *Leavenworth Daily Conservative*, September 12, 1861.

4. Letter dated Fort Scott, September 4, 1861, Lawrence *Republican*, September 19, 1861.

5. The stories of the mule raid and the Drywood battle are compiled from these sources: Brigadier General A. E. Steen's report, *Liberty* (Missouri) *Tribune*, September 13, 1861; letter dated Fort Scott, September 4, 1861, *Leavenworth Daily Conservative*, September 12, 1861; letter dated Fort Scott, September 4, 1861, Lawrence *Republican*, September 19, 1861; Moonlight to H. P. Scott, September 6, 1861, September 12, 1861, Leavenworth *Daily Times*; report of Colonel J. T. Hughes, September 4, 1861, ibid., September 12, 1861; *History of Vernon County, Missouri*, 279–86; Anderson, *Memoirs*, 50–53.

Wiley Britton wrote that immediately following the raid on the mule herd, Lane formed the men into a hollow square "as if expecting a charge of the enemy every moment" and stayed so deployed for about an hour. Infantry formed in a hollow square was a Napoleonic tactic utilized to repel cavalry charges. This tactic would have been consistent with Lane's Mexican War experience. Wiley Britton, *Pioneer Life in Southwest Missouri* (Columbia: State Historical Society of Missouri, 1923), 170. The captured teamsters were released within a month. Price to Lane, October 16, 1861, *OR* Series II, 1:134.

6. W. P. Barlow, of Guibor's Missouri battery, stated that one of the two guns of the battery was left with only two able men and was forced to retire from the Drywood battlefield. *History of Vernon County*, 285. In an account written just after the war, Moonlight claimed his battery had changed position twelve times and fired thirty-nine rounds. Lindberg and Matthews, "'The Eagle of the 11th Kansas,'" 8.

7. E. S. W. Drought, of Williams's company, wrote fifty years later that Montgomery's bugler sounded the retreat; in this regard his memory appears faulty. Drought, "James Montgomery," 343. Drought wrote that his company was armed with Sharps rifles.

8. Prince to Kelton, September 5, 1861; Lane to Prince, September 3, 1861, *OR* 3:162–63; Price to Jackson, September 4, 1861, *OR* 53:435–36; Anderson, *Memoirs*, 52.

The regimental official history identified Greeno's company as participating in this fight. *Military History of Kansas Regiments*, 120. The contemporary account from which the home guard's participation was gleaned identified them only as "irregulars."

9. Letter dated Fort Scott, September 4, 1861, *Leavenworth Daily Conservative*, September 12, 1861; letter dated Fort Scott, September 4, 1861, Lawrence *Republican*, September 19, 1861; Lane to Prince, September 4, 1861, *OR* 3:163–64; Huntoon to My Dear Wife, September 4, 1861, Andrew Jackson Huntoon papers; "Sketches of Early History," *Humboldt Union*, March 21, 1918; Patrick Gorman interview, January 20, 1908, Sixth Kansas Cavalry collection.

Watson Stewart, the militiaman who authored the "Sketches of Early History," wrote that the Seventh Regiment Kansas State Militia had been ordered to Fort

Scott but was redirected to Barnesville and Fort Lincoln before the regiment reached Fort Scott. However, in the absence of any other militia who could have entered Fort Scott to reinforce Montgomery, it appears that a substantial part of the regiment did make it into Fort Scott.

10. Trego to My Dear Wife, September 5, 1861, in Langsdorf, "The Letters of Joseph H. Trego," 290. As Trego was writing the letter, he noted taking a long pause to listen to Zulasky sing "Annie Laurie" and then added, "Zulavsky is at the piano again getting off some of his Hungarian songs." The different spellings of the adjutant's name are Trego's.

11. M. to Friend Speer, September 15, 1861, in the September 26, 1861, Lawrence *Republican*; Trego to Dear Wife, September 5, 1861, in Langsdorf, "The Letters of Joseph H. Trego," 293. The Lawrence *Republican* of September 19, 1861, and January 8, 1862, identify Reverend H. H. Moore as its correspondent.

12. Moonlight to H. P. Scott, September 6, 1861, Leavenworth *Daily Times*, September 12, 1861; Lane to Prince, September 4, 1861, *OR* 3:163–64; Huntoon to My Dear Wife, September 4, 1861, Andrew Jackson Huntoon papers; Huntoon to My Beloved Wife & Boy, September 15, 1861, ibid.; "Muster-Out Roll of Captain Zacheus Gower's Company"; Chandler to Dear Friend [Rev. J. S. Brown], September 25, 1861, in John Stillman Brown Family papers. The hospital had been moved to Mapleton, under the supervision of brigade surgeon Rufus Gilpatrick. Among the patients were two men injured in fights, one stabbed in the back, and the other hit over the head with a spade. Daniel Chandler recorded that the man hit with the spade died of inflammation of the brain at the Mapleton hospital, and his assailant was at-large. Chandler to Dear Friend [Rev. J. S. Brown], September 25, 1861, ibid. Another man had a finger shot off accidentally. At Fort Lincoln were the two Iowa companies of the Fifth regiment (Garrett Gibson's and Samuel Thompson's), which Lane placed under the temporary command of Lieutenant George S. Hollister.

13. Price to Jackson, September 4, 1861, *OR* 53:435–36; *History of Vernon County, Missouri*, 287; Anderson, *Memoirs*, 53, 59–60; report of Colonel J. T. Hughes, September 4, 1861, *Liberty* (Missouri) *Tribune*, September 13, 1861, and Leavenworth *Daily Times*, September 12, 1861. Price's report was also published in the *New York Tribune* (semi-weekly), September 17, 1861, p. 1.

14. "The Frightful Tragedy of Platte Bridge" and "From Platte River Bridge," *Leavenworth Daily Conservative*, September 5, 1861.

15. Galbreath, "Barclay Coppoc," 479–81; Dickinson diary, entry of September 17, 1861.

16. "Our Kansas Letter," *Chicago Tribune*, March 27, 1862; Leslie, *The Devil Knows How to Ride*, 71–77; Keeler, "Owen Brown's Escape from Harpers Ferry," 342–65.

17. Galbreath, "Barclay Coppoc," 469–70, 473–76; *History of Cedar County, Iowa*; *A Directory of the Kansas Historical Exhibit*; Oates, *To Purge This Land with Blood*, 288, 302, 309, 316, 326.

18. D. Jonathan White, "'What We Have to Expect': Harper's Ferry, Extradition, and Secession" (unpublished manuscript and speech given to the Civil War Roundtable of Eastern Kansas, April 28, 2005).

19. Lane to Prince, September 3, 1861, *OR* 3:163; Lane to Prince, September 4, 1861, ibid., 163–64; Prince to Peabody, September 5, 1861, ibid., 164–65; Prince to Kelton, September 5, 1861, ibid., 162.

20. Lane to Prince, September 5, 1861, *OR* 3:164; Prince to Frémont, September 7, 1861, *OR* Series II, 1:225; Lane to Prince, September 7, 1861, *OR* 3:475; Prince to Lane, September 9, 1861, "Fort Leavenworth, Kansas Letter Book."

21. Letter dated Barnesville, September 9, 1861, *Leavenworth Daily Conservative*, September 17, 1861.

22. Ibid.; letter from Kansas, September 9, 1861, Lawrence *Kansas State Journal*, September 12, 1861.

23. Prince to Lane, September 9, 1861, *OR* Series II, 1:225.

24. Letter dated Barnesville, September 9, 1861, *Leavenworth Daily Conservative*, September 17, 1861.

25. Cutler, *History of the State of Kansas*, 1:669; "Personal Memoirs of Watson Stewart," 37; Lane to Prince, September 12, 1861, *OR* 3:490. Dr. George Lisle, who said he knew Mathews, stated Mathews was not present during the raid. Case, *History of Labette County, Kansas*, 22, 30.

26. High Private to Editor Republican, Lawrence *Republican*, September 26, 1861; "Personal Memoirs of Watson Stewart," 37. Augustus Wattles claimed he was with the expedition pursuing Mathews. According to Wattles Mathews was in the company of sixty men when found, and in the ensuing fight ten were killed. These numbers appear greatly inflated. Wattles also reported that on Mathews's body was found a commission from McCulloch authorizing him to enlist Indians to operate on the border. Wattles to Dole, September 25, 1861, in Abel, *The American Indian in the Civil War*, n109, 53–54.

27. High Private to Editor Republican, Lawrence *Republican*, September 26, 1861; Case, *History of Labette County, Kansas*, 22–23, 30. Mathews's trading post was located at present-day Oswego, Kansas.

28. "Personal Memoirs of Watson Stewart," 37–38; "Sketches of Early History," *Humboldt Union*, March 21, 1918; Cutler, *History of the State of Kansas*, 1:669, 2:1106.

29. *Military History of Kansas Regiments*, 119–20; Britton, *The Civil War on the Border*, 1:297. Two additional companies were raised and would join the Sixth by October. These were the companies of David Mefford and Charles F. Clarke.

30. Prince to Lane, September 9, 1861, *OR* 3:483; Berry to Prince, September 9, 1861, ibid., 483.

31. Prince to Lane, September 9, 1861, *OR* 3:483; Lane to Prince, September 10, 1861, ibid.; Lane to Prince, September 12, 1861, ibid., 490; Lane to Commandant of Post, September 14, 1861, ibid., 492–93; Lane to Prince, September 10, 1861, "James Henry Lane Letters." Both the Anderson County court clerk and

sheriff informed Judge Solon O. Thacher it was impossible to conduct court business because, on the solicitation of Lane, the citizens of Anderson—including lawyers, litigants, jurymen, and witnesses—had fled, en masse, to Fort Scott and the vicinity." Courts in the Franklin District," Lawrence *Republican,* September 12, 1861.

32. Trego to My Dear Wife, September 5, 1861, addendum dated September 12, 1861, in Langsdorf, "The Letters of Joseph H. Trego," 293–94; Trego diary, entry of September 13, 1861.

33. "Record of Events," William Creitz diary; Lane to Richy [*sic*], September 17, 1861, in Cory, "The Sixth Kansas Cavalry and Its Commander," 224.

34. Davis to Frémont, September 6, 1861, *OR* 3:472; Prince to Frémont, September 7, 1861, *OR* 3:475; letter from Maumee, September 4, 1861, *Leavenworth Daily Conservative,* September 13, 1861. The only casualty of the Shelbina fight was Captain James McClure of the Second Kansas Infantry, who had his leg taken off by a cannon ball. According to Maumee, Woodruff belonged to "Capt. Rose's Browning Rangers." The *Roll of the Officers and Enlisted Men* misidentified William Rose as William Bruce. See "Capt. Rose's Company," "Another Fight in Missouri," "A Skirmish at Osceola, Mo.," and "Major William Rose" in the Quincy, Illinois, *Daily Herald,* July 31, September 28, October 7, and November 30, 1861.

35. Frémont to Pope, September 6, 1861, *OR* 3:472–73; Frémont to Sturgis, September 6, 1861, *OR* 3:473–74.

36. Dickinson, "War Notes" and diary, entries of September 13, 14, 1861.

37. Lane to Commandant of Post, September 14, 1861, *OR* 3:492–93; Huntoon to My Loving Lizzie, September 17, 1861, Andrew Jackson Huntoon papers; Lane to Prince, September 16, 1861, "James Henry Lane Letters"; Lane to Prince, September 17, 1861, *OR* 3:498–99; Prince to —, September 15, 1861, "James Henry Lane Letters."

38. "To Commanders of Regiments Battalions Companies & Squads," September 17, 1861, "James Henry Lane Letters"; Dickinson, "War Notes" and diary, entry of September 17, 1861.

39. C.L.T. to Friend Shepherd, September 18, 1861, *Wabaunsee* (Kansas) *Patriot,* September 28, 1861; M. to Friend Speer, September 18, 1861, Lawrence *Republican,* September 26, 1861; X.Y. to Eds. Journal, September 18, 1861, Lawrence *Kansas State Journal,* September 26, 1861; "Record of Events," William Creitz diary; [Lions Club of Freeman, Missouri], *Freeman at 100,* 6–7, reprinting the *Cass County Democrat* of June 10, 1926; *History of Vernon County, Missouri,* 289. Copeland had only been with the regiment since August 30. Terrill soon died of pneumonia at Barnesville, Kansas, on February 25, 1862. Joseph Trego wrote before Johnson's death: "Col. Johnson was so wrought up that if he had had command at Dry-wood we would have all been killed or taken prisoners." Trego to My Dear Wife, September 5, 1861, addendum dated September 12, 1861, in Langsdorf, "The Letters of Joseph H. Trego," 294. Another trooper claimed Johnson was preparing to charge when Montgomery ordered the retreat. Drought, "James Montgomery," 343.

40. C.L.T. to Friend Shepherd, September 18, 1861, *Wabaunsee* (Kansas) *Patriot*, September 28, 1861; Porter, "Personal Reminiscences"; Trego diary, entry of September 18, 1861; obituary of John Edward Berry, *Cass County* (Missouri) *Democrat*, August 16, 1936; private communication from Chris Tabor of Butler, Missouri, to author, May 9, 2006. Moonlight claimed his cannon accompanied the cavalry charge and that after Johnson was killed, he, as the senior officer, took command and moved the men onto clear ground, where they opened up on the ravine with the howitzer and rifles. Lindberg and Matthews, "'The Eagle of the 11th Kansas,'" 11.

Daniel Chandler, hospital steward at the Mapleton hospital, was sent from that place on September 23 to care for the men wounded at Morristown. He identified three as being severely wounded: one shot in the back, one man with two buckshot in the face, and the third with a thigh wound. On September 28 he returned to Mapleton with fifteen sick and wounded in three ambulances. Chandler to Dear Friend [Rev. J. S. Brown], September 25, 1861, and addendum to same dated September 28, in John Stillman Brown Family papers.

41. "The Burning of Hampton," *Harper's Weekly*, August 31, 1861, 554; "March of Our Troops Down the Peninsula, and the Burning of Hampton," *Richmond* (Virginia) *Daily Dispatch*, August 12, 1861; "Delayed," Leavenworth *Daily Times*, October 2, 1861; Palmer, "The Black-flag Character of War on the Border," 456; Dickinson, "War Notes"; "Position of Lane and Sturgis," *New York Times*, October 13, 1861, p. 1, quoting the *Chicago Tribune* (daily), October 10, 1861.

Various accounts state the number of men captured was from five to ten. Two of the prisoners were released because of their youth; one account credits Montgomery with their release. [Lions Club of Freeman, Missouri], *Freeman at 100*, 6–7, reprinting the *Cass County Democrat* of June 10, 1926; Drought, "James Montgomery," 343.

42. Jarboe, "John Ritchie," 10, 15–20, 22–23, 27–29, 34–35, 61; Giles, *Thirty Years in Topeka*, 42, 52; *Kansas Constitutional Convention*, 76, 147, 181–82, 273, 298–99, 325, 514–15.

43. "Prominent Members of the Constitutional Convention," Leavenworth *Daily Times*, July 27, 1859.

44. Jarboe, "John Ritchie," 15–36, 61; "Slave Hunting," Topeka *Kansas Tribune*, November 7, 1855; Hinton, *John Brown and His Men*, 224.

45. Jarboe, "John Ritchie," 36–37; Giles, *Thirty Years in Topeka*, 52, 64–66; Topeka *Kansas State Record*, Extra edition, April 23, 1860.

46. "Record of Events," William Creitz diary.

47. Bryant to Dear Brother, May 9, 1861, in Murray and Rodney, "The Letters of Peter Bryant," 348; Creitz to Col. James Redpath, December 17, 1859, Richard Hinton collection, Box 1, Folder 10; "Col. Ritchey—Capt. Creitz," *Topeka Tribune*, December 28, 1861.

48. Bond to Dear Friend Roland, October 14, 1861, Rowland Mantor papers.

49. Lane to Richy [*sic*], Head Quarters, West Point, September 17, 1861, James Henry Lane papers; Lane to Prince, August 16, 1861, "James Henry Lane Letters." The *Roll of the Officers and Enlisted Men* dates Weer's muster as August 19.

50. "Proclamation of Gen. Lane," *Leavenworth Daily Conservative*, September 26, 1861; Lane's speech, ibid., October 5, 1861. A portion of Lane's proclamation was reprinted with apparent approval in the Canton (Ohio) *Stark County Republican*, November 6, 1861.

51. Drought, "James Montgomery," 342.

52. Trego diary, entry of September 13, 1861.

53. Letter from Sojer, July 20, 1861, *Leavenworth Daily Conservative*, July 25, 1861; Rover to Editor Times, Leavenworth *Daily Times*, July 16, 1861; N to Friend X, Lawrence *Kansas State Journal*, July 18, 1861; M. to Friend Speer, September 30, 1861, Lawrence *Republican*, October 3, 1861. Only about half of the Kansas men were horsewhipped, as darkness cut the ceremony short. By November the First Kansas had resumed foraging; Captain Job Stockton of Company G wrote a humorous piece regarding the regiment. Among other claims, he said of the soldier of the First: "No sooner hath he passed the sentry's beat than he striketh a 'bee-line' for the nearest hen roost, and seizing a pair of plump pullets, returneth, soliloquizing to himself: 'The noise of a goose saved Rome; how much more the flesh of chicken preserveth the soldier.'" Leavenworth *Daily Times*, November 23, 1861.

54. "Position of Land and Sturgis," *New York Times*, October 13, 1861, p. 1, quoting the October 10, 1861, *Chicago Tribune*.

55. Trego to My Dear Wife, September 25, 1861, and Trego to My Dear Little Wife, November 12, 1861, addendum of November 20, 1861, in Langsdorf, "The Letters of Joseph H. Trego," 295, 298–300.

56. Halpine to Halleck, March 14, 1862, *OR* 8:615–17.

57. Prince to Lane, September 17, 1861, "Fort Leavenworth, Kansas Letter Book"; Frémont to Lane, September 18, 1861, and Frémont to Sturgis, September 18, 1861, *OR* 3:500.

58. Frémont to Lane, September 20, 1861, *OR* 3:181; Prince to Lane, September 20, 1861, *OR* 3:181–82; M. to Friend Speer, September 25, 1861, Lawrence *Republican*, October 3, 1861; Drought, "James Montgomery," 343; Dickinson, "War Notes" and diary, entry of September 21, 1861.

Dickinson recorded that two men of Foreman's company had been given a furlough at Papinsville and captured and executed by rebels. The *Roll of the Officers and Enlisted Men* only documents one such death, that being William Vance, of "Papesville," Missouri, killed by guerillas on September 18 in Bates County. Dickinson, "War Notes" and diary, entry of September 21, 1861.

59. The primary sources for this and the subsequent paragraphs in chapter 5 relating to Osceola are: letter from H.D.L. dated September 27, 1861 in Moore, *Rebellion Record*, 149–50; Weidemeyer, "Memoirs of a Confederate Soldier"; M. to Friend Speer, Lawrence *Republican*, October 3, 1861; letter from Kansas, September 23, 1861, Lawrence *Kansas State Journal*, September 26, 1861; "Record of Events," William Creitz diary; "The Raid of Osceola, September 21,1861," *Memphis Daily Appeal*, April 13, 1862, p. 1; William T. Johnson memoir; Lewis, "Kansas Jayhawker's

Raid Upon Osceola, October, 1861," 54–55; Trego diary, entry of September 25, 1861; Creitz, "History of Company 'A' Fifth Kansas Cavalry Volunteers."

60. William T. Johnson memoir.

61. Ibid.

62. Connelley, *Quantrill and the Border Wars*, n2, 199–200. Connelley attributed this story to a conversation he had with Cyrus Leland. Moonlight also claimed to have fired twelve shells into the courthouse. Lindberg and Matthews, "'The Eagle of the 11th Kansas,'" 11.

63. "News from the West," *Chicago Tribune* (weekly), October 10, 1861, p. 1; Palmer, "The Black-flag Character of War on the Border," 457; "The Raid of Osceola, September 21, 1861," *Memphis Daily Appeal*, April 13, 1862, p. 1; Drought, "James Montgomery," 343; letter from H.D.L., in Moore, *Rebellion Record*, 150.

64. Letter from Galway, October 27, 1861, *New York Times*, November 9, 1861, p. 2.

65. The two most likely candidates to have possessed any wealth were R. C. Vaughan (not *Vaughn*), age twenty-four, a tinner (or tanner), who owned $7,400 in personal property, and George M. Vaughan, age twenty-four, a druggist, with personal property valued at $150.

66. Castel, "Kansas Jayhawking Raids" 1–11; Castel, *A Frontier State at War*, 54; Goodrich, *Black Flag*, 18, 51; Goodrich, *Bloody Dawn*, 48, 59; Fisher, *The Gun and the Gospel*, 164–65; "Funeral of Col. H. P. Johnson," Leavenworth *Daily Times*, September 21, 1861; "The Funeral of Colonel Johnson," *Leavenworth Daily Conservative*, September 21, 1861; Leslie, *The Devil Knows How to Ride*, 92–93.

Fisher announced Johnson's funeral in the September 20 editions of the *Daily Times* and the *Daily Conservative*, and in these papers the First Regiment Kansas State Militia was ordered to assemble for the funeral procession. The day of the funeral, the militia was augmented by the Volunteers of the Second Kansas Infantry.

67. "The Raid on Osceola, September 21, 1861," *Memphis Daily Appeal*, April 13, 1862, p. 1.

68. M. to Friend Speer, September 25, 1861, Lawrence *Republican*, October 3, 1861; "The Raid on Osceola, September 21, 1861," *Memphis Daily Appeal*, April 13, 1862.

Chaplain Moore ("M.") was the author of the quoted phrase ("it was traitorous to the core . . . ") that supposedly justified the burning of the town. In a subsequent letter to the *Missouri Democrat*, he added another justification: "We hoped to draw the enemy back from the Missouri River upon us, and give the rebels generally the benefits of the terror of our arms." This letter contained the misrepresentation that only the business portion of the town was put to the torch. "Additional from Kansas City," *New York Times*, October 14, 1861, p. 1.

69. Goodrich, *Black Flag*, 16, 18; Leslie, *The Devil Knows How to Ride*, 93. Although slaves were not individually enumerated in the census, St. Clair County as a whole had 278 slaves in 1860. *Population of the United States in 1860*, 297. This source does not separate the population of the town of Osceola from Osceola township. The latter population was given at 1,794, which appears to be whites only.

70. M. to Friend Speer, September 25, 1861, Lawrence *Republican*, October 3, 1861; Weidemeyer, "Memoirs of a Confederate Soldier," 64–65.

71. M. to Friend Speer, September 25, 1861, Lawrence *Republican*, October 3, 1861; Dickinson, "War Notes" and diary, entry of September 22, 1861; Frémont's Proclamation, August 30, 1861; Lincoln to Frémont, September 2, 1861; Frémont to the President, September 8, 1861; Lincoln to Frémont, September 11, 1861; *OR* 3:466–67, 469–70, 477–78, 485–86.

Chaplain Moore wrote that on the return march, Lane carried his proclamation ("To the People of Western Missouri") and distributed copies among the people. M. to Friend Speer, September 25, 1861, Lawrence *Republican*, October 3, 1861.

72. Dickinson, "War Notes."

73. M. to Friend Speer, September 25, 1861, Lawrence *Republican*, October 3, 1861; Dickinson diary entry for September 25, 1861; letter from H.D.L., in Moore, *Rebellion Record*, 150.

74. Dickinson, "War Notes" and diary, entry of September 26, 1861; Trego diary, entry for September 25, 1861.

75. Chandler to Dear Friend [Rev. J. S. Brown], September 25, 1861, addendum dated September 28, in John Stillman Brown Family papers; Britton, *The Civil War on the Border*, 1:148; Dickinson diary, entry of September 22, 1861; letter from H.D.L., in Moore, *Rebellion Record*, 150.

76. Lane to Frémont, September 24, 1861, *OR* 3:196, 504; Plumly to Scott, October 3, 1961, ibid., 516–17.

77. Letter from Galway, October 27, 1861, *New York Times*, November 9, 1861, p. 2.

78. Paludan, "The Better Angels of Our Nature," 5–6.

Chapter 6. Frémont's Grand Army

1. Lane to Frémont, September 25, 1861, "James Henry Lane Letters": Lane to Frémont, September 24, 1861, *OR* 3:505–506. On October 4, at Kansas City, Captain Thomas Bickerton obtained from the Kansas militia a cannon known as the Topeka Gun. It was described as a four- or six-pound brass piece that had been purchased by the Scott Club of Milwaukee, Wisconsin, and christened "Liberty." Presumably this had been provided to Free State forces during the territorial strife. Receipt, dated October 4, 1861, in History/Cannon/Topeka collection, KSHS; John B. Coffin to F. G. Adams, December 21, 1879, ibid.

2. Prince to Lane, September 23, 1861, *OR* 3:184; Prince to Gen'l, September 23, 1861, James Lane collection, Box 1, Folder 7, Spencer Research Library; Prince to Lane, October 8, 1861, "Fort Leavenworth, Kansas Letter Book."

3. Starr, *Jennison's Jayhawkers*, 80; Dickinson, "War Notes" and diary, entry of September 30, 1861; unsigned letter dated Kansas City, October 2, 1861, Leavenworth (weekly) *Conservative*, October 10, 1861.

4. Anthony to Dear Brother, October 1, 1861, in Langsdorf and Richmond, "Letters of Daniel R. Anthony," 351–70; letter from Epaphroditus, October 8,

1861, *Leavenworth Daily Conservative,* October 11, 1861; Trego to My Dear Wife, October 2, 1861, in Langsdorf, "The Letters of Joseph H. Trego," 296; letter dated Kansas City, September 30, 1861, Leavenworth (weekly) *Conservative,* October 10, 1861; Starr, *Jennison's Jayhawkers,* 81.

On October 10 Anthony took a steamboat to Parkville where he and his men captured the town by surprise and arrested a number of civilians, some fourteen of whom were released by Prince later that month. Letter from Epaphroditus, October 11, 1861, *Leavenworth Daily Conservative,* October 13, 1861; Moore diary, entry of October 12, 1861; "From Kansas," *Chicago Tribune* (daily), October 31, 1861, p. 1.

5. "Demagogery," Lawrence *Republican,* October 3, 1861; Trego to My Dear Wife, October 2, 1861, in Langsdorf, "The Letters of Joseph H. Trego," 297; Dickinson, "War Notes" and diary, entry of October 2, 1861; Huntoon to My Dearly Beloved Wife & Boy, October 13, 1861, Andrew Jackson Huntoon papers; Starr, *Jennison's Jayhawkers,* 81.

The hospital had been moved to Mapleton in late September, under the supervision of brigade surgeon Rufus Gilpatrick. Among the patients were two men injured in fights, one stabbed in the back, and the other hit over the head with a spade. Hospital steward Daniel Chandler recorded that the man hit with the spade died of inflammation of the brain, and his assailant was at large. Chandler to Dear Friend [Rev. J. S. Brown], September 25, 1861, in John Stillman Brown Family papers. Another man had a finger shot off accidentally.

6. Dickinson, "War Notes" and diary, entries of October 2, 4, 1861.

7. Ibid., October 5, 6, 9, 1861.

8. Ibid., October, 8, 1861.

9. Moore diary, entry of October 2, 1861; "Rough on Secesh," *Leavenworth Daily Conservative,* October 11, 1861.

10. Letter from Epaphroditus, October 8, 1861, *Leavenworth Daily Conservative,* October 11, 1861; Moore diary, entries of October 2, 5, 9, 10, 1861; Trego diary, entry of October 3, 1861; Dickinson, "War Notes" and diary, entries of October 5, 7, 1861; *Roll of the Officers and Enlisted Men of the Third, Fourth, Eighteenth, and Nineteenth Kansas Volunteers,* 47.

11. Letter from J.[F.]V. to Ed. Times, October 3, 1861, Leavenworth *Daily Times,* October 5, 1861; Lane to Frémont, October 3, 1861, *OR* 3:515–16; "Position of Lane and Sturgis," *New York Times,* October 13, 1861, p. 1, quoting the *Chicago Tribune,* October 10, 1861.

12. Lane to Frémont, October 3, 1861, *OR* 3:515–16; Lane to Sturgis, October 3, 1861, ibid., 516.

13. Lane to Sturgis, October 3, 1861, *OR* 3:516; Trego to My Dear Wife, October 2, 1861, in Langsdorf, "The Letters of Joseph H. Trego," 296; letter from M., October 10, 1861, Lawrence *Republican,* October 17, 1861; Trego diary, entry of October 16, 1861.

14. Frémont to Sturgis, September 29, 1861, *OR* 3:521; Sturgis to Lane, October 4, 1861; *OR* 3:520; Lane to Sturgis, October 4, 1861; *OR* 3:521; "General Blunt's Account of His Civil War Experiences," 215; Moore diary, entry of October 5, 1861; Trego diary, entries of October 6, 7, 1861.

15. Eaton to Lane and Sturgis, October 6, 1861, *OR* 3:522.

16. Letter from Epaphroditus, October 8, 1861, *Leavenworth Daily Conservative*, October 11, 1861.

17. *Leavenworth Daily Conservative*, October 9, 1861. The speech was also fully reported in the *New York Tribune* (semi-weekly), October 21, 1861, p. 3, and slightly different versions in "Meeting at Stockton's Hall," Leavenworth *Daily Times*, October 9, 1861, and "Jim Lane's Speech in Kansas," Richmond (Virginia) *Daily Dispatch*, October 30, 1861.

18. Letter from H.D.F., October 11, 1861, *Leavenworth Daily Conservative*, October 12, 1861; Dickinson, "War Notes" and diary, entry of October 11, 1861.

19. "Letter from Gov. Robinson," Leavenworth *Daily Times*, October 13, 1861; "The Soldiers of Kansas Brand Gov. Robinson as a Base Slanderer, a Traitor, and a Coward," *Leavenworth Daily Conservative*, October 18, 1861.

20. Lane to Lincoln, October 9, 1861, *OR* 3:529–30.

21. Robinson to Lincoln, October 10, 1861, Abraham Lincoln papers.

22. Coffin and Delahay to Lincoln, October 21, 1861, Abraham Lincoln papers.

23. Castel, *A Frontier State at War*, 68–70, 71–77.

24. Offley to Bowman, October 10, 1861, Charles S. Bowman papers, Box 1, "Correspondence of Special Interest." Rose and his company were in Quincy, Illinois, and Canton, Missouri, the preceding August. Letter from Maumee, August 18, 1861, *Leavenworth Daily Conservative*, August 22, 1861; Leavenworth *Daily Times*, August 18, 1861, quoting the St. Louis *Democrat*. These sources described Rose as an "old Mexican soldier" and "ex-constable, ex-Benedict" who "has distinguished himself in two battles over in Missouri within the last ten days." Prince noted Rose's appearance on August 31, and on September 4 he wrote he had dispatched Rose's company to report to Lane, and an ammunition wagon for Montgomery was being escorted by Captain Rose. Prince to Lane, August 31 and September 4, 1861, "Fort Leavenworth, Kansas Letter Book."

25. McKeever to McKinstry, September 24, 1861, *OR* 3:504.

26. M. to Friend Speer, October 14, 1861, Lawrence *Republican*, October 17, 1861.

27. Trego diary, entry of October 14, 1861.

28. "Record of Events," William Creitz diary; Sam Slick to Ed. Times, October 22, 1861, Leavenworth *Daily Times*, November 6, 1861.

29. M. to Friend Speer, October 28, 1861, Lawrence *Republican*, November 7, 1861.

30. Moore diary, entry of October 16–17, 1861.

31. Ibid., October 18, 20, 1861.

32. Halpine to Weed, October 17, 1861, Abraham Lincoln papers; General Orders no. 23, Headquarters Western Department, October 20, 1861, *OR* 3:539–40.

33. Moore diary, entry of October 15, 1861; Nichols and Hauptman, "Warriors for the Union," 34–41; Statement of William P. Chandler, in the *Leavenworth Daily Conservative*, October 29, 1861; "Southern Kansas," *New York Times*, November 8, 1861, quoting the Leavenworth (weekly) *Conservative* of October 30, 1861; letter from Galway, October 27, 1861, ibid., November 9, 1861, p. 2.

34. Sam Slick to Ed. Times, October 22, 1861, Leavenworth *Daily Times*, November 6, 1861; Trego diary, entry of October 16, 1861; C. to Mr. Beal, November 6, 1861, in Patrick, "Reporting from an Enemy's Land," 328–29; Speer, *Life of Gen. James H. Lane*, 329. W. H. H. Dickinson noted that at Pleasant Hill, he "saw more handsome women" than he had seen since leaving Ohio. Dickinson, "War Notes" and diary, entry of October 17, 1861.

35. Sam Slick to Ed. Times, October 22, 1861, Leavenworth *Daily Times*, November 6, 1861.

36. Trego diary, entry of October 19, 1861; M. to Friend Speer, October 24, 1861, Lawrence *Republican*, December 7, 1861.

37. "The Raid of Osceola, September 21,1861," *Memphis Daily Appeal*, April 13, 1862, p. 1; "Generals Lane and Sturgis—Their Policies Compared," *Chicago Tribune* (daily), November 1, 1861, p. 2. Lieutenant Johnson was described as "scarcely advanced to manhood—so young and yet so old in wickedness. He belongs to a good family in Indiana, and his brother-in-law, who was evidently ashamed of his conduct, said he was astonished at his rapid march in evil, and acknowledged that he would 'not only steal, but lie about it afterward.'"

38. Dickinson, "War Notes" and diary, entry of October 21, 1861.

39. M. to Friend Speer, October 24, 1861, Lawrence *Republican*, December 7, 1861; Moore diary, entry of October 21, 1861.

40. Trego to My Dear Wife, October 28, 1861, in Langsdorf, "The Letters of Joseph H. Trego," 297–98; Trego diary, entry of October 23, 1861.

41. "The Raid of Osceola, September 21,1861," *Memphis Daily Appeal*, April 13, 1862, p. 1.

42. "Generals Lane and Sturgis—Their Policies Compared," *Chicago Tribune* (daily), November 1, 1861, p. 2.

43. Uncaptioned story, Canton (Ohio) *Stark County Republican*, December 25, 1861.

44. Moore diary, entry of October 23, 1861; Trego to My Dear Wife, October 28, 1861, in Langsdorf, "The Letters of Joseph H. Trego," 297; statement of correspondent of the *New York Times*, in the Leavenworth *Daily Times*, November 16, 1861; statement of William P. Chandler, in the *Leavenworth Daily Conservative*, October 29, 1861.

45. Welch, *Border Warfare*, 33–34, 39, 43–44, 51, 58–59, 124–27, 201; "Certificate of Enlistment of U.S. Soldiers in O. P. Bayne's Company, Camp near Mound

City, December 12, 1861," Papers Relating to Individual Units—Third Kansas Infantry, Box 2, Folder 15; R. to Mr. Speer, November 10, 1861, Lawrence *Republican*, November 14, 1861.

"R" apparently thought little of Bayne's men: "I forbear to comment on the general character and conduct of the men under Capt. Bayne at *this time*." The "Certificate of Enlistment," signed by Bayne and Montgomery, claimed the company had been mustered into the U.S. service. As it also gave the section and range of where each man lived, it appears that this was executed to claim some sort of a land bounty. It was claimed in the fall of 1861, when Bayne's company went into Missouri and captured a number of secesh, seven of whom Bayne executed, allegedly for their having been part of the 1858 Marais des Cygnes massacre of five Free State men. Robley, *History of Bourbon County*, 176–77.

46. Dickinson, "War Notes" and diary, entry of October 15, 1861; M. to Friend Speer, October 24, 1861, Lawrence *Republican*, December 7, 1861.

47. Eaton to Lane, October 24, 1861, *OR* 3:554; letter from Galway, October 27, 1861, *New York Times*, November 9, 1861, p. 2; A. T. Ward to My Dear Sister, October 27, 1861, A. T. Ward papers; A. to Messrs. Editors, November 3, 1861, Lawrence *Kansas State Journal*, November 14, 1861; "Record of Events," William Creitz diary; Trego to My Dear Wife, October 28, 1861, in Langsdorf, "The Letters of Joseph H. Trego," 297; Moore diary, entries of October 24–27, 1861.

48. "General Blunt's Account of His Civil War Experiences," 216.

49. Letter from Galway, October 27, 1861, *New York Times*, November 9, 1861, p. 2. Excerpts were also printed in "Gen. Lane and His Army," *Harper's Weekly*, November 23, 1861, p. 738, and the Leavenworth *Daily Times*, November 16, 1861.

50. Moore diary, entries of October 4, 28, 1861. Dickinson attributed the arrest order to Sturgis. Moore would have been in a better position to divine the source of the order. Dickinson wrote on October 27, "[Sturgis] made a speech to the guards last night & I had a good chance to see him. He has given every rebel a voucher for every chicken duck hog sheep horse slave & every thing we have taken since leaving Kansas City." Dickinson, "War Notes."

51. Weer to Prince, October 29, 1861, Charles S. Bowman papers, Box 1, "Miscellaneous Papers June 1861–March 1862."

52. Dickinson, "War Notes.

53. Eaton to Hunter, October 30, 31, 1861, *OR* 3:557–58; Dorsheimer, "Frémont's Hundred Days in Missouri," 377.

54. Letter from Galway, October 27, 1861, *New York Times*, November 9, 1861, p. 2.

55. "General James H. Lane," *Chicago Tribune* (daily), October 22, 1861, p. 2; "What Gen. Lane is Doing," Lawrence *Republican*, November 7, 1861; letter dated Camp Lyon, Springfield, Missouri, November 2, 1861, *New York Tribune* (semi-weekly), November 15, 1861, p. 6.

56. "Speech of General James H. Lane," *Leavenworth Daily Conservative*, January 29, 1862; "Our Kansas Letter," *Chicago Tribune* (daily), February 5, 1862, p. 2;

"Gen. Lane's Speech," *Tipton* (Iowa) *Advertiser,* February 13, 1862; "The Campaign in Kansas," *New York Times,* December 27, 1861, p. 2.

57. Bryant to Dear Brother, May 9, September 1 and October 13, 1861, in Murray and Rodney, "The Letters of Peter Bryant," 348–51.

58. Ward to My Dear Sister, October 27, 1861, A. T. Ward papers.

59. Cutler, *History of the State of Kansas,* 1:669; "Personal Memoirs of Watson Stewart," pp. 38–39; Watson Stewart, "Sketches of Early History," *Humboldt Union,* March 21, 1918; Blair, *The History of Johnson County,* 140–43; "Retaliation Once More!" Lawrence *Kansas State Journal,* October 24, 1861.

60. E. to Editor Republican, October 31, 1861, Lawrence *Republican,* November 7, 1861; Bowman to Halpine, January 20, 1862, Charles S. Bowman papers, Box 1, "Muster Orders June 1861–Sept 1862"; Hollister to Halpine, ibid., February 4, 1862; R. to Mr. Speer, November 10, 1861, Lawrence *Republican,* November 14, 1861.

61. R. to Mr. Speer, November 10, 1861, Lawrence *Republican,* November 14, 1861.

62. Huntoon to wife, October 6, 13, 20, 31, 1861, Andrew Jackson Huntoon papers.

Chapter 7. Lane the Liberator

1. Cameron to Dear Sir [Lincoln], October 14, 1861, Abraham Lincoln papers; Monaghan, *Civil War on the Western Border,* 199–200; Lincoln to Curtis, October 24, 1861, *OR* 3:553.

2. Frémont, "In Command in Missouri," 286; Lane to Colonels of Regiments and Commandants of Battalions & Companies, November 2, 1861, "Records Relating to Individual Units—Fifth Kansas Cavalry," Box 2, Folder 17.

3. Basler, *The Collected Works of Abraham Lincoln,* 4:562–63; General Orders no. 18, October 24, 1861, *OR* 3:553; General Orders no. 28, November 2, 1861, ibid., 559.

4. A. to Messrs. Editors, [November] 3, 1861, November 14, 1861, *Kansas State Journal.* William Dorsheimer recorded, "General McKinstry designed to make a reconnoissance in force with his whole division towards Wilson's Creek; but yielding to the solicitations of the chief officers, and in view of the imminence of battle, to-day General Frémont resumed the command, and ordered McKinstry not to make his reconnoissance." Dorsheimer, "Frémont's Hundred Days in Missouri," 380.

5. Frémont, "In Command in Missouri," 287–88. The Delaware refused to serve under anyone but Frémont, who subsequently discharged them from the service at Sedalia. Fall Leaf would go on to raise Company D of the loyal Second Indian Home Guard regiment, and later serve as scout under Blunt. Nichols and Hauptman, "Warriors for the Union," 34–41.

6. Dickinson, "War Notes" and diary, entry of October 6, 1861.

7. Moore diary, entry of November 5, 1861; letter from Galway, November 6, 1861, *New York Times*, November 14, 1861, p. 3. Galway greatly exaggerated Ritchie's strength as a thousand men.

8. M. to Friend Speer, November 8, 1861, Lawrence *Republican*, November 21, 1861.

9. Ibid.; "Gen. Lane's Speech," *Leavenworth Daily Conservative*, November 17, 1861. Lane's speech was also fully reported in the *New York Tribune* (semi-weekly), November 19, 1861, p. 8, and the *Chicago Tribune* (daily), November 18, 1861, p. 2.

10. M. to Friend Speer, November 8, 1861, Lawrence *Republican*, November 21, 1861.
Lane's speech to the Twenty-fourth Indiana Regiment was given from the balcony of his new headquarters, the home of a Major Berry. The major and three of his sons were away serving in the rebel army, while the ladies of his family remained in the home, forced to share it with the despised Lane. The ladies left the building to listen to Lane's speech, but on reentering afterward "were astounded to find that all the negroes in the family (five) had embraced the opportunity afforded by their brief absence to run away!...Yesterday morning the ladies were reduced to the melancholy necessity of preparing their own breakfast! During the day they were searching diligently through Lane's camp for their evanescent chattels, but not, I think, with very brilliant prospects of success." Judge Advocate Moore claimed the blacks did not so much run away as were taken by the "boys," and as a result Lane got no breakfast the following day. Letter dated Camp Lyon, Springfield, Missouri, November 9, 1861, *New York Tribune* (semi-weekly), November 19, 1861, p. 1; Moore diary, entries of November 7, 8, 1861.

11. Letter dated Washington, December 2, 1861, *New York Tribune* (semi-weekly), December 3, 1861, p. 4.

12. *Congressional Globe*, 37th Congress, 1st sess., 190. In a speech in Chicago on January 22, Lane proposed resettling former slaves on the Gulf Coast under paternalistic government supervision, thus preventing any competition between white and black labor. "Gen. Lane on His Way Westward," *New York Times*, January 29, 1862, p. 3.

13. "From Kansas," *Chicago Tribune* (daily), November 9, 1861, p. 2, quoting the Missouri *Democrat*; "From Kansas," ibid., November 1, 1861, p. 1.

14. Castel, "Civil War Kansas and the Negro," 126; Berwanger, *The Frontier Against Slavery*, 22–23, 32–34, 43–45, 106–17.

15. "Contraband Schools," *Leavenworth Daily Conservative*, January 5, 1862.

16. Blanton to Messrs. Editors, October 22, 1855, Lawrence *Kansas Free State*, October 29, 1855; "Journal of the Leavenworth Constitutional Convention," April 1, 1858.

17. *Kansas Constitutional Convention*, 121, 147, 176–78, 181–82, 193, 277, 294, 298, 301.

18. Statement of H. D. Fisher, *Leavenworth Daily Conservative*, November 21, 1861; "The Contrabands," Leavenworth *Daily Times*, December 22, 1861.

19. "Affairs in Kansas," *New York Times*, November 11, 1861, p. 3; untitled article, Leavenworth *Daily Times*, December 22, 1861.

20. Wood to Stearns, November 19, 1861, George Luther Stearns papers; "Contraband Schools," *Leavenworth Daily Conservative*, January 5, 1862; "What's To Be Done with Them?" Leavenworth *Daily Times*, December 21, 1861.

21. M. to Friend Speer, December 6, 1861, Lawrence *Republican*, December 12, 1861. In February 1862, to provide employment for the escaped slaves, the newly formed Kansas Emancipation League in Leavenworth offered to assist employers "in want of Colored help, male and female, farm laborers, teamsters, house servants, hotel waiters, porters, cooks, chambermaids &c." It is unknown how successful this program was. "Labor Exchange" advertisement, *Leavenworth Daily Conservative*, February 13, 1862.

22. "Excluding Slaves," Lawrence *Republican*, February 6, 1862.

23. Ibid.

24. "Contraband," Leavenworth *Daily Times*, December 31, 1861; Lincoln to the Commander of the Department of the West, October 24, 1861, *OR* 3:553–54.

25. "A Question," Leavenworth *Daily Times*, December 22, 1861.

26. Wright to wife, November 25, 1861, Clark Wright papers; "Resolution Presented to General Halleck by Union Loyalists in Southwest Missouri," November 20 (about), 1861, *OR* 8:370–71. Among the petitioners to Halleck was Nathan Bray of Barton County, who was mentioned in a previous chapter as leading a company of Unionists.

27. Moore diary, entry of November 9, 1861; "Neugent's Regiment Again," Leavenworth *Daily Times*, January 17, 1862; H. H. Moore to Friend Speer, November 19, 1861, Lawrence *Republican*, November 21, 1861; "John Brown. A Lecture Delivered in Topeka in 1893 By J. K. Hudson," Joseph Kennedy Hudson papers, Miscellaneous Material folder.

28. H. H. Moore to Friend Speer, November 19, 1861, Lawrence *Republican*, November 21, 1861.

29. The story of the Black Brigade is taken from these sources: H. H. Moore to Friend Speer, November 19, 1861, Lawrence *Republican*, November 21, 1861; statement of H. D. Fisher, *Leavenworth Daily Conservative*, November 21, 1861; Fisher, *The Gun and the Gospel*, 166–67; "John Brown. A Lecture Delivered in Topeka in 1893 By J. K. Hudson," Joseph Kennedy Hudson papers, Miscellaneous Material folder.

30. H. H. Moore to Friend Speer, November 19, 1861, Lawrence *Republican*, November 21, 1861; statement of H. D. Fisher, *Leavenworth Daily Conservative*, November 21, 1861; Fisher, *The Gun and the Gospel*, 166–67.

31. Dickinson, "War Notes. Dickinson identified three of the recruits: Charley Bonsall, Sam Hudson, and W. Sharpnack.

32. Moore diary, entry of November 14, 1861; Cutler, *History of the State of Kansas*, 1:669; "Record of Events," William Creitz diary; Trego diary, entry of November 15, 1861; General Orders no. 1, Headquarters Department of the

Missouri, November 19, 1861, *OR* 8:369, 370; letter from H.J., December 1, 1861, *New York Times*, December 17, 1861, p. 3.

In a move evidently inspired by Lane, Representative Mark Delahay wrote to Lincoln, alleging that Robinson was a traitor. Ostensibly the purpose of the letter was to request that the governor be deprived of any authority to organize the regiments being raised for service in New Mexico. Delahay suggested that Hunter was a man better suited for the task, one who enjoyed their confidence and respect. Delahay to Lincoln, November 30, 1861, Charles and Sara Robinson papers.

Among Hunter's first acts was to ask Washington for "authority to muster into the service a Brigade of Kansas Indians to assist the Creeks Seminoles & Chickawas [sic] [in the Indian Territory] in adhering to their loyalty." He did not receive permission. Hunter to Lorenzo Thomas, November 27, 1861, Abraham Lincoln papers.

Napoleon Blanton's company received reinforcements with the transfer on November 26 of eighteen men from Henry Dudley's company and twelve from Dr. George A. Miller's company. These were the militia companies that had been raised in Humboldt following the sack of that town September 8. *Roll of the Officers and Enlisted Men of the Third, Fourth, Eighteenth, and Nineteenth Kansas Volunteers*, 83–86.

Captain Miller was mustered August 28, 1862, as assistant surgeon of the Tenth Kansas Infantry.

33. Letter from Brigade, November 25, 1861, *Chicago Tribune* (daily), November 27, 1861, p. 2; "Movements of Gen. Lane," *New York Times*, November 28, 1861, p. 1; "Gen. Lane in Boston," ibid., November 29, 1861, p. 1; untitled article, Leavenworth *Daily Times*, November 26, 1861.

34. Trego diary, entry of November 23, 1861; E. E. Harvey to Montgomery, December 1, 1861, James Montgomery collection; Trego to My Dear Little Wife, November 12, 1861, addendum of November 18, in Langsdorf, "The Letters of Joseph H. Trego," 298–99.

35. "Artillery for Lane's Brigade," Leavenworth *Daily Times*, October 11, 1861; "The Gibbon Battery," ibid., October 15, 1861; Moore diary, entry of November 15, 1861; Lindberg and Matthews, "'The Eagle of the 11th Kansas,'" 14–17; letter from H.J., December 1, 1861, *New York Times*, December 17, 1861, p. 8; "Capt. Moonlight's Letter to Oldham," *Leavenworth Daily Conservative*, December 3, 1861. Gordon's men audaciously stopped and robbed the train again the following night. Letter from H.J., December 1, 1861, *New York Times*, December 17, 1861, p. 8.

36. "Escape of Capt. Moonlight," Leavenworth *Daily Times*, December 3, 1861; Kelton to Commanding Officer, Camp Chase, Ohio, June 5, 1862, *OR* Series III, 3:653.

37. "How the Rebels in Missouri Are Treated," *New York Times*, December 15, 1861, p. 2; *Chicago Tribune* (daily), December 11, 1861, p. 2; Moore diary, entry of December 1, 1861.

38. "Linn County Pillaged by Rebels," Lawrence *Republican*, November 7, 1861, quoting the Leavenworth *Conservative*; "Invasion of Southern Kansas!" Leavenworth

Daily Times, November 5, 1861, quoting the *Osawatomie Herald*; Cutler, *History of the State of Kansas*, 2:1106; "From Kansas," *Chicago Tribune* (daily), November 10, 1861, p. 1.; "More Troubles in Linn County," Leavenworth *Daily Times*, November 17, 1861; Samuel Reader to My Dear Brother Frank, December 1, 1861, "Letters of Samuel James Reader," 49–50.

The brigade in late September had been credited with killing the "notorious" Locke; it is unknown if the two were one and the same.

39. "Fight at Big Creek, Cass Co., Mo.," Lawrence *Republican*, November 7, 1861; Trego to My Dear Little Wife, November 12, 1861, addendum of November 18, in Langsdorf, "The Letters of Joseph H. Trego," 298–99.

The roster of Trego's company (Captain Henry Seaman, Third regiment) suggests two possibilities for the dead man mentioned by Trego: Albert or Harmon Stockham. Both were of Mound City, and both had enlisted in July and had been discharged for disability upon the order of Montgomery on August 31 and September 17, respectively.

40. "A Lick at Jayhawkers," Leavenworth *Daily Times*, November 24, 1861, quoting the *Osawatomie Herald*; letter from Kansas, December 2, 1861, Lawrence *Kansas State Journal*, December 5, 1861; "From Linn County," Leavenworth *Daily Times*, December 7, 1861; "From Southern Kansas," Leavenworth *Daily Times*, December 10, 1861. The missing men were identified as Manard, Hart, and Barr, all from Mound City. Trego wrote of a similar, and possibly the same, raid. He described a party of seventy-five Kansans who "gathered up a lot of stock and several wagonloads of plunder, a load or two of salt." He named Baine Corbins, Jim Manor, and By Hildreth as among the Kansas dead. Trego to My Dear Little Wife, November 12, 1861, addendum of November 18, in Langsdorf, "The Letters of Joseph H. Trego," 298–99. However, "From Southern Kansas" recounted that By Hildreth arrived in Mound City on November 30 from Leavenworth with a load of liquor for his saloon.

41. Ritchie to Montgomery, November 24, 1861, and Montgomery to Ritchie, November 29, 1861, "Records Relating to Individual Units—Fifth Kansas Cavalry," Box 2, Folder 17; "Record of Events," William Creitz diary. Ritchie's letter mentioned his men "reported five or six houses burned." It is impossible to discern whether this means they burned the houses or found them burned.

42. Trego diary, entry of November 23, 1861; letter from Kansas, December 2, 1861, Lawrence *Kansas State Journal*, December 5, 1861; Montgomery to Ritchie, November 29, 1861, "Records Relating to Individual Units—Fifth Kansas Cavalry," Box 2, Folder 17. Ritchie advised Montgomery in a letter dated November 29 he would draw rations for six days and then move together with Moonlight's howitzer. "Records Relating to Individual Units—Fifth Kansas Cavalry," Box 2, Folder 17.

43. Price to Polk, December 23, 1861, *OR* 8:729–30.

44. "Proclamation to the People of Central and North Missouri," November 26, 1861, *OR* 8:695–97. This also appeared in the *New York Times*, December 1, 1861, p. 1, and the *Chicago Tribune* (daily), December 1, 1861, p. 1.

Chapter 8. Visitations of Mercy

1. Letter from Jack, December 4, 1861, *Leavenworth Daily Conservative*, December 7, 1861; "The Rebels Threaten Kansas," *New York Times*, December 18, 1861, p. 6; Thrasher diary entries of December 3, 6, 12, 18, 1861.

2. E. E. Harvey to Montgomery, December 1, 1861, James Montgomery collection; Flanders to Dear Brother, December 3, 1861, in Swenson, *Civil War Letters Written by George Edwin Flanders*, 1: 1.

3. Thrasher diary, entry of December 3, 1861; uncaptioned story, *Leavenworth Daily Conservative*, December 7, 1861; *Ashtabula* (Ohio) *Weekly Telegram*, January 18, 1862. Allen was mustered out on February 13, 1862; when the Third Kansas was disbanded in the spring of 1862, the rest of his company was transferred to Company C of the Tenth Kansas Infantry. Allen had been identified by John Brown, Jr., as a man to whom abolitionist circulars could be safely sent and who could be relied upon "faithfully"; another man so identified was Augustus Wattles of Mound City. John Brown, Jr., to Stearns, May 11, 1861, George Luther Stearns papers.

At the time of his capture, Allen had been on detached service since November 25; he never returned to his company. In his absence, command had fallen onto Second Lieutenant Joseph K. Hudson (First Lieutenant Barclay Coppoc having been killed in September), but Hudson had been ordered to report to Hunter for a six-month term as a recruiting officer. However Ordnance Office records state Hudson commanded until January 4, 1862, when he was put on detached service. The company morning reports for January and February 1862 were signed by Lieutenant C. Kille as the commanding officer; Allen was listed on these as being on detached service. Strangely, the report of the Kansas Adjutant General identifies Clayton Kille only as a private. The morning reports also indicate that on February 11, 1862, Lieutenant Morse assumed command of the company by order of Colonel Montgomery; this apparently was Second Lieutenant Orlin C. Morse of Seaman's company. However the Ordnance Office record states Company C was consolidated with Company A on February 13 and was then commanded by Captain John Foreman. Montgomery to Hudson, January 4, 1862, Charles S. Bowman papers, Box 1, "Miscellaneous papers June 1861–March 1862"; undated Ordnance Office report, Joseph Kennedy Hudson papers, collection 395, 1861–1898 folder; "Morning Reports of Captain William R. Allen's Company, Third Regiment Kansas Volunteers," January and February 1862, James M. Harvey collection (oversize).

4. General Orders no. 2, Head Quarters Department of Kansas, December 2, 1861, Leavenworth *Daily Times*, December 5, 1861; "Address of Ex-Governor James W. Denver," 365; Barns, *Denver, the Man*, 202–203, 208–209; Denver to Lewis Cass, June 7, 23, 1858, in "Governor Denver's Administration," 528–35; Speer, *Life of Gen. James H. Lane*, 173; letter from H.J., December 1, 1861, *New York Times*,

December 17, 1861, p. 3; "Affairs in Kansas," ibid., December 20, 1861, p. 1; "Affairs in Kansas," ibid., December 21, 1861, pp. 2–3; "The War on the Kansas Frontier," Leavenworth *Daily Times*, January 7, 1862, quoting the *New York Times*; untitled article, ibid., December 27, 1861.

5. "General Orders no. 1, Head Quarters Post at Kansas City, Mo., December 7, 1861," broadside, KSHS."

6. Thrasher diary, entry of December 10, 1861; Weer to Captain, December 20, 1861, James M. Harvey papers, Box 1, correspondence 1861–1865; "Muster Roll of Captain James M. Harvey's Company," March 4, 1862; Montgomery to Lane, December 8, 1861, *OR* 8:415–16.

The muster roll dated December 31, 1861, stated Harvey's company had been at Osawatomie from November 29 to December 5. Weer was called to Washington to present evidence in connection with the contest for Lane's Senate seat. *Congressional Globe*, 37th Congress, 2d sess., 128, 263.

7. "Record of Events," William Creitz diary; Moore diary, entry of December 7, 1861.

8. "Col. Ritchey—Capt. Creitz," *Topeka Tribune*, December 28, 1861; Special Orders no. 17, Head Quarters Troops in Kansas, December 17, 1861, in John Ritchie compiled military service file, Fifth Kansas Cavalry; Barns, *Denver, the Man*, 220–21; "Record of Events," William Creitz diary. Ill feelings toward Ritchie still existed in February. George Flanders noted "Apostle John" had reportedly gotten a position as major on Lane's staff, which suited the men well because they would no longer have direct contact with him. Flanders to Dear Mother, February 10, 1862, in Swenson, *Civil War Letters Written by George Edwin Flanders*, 1:3–4. The Adjutant General's report for Company C states Summers was promoted to major on September 10, 1861. If this was true, Hunt would not have been the senior officer following Ritchie's resignation. It is possible Summer was promoted after Ritchie resigned, but the promotion was backdated to September 10. A letter from a civilian dated December 13 stated that Ritchie resigned "owing to the intrigue of some of the field officers." "Affairs in Kansas," *New York Times*, December 21, 1861, pp. 2–3.

9. *Roll of the Officers and Enlisted Men*, 8–9, 50–53.

10. Letter from Jack, December 4, 1861, *Leavenworth Daily Conservative*, December 7, 1861.

11. Letter from Galway, November 1, 1861, *New York Times*, November 11, 1861, pp. 2–3.

12. Sherman to John Sherman, January 9, 1862, in Simpson and Berlin, *Sherman's Civil War*, 183.

13. E. to Friend Speer, December 6, 1861, Lawrence *Republican*, December 12, 1861; Britton, *The Civil War on the Border*, 1:183–85; *History of Vernon County, Missouri*, 296–98. *History of Vernon County* mistakenly places this event as occurring in February 1862.

14. *History of Vernon County, Missouri*, 298–99; Judson to Jennison, December 24, 1861, *New York Times*, January 8, 1862, p. 8; Judson to Price, December 13, 1861, *OR* Series II, 1:152; Judson to Price, December 23, 1861, ibid., 154–55. The return to duty was short-lived for one of the men: James C. Alsup deserted the following April.

15. Montgomery to Lane, December 8, 1861, *OR* 8:415–16.

16. Wm. H. Fisher to Editor Republican, December 12, 1861, Lawrence *Republican*, December 19, 1861. Captain Miller may have been Dr. George Miller of the Humboldt militia or Adoniram Miller with his Fifth regiment recruits. Because both were described as scouts, it was probably the former.

17. Special Orders no. 8, Headquarters Troops in Kansas, December 10, 1861, *OR* 8:423.

18. "Three Rebels Killed," Leavenworth *Daily Times*, December 10, 1861; "The Rebellion in Missouri," *New York Times*, December 13, 1861, p. 8; "Skirmish in Cass Co. Mo.," *Leavenworth Daily Conservative*, December 10, 1861; "Skirmishing on the Kansas Border," *New York Times*, December 15, 1861, p. 2, quoting the Leavenworth *Times*; Huntoon to My Dear Wife, December 22, 1861, Andrew Jackson Huntoon papers.

19. "Affairs in Kansas," *New York Times*, January 5, 1862, p. 2; E. to Friend Speer, December 6, 1861, Lawrence *Republican*, December 12, 1861. The *Richmond (Virginia) Daily Dispatch* of January 3, 1862, "One Hundred Houses of Rebels Burnt," quoted the Boston *Traveller*, which reported it had received a letter from its correspondent with the army of the West. The letter writer claimed Fitzpatrick was a rebel captured in a skirmish, and he had killed a Federal officer and shot a Methodist preacher who was standing guard over him. He was tried, condemned to death by Jennison, and "died game, shouting for Jeff. Davis and the South as he fell pierced with the bullets of the soldiers."

20. "Affairs in Kansas," *New York Times*, December 21, 1861, pp. 2–3; "The Campaign in Kansas," ibid., December 27, 1861, p. 2. The latter writer, who signed himself "Subaltern," may have been a military man.

21. *Governor's Annual Message: Kansas, 1862*.

22. Cutler, *History of the State of Kansas*, 2:1106–1107; letter dated Mound City, December 16, 1861, Lawrence *Kansas State Journal*, December 19, 1861; Goodrich, *Black Flag*, 20; letter from Your Own, December 14, 1861, *Leavenworth Daily Conservative*, December 17, 1861; letter dated Mound City, December 16, 1861, Lawrence *Kansas State Journal*, December 19, 1861; "From Southern Kansas," *Leavenworth Daily Conservative*, December 21, 1861; "The War on the Border," *Chicago Tribune* (daily), December 26, 1861, p. 3.

23. Dickinson, "War Notes"; Thrasher diary, entry of December 12, 1861. Dickinson wrote that Lupton's son had been murdered while visiting his sick mother. The *Roll of Officers and Enlisted Men* only lists a Columbus C. Lupton, of Papinsville, survived at least long enough to be assigned to the Tenth Kansas in April.

24. M. A. Vansickle to Dear Friend, December 15, 1861, John Henry Vansickle collection; "The War on the Border," *Chicago Tribune* (daily), December 26,

1861, p. 3; M. to Friend Speer, December 15, 1861, Lawrence *Republican*, December 26, 1861; Thrasher diary, entry of December 12, 1861.

25. Letter dated Mound City, December 16, 1861, Lawrence *Kansas State Journal*, December 19, 1861.

26. "The War on the Border," *Chicago Tribune* (daily), December 26, 1861, p. 3; M. to Friend Speer, December 15, 1861, Lawrence *Republican*, December 26, 1861; *Roll of Officers and Enlisted Men*, 38, 53. Luther Thrasher wrote that Smalley, "that gasometer," was on an unauthorized scout. Thrasher diary, entry of December 14, 1861.

27. Thrasher diary, entries of December 12, 14, 1861; M. to Friend Speer, December 15, 1861, Lawrence *Republican*, December 26, 1861.

28. M. to Friend Speer, December 15, 1861, Lawrence *Republican*, December 26, 1861; Trego to My Dear Wife, December 18, 1861, in Langsdorf, "The Letters of Joseph H. Trego," 300–301; "The War on the Border," *Chicago Tribune* (daily), December 26, 1861, p. 3; letter dated Mound City, December 16, 1861, Lawrence *Kansas State Journal*, December 19, 1861.

Not every building in Papinsville was burned; a Wisconsin trooper passing through the following September described it as "a small town, but the best portion of the town had been burnt by Kansas troops." Brophy, *In the Devil's Dominions*, p. 24.

29. M. to Friend Speer, December 18, 1861, Lawrence *Republican*, December 26, 1861.

30. Letter from Your Own, December 14, 1861, *Leavenworth Daily Conservative*, December 17, 1861; letter dated Mound City, December 16, 1861, Lawrence *Kansas State Journal*, December 19, 1861; M. to Friend Speer, December 18, 1861, Lawrence *Republican*, December 26, 1861; Thrasher diary, entry of December 17, 1861; Moore diary, entries of December 17, 30, 1861; Robinson to Denver, December 28, 1861, Charles S. Bowman papers, Box 1, "Governor's Correspondence, Aug 1861–Feb 1862"; letter from Maumee, January 12, 1862, *Leavenworth Daily Conservative*, January 18, 1862; Bondi, *Autobiography*, 77–78.

Camp Defiance was located on the southern border of Linn County, about eight miles from the state line. "Our Kansas Letter," *Chicago Tribune*, March 27, 1862.

Robinson would ask that E. P. Sheldon be mustered as assistant surgeon of the Fifth, W. A. Jenkins as major of the Fifth, and once again that Powell Clayton be mustered into the Fifth, this time as lieutenant colonel. Robinson to Prince, January 4, 31, 1862, and February 27, 1862, in Charles S. Bowman papers, Box 1, "Governor's Correspondence, August 1861–February 1862."

31. Anthony to Dear Sister, December 26, 1861, in Langsdorf and Richmond, "Letters of Daniel R. Anthony," 351–70; letter from the Eighth, December 31, 1861, *Leavenworth Daily Conservative*, January 4, 1862; Jayhawker to Ed. Enterprise, January 1, 1862, in Patrick, "This Regiment Will Make a Mark," 50–58; "Operations in Western Missouri," *New York Times*, January 6, 1862, p. 8.

32. Mooney, *History of Butler County, Kansas*, 69–70, 104; Cutler, *History of the State of Kansas*, 2:900, 1431; "Irregular Troops," *Leavenworth Daily Conservative*, December 31, 1861; "Reorganization of the Kansas Regiments" and "From the Neosho Battalion," ibid., January 4, 1862.

Fort Row "consisted of three block houses, 16 x 24 feet, made of heavy logs, and enclosed with pickets six feet high. An embankment was thrown up on all sides, and the company went into winter quarters." Cutler, *History of the State of Kansas*, 2:900. It was also described: "One side was protected by the insurmountable bank of the river, and the other 3 sides by blockhouses, each 16 by 24 feet, constructed of heavy logs. Embankments were thrown up on all sides and the company went into winter quarters." Blackmar, *Kansas*, 2: 922.

33. M. to Friend Speer, December 18, 1861, Lawrence *Republican*, December 26, 1861; letter from Citizen, December 29, 1861, *Leavenworth Daily Conservative*, January 3, 1862.

34. *Congressional Globe*, 37th Congress, 2d sess., 128, 263; General Orders no. 1, Head Quarters, Wyandotte, Kansas, December 25, 1861, *Wyandotte Gazette*, January 11, 1862. In the same issue of the *Wyandotte Gazette*, two recent deaths in the Kansas City military hospital of Fourth Regiment men were announced: Lycargus Alexander, age seventeen, and Joseph Alexander, age nineteen, both of Company A. The "Tri-monthly report of Kansas Volunteers for the 10th day of January, 1862" stated an average of seven men per company in the Fourth were sick. *OR* Series III, 1:787.

35. Letter dated Kansas City, November 15, 1861, *Leavenworth Daily Conservative*, November 20, 1861.

36. Letter from Kansas, December 20, 1861, *Leavenworth Daily Conservative*, December 25, 1861.

37. Dickinson, "War Notes"; Moore diary, entries of December 25–26, 1861.

38. Huntoon to My Dear Wife, December 22, 25, 1861, Andrew Jackson Huntoon papers; "Operations in Western Missouri," *New York Times*, January 8, 1862, p. 8.

39. Trego to My Dear Little Wife, December 28, 1861, addendum of December 29, 1861, in Langsdorf, "The Letters of Joseph H. Trego," 301–302; Moore diary, entries of December 30, 1861, and January 29, 1862.

40. "Expedition to Walker's," *Wyandotte Gazette*, January 4, 1862.

41. Lane's Tremont Temple speech, Leavenworth *Daily Times*, December 11, 1861; letter from Kansas, December 2, 1861, Lawrence *Kansas State Journal*, December 5, 1861; "From Southern Kansas," Leavenworth *Daily Times*, December 10, 1861; "Tells of Smashing Early Day Saloon, Mound City (Kansas) *Republic*, July 6, 1939; Connelley, *A Standard History of Kansas* 2:798; Wm. H. Fisher to Editor Republican, December 12, 1861, Lawrence *Republican*, December 19, 1861; letter from Carlyle, December 22, 1861, *Leavenworth Daily Conservative*, December 27, 1861; Bondi, *Autobiography*, 74. John A. Parker of Adoniram Miller's company

served as bugler until he received a severe thigh wound on September 11, 1864, at Cross Roads, Arkansas. He was mustered out of the Fifth on December 2, 1865; as this was well after the rest of the regiment had been mustered out, he was likely taking a long time to recuperate from his wound. Oliver G. Triplett of Jenkins's company died of dysentery on September 27, 1864. *Report of the Adjutant General of the State of Kansas, 1861–65*, 1:146, 155, 156.

42. M. to Editor Times, January 4, 1862, Leavenworth *Daily Times*, January 11, 1862; M. to Friend Speer, January 4, 1862, Lawrence *Republican*, January 9, 1862; letter from J.B., January 14, 1862, *Leavenworth Daily Conservative*, January 18, 1862.

43. G. A. Crawford, Chas. Sims and Mark Delahay to Gen. J. H. Lane, December 6, 1861, Abraham Lincoln papers.

44. Robinson to Denver, December 28, 1861, Kansas Adjutant General records, "General Correspondence 1861–1862"; "Reorganization of the Kansas Regiments," *Leavenworth Daily Conservative*, January 4, 1862. In addition, four companies of Newgent's Cass County (Missouri) Home Guard regiment, whose companies had originally been raised in Kansas, were transferred to the then-forming Ninth Kansas Volunteers. Although this transfer was later held to be illegal, and may have existed only on paper, it served its short-term purpose of giving the illusion the Ninth (later redesignated as the Second Kansas Cavalry) was at full strength.

45. Bondi, *Autobiography*, 74–75. One assumes the muskets were smoothbores as the men would have known that to do this to rifled guns would harm the ballistics.

46. *Roll of the Officers and Enlisted Men*, 70; General Orders no. 3, Department of Kansas, December 31, 1861; "From the Kansas Brigade," *Leavenworth Daily Conservative*, January 30, 1862.

47. "A Serenade and Speeches," *New York Times*, December 3, 1861, p. 1.

48. *New York Tribune* (semi-weekly), December 3, 1861, p. 4

49. "Serenade to Senator Lane," *New York Times*, December 5, 1861, p. 1.

50. Lane's Tremont Temple speech, Leavenworth *Daily Times*, December 11, 1861.

51. *Congressional Globe*, 37th Congress, 2d sess., 115, 127–30, 263, 290–97, 336–40, 359–64.

52. *Congressional Globe*, 37th Congress, 2d sess., 129; "Gen. Lane's Commission," Leavenworth *Daily Times*, July 30, 1861; *Congressional Globe*, 37th Congress, 2d sess., 341; Certificate from the Adjutant General of Indiana, March 31, 1910, James Henry Lane papers. On October 7, 1862, by which time Lane had been appointed a recruiting commissioner, Major General Samuel Curtis wrote to Halleck, "General J. H. Lane, of Kansas, has raised three regiments. He has a commission for a brigadier-general from Indiana. Can I detail and give him a temporary command? Blunt recommends it and favors it." *OR* 13:715.

Chapter 9. Monotony and Mutiny

1. Dickinson, "War Notes."
2. Hatch, *The Blue, The Gray, & The Red*, 2–19; Cutler to Dole, November 4, 1861, in Abel, *The American Indian in the Civil War, 1862–1865*, n141, 65–66.
3. Collamore to Dole, April 21, 1862, *OR* Series II, 4:11–12.
4. Campbell to Barnes, February 5, 1862, *OR* Series II, 4:6–7. See also O. S. Coffin to William G. Coffin, January 26, 1862, in Abel, *The American Indian in the Civil War, 1862–1865*, n174, 83. Campbell took a census of the Indians encamped on the Verdigris River and counted 3,168 Creek, 53 slaves owned by the Creek, 38 free blacks who were members of the Creek tribe, 777 Seminole, 136 Quapaw, 50 Cherokee, 31 Chickasaw, and "some few Kickapoos and other tribes—about 4,400 all."
5. "Interview with the Indians," February 6, 1862 Lawrence *Republican*, quoting the Leavenworth *Conservative*.
6. Collamore to Dole, April 21, 1862, *OR* Series II, 4:12. Collamore reported that the government bacon provided to the refugees had been condemned at Fort Leavenworth and was not fit for a dog. Collamore took a census and counted 5,000 Creek, 1,096 Seminole, 140 Chickasaw, 315 Quapaw, 544 Uchee, 84 Keechie, 197 Delaware, 17 Ionies, 3 Caddoe, 5 Wichita, and 240 Cherokee—approximately 7,600 in all.
7. Letter from W. G. Coffin, April 12, 1862, *Leavenworth Daily Conservative*, April 16, 1862. Coffin noted, regarding the bathing ceremony, that "should any die that have gone through the operation, he had either not vomited enough, not danced hard enough, not stayed in the water long enough, or some other defect in the performance. The thing itself is all right and perfect if only performed properly in all its parts. The only reason they lost the last battle, they most religiously believe, was because the enemy came upon them before they had time to take medicine and go through the enchantments."
8. Collamore to Dole, April 21, 1862, *OR* Series II, 4:12.
9. Moore diary, entries of January 2, 4, 5, 9, 10, 11, 13, 21, 1862; Clarke to Williams, undated, Henry Miles Moore collection, Box 1; letter from R. Gilpatrick, January 8, 1862, ibid.; Special Orders no. 13, Head Quarters Troops in Kansas, December 16, 1861, ibid.; "Muster Out Roll of Eli Snyder's Infantry" and "Muster Out Roll of Jno. E. Stewart Cavalry."
10. Moore diary, entries of January 9, 10, 13, 1862.
11. "Headquarters Troops in Kansas," December 27, 1861, Henry Miles Moore collection, Box 1; Moore diary, entries of January 17–18, 20, 1862. It was also reported that an unidentified man was tried for treason by a drum-head court-martial and ordered to be shot but escaped the morning of January 14. Dickinson, "War Notes."
12. M. to Friend Speer, January 9, 1862, Lawrence *Republican*, January 16, 1862; "General Blunt's Account of His Civil War Experiences," 215; letter from

Maumee, January 12, 1862, *Leavenworth Daily Conservative*, January 18, 1862; letter from J.B., January 14, 1862, ibid., January 18, 1862.

13. Huntoon to My Dear Wife, January 30, 1862, Andrew Jackson Huntoon papers; J. H. Vansickle to Dear Sir, January 9, 1862, John Henry Vansickle collection, Spencer Research Library; Moore diary, entries of January 21, 24–25, 1862. Moore's diary contains a copy of Denver's General Orders no. 10, Headquarters Department of Kansas, January 25, 1862, which revoked the furloughs.

14. M. to Friend Speer, January 9, 1862, Lawrence *Republican*, January 16, 1862; letter from Maumee, January 12, 1862, *Leavenworth Daily Conservative*, January 18, 1862; letter from J.B., January 14, 1862, ibid., January 18, 1862; Flanders to Dear Mother, February 10, 1862, in Swenson, *Civil War Letters Written by George Edwin Flanders*, 1:3.

15. "From the Kansas Brigade," *Leavenworth Daily Conservative*, January 30, 1862; Bondi, *Autobiography*, 76, 78. At the time of Stephenson's death, Bickerton was being treated at the Mound City Hotel for "rheumatism, affection of the kidney, and dropsy. He has had an operation performed, which affords temporary relief, but from present indications the Captain will be compelled ere long to retire." "From the Kansas Brigade," ibid. He was mustered out of the service February 15, 1862. Rice was discharged on account of disability on December 25, 1861, at Mound City, Illinois.

16. Moore diary, entry of January 17, 1862.

17. "Record of Events," William Creitz diary; letter from H. D. Fisher, January 31, 1862, *Leavenworth Daily Conservative*, February 6, 1862.

18. Anthony to Dear Sister, February 3, 1862, in Langsdorf and Richmond, "Letters of Daniel R. Anthony," 351–70; letter from Sojer, January 4, 1862, *Leavenworth Daily Conservative*, January 7, 1862; letter from Peter, January 12, 1862, ibid., January 16, 1862; Jayhawker to Mr. Beal, January 15, 1862, in Patrick, "This Regiment Will Make a Mark," 50–58.

19. Bondi, *Autobiography*, 75, 76–77.

20. "Record of Events," William Creitz diary.

21. Boutwell, "A Veteran's History of His Unrequited Service to this Republic"; Boutwell, "A Plea for Justice." Sheldon mustered in as assistant surgeon at the request of Robinson. Robinson to Prince, January 4, 1862, Charles S. Bowman papers, Box 1, "Governor's Correspondence, Aug 1861–Feb 1862."

The situation with "Company X" appears to be what Halpine referred to when he claimed the men of the brigade constituted a "mutinous rabble, taking votes as to whether any troublesome or distasteful order should be obeyed or defied." Halpine to Halleck, March 14, 1862, *OR* 8:615–17.

22. Huntoon to My Dear Wife, January 23, 1862, January 30, 1862, and March 22, 1862, Andrew Jackson Huntoon papers.

23. Flanders to Dear Brother, March 17, 1862, in Swenson, *Civil War Letters Written by George Edwin Flanders*, 1:10; Flanders to Dear Brother, March 29, 1862, ibid.,

1:14; Flanders to Dear Brother, April 29, 1863, ibid., 2:92; Joel Moody to James G. Blunt, September 11, 1862, in John Ritchie compiled military service file, Fifth Kansas Cavalry; "Battle of Pine Bluff, Ark.," Leavenworth *Daily Times*, November 18, 1863.

24. Moore diary, entries of January 24–26, 1862.

25. Moore diary, entry of January 30, 1862; General Orders no. 9, Head Quarters Department of Kansas, January 17, 1862, Leavenworth *Daily Times*, January 24, 1862. Special Orders no. 40, Head Quarters, Department of Kansas, January 13, 1862, dictated that in compliance with Special Orders no. 1, Head Quarters, U.S. Army, January 2, 1862, Lieutenant Bowman was ordered to remuster the Third, Fourth, and Fifth regiments. Charles S. Bowman papers, Box 3, "Special Orders (no particular headquarters)."

26. General Orders no. 7, Head Quarters Department of Kansas, January 13, 1862, James W. Denver collection, "Correspondence 1862" folder; Barns, *Denver, the Man*, 284; Robinson to Dear Genl, January 14, 1862, James W. Denver collection, "Correspondence 1862" folder.

27. "Speech of General James H. Lane," *Leavenworth Daily Conservative*, January 29, 1862; "Our Kansas Letter," *Chicago Tribune* (daily), February 5, 1862, p. 2; "Gen. Lane's Speech," *Tipton* (Iowa) *Advertiser*, February 13, 1862.

28. Ibid.

29. General Orders no. 11, Headquarters Department of Kansas, January 27, 1862, *OR* 8:529.

Chapter 10. Dissolution

1. Halleck to Hunter, February 2, 1862, *OR* 8:829.

2. Bishop, *Loyalty on the Frontier*, 47–50.

3. Letter from Kansas, February 10, 1862, Lawrence *Kansas State Journal*, February 20, 1862; letter from Sojer, February 15, 1862, *Leavenworth Daily Conservative*, February 21, 1862; Moore diary, entries of February 3–4, 6–8, 1862; Dickinson, "War Notes"; Archives of the Adjutant General of Ohio, "Correspondence to the Governor and Adjutant General of Ohio."

On July 7, 1862, Stanton Weaver wrote to the governor of Ohio, requesting authority to raise a company. He indicated that despite his wound, he could still handle a revolver in his left hand and could give as severe a cut with the sword as ever. He would eventually serve in Company G of the 104th Ohio Infantry as first sergeant and then as first lieutenant.

4. Moore diary, entry of February 3, 1862; "Our Kansas Letter," *Chicago Tribune*, March 27, 1862.

5. Huntoon to My Dear Wife, January 30, 1862, Andrew Jackson Huntoon papers; Huntoon to Beloved Lizzie and Prentiss, February 7, 1862, ibid.; Flanders to Dear Mother, February 10, 1862, in Swenson, *Civil War Letters Written by George*

Edwin Flanders, 1:4; *Report of the Adjutant General of the State of Kansas, 1861–65*, 1:146; Descriptive Roll Sixth Kansas Cavalry.

Pardia is identified as Pardier Marcellena in the roster of the Fifth in the *Roll of the Officers and Enlisted Men*. I have chosen to go with Marcellia Pardia, as this is the name listed in the roster of the Sixth in the *Report of the Adjutant General of the State of Kansas, 1861–65*, 1:209, the descriptive roll of the Sixth, and at the Fort Scott National Cemetery.

     6. Moore diary, entry of February 9, 1862; letter from Kansas, February 10, 1862, Lawrence *Kansas State Journal*, February 20, 1862; "Gen. Hunter's Department," *New York Times*, February 1, 1862, p. 1; Robinson to Stanton, May 23, 1862, *OR* Series III, 2:65–66. Hunter's order also stated the new Second Kansas Cavalry was to be consolidated with the First New Mexico regiment, with Colonel Robert H. Graham to command it.

     7. Moore diary, entry of February 14, 1862; undated Ordnance Office report, Joseph Kennedy Hudson papers, collection 395, 1861–1898 folder; Special Orders Head Quarters Kansas Third, February 10, 1861, Henry Miles Moore collection; Moore diary, entry of February 10, 1862.

     8. Letter from Maumee, February 21, 1862, *Leavenworth Daily Conservative*, February 25, 1862; Moore diary, entries of October 1–2, 23, December 16, 1861, January 1, February 10–12, 16, 1862; Commission from Governor Robinson dated October 1, 1861, Special Orders Head Quarters Kansas Brigade, October 1, 1861, Certificate by Thomas Moonlight, October 23, 1861, Certificate by Montgomery, Headquarters Army of the Western Border, November 15, 1861, Special Orders Headquarters Kansas Third, February 10, 1862, Moore to Major Martin, February 11, 1862, all in Henry Miles Moore collection, Box 1. Maumee wrote that Moore asked for a discharge due to poor health.

     9. *Roll of the Officers and Enlisted Men*, 8–9, 50–53; J. H. Vansickle to Dear Sir, January 9, 1862, and February 18, 1862, John Henry Vansickle collection. Vansickle's February 18 letter indicated he was in Company K of the Third.

     10. Dickinson, "War Notes."

     11. Special Orders no. 101, Headquarters Department of Kansas, February 15, 1862, Charles S. Bowman papers, Box 3, "Special Orders (no particular headquarters)"; letter from Sojer, February 15, 1862, *Leavenworth Daily Conservative*, February 21, 1862; letter from Maumee, February 21, 1862, ibid., February 25, 1862; Moore diary, entry of February 13, 1862.

     12. Moore diary, entry of February 15, 1862; letter from Maumee, February 21, 1862, *Leavenworth Daily Conservative*, February 25, 1862.

     13. Letter dated Camp Denver, February 17, 1862, *Leavenworth Daily Conservative*, February 22, 1862; Bondi, *Autobiography*, 77–78; "Record of Events," William Creitz diary; Summers to Hunter, February 18, 1862, Charles S. Bowman papers, Box 2, "Officers Muster Orders Aug 1861–Nov 1862"; Robinson to Prince, March 7, 1862, Charles S. Bowman papers, Box 1, "Governor's Correspondence, March 1862–December 1862."

Robinson wrote to Lynde, enclosing Summers's resignation. Robinson to Lynde, March 20, 1862, Charles S. Bowman papers, Box 1, "Governor's Correspondence, March 1862–December 1862." Bondi noted that at the same time Summers resigned, so too did Captain Adoniram Miller and Lieutenants McGinnis and Rush of his company.

14. Letter from Maumee, February 21, 1862, *Leavenworth Daily Conservative*, February 25, 1862; Bondi, *Autobiography*, 78; letter from H. D. Fisher, February 23, 1862, *Leavenworth Daily Conservative*, February 26, 1862; letter from Maumee, March 4, 1862, ibid., March 9, 1862; General Orders No. 14, Headquarters Department of Kansas, February 1, 1862, Special Orders No. 100, Headquarters Department of Kansas, February 15, 1862, Halpine to Deitzler, February 28, 1862, *OR* 8:541, 557–58, 573–74; "Our Kansas Letter," *Chicago Tribune*, April 4, 1862.

The reference to "loose dirt" probably refers to horse dung. Halpine's February 28 letter mentions that Jennison outranked Deitzler; this would refer to their dates of rank as acting brigadiers.

15. General Orders no. 26, Headquarters Department of Kansas, February 28, 1862, Kansas Adjutant General records, "General Correspondence 1861–1865"; *OR* 8:617; Halpine to Halleck, March 14, 1862, *OR* 8:615–17.

16. Company F, Fifth Cavalry, had been commanded by Greenville Watson, who resigned March 23, 1862, after his company was transferred to the Tenth Kansas Infantry; it is unclear why he was not listed as company commander in General Orders no. 26. As Company F was understrength upon remuster, Thompson was mustered out as captain and remustered as first lieutenant, then again promoted to captain March 17, 1862.

17. Halleck to Robinson, March 21, 1862, Kansas Adjutant General Records, "Tenth Regiment Correspondence, Field & Staff 1863–1877."

18. Lindberg and Matthews, "'The Eagle of the 11th Kansas,'" 18.

19. Robinson to Stanton, May 23, 1862, *OR* Series III, 2:65; Flanders to Dear Brother, March 17, 1862, in Swenson, *Civil War Letters Written by George Edwin Flanders*, 1:10; "Record of Events," William Creitz diary.

20. Flanders to Dear Mother, February 10, 1862, in Swenson, *Civil War Letters Written by George Edwin Flanders*, 1:4; General Orders no. 17, Headquarters Department of Kansas, February 8, 1862, *OR* 8:547–48; "Martial Law—The State," Leavenworth *Daily Times*, February 9, 1862.

21. Leslie, *The Devil Knows How to Ride*, 106–11; Goodrich, *Black Flag*, 29–30; Connelley, *Quantrill and the Border Wars*, 199.

22. Connelley, *A Standard History of Kansas*, 3:1204.

23. "The Recent Outrages," *Leavenworth Daily Conservative*, March 13, 1861; Leslie, *The Devil Knows How to Ride*, 108–14.

24. Halpine to Halleck, March 14, 1862, *OR* 8:614.

25. Ibid., 615–17.

26. Ibid. On November 22, 1861, T. J. Weed had written to Montgomery that the services of a Lieutenant Anderson were being provided, apparently to train

company commanders and clerks in their ministerial duties. However, Weed wrote that no fund existed by which to pay Anderson, and he suggested the company commanders could individually make such financial arrangements directly with Anderson. James Montgomery papers, KSHS.

27. Letter from Carlyle dated December 22, 1861, *Leavenworth Daily Conservative*, December 27, 1861; Thrasher diary, entries of December 3, 4, 5, 6, 7, 11, 18, 19, 1861. Another source for adverse information may have been complaints passed on by Secretary of War Cameron, given to him while he was in St. Louis in late October. "The Outrages of Gen. Lane," *Richmond* (Virginia) *Daily Dispatch*, October 25, 1861, reprinting the St. Louis *Republican*.

28. Halleck to Stanton, March 7, 1862, *OR* 8:831–32; President's War Orders no. 3, March 11, 1862, ibid.,605–606; Special Orders no. 54, War Department, March 13, 1862, ibid., 612; Halpine to Halleck, March 14, 1862, ibid., 614; General Orders no. 7, Headquarters Department of the Mississippi, March 19, 1862, ibid., 832. Excepted from Denver's command was Deitzler's brigade, which was intended for service with Curtis in Arkansas.

29. Special Orders no. 54, War Department, March 13, 1862, *OR* 8:612; General Orders no. 7, Headquarters Department of the Mississippi, March 19, 1862, ibid., 832; Lincoln to Halleck, March 21, 1862, *OR* 53: 516; E. A. Hitchcock to Halleck, March 22, 1862, *OR* 8:832–33; Stanton to Halleck, March 26, 1862, *OR* 53:516; Halleck to Stanton, March 26, 1862, ibid.

30. Halleck to Stanton, March 28, 1862, *OR* 8:647–48.

31. Special Orders no. 49, Headquarters Department of the Mississippi, March 28, 1862, *OR* 53:517; Lincoln to Halleck, April 4, 1862, Abraham Lincoln papers; Halleck to Sturgis, April 6, 1862, *OR* 8:668; General Orders no. 4, Headquarters District of Kansas, April 10, 1862, *OR* 8:683.

Halleck instructed Denver: "Report immediately what means you have for arming friendly Indians, and how many it will be safe to arm." Halleck to Denver, April 5, 1862, *OR* 8:664–65. Denver objected: "The dictates of humanity ought to prompt any civilized community to avoid the employment of savages in their wars. . . . It is utterly ridiculous to talk about controlling savages in time of war. . . . It is no sense to talk about reducing the Indians to the laws and customs regulating civilized warfare. The officers commanding them will be compelled to conform themselves to their (the Indians) mode of warfare as every instance of the kind on record will prove." Denver to Halleck, April 14, 1862, ibid., 287.

32. Stevens to Dear Genl, April 11, 1862, James W. Denver collection, "Correspondence 1861" folder; R. S. Stevens to Denver, April 11, 1862, in Barns, *Denver, the Man*, 285–86.

33. Letter from Pick, March 9, 1862, Lawrence *Kansas State Journal*, March 13, 1862; Halpine to Butler, March 4, 1862, Kansas Adjutant General records, "General Correspondence 1861–1862"; "General Blunt's Account of His Civil War Experiences," 218. Among others losing rank was hospital steward Daniel Chandler, who

was reduced to a private in Napoleon Blanton's company; he was promoted to hospital steward in the Third Indian Home Guard in October 1862.

34. *Military History of Kansas Regiments*, 120–21; J. H. Vansickle to Dear Sir, April 19, 1862, M. A. Vansickle to Dear Father, June 22, 1862, J. H. Vansickle to Dear Sir, July 4, 1862, John Henry Vansickle collection; *Roll of the Officers and Enlisted Men*, 8–9, 50–53.

Lieutenant Hollister had mustered in the original three Fort Scott companies as home guards, but he claimed that when the Sixth regiment was organized, these three were remustered without their service being limited to that of home guards. Nonetheless, Lieutenant Bowman was ordered on February 4 to muster out the home guards. Bowman to Halpine, January 20, 1862, Hollister to Halpine, February 4, 1862, Charles S. Bowman papers, Box 1, "Muster Orders June 1861–September 1862"; Halpine to Bowman, February 4, 1862, Charles S. Bowman papers, Box 3, "Headquarters, Dept of KS Special Orders Sept 1861–Jan 1863." The apparent delay is unexplained.

Vansickle was killed the next year when he was with a group of citizens who were hunting down a thief named Reuben Forbes. Forbes opened fire from a hiding place in the brush, wounding two men and killing Vansickle with a "load of buckshot 2 of which struck him in the neck. One shot passed through his windpipe and the jugular vein." Both shots lodged between his shoulders. "He lived but a few minutes and spoke only about five words after he was shot." Forbes was then killed. "He was shot all to pieces. From 20 to 30 balls passed through his body." "Terrible Scenes in Bourbon County," Lawrence *Kansas State Journal*, June 18, 1863; Goodrich, *Black Flag*, 116–17.

35. Special Orders no. 80, War Department, April 12, 1862, *OR* Series III, 2:16. Attorney general Edwin Bates later concluded that while Robinson had the authority to fill officer vacancies, he did not have the power to either muster an officer out of the service or to remove him from a position once that officer had entered the U.S. service. Bates to Stanton, June 16, 23, 1862, *OR* Series III, 2: 149–52, 169–70.

36. Blunt to Stanton, May 27, 1862, *OR* Series III, 2:83–84; Robinson to Stanton, May 23, 1862, ibid., 65–66.

37. Thomas to Blunt, May 30, 1862, *OR* Series III, 2:49.

Chapter 11. The Great Southern Expedition

1. "The Great Southern Expedition," *Topeka State Record*, July 26 and August 9, 1871; Giles, *Thirty Years in Topeka*, 108–11.

2. Ibid.

3. Order dated Head Quarters, Kan. Brig., Camp Mitchell, October 3, 1861, Daniel H. Horne papers; "Gen. Lane to Retake Fort Smith," *Leavenworth Daily Conservative*, May 11, 1861; Samuel Reader to My Dear Brother Frank, May 12, 1861,

"Letters of Samuel James Reader," 30–31; "Latest News by Mail," *Richmond* (Virginia) *Daily Dispatch*, May 11, 1861.

4. Samuel Reader to My Dear Brother Frank, May 12, 1861, "Letters of Samuel James Reader," 30–31. For background information on Horne, see "At Rest in Peace," Oceanside, California, *Blade*, April 28, 1894; Cutler, *History of the State of Kansas*, 1:544, 545; Blackmar, *Kansas*, 2:812.

5. "Meeting at Stockton's Hall," Leavenworth *Daily Times*, October 9, 1861.

6. "Gen. Lane on His Way Westward," *New York Times*, January 29, 1862, p. 3.

7. "The Great Southern Expedition," *Topeka State Record*, July 26 and August 9, 1871; Giles, *Thirty Years in Topeka*, 108–11.

8. Coffin and Delahay to Lincoln, October 21, 1861, Abraham Lincoln papers; B. F. Wade, Z. Chandler, and D. Kilgore to Lincoln, November 7, 1861, ibid.

9. Gamble to Cates, November 21, 1861, *OR* 17, part 2:92; Hall to Lincoln, October 18, 1861, Abraham Lincoln papers.

10. Chase to Lincoln, November 9, 1861, Abraham Lincoln papers.

11. "McClellan's Report of the Operations of the Army of the Potomac from July 27, 1861, to November 9, 1862," *OR* 5:8–9; Thomas to Hunter, November 26, 1861, *OR* 8:379.

McClellan proposed to Lincoln: "Another independent movement that has often been suggested, and which has always recommended itself to my judgment. I refer to a movement from Kansas and Nebraska through the Indian Territory upon Red River and Western Texas, for the purpose of protecting and developing the latent Union and free-State sentiment well known to predominate in Western Texas, and which, like a similar sentiment in Western Virginia, will, if protected, ultimately organize that section into a free State."

12. Miller, *Lincoln's Abolitionist General*, 79. Hunter must have expressed the same sentiment to Secretary of War Cameron. In a letter to Hunter, Cameron stated: "Your views upon the slavery question as connected with this war must, it seems to me, meet the approval of all men who are not controlled by the magical power of the slave interests. I believe that the war can be only successfully terminated by carrying out the policy which is indicated in your letter." Cameron to Hunter, January 3, 1862, *OR* 53:512.

13. Hunter to Thomas, December 11, 1861, *OR* 8: 428; McClellan to Hunter, December 11, 1861, ibid., 428–29.

14. Hunter to McClellan, December 19, 1861, *OR* 8:450–51.

15. Trickett, "The Civil War in the Indian Territory, 1862," 60; Rafuse, "Typhoid and Tumult," 1–16.

16. Stevens to Denver, December 4, 9, 1861, in Barns, *Denver, the Man*, 280–81. The originals of these two letters are found in the James W. Denver collection, "Correspondence 1861" folder.

17. Stevens to Dear Genl, December 21, 1861, James W. Denver collection, "Correspondence 1861" folder.

18. Halleck to McClellan, December 19, 1861, *OR* 8:448–50; "James H. Lane a Major General," *Leavenworth Daily Conservative*, December 18, 1861. In an endorsement to Halleck's letter, Lincoln commented, "I am sorry General Halleck is so unfavorably impressed with General Lane."

19. Basler, *The Collected Works*, 5:71; Ainsworth to Martin, March 26, 1910, and Ainsworth to Anthony, Jr., March 26, 1910, James Henry Lane papers; "Gen. Lane's Appointment," *New York Times*, December 19, 1861, p. 1; "Appointments Confirmed by the U.S. Senate," *Richmond* (Virginia) *Daily Dispatch*, December 30, 1861. Ainsworth's letter to Martin is also found in Cory, "The Sixth Kansas Cavalry and Its Commander," 225.

20. "The Western Department," Leavenworth *Daily Times*, December 25, 1861; "The Campaign in Kansas," *New York Times*, December 27, 1861, p. 2; "The War on the Kansas Frontier," ibid., December 24, 1861, p. 4.

21. Cameron to Hunter, January 3, 1862, *OR* 53:512–13. Cameron also commented, "Your views upon the slavery question as connected with this war must, it seems to me, meet the approval of all men who are not controlled by the magical power of the slave interests."

22. Lane to Hunter, January 3, 1862, *OR* 8:482. In a letter dated December 31, 1861, to Surgeon General C. A. Finley, Assistant Adjutant General E. D. Townsend wrote: "I have respectfully to inform you that four regiments of infantry, seven regiments of cavalry, three batteries of artillery, besides Kansas troops, from 8,000 to 10,000, and about 4,000 Indians, forming an aggregate of about 27,000 troops, are ordered to be concentrated near Fort Leavenworth, for whom medical supplies, blanks, &c., will be required at an early day." *OR* 8:576. Hunter was not adverse to arming Indians. He had in a letter to Adjutant General Thomas dated December 9, 1861, requested permission to muster in loyal Indians to assist the loyal Creeks, Seminoles, and Chickasaws in the Indian Territory. The request was denied. Miller, *Lincoln's Abolitionist General*, 78–79.

23. Cameron to Hunter, January 3, 1862, *OR* 53:512–13.

24. "The Campaign in Kansas," *New York Times*, December 27, 1861, p. 2; "Gen. Lane's Department," *New York Times*, January 3, 1862, p. 5; "Gen. Lane's Campaign," ibid., p. 1; "Gen. Lane's Expedition," ibid., p. 8; Gen. Lane's Expeditionary Corps," ibid., January 12, 1862, p. 1, reprinting the *Chicago Tribune* (daily) of January 8, 1862 ("Jim Lane's Great Expedition").

25. "Latest from Washington," *Leavenworth Daily Conservative*, December 29, 1861; "Gen. Lane's Position," *Lawrence Republican*, January 9, 1862.

26. "Gen. Lane's Expedition," *Lawrence Republican*, January 16, 1862; "Gen. Lane," *Tipton* (Iowa) *Advertiser*, January 16, 1862; "Sketches from the Seat of War," *Jewish Messenger*, January 1862. The latter source was found at www.jewish-history.com/sketches.html and the month of its publication provided courtesy of L. M. Berkowitz.

27. "The Character of the War on the Western Frontier," Little Rock *Arkansas True Democrat,* January 30, 1862, p. 2; "Jim Lane's Command," *Richmond* (Virginia) *Daily Dispatch,* January 16, 1862.

28. "Gen. Lane's Programme," *Chicago Tribune* (daily), January 23, 1862, p. 2, and "Lane's Brutal Plans Endorsed by General M'Clellan," *Richmond* (Virginia) *Daily Dispatch,* January 25, 1862, both quoting the *New York Post*; Leavenworth *Daily Times,* January 26, 1862, quoting the *New York Tribune.*

29. Thomas to Hunter, January 24, 1862, *OR* 8:525–26.

30. Miller, *Lincoln's Abolitionist General,* 83–84.

31. "Gen. Lane on His Way Westward," *New York Times,* January 29, 1862, p. 3; "Gen. Lane in Chicago," *Chicago Tribune* (daily), January 23, 1862, p. 4.

32. "Died," Lawrence *Republican,* February 6, 1862; "Gen. James H. Lane," *Chicago Tribune* (weekly), February 6, 1862, p. 2, quoting the *Quincy Whig.*

33. "Speech of General James H. Lane," *Leavenworth Daily Conservative,* January 29, 1862. This was also reported in "Our Kansas Letter," *Chicago Tribune* (daily), February 5, 1862, p. 2, and "Gen. Lane's Speech," *Tipton* (Iowa) *Advertiser,* February 13, 1862.

34. Ibid.

35. General Orders no. 11, Headquarters Department of Kansas, January 27, 1862, *OR* 8:529–30.

36. Hunter to Halleck, February 8, 1862, *OR* 8:829–31.

37. Delahay to Lincoln, January 28, 1862, Abraham Lincoln papers.

38. Ho-po-eith-le-yo-ho-la and A-luk-tus-te-nu-ke to Lincoln, January 28, 1862, *OR* 8:537.

39. *Senate Journal of the Legislative Assembly of the State of Kansas,* 69–71; *House Journal, 1862* [Kansas], 126; House of Representative State of Kansas to the President of the United States, February 6, 1862, Abraham Lincoln Papers; House of Representatives State of Kansas to Hon. S.C. Pomeroy, February 6, 1862, ibid.

40. Miller, *Lincoln's Abolitionist General,* 50–52, 71, 73; Hunter to Lincoln, October 20, 1860, Abraham Lincoln papers; Lincoln to Hunter, December 31, 1861, *OR* 53:511.

41. Lincoln to Stanton, January 31, 1862, *OR* 8:538.

42. Stanton to Dana, February 1, 1862, quoted in Trickett, "The Civil War in the Indian Territory, 1862," 60, 62.

43. Hunter to Halleck, February 8, 1862, *OR* 8:829–31. A number of men had been appointed as "Aides-de-camp for service under Brigadier General Lane." Among these were Colonel William H. Merritt; Lieutenant Judson Kilpatrick; Majors T. J. Weed, Champion Vaughan, John Ritchie, and Verplanck Van Antwerp; and a number of captains. Kilpatrick went to Kansas in January upon the representation he was to be chief of artillery for the expedition. These men were appointed on January 29–30. The War Department later granted them honorable discharges. Special Orders no. 61, War Department, March 21, 1862, Charles S.

Bowman papers, Box 3, "Special Orders (no particular headquarters) 1861–March 1862"; "Hugh Judson Kilpatrick," in Wilson and Fiske, *Appleton's Cyclopedia of American Biography*.

The *Leavenworth Daily Conservative* of January 8, 1862, reported that Champion Vaughan and T. J. Weed had been appointed to McClellan's staff and then transferred to General Lane. The *Conservative* of January 24, in "Gen. Lane's Staff," identified the following men as having been appointed by McClellan and then detailed to Hunter who was in turn to detail them to Lane's staff: Colonel William H. Merritt; Lieutenant Colonel Judson Kilpatrick; Majors John Ritchie, Vevan Antwerp, T. J. Weed, and Champion Vaughn; Captains J. R. McClure, William Kyle, William A. Phillips, A. P. Russell, and William O'Donnell; and ten lieutenants.

44. Hunter to Halleck, February 8, 1862, *OR* 8:829–31.

45. Hunter to Stanton, February 1, 1862; Hunter to Lincoln, February 4, 1862, Abraham Lincoln papers.

46. Connelley, *The Provisional Government of Nebraska Territory*, 134. Guthrie was not close to Lane; on the contrary his diary is full of complaints of slights and double-dealing by Lane.

47. *Congressional Globe*, 37th Congress, 2d sess., 307; "Gens. Lane and Hunter," *New York Times*, February 7, 1861, p. 1; Pomeroy to James H. Lane, Jr., February 6, 1862, James Lane collection, Box 1, Folder 14, Spencer Research Library.

48. Medill to Lincoln, February 9, 1862, Abraham Lincoln papers.

49. Lincoln to Hunter and Lane, February 10, 1862, *OR* 8:551.

50. Hunter to Lane, February 13, 1862; Lane to Hunter, February 13, 1862, Abraham Lincoln papers.

51. Hunter to Lane, February 13, 1862, Abraham Lincoln papers.

52. Hunter to Lincoln, February 14, 1862, Abraham Lincoln papers.

53. McClellan to Halleck, February 12, 1862, *OR* 53:513, McClellan to Halleck, February 13, 1862, *OR* 8:555.

54. Halleck to Hunter, February 13, 1862, *OR* 8:554–55.

55. Letter from Lane, February 26, 1862, *Leavenworth Daily Conservative*, February 28, 1862, quoted in Cory, "The Sixth Kansas Cavalry and Its Commander," 226–27; *Senate Journal of the Legislative Assembly of the State of Kansas*, 69–71; *House Journal, 1862* [Kansas], 164–66.

56. Connelley, *The Provisional Government of Nebraska Territory*, 131–33, 141.

57. Special Orders no. 49, Headquarters Department of the Mississippi, March 28, 1862, *OR* 53:517; General Orders no. 4, Headquarters District of Kansas, April 10, 1862, *OR* 8:683; Halleck to Sturgis, April 6, 1862, *OR* 8:668; Lane and Pomeroy to Lincoln, April 24, 1862, Abraham Lincoln papers; General Orders no. 12, Headquarters District of Kansas, May 5, 1862; General Orders no. 1, Headquarters Department of Kansas, May 5, 1862, *OR* 13:370.

58. Castel, *A Frontier State at War*, 82–83.

59. Ibid., 84.

Conclusion

1. McCullough, *Truman*, 30.
2. Ibid., 30–31; "Expedition to Walker's," *Wyandotte Gazette*, January 4, 1862.
3. McCullough, *Truman*, 30, 72.
4. Goodrich, *Black Flag*, 16; Castel, *A Frontier State at War*, 53; Castel, *General Sterling Price*, 60.
5. Stringfellow, "Jim Lane," 274. "Stringfellow's" article was reprinted in the Topeka *Kansas State Record*, March 2, 1870. His claims were given the patina of authenticity by being repeated in Professor Leverett Wilson Spring's book, *Kansas: The Prelude to the War for the Union*, 276.
6. Halleck to Lincoln, January 6, 1862, Abraham Lincoln papers.
7. Letter dated Camp Lyon, Springfield, Missouri, November 2, 1861, *New York Tribune* (semi-weekly), November 15, 1861, p. 6; "The War in Missouri," *Harper's Weekly*, November 16, 1861, 722.
8. Halpine to Weed, October 17, 1861, Abraham Lincoln papers.
9. Ibid.
10. "Operations in Western Missouri," *New York Times*, January 6, 1862, p. 8. About the same time, Colonel John A. Martin of the Kansas Eighth recorded a nearly identical description of the countryside. Goodrich, *Black Flag*, 27.
11. Sheridan, "From Slavery in Missouri to Freedom in Kansas," 28–47; Margaret J. Hays to Dear Mother, June 6, 1861, and September 26, 1861, private collection of Marian Franklin, Laytonville, California; "Affairs in Kansas," *New York Times*, November 11, 1861, p. 3; Nelson, "Missouri Slavery, 1861–1865," 260–74, 267, 269; private correspondence with Chris Tabor of Butler, Missouri, January 5, 2005.
12. Bowen, "Guerrilla War in Western Missouri, 1862–1865," 49–50.
13. Margaret J. Hays to Dear Mother, September 26, 1861, private collection of Marian Franklin, Laytonville, California.
14. Frémont, "In Command in Missouri," 287; Eaton to Price, November 2, 1861, *OR* 3:563–64; Little to Frémont, November 5, 1861, ibid., 565; Halleck to Thomas, November 7, 1861, ibid., 561–62; Hunter to Price, November 7, 1861, ibid., 565; General Orders no. 2, Headquarters Department of the Missouri, March 13, 1862, *OR* 8:611–12.
15. *Congressional Globe*, 37th Congress, 2d sess., 110–11. This speech was reprinted in the December 24, 1861, *Richmond* (Virginia) *Daily Dispatch*, "The Slavery Question in the Federal Congress," and the January 12, 1862, *Chicago Tribune* (daily), "Gen. Lane's Speech in the Senate," p. 2.
16. Two hundred portable corn mills were purchased by the government at Lane's request and sent to Fort Leavenworth. Meigs to the Secretary of War, November 18, 1862, *OR* Series III, 2:801.
17. *Congressional Globe*, 37th Congress, 1st sess., 192; M. to Friend Speer, November 8, 1861, Lawrence *Republican*, November 21, 1861; "Gen. Lane's Speech,"

Leavenworth Daily Conservative, November 17, 1861; *Congressional Globe,* 37th Congress, 2d sess., 110–11; Leavenworth *Daily Times,* June 12, 1862; "Speech of General James H. Lane," *Leavenworth Daily Conservative,* January 29, 1862; "Our Kansas Letter," *Chicago Tribune* (daily), February 5, 1862, p. 2; "Gen. Lane's Speech," *Tipton* (Iowa) *Advertiser,* February 13, 1862. Lane's Springfield speech was fully reported in *New York Tribune* the (semi-weekly), November 19, 1861, p. 8, and the *Chicago Tribune* (daily), November 18, 1861, p. 2.

18. Orders no. —, Headquarters Army of the West, July 26, 1861, *OR* 3:407; "Proclamation," Headquarters Western Department, August 30, 1861, *OR* 3:466–70; Lincoln to Frémont, September 11, 1861, *OR* 3:485–86; General Orders no. 23, Headquarters Western Department, October 20, 1861, *OR* 3:539–40.

19. General Orders no. 8, Headquarters Department of the Missouri, November 26, 1861, *OR* Series II 1:137; Neely, *The Fate of Liberty,* 44–46; General Orders no. 24, December 12, 1861, *OR* Series II, 1:150–51; General Orders no. 13, Headquarters Department of the Missouri, December 4, 1861, *OR* 8:405–407.

20. General Orders no. 32, Headquarters Department of the Missouri, December 22, 1861, *OR* 8:463–64, *OR* Series II, 1:237.

21. Pope to Frémont, July 16, 1861, *OR* 3:396; "Notice," July 21, 1861, ibid., 403–404; Pope to Stevenson, August 2, 1861, ibid., 421; Pope to Frémont, August 25, 1861, ibid., 456–57; Pope to Commanding Officer, August 2, 1861, ibid., 421–22.

22. Pope to Kelton, August 17, 1861, *OR* 3:447–48. Secessionists soon learned to manipulate these policies to harm loyal men. Hayward to Frémont, August 25, 1861, *OR* 3:433–35; Hayward to Brooks, August 13, 1861, ibid., 458.

23. Grant to McMackin, August 12, 1861, *OR* 3:438–39; Simon, *The Papers of Ulysses S. Grant,* 2:136–37; Grant to Worthington, August 26, 1861, *OR* Series II, 1:217; Grant to Oglesby, November 3, 1861, *OR* 3:268.

At least three times—in December, January, and February—Grant cautioned subordinates against taking private property. In one instance he directed that property taken be returned to its owners, and in another he had an offending captain arrested. He felt strongly enough about this to write, "In cases of outrageous marauding I would fully justify shooting the perpetrators down if caught in the act—I mean our own men as well as the enemy." Grant to Ross, December 4, 1861, *OR* Series II, 1:233; Grant to Paine, January 23, 1862, *OR* Series II, 3:211; Grant to Kelton, February 22, 1862, ibid., 300.

24. Grant to Butler, August 23, 1861, *OR* 3:452–53; testimony of H. M. Day, February 14, 1862, *OR* Series II, 1:320; Simon, *The Papers of Ulysses S. Grant,* 2:136–37; Rawlins to Wood, September 25, 1861, *OR* Series II, 1:511; Grant to McKeever, September 26, 1861, *OR* 3:197; Grant to McKeever, September 26, 1861, *OR* Series II, 2:79; Grant to Worthington, August 26, 1861, *OR* Series II, 1:217.

25. Grant to Paine, January 11, 1862, *OR* 8:494–95; Thompson to Polk, January 18, 1862, ibid., 737. It is unclear how long the citizens were kept in tents and away from their homes.

26. Dodge to Greusel, November 4, 1861, *OR* 3:255; Dodge to McKeever, November 8, 1861, ibid.; "National Operations in Texas County," *New York Times*, November 11, 1861, p. 8.

27. As an example of the limits to which "lawful" warfare can be stretched, in World War II the British adopted the policy of "de-housing" the German civilian population by destroying their homes through area bombing. This necessarily inflicted massive civilian casualties. The U.S. Air Force targeted civilians to a lesser degree, the fire bombing of Dresden being the most notorious example. A wartime English author, arguing that "the old clear distinction between soldiers and civilians has been obscured," justified the intentional targeting of not only German industrial workers but also "transport workers, as well as all the civilians enrolled in the service of passive defence—the fire-fighters, the rescue parties, the demolition squads." (The logical extension of such a policy would allow the bombing of farmers who grow crops that feed munitions workers and the army—in fact, it could justify killing just about anyone.) In the war against Japan, the United States began fire-bombing Japanese cities on the theory that entire cities should be destroyed in order to eradicate widely dispersed small factories and to break the enemy's will to resist. The March 1945 raid against Tokyo killed more than eighty-three thousand people, injured more than forty thousand, and left up to one million homeless. To my knowledge, the aerial bombing practices of the Allies have never been officially repudiated and stand as precedent as an acceptable method of conducting war. Murray, "Did Strategic Bombing Work?"; 494–512; Spaight, *Bombing Vindicated*, 78, 112, 115; Haulman, *Hitting Home: The Air Offensive Against Japan*, 22.

28. Thomas Hardy, *Times Laughingstocks and Other Verses* (MacMillan and Co., 1919).

Appendix A. Necrology

1. Salomon to Blunt, July 20, 1862, *OR* 13:484–85. Salomon wrote that Weer was "a man abusive and violent in his intercourse with his fellow-officers, notoriously intemperate in habits, entirely disregarding military usages and discipline, always rash in speech, act and orders, refusing to inferior officers and their reports that consideration which is due an officer of the U.S. Army."

2. *Military History of Kansas Regiments*, 287–21.

3. Trego to My Dear Wife, June 1, 1862, in Langsdorf, "The Letters of Joseph H. Trego," 303–304; Holcombe, *History of Greene County, Missouri*, 416–17.

4. *Military History of Kansas Regiments*, 108–18.

5. Ibid., 119–50; Fisher, "The First Kansas Colored," 121–28.

6. Curtis to Blunt, Herron, and Schofield, December 23, 1862, *OR* 22, part 1:858; Scott to Maxey, April 12, 1864, *OR* 34, part 3: 762–63; Scott to McCulloch, April 12, 1864, ibid., 774.

7. "General Blunt's Account of His Civil War Experiences," 222–35, 242–53, 262–64.

8. Ibid., 211; Collins, *General James G. Blunt*, 208–12, 218–22. In a case that made its way to the United States Supreme Court, Blunt's brother Elbridge G. Blunt sued the administrator of James Blunt's estate over a note by James payable to Elbridge, made in Chicago on July 1, 1875, in the amount of $3,204.34 "in settlement for work previously done by the plaintiff for the maker." The issue was whether collection was barred by the statute of limitations. The Supreme Court remanded the matter to the circuit court to allow the plaintiff to try to establish facts that would overcome the statute of limitations defense. *Bauserman v. Blunt*, 147 U.S. 647 (1893).

9. Cutler, *History of the State of Kansas*, 1:302–303; report of Blunt, December 24, 1864, *OR* vol. 41, part 1:571–72.

10. Marsh to Hardie, April 13, 1864, *OR* Series 2, 7:43; Clarke to Hoffman, April 24, 1864, ibid., 84–86; Hoffman to Halleck, May 29, 1864, ibid., 175–76.

11. Manning, "The Kansas Senate of 1865 and 1866," 363; "Died," *Wyandotte Gazette*, March 2, 1867. Weer's body was taken to Alton, Illinois, for burial.

12. Thomas to Halleck, April 4, 1862, *OR* 8:659–60; Second Brigade to Dear Journal, September 15, 1862, Lawrence *Kansas State Journal*, October 2, 1862; X to Editor Republican, September 22, 1862, Lawrence *Republican*, October 2, 1862; Weer to Moonlight, September 12, 1862, *OR* 13:627; Blunt to Caleb B. Smith, November 21, 1862, Abraham Lincoln papers; Curtis to Pleasonton, October 26, 1864, *OR* 41, part 1:339–40; Pleasonton to Curtis, October 27, 1864, ibid., part 4:286; Curtis to Pleasonton, October 27, 1864, ibid., part 4:286–87; John Ritchie compiled military service file, Second Indian Home Guard.

13. Jarboe, "John Ritchie," 48–68; Blunt to Caleb B. Smith, November 21, 1862, Abraham Lincoln papers.

14. Stephenson, *The Political Career of General James H. Lane*, 127–29.

15. Goodrich, *Bloody Dawn*, 95–97, 155.

16. Castel, *A Frontier State at War*, 200–201.

17. Waugh, *Reelecting Lincoln*, 185–87; Stoddard, "The Story of a Nomination," 272–73.

18. Stephenson, *The Political Career of General James H. Lane*, 152–59. Jack Henderson claimed a role in Lane's suicide. He said he obtained evidence of a $60,000 payoff to Lane for Lane's part in pushing through a bill for the removal of refugee Indians in Kansas, and was about to expose Lane in Congress. Allegedly Lane was warned of this by Charles Sumner; Lane "arose at once and said he had a dispatch from home announcing illness in his family, and asked leave of absence for ten days. He went back to Kansas, and three or four days after he arrived there committed suicide." Henderson also claimed Lane had sabotaged Henderson's appointment as superintendent of the Pueblo Indians. I have been unable to confirm or discredit either allegation. "Jack Henderson: A Border Ruffian's Recollections of Kansas," Arkansas City (Kansas) *Traveler*, March 5, 1879.

Appendix B. Brigade Staff

1. Sources for the men are as follows:

Adams: Basler, *The Collected Works*, 4:476.

Ainsworth: Typed copy of an original reminiscence dated 1904, Richard M. Ainsworth collection; Lawrence *Republican*, December 19, 1861; Hill, *A History of the State of Oklahoma*, 2:40–41.

Anderson: Untitled article, *Leavenworth Daily Conservative*, September 26, 1861; "Proclamation of Gen. Lane," ibid., September 26, 1861.

Chandler: Untitled article, *Leavenworth Daily Conservative*, October 29, 1861; untitled article, ibid., October 29, 1861.

Cutler: *OR* 3:164.

Davis and McCall: "Appointments," *Leavenworth Daily Conservative*, August 17, 1861; untitled article, Leavenworth *Daily Times*, August 18, 1861; J. J. Sears to Montgomery, December 12, 1861, James Montgomery papers, Montgomery 1861 folder.

Ege: Untitled article, *Leavenworth Daily Conservative*, August 7, 17, 1861.

Ellis: Connelley, *A Standard History of Kansas*, 3:1204.

Gilpatrick: Henry Miles Moore papers; Fisher to Editor Republican, December 12, 1861, Lawrence *Republican*, December 19, 1861; *Leavenworth Daily Conservative*, December 27, 1861; Basler, *The Collected Works*, 4:476.

Insley: Letter from Maumee, August 18, 1861, *Leavenworth Daily Conservative*, August 22, 1861; letter from Maumee, September 4, 1861, ibid., September 13, 1861.

Loring: Lane to Scott, September 6, 1861, James Lane collection, Box 1, Folder 7, Spencer Research Library.

Moore: Henry Miles Moore papers.

Parrott: *OR* 3:447.

Pomeroy: "Arrival of Military Officers," Leavenworth *Daily Times*, August 2, 1861.

Undergraff: "Appointments," *Leavenworth Daily Conservative*, August 17, 1861; Basler, *The Collected Works*, 4:476.

George Weed: "Weekly Report of Geo. W. Weed Ordnance Segt K. B. for the Week Ending Dec 2nd 1861," James Montgomery papers, Montgomery 1861 folder; T .J. Weed to Geo. W. Weed, October 5, 1861, Collection 2.16, "Papers Relating to Individual Units— Fourth Infantry."

Dr. T. J. Weed: Untitled article, *Leavenworth Daily Conservative*, October 30, 1861; "Affairs in Kansas," *New York Times*, November 11, 1861, p. 3.

Wilder: Basler, *The Collected Works*, 4:476.

Insley, T. J. Weed, Gilpatrick, Anderson, Kerr, and Loring are identified in "The Soldiers of Kansas Brand Gov. Robinson as a Base Slanderer, a Traitor, and a Coward," *Leavenworth Daily Conservative*, October 18, 1861.

2. "Arrival of Military Officers," Leavenworth *Daily Times*, August 2, 1861; "Brigadier-General J. H. Lane," *Leslie's Illustrated Newspaper*, August 17, 1861, p. 24.

3. "From Kansas," *Chicago Tribune* (daily), November 10, 1861; untitled article, Leavenworth *Daily Times*, November 15, 1861. In the former article de Vecchi was described as a "late Artillerist" of Lane's staff.

Appendix C. Brigade Casualties

1. McPherson, *Battle Cry of Freedom*, 485–88.
2. The *Roll of the Officers and Enlisted Men* gives the date as September 22; it is assumed this is a transcription error.
3. The *Report of the Adjutant General* lists Schultz as having been killed in October near Butler, Missouri, and Francis Miller as having been killed at West Point, Missouri, in October.
4. Information for Isaac H. Gray, Charles Coger (March 3), Jacob L. Vanwert (March 1), and Brice A. Jackson (March 19), comes exclusively from the *Report of the Adjutant General*.
5. The *Report of the Adjutant General* lists Allen as having died of typhoid fever October 20 at Fort Scott.

Bibliography

Manuscripts

Ainsworth, Richard M. Collection. Kansas State Historical Society.
[Boutwell, Daniel W.] "A Plea for Justice for One Court-Martialed, Sentenced, and Shot, Reported as a Deserter, and Afterward, as a Private Citizen, Through Bravery and Heroism in Time of Danger, Saved Millions of Stores for the U.S. Government." N.p.: n.p., 1909. Biographical Pamphlets. Kansas State Historical Society.
———. "A Veteran's History of His Unrequited Service to this Republic." Biographical Pamphlets. Kansas State Historical Society.
Bowman, Charles S. Papers. Kansas State Historical Society.
Brown Family, John Stillman. Papers. Microfilm MS 566. Kansas State Historical Society.
Creitz, William A. Diary. Kansas State Historical Society.
———. "History of Company 'A' Fifth Kansas Cavalry Volunteers." Kansas State Historical Society.
Denver, James W. Collection. Kansas State Historical Society.
Descriptive Roll 10th Kansas Infantry. Microfilm AR 116. Kansas State Historical Society.
Dickinson, William H. H. Diary. Manuscript 255. K. Ross Toole Archives, Mansfield Library, University of Montana, Missoula.
———. "War Notes." Manuscript 255. K. Ross Toole Archives, Mansfield Library, University of Montana, Missoula. This collection contains two handwritten documents: one is a contemporarily created diary, and the second, which

I have dubbed "War Notes," appears to have been a reminiscence that drew upon contemporary writings.

Fifth Kansas Cavalry. Collection 2.17. Kansas State Historical Society.

"Fort Leavenworth, Kansas Letter Book, 1861–1863," Western Historical Manuscript Collection, University of Missouri, collection C 1103.

Harvey, James M. Papers. Kansas State Historical Society.

———. Collection (oversize). Kansas State Historical Society.

Hays, Margaret. Letters. Private collection of Marian Franklin, Laytonville, California.

Hinton, Richard. Collection. Kansas State Historical Society.

Horne, Daniel H. Papers. Kansas State Historical Society.

Hudson, Joseph Kennedy. Papers. Collection 395. Kansas State Historical Society.

Hyatt, Thaddeus. Papers. Microfilm MS 87. Kansas State Historical Society.

Huntoon, Andrew Jackson. Papers. Collection 398. Kansas State Historical Society.

Isely, Christian. Papers, Microfilm MS 139.03. Kansas State Historical Society.

———. Papers. Wichita State University special collections.

Johnson, William T. Memoir. Typescript copy. Western Historical Collection. State Historical Society of Missouri, Columbia..

"Journal of the Leavenworth Constitutional Convention, April 1, 1858." Kansas State Historical Society.

"James Henry Lane Letters to William E. Prince." Beinecke Rare Book and Manuscript Library, Yale University. Collection WA MSS S-1676 P9365.

Lane, James. Collection. Spencer Research Library, University of Kansas, Lawrence.

Lane, James Henry. Papers. Kansas State Historical Society.

Levinson, Irving W. "Occupation and Stability Dilemmas of the Mexico War: Origins and Solutions." Paper presented at the Combat Studies Institute, U.S. Army Command and General Staff College, Fort Leavenworth, Kansas, August 5–7, 2003. Kansas State Historical Society.

Lincoln, Abraham. Papers. Library of Congress.

Mantor, Rowland. Papers. Collection 430. Kansas State Historical Society.

Montgomery, James. Collection. Kansas State Historical Society.

Moonlight, Thomas. Collection. Kansas State Historical Society.

Moore, Henry Miles. Collection. Kansas State Historical Society.

———. Diary. Microfilm MS 33. Kansas State Historical Society.

Muster Out Rolls of Third, Fourth, Fifth, and Sixth Kansas Regiments. Microfilm AR 118. Kansas State Historical Society.

"Papers Relating to Individual Units—Third Kansas Infantry." Kansas State Historical Society.

"Personal Memoirs of Watson Stewart." Kansas State Historical Society.

Porter, David. "Personal Reminiscences of the Civil War." A paper read by Dr. David R. Porter before the Loyal Legion, Department of Missouri, at Kansas City, in September, 1916. Kansas State Historical Society.

"Records Relating to Individual Units—Fifth Kansas Cavalry." Kansas State Historical Society.
Robinson, Charles and Sara. Papers. Microfilm MS 640, roll 1. Kansas State Historical Society.
Sixth Kansas Cavalry. Collection. Kansas State Historical Society.
Stearns, George Luther. Papers. Microfilm MS 171. Kansas State Historical Society.
Trego, Joseph. Diary, 1861–63. Microfilm MS 1008. Kansas State Historical Society.
Vansickle, John Henry. Collection. Spencer Research Library, University of Kansas, Lawrence.
Ward, A. T. Papers. Microfilm MS 1183.03. Kansas State Historical Society.
Wright, Clark. Papers. Pearce Civil War Collection, Navarro College, Corsican, Tex.

Archives

Archives of the Adjutant General of Ohio. "Correspondence to the Governor and the Adjutant General of Ohio." Series 147, vol. 43. Ohio Historical Society.
Kansas State Historical Society
    "Governor's Office—Correspondence Files—Governor Robinson. Box 1.1, Folder 13, Military Affairs."
    Kansas Adjutant General records. "General Correspondence 1861–1862."
    ———. "General Correspondence 1861–1865."
    ———. "Tenth Regiment Correspondence, Field & Staff 1863–1877."
National Archives and Records Administration
    "Fort Leavenworth Letters Sent, December 1845 to December 1870." Record Group 94.
    John Ritchie compiled military service file. Fifth Kansas Cavalry.
    ———. Second Indian Home Guard.
    Thrasher, Luther. Diary. In "Regimental Letter, Endorsement & Order Book." Record Group 94. Bound Records. 10th Kansas Infantry.

Court Records

Lane, James H. Probate estate. File #1445. District Court of Douglas County, Kansas.
Index to Deeds No. 2—Grantor. Douglas County, Kansas, Register of Deeds, Lawrence.

Newspapers

Arkansas City (Kansas) *Traveler*
Ashtabula (Ohio) *Weekly Telegram*
Augusta (Georgia) *Daily Constitutionalist*
Canton (Ohio) *Stark County Republican*

Chicago Tribune (daily)
Chicago Tribune (weekly)
Congressional Globe. 37th Congress, 1st and 2d sessions.
Dallas *Herald*
Doniphan *Kansas Crusader of Freedom*
Ellsworth (Maine) *Herald*
Fort Scott *Democrat*
Frank Leslie's Illustrated Newspaper
Harper's Weekly
Humboldt Union
Lawrence *Kansas State Journal*
Lawrence *Republican*
Leavenworth (weekly) *Conservative*
Leavenworth Daily Conservative
Leavenworth *Daily Times*
Lecompton Union
Liberty (Missouri) *Tribune*
Little Rock *Arkansas True Democrat*
Memphis Daily Appeal
Mound City (Kansas) *Republic*
New York *The Jewish Messenger*
New York Times
New York Tribune (daily)
New York Tribune (semi-weekly)
Olathe *Mirror*
Paulding (Mississippi) *Eastern Clarion*
Richmond (Virginia) *Daily Dispatch*
Tipton (Iowa) *Advertiser*
Topeka *Daily State Record*
Topeka *Kansas State Record*
Topeka Tribune
Houston *Tri-Weekly Telegraph*
Wabaunsee (Kansas) *Patriot*
White Cloud *Kansas Chief*
Wyandotte Gazette

Books and Pamphlets

Abel, Annie Heloise. *The American Indian in the Civil War, 1862–1865.* Lincoln: University of Nebraska Press, 1992. Reprint of vol. 2, *The American Indian as Participant in the Civil War,* 1919.

Anderson, Ephraim McD. *Memoirs: Historical and Personal; Including the Campaigns of the First Missouri Brigade.* St. Louis: Times Printing Co., 1868.

Barns, George C. *Denver, the Man: The Life, Letters, and Public Papers of the Lawyer, Soldier, and Statesman.* Wilmington, Ohio: n.p., 1949.
Basler, Roy C., ed. *The Collected Works of Abraham Lincoln.* 5 vols. New Brunswick, N.J.: Rutgers University Press, 1952–55.
Berlin, Ira, and Barbara J. Fields, Steven F. Miller, Joseph P. Reidy, and Leslie S. Rowland, eds. *Free at Last: A Documentary History of Slavery, Freedom, and the Civil War.* New York: New Press, 1992.
Berwanger, Eugene H. *The Frontier Against Slavery: Western Anti-Negro Prejudice and the Slavery Extension Controversy.* Urbana: University of Illinois Press, 1967.
Biographical and Historical Record of Ringgold and Decatur Counties, Iowa. Chicago: Lewis Publishing Co., 1887.
Birtle, Andrew J. *U.S. Army Counterinsurgency and Contingency Operation Doctrine 1860–1941.* Washington, D.C.: Center of Military History, 1998.
Bishop, A. W. *Loyalty on the Frontier, or Sketches of Union Men of the Southwest; with Incidents and Adventures in Rebellion on the Border.* St. Louis: R. P. Studley and Co., 1863.
Blackmar, Frank W., ed. *Kansas: A Cyclopedia of State History.* 2 vols. Chicago: Standard Publishing Co., 1912.
Blair, Ed. *The History of Johnson County.* Lawrence, Kans.: Standard Publishing Co., 1915.
Bondi, August. *Autobiography of August Bondi, 1833–1907.* Galesburg, Ill.: Wagoner Printing Co., 1910.
Brewerton, G. Douglas. *The War in Kansas: A Rough Trip to the Border.* New York: Derby & Jackson, 1856.
Britton, Wiley. *Pioneer Life in Southwest Missouri.* Columbia: State Historical Society of Missouri, 1923.
———. *The Civil War on the Border.* Vol. 1, 1861–1862. New York: G. P. Putnam's Sons, 1899. Reprint, Ottawa: Kansas Heritage Press, 1994.
Brophy, Patrick, ed. *In the Devil's Dominions: A Union Soldier's Adventures in "Bushwhacker Country."* Nevada, Mo.: Vernon County Historical Society, 1998.
Browne, Francis Fisher. *The Every-Day Life of Abraham Lincoln.* Chicago: Browne & Howell Co., 1913.
Brownlee, Richard S. *Gray Ghosts of the Confederacy: Guerrilla Warfare in the West, 1861–1865.* Baton Rouge: Louisiana State University Press, 1958.
Burlingame, Michael, and John R. Turner Ettlinger. *Inside Lincoln's White House: The Complete Civil War Diary of John Hay.* Carbondale: Southern Illinois University Press, 1997.
Case, Nelson. *History of Labette County, Kansas.* Topeka, Kans.: Crane & Co., 1893.
Castel, Albert. *A Frontier State at War: Kansas 1861–1865*, Ithaca, N.Y.: Cornell University Press, 1958.
———. *General Sterling Price and the Civil War in the West.* Baton Rouge: Louisiana State University Press, 1968.

Catton, Bruce. *A Stillness at Appomattox*. New York: Doubleday & Co., 1953.

———. *This Hallowed Ground: The Story of the Union Side of the Civil War*. Garden City, N.Y.: Doubleday & Co., 1956.

Collins, Robert. *General James G. Blunt: Tarnished Glory*. Gretna, La.: Pelican, 2005.

Connelley, William E., ed. *The Provisional Government of Nebraska Territory and the Journals of William Walker*. Lincoln, Neb.: State Journal Co., 1899.

———. *Quantrill and the Border Wars*. Cedar Rapids, Iowa: Torch Press, 1910.

———. *A Standard History of Kansas and Kansans*. 5 vols. Chicago: Lewis Publishing Co., 1918.

[Cutler, William G., ed.] *History of the State of Kansas*. 2 vols. Chicago: A. T. Andreas, 1883.

Deane, Frank P., ed. *My Dear Wife . . . The Civil War Letters of David Brett Union Cannoneer*. Little Rock, Ark.: Pioneer Press, 1964.

A Directory of the Kansas Historical Exhibit in the Kansas State Building at the World's Columbian Exposition, 1893. Topeka, Kans.: n.p., 1893.

Eldridge, Shalor Winchell. *Recollections of Early Days in Kansas*. Vol. 2. Publications of the Kansas State Historical Society, Topeka, Kans.: Imri Zumwalt, State Printer, 1920.

Fisher, H[ugh] D[unn]. *The Gun and the Gospel*. Chicago: Medical Century Co., 1899.

Ford, Leicester. *The Works of Thomas Jefferson*. Vol. 11. New York and London: P. Putnam's Sons, 1904–05.

Frémont, John C. "In Command in Missouri." Pp. 278–88, in *Battles and Leaders of the Civil War*, edited by Robert Underwood Johnson and Clarence Clough Buel. 4 vols. New York: The Century Co., 1887. Reprint, Secaucus, N.J.: Castle Books, 1982.

Gaeddert, G. Raymond. *The Birth of Kansas*, Topeka, Kans.: Kansas State Printing Plant, 1940.

Gates, Paul Wallace. *Fifty Million Acres: Conflict Over Kansas Land Policy, 1854–1890*. New York: Arno Press, 1954.

Giles, Fry W. *Thirty Years in Topeka: A Historical Sketch*, Topeka, Kans.: Geo. W. Crane, 1886. Reprint, Topeka, Kans.: Capper Special Services, 1960.

Goodlander, C. W. *Memoirs and Recollections of C. W. Goodlander of the Early Days of Fort Scott*. Fort. Scott: Monitor Printing, 1900.

Goodrich, Thomas. *Bloody Dawn: The Story of the Lawrence Massacre*. Kent, Ohio: Kent State University Press, 1991.

———. *Black Flag: Guerrilla Warfare on the Western Border, 1861-1865*, Bloomington: Indiana University Press, 1995

———. *War to the Knife: Bleeding Kansas, 1854–1861*. Mechanicsburg, Penn.: Stackpole, 1998.

Governor's Annual Message: Kansas, 1862. N.p: n.p., n.d.

Hatch, Thom. *The Blue, The Gray, & The Red: Indian Campaigns of the Civil War*. Mechanicburg, Penn.: Stackpole, 2003.

Haulman, Daniel L. *Hitting Home: The Air Offensive against Japan*. Washington, D.C.: Government Printing Office, 1999.

Hill, Luther B. *A History of the State of Oklahoma*, Vol. 2. Chicago: Lewis Publishing Co., 1908.

Hinton, Richard J. *John Brown and His Men*. New York and London: Funk & Wagnalls Co., c1894.

History of Cedar County, Iowa. Chicago: Western Historical Co., 1878.

History of Vernon County, Missouri. St. Louis: Brown & Co., 1887.

Holcombe, R. I., ed. *History of Greene County, Missouri*. St. Louis: Western Historical Co., 1883.

House Journal, 1862 [Kansas]. N.p.: n.p., n.d.

Hunt, George D. *History of Salem and the Immediate Vicinity*. Salem, Ohio: n.p., 1898.

Johnson, W. A. *The History of Anderson County, Kansas, from its First Settlement to Fourth of July, 1876*. Garnett, Kans.: Kauffman & Iler, 1877.

Kansas Constitutional Convention. Topeka, Kans.: Kansas State Printing Plant, 1920.

Kent, James. *Commentaries on American Law*. Vol. 1. New York: O. Halstead, 1826.

Kiper, Richard L. *Major General John Alexander McClernand: Politician in Uniform*. Kent, Ohio: Kent State University Press, 1999.

Leslie, Edward E. *The Devil Knows How to Ride*. New York: Random House, 1996.

Lewis, Mrs. M. E. "Kansas Jayhawker's Raid Upon Osceola, October, 1861." Pp. 54–55 in [United Daughters of the Confederacy, Missouri Division], *Reminiscences of Missouri Women during the Sixties*. Jefferson City, Mo.: Hugh Stevens Printing Co., 1913.

[Lions Club of Freeman, Missouri], *Freeman at 100*. Freeman, Mo.: 1970.

McCullough, David. *Truman*, New York: Simon & Schuster, 1992.

McPherson, James M. *Battle Cry of Freedom: The Civil War Era*. New York: Oxford University Press, 1988.

Military History of Kansas Regiments During the War for the Suppression of the Great Rebellion. Leavenworth, Kans.: W. S. Burke, 1870.

Miller, Edward A. Jr. *Lincoln's Abolitionist General: The Biography of David Hunter*. Columbus: University of South Carolina Press, 1997.

Monaghan, Jay. *Civil War on the Western Border, 1854–1865*. Boston: Little, Brown, 1955.

Mooney, Volney P. *History of Butler County, Kansas*. Lawrence, Kans.: Standard Publishing Co., 1916.

Moore, Frank, ed. *Rebellion Record: A Diary of American Events: Documents and Narratives*. Vol. 3. New York: G. P. Putnam, 1862.

Morgan, Perl W., ed. *History of Wyandotte County, Kansas, and Its People*. Chicago: The Lewis Publishing Co., 1911.

Murray, Williamson R. "Did Strategic Bombing Work?" Pp. 494–512 in *No End Save Victory: Perspectives on World War II*, edited by Robert Cowley. New York: G. P. Putnam's Sons, 2001.

Neely, Mark E., Jr. *The Fate of Liberty: Abraham Lincoln and Civil Liberties*. New York: Oxford University Press, 1991.

Oates, Stephen B. *To Purge This Land with Blood. A Biography of John Brown*. Amherst: University of Massachusetts Press, 1984.

Oliva, Leo E. *Fort Scott on the Indian Frontier*. Topeka, Kans.: Kansas State Historical Society, 1984.

Paludan, Philipp Shaw. "The Better Angels of Our Nature. Lincoln, Propaganda and Public Opinion in the North During the American Civil War." A talk given at the Fifteenth Annual R. Gerald McMurtry Lecture, the Lincoln Museum, Fort Wayne, Indiana, 1992.

Phillips, Christopher. *Damned Yankee: The Life of General Nathaniel Lyon*. Columbia: University of Missouri Press, 1990.

Phillips, William. *The Conquest of Kansas, by Missouri and Her Allies*. Boston: Phillips, Sampson and Co., 1856.

Population of the United States in 1860; Compiled from the Original Returns of the Eighth Census. Washington, D.C.: Government Printing Office, 1864.

Price, Richard Scott. *Nathaniel Lyon: Harbinger from Kansas*. Springfield, Mo.: Wilson's Creek National Battlefield Foundation, 1990.

Remini, Robert V. *Andrew Jackson and His Indian Wars*. New York: Viking, 2001.

Report of the Adjutant General of the State of Kansas, 1861–65. 2 vols. Topeka, Kans.: J. K. Hudson Printing Co., 1896.

Richardson, Albert D. *Beyond the Mississippi: From the Great River to the Great Ocean*, Hartford, Conn.: American Publishing Co., 1867.

Richmond, Robert W. *Kansas: A Land of Contrasts*. St. Charles, Mo.: Forum Press, 1974.

Robley, T. F. *History of Bourbon County, Kansas, to the Close of 1865*. Fort Scott, Kans: Monitor Book & Printing, 1894.

Rogers, William B., and N. G. Rogers, *Souvenir History of Mercer County, Missouri, and Dictionary of Local Dates*. Trenton, Mo.: W. B. Rogers Printing Co., 1911.

Roll of the Officers and Enlisted Men of the Third, Fourth, Eighteenth, and Nineteenth Kansas Volunteers. Topeka, Kans.: W. Y. Morgan, 1902. Reprint of Appendix 4 of Adjutant General's Thirteenth Biennial Report.

Senate Journal of the Legislative Assembly of the State of Kansas, at Its Second Session Commenced at the City of Topeka, January 14, and Concluded March 6, A.D.1862. Lawrence, Kans.: State Journal, 1862.

Simon, John Y., ed. *The Papers of Ulysses S. Grant*. Carbondale: Southern Illinois University Press, 1967–85.

Simpson, Brooks D., and Jean V. Berlin, eds. *Sherman's Civil War: Selected Correspondence of William T. Sherman, 1860–1865*. Chapel Hill: University of North Carolina Press, 1999.

Spaight, J. M. *Bombing Vindicated*, London: Geoffrey Bles, 1944.
Speer, John. *Life of Gen. James H. Lane: "The Liberator of Kansas."* Garden City, Kans.: John Speer, Printer, 1896.
Spring, Leverett Wilson. *Kansas: The Prelude to the War for the Union.* Boston: Houghton, Mifflin and Co., 1885.
Starr, Stephen Z. *Jennison's Jayhawkers: A Civil War Cavalry Regiment and Its Commander.* Baton Rouge: Louisiana State University Press, 1973.
Stephenson, Wendell Holmes. *The Political Career of General James H. Lane.* Vol. 3. Publications of the Kansas State Historical Society. Topeka, Kans.: B. P. Walker, State Printer, 1930.
Swenson, Virginia, compiler. *Civil War Letters Written by George Edwin Flanders During His Service in the Kansas Volunteer Cavalry.* 2 vols. Topeka, Kans: n.p., 1989.
[U.S. Senate]. *Select Committee on the Harpers Ferry Invasion.* Rep. Com. No. 278, 36th Congress, 1st Session, 1860.
Villard, Oswald Garrison. *John Brown, 1800–1859: A Biography Fifty Years After.* Boston: Houghton Mifflin, 1910.
The War of the Rebellion: A Compilation of the Official Records of the Union and Confederate Armies. 128 vols. Washington, D.C.: Government Printing Office, 1880–1901.
Warren, Charles. *The Supreme Court in United States History.* 3 vols. Boston: Little, Brown, 1922.
Waugh, John C. *Reelecting Lincoln: The Battle for the 1864 Presidency.* New York: Crown, 1997.
Weidemeyer, John M. "Memoirs of a Confederate Soldier." Pp. 61–65 in [United Daughters of the Confederacy, Missouri Division], *Reminiscences of Missouri Women During the Sixties.* Jefferson City, Mo.: Hugh Stevens Printing Co., 1913.
Welch, G. Murlin. *Border Warfare in Southeastern Kansas 1856–1859.* Pleasanton, Kans.: Linn County Publishers, 1977.
Wilder, D. W. *The Annals of Kansas 1854–1885.* Topeka, Kans.: T. Dwight Thacher, 1886.
Wilson, James Grant, and John Fiske, eds. *Appleton's Cyclopedia of American Biography,* New York: Appleton and Co., 1887–89.

Articles

Addicott, Jeffrey F. "Operation Desert Storm: R. E. Lee or W. T. Sherman?" *Military Law Review* 136 (Spring 1992): 115–35.
"Address of Ex-Governor James W. Denver." *Transactions of the Kansas State Historical Society, 1883–1885* 3 (1886): 359–66.
Atherton, Lewis E. "Daniel Howell Hise, Abolitionist and Reformer." *Mississippi Valley Historical Review* 26 (December 1939): 343–58.
Barnes, Lela, ed. "An Editor Looks at Early-Day Kansas. The Letters of Charles Monroe Chase." *Kansas Historical Quarterly* 26 (Summer 1960): 113–51.

Berneking, Carolyn. "Letters from Robert Gaston Elliott," *Kansas Historical Quarterly* 43 (Autumn 1977): 282–96.

Beszedits, Stephen. "Notable Hungarians and Their Contributions in the Civil War," http://suvcw.org/mollus/art14.htm, and "Prominent Hungarians of the American Civil War, http://www.hccc.org/A2e/A20303b.shtml. Both accessed August 21, 2006.

Bowen, Don R. "Guerrilla War in Western Missouri, 1862–1865: Historical Extensions of the Relative Deprivation Hypothesis." *Comparative Studies in Society and History* 19 (1977): 30–51.

Brinsfield, John W. "The Military Ethics of General William T. Sherman: A Reassessment." *Parameters: Journal of the US Army War College* 12 (June 1982): 36–48.

Castel, Albert. "Kansas Jayhawking Raids Into Western Missouri in 1861." *Missouri Historical Review* 54 (October 1959): 1–11.

———. "Civil War Kansas and the Negro." *Journal of Negro History* 51 (1966): 125–38.

Cory, Charles E. "The Sixth Kansas Cavalry and Its Commander." *Collections of the Kansas Historical Society, 1909–10* 11 (1910): 217–38.

Dirck, Brian R. "By the Hand of God: James Montgomery and Redemptive Violence." *Kansas History* 27 (Spring–Summer 2004): 100–15.

[Dorsheimer, William.] "Fremont's Hundred Days in Missouri." *Atlantic Monthly* 9 (March 1862): 115–25, 247–58, 372–84.

Drought, E. S. W. "James Montgomery." *Transactions of the Kansas State Historical Society, 1897–1900* 6 (1901): 342–43.

Fisher, Mike. "The First Kansas Colored—Massacre at Poison Springs." *Kansas History* 2 (Summer 1979): 121–28.

Galbreath, C. B. "Barclay Coppoc." *Ohio History* 30 (October 1921): 459–81.

"General Blunt's Account of His Civil War Experiences." *Kansas Historical Quarterly* 1 (May 1932): 211–65.

"Governor Denver's Administration." *Transactions of the Kansas State Historical Society, 1889–'96* 5 (1896): 464–61.

Gower, Calvin W. "Gold Fever in Kansas Territory: Migration to the Pike's Peak Gold Fields, 1858–1860." *Kansas Historical Quarterly* 39 (Spring 1973): 58–74.

Hoole, William Stanley, ed. "A Southerner's Viewpoint of the Kansas Situation, 1856–57: The Letters of Col. A. J. Hoole, C.S.A." *Kansas Historical Quarterly* 3 (February 1934): 43–56.

Hougen, Harvey R. "The Marais des Cygnes Massacre and the Execution of William Griffith." *Kansas History* 8 (Summer 1985): 74–94.

Jarboe, Mary Ritchie. "John Ritchie, Portrait of an Uncommon Man." Pp. 7–70 in *Bulletin of the Shawnee County Historical Society* 66 (November 1991).

Keeler, Ralph. "Owen Brown's Escape from Harper's Ferry." *Atlantic Monthly* 33 (March 1874): 342–65.

Langsdorf, Edgar, ed. "The Letters of Joseph H. Trego, 1857–1864, Linn County Pioneer. Part Two, 1861, 1862." *Kansas Historical Quarterly* 19 (August 1951): 287–309.

Langsdorf, Edgar, and Robert W. Richmond, eds. "Letters of Daniel R. Anthony, 1857–1862. Part Three, October 1, 1861–June 7, 1862." *Kansas Historical Quarterly* 24 (Autumn 1958): 351–70.

Langsdorf, Erich. "Jim Lane and the Frontier Guard." *Kansas Historical Quarterly* 9 (February 1940): 13–25.

"Letters of John and Sarah Everett, 1854–1864." *Kansas Historical Quarterly* 8 (May 1939): 143–74.

"Letters of Samuel James Reader, 1861–1863: Pioneer of Soldier Township, Shawnee County." *Kansas Historical Quarterly* 9 (February 1940): 13–25.

Lewis, Lloyd. "The Man the Historians Forgot." *Kansas Historical Quarterly* 8 (February 1939): 85–103.

Lindberg, Kip, and Matt Matthews, eds. "'The Eagle of the 11th Kansas': Wartime Reminiscences of Colonel Thomas Moonlight." *Arkansas Historical Quarterly* 62 (Spring 2003): 1–41.

Manning, Edwin C. "The Kansas Senate of 1865 and 1866." *Transactions of the Kansas State Historical Society, 1905–1906* 9 (1906): 359–75.

Murray, Donald M., and Robert M. Rodney, eds. "The Letters of Peter Bryant, Jackson County Pioneer: First Installment, 1854–1861." *Kansas Historical Quarterly* 27 (Autumn 1961): 320–52.

Neely, Mark E., Jr. "Was the Civil War a Total War?" *Civil War History* 37 (1991): 5–28.

Nelson, Earl J. "Missouri Slavery, 1861–1865." *Missouri Historical Review* 28 (1934): 260–74.

Nichols, Deborah, and Laurence M. Hauptman, "Warriors for the Union." *Civil War Times Illustrated* 35 (February 1997): 34–41.

Palmer, H. E. "The Black-flag Character of War on the Border." *Transactions of the Kansas State Historical Society, 1905–1906* 9 (1906): 455–66.

Patrick, Jeffrey L. "Reporting from an Enemy's Land: The Indiana Letters of 'Chincoupin.'" *Missouri Historical Review* 90 (April 1996): 309–29.

———. "This Regiment Will Make a Mark." *Missouri Historical Review* 90 (April 1996): 50–58.

Rafuse, Ethan S. "Typhoid and Tumult: Lincoln's Response to General McClellan's Bout with Typhoid Fever During the Winter of 1861–62." *Journal of the Abraham Lincoln Association* 18 (Summer 1997): 1–16.

Sheridan, Richard B. "From Slavery in Missouri to Freedom in Kansas: The Influx of Black Fugitives and Contrabands Into Kansas, 1854–1865." *Kansas History* 12 (Spring 1989): 28–47.

Stoddard, W. O. "The Story of a Nomination." *North American Review* 138 (March 1884): 263–74.

Stringfellow, Jacob [Verres Nicholas Smith]. "Jim Lane." *Lippincott's Magazine* 5 (March 1870): 266–78 (also in the Topeka *Kansas State Record*, March 2, 1870).

Tidball, Eugene C. "The View from the Top of the Knoll: Capt. John C. Tidball's Memoir of the First Battle of Bull Run." *Civil War History* 44 (September 1998): 175–93.

Trickett, Dean. "The Civil War in the Indian Territory, 1862." *Chronicles of Oklahoma* 19 (March 1941): 55–69.

Williams, Glenn F. "The Battle of Newtown, 29 September 1779: An Aggressive Attack Carried Out with Audacity." *On Point: The Journal of Army History* 12 (Fall 2006): 8–15.

Index

Adams, Henry J., 259
Ainsworth, Richard M., 259
Alcohol, abuse of in Lane's Brigade, 70, 182, 183, 203–204
Aldeman, Pvt. (Union), 206
Allen, Norman, 209
Allen, William R., 40, 50, 52, 59, 87, 158, 204, 205–206, capture and escape, 166–67
Aluktustenuke (Seminole chief), 231
Amnesty Act, 23
Anderson, Jeremiah G., 20
Anderson, T. J., 259
Anthony, Daniel R., 110
Arms, Leonard, 92
Army of the Western Border, 159
Arthur, Lieut. (Union), 206
Arthur, James M., 203
Asboth, Alexander, 118, 148, 242
Atchison, Kans., 166
Aubry, Kans., 58, 211
Aunt Cin (slave), 99
Austin, Mo., 45

Baird, Absolom, 229
Ball's Mill, Mo., 42, 61, 64, 67
Balltown, Mo., 67
Barnes, George Washington, 98
Barnesville, Kans., 26, 74, 77, 81, 85, 173, 178, 204
Bayne, Oliver P., 20, 21, 119, 126, 163, 169, 178, 179–80
Berry, M. P., 85
Besin, Pvt. (Union), 206
Bickerton, Thomas, 49, 52, 56, 59, 67, 206
Bird, S., 185
Bird's Point, Mo., 248
"Black Brigade," 156–58
Blacks, Kansans' attitudes toward, 17, 59–60, 126, 151–55
Blair, Charles W., 31
Blanton, Napoleon B., 63, 152
Blunt, James G., 53–55, 83–84, 113, 114, 116, 127, 182, 194, 204, 206, 216, 217, 218, 237–38, 253–55
Bolivar, Mo., 101

Bond, David P., 53, 93–94
Bondi, August, 183, 186, 195–96, 197, 207
Bonham, Daniel (slave), 157
Bonsall, Charley, 203
Booneville, Mo., 30, 34
Boutwell, Daniel W., 198–99
Bowles, John, 112, 182, 193, 194
Bowman, C. S., 199–200, 204, 205, 206
Boyce, Capt. (Union), 133
Boyd, John J., 65, 185
Bradley, Eli, 203–204
Bray, Nathan, 56–57
Britton, Wiley, 56–57, 84, 106
Broadhead, John F., 52, 56, 182
Brooklyn, Kans., 161
Brooks, Lieut. (Union), 206
Brown, A. W. J., 216
Brown, Ansel D., 61, 193, 206
Brown, Owen, 79, 80
Brown, John, 20, 22, 41, 43, 45, 50, 54, 80, 90, 92, 186
Brown, John, Jr., 40, 50, 158, 197
Brown, Lieut. (Union), 206
Brown, Wealthy, 50
Bryant, Peter, 131
Buell, Don Carlos, 223
Burris, John T., 116, 169, 180–81, 182, 200, 216, 217, 218, 251
Butler, Benjamin F., 7, 71
Butler, Mo., 86, 104; sacked, 176

Cameron, Mo., 29
Cameron, Simon, 33, 35, 57, 147, 159, 188, 224, 226–27, 232
Camp Alert, Kans., 14
Camp Defiance, Kans., 178, 183, 190, 195, 196, 204
Camp Denver, Kans., 195, 204
Camp Hunter, Kans., 207
Camp Lane, Kans., 39
Camp Montgomery, Mo., 109

Camp Prince, Mo., 45
Camp Union, Kans., 45
Campbell, A. B., 191
Campbell, William T., 31, 41, 84, 119, 216
Cansdell, Argent K., 193, 194
Carthage, Mo., 41 199, 210
Cass County Home Guards, 45, 65, 156, 168, 179, 182, 243, 244
Cassville, Mo., 149
Chandler, Daniel, 64–65, 77, 105–106
Chandler, William P., 259
Chandler, Zachariah, 222
Chase, Salmon, 222
Cherokee Neutral Lands, 13, 57, 59, 66, 133, 207
Chickasaw Nation, 190
Chillicothe, Mo., 52
Christian, James, 19
Christmas, 1861, celebrated, 181–82
Clark, Frank, 93
Clark, John R., 40, 75, 252
Clarke, Charles F., 133, 210
Clarke, Charles S., 179, 208
Clay, Cassius, 26
Clay Guards, 26
Clayton, Powell, 178, 207, 214
Clear Creek, Mo., 172
Clem, John, 161, 175
Cleveland, Marshal, 45, 175
Clinton, Mo., 122
Cloud, William F., 217, 218
Coe, Elias, 182
Coffin, William G., 117, 192, 221–22
Coleman, Charles F., 179
Coleman, Robert, 46
Collamore, George, 191
Columbus, Mo., 197
"Commissary Cart Wilder," 221
"Company X," 197–98
Conway, Martin F., 36, 234
Cook, John, 79

Cooper, Pvt. (Union), 206
Copeland, James M., 89
Coppoc, Barclay, 50, 78–80, 261
Coppoc, Edwin, 79
Cottonwood River, Kans., 191
Courts-martial, in Lane's Brigade, 112–13, 183–84, 193–94, 205
Covode, John, 230, 234
Crawford, George A., 117
Creek Nation, 190, 231
Creitz, William F., 86, 88–89, 92–93, 119, 120, 127, 131, 149, 158, 163, 170, 178, 196, 197–98, 207
Crescent Hill, Mo., 46
Crittenden-Johnson Resolution, 7, 37
Cummings, Dr. (rebel), 202
Cummins, Thomas, 67
Curtis, Samuel, 147–48, 208
Cutler, Abram, 259
Cutler, George A., 192

Dana, Charles A., 232
Davies, Thomas A., 214, 215
Davis, Jefferson C., 86
Deane, Abner, 45, 48
Deitzler, George W., 31, 154, 208, 214
Delahay, Mark, 19, 27, 62, 117, 184, 221–22, 231
Delaware Indians, 121, 122–23, 149
Denver, James W., 167, 169–70, 173–74, 178, 194, 195, 200, 213, 214, 215, 216, 224, 225, 226, 237
Department of Kansas (First), 158–59
Department of Kansas (Second), 237, 253
Department of the Mississippi, 214
Department of the Missouri, 4, 159, 247, 253
Department of the South, 214
Dickinson, William Henry Harrison, 40, 79, 90, 98, 104–105, 106, 111–12, 127, 129, 149, 181, 206

District of Kansas, 214, 237, 254
District of the Border, 254
District of the Frontier, 254
District of the Upper Arkansas, 255
Dixon, (rebel), 182
Dobyns, Henry M., 83, 174
Dodge, Grenville, 248–49
Dorsheimer, William, 129
Doubleday, Charles, 207
Doudna, Willoughby, 179
Downing, John, 205, 206
Drywood, battle of, 74–76, 211
Drywood Creek, Kans., 207, 210
Drywood Creek, Mo., 44, 56
Dudley, Henry, 84
Durno, W. W., 177

Easley, Thomas, 77
Eaton, Joseph H., 148
Ege, A. G., 259
Eighth Kansas Infantry, 173, 179, 182, 213
Eight Iowa Infantry, 179
Eleventh U.S. Colored Troops, 254
Ellenwood, Lieut. (Union), 166
Ellis, Abraham, 58, 211–12, 259
Ervin, William, 88
Eves, Capt. (Union), 206
Ewing, Thomas, Jr., 27, 117

Fail, William B., 69
Fall Leaf, Capt. (Panipakuxwe, Delaware chief), 121
Fall River, Kans., 86, 191
Fifth Kansas Cavalry, 39, 52, 53, 63,65, 74, 81, 83, 86, 115, 118, 162–63, 166, 168, 173, 178, 196–97, 200, 207, 213, 252; reorganized (First), 185; reorganized (Second), 206, 208–10
First Battalion Kansas Cavalry, 179
First Kansas Battery, 210

First Kansas Colored Infantry, 244, 253, 257–58
First Kansas Infantry, 31, 87, 95, 154, 178, 208, 213
First New Mexico Kansas Volunteers, 209
Fish, Reeder, 156
Fish Creek, Kans., 65
Fisher, Hugh, 52, 102, 115, 116, 152, 156, 196
Fitzpatrick, Henry, 174
Five Civilized Tribes, 30
Flanders, George, 195, 199
Fleming, Elijah K., 209
Flesher, Henry, 179
Fletcher, James, 221
Flint, Capt. (Union), 76
Ford, Capt. (Union), 83
Fording, C., 79
Foreman, John, 41, 48, 49, 52, 105, 175, 205–206
Fort Bayne, Kans., 54, 126
Fort Lane, Kans., 85, 134
Fort Larned, Kans., 14
Fort Leavenworth, Kans., 14, 41, 210, 212
Fort Lincoln, Kans., 48, 64, 66, 76–77, 81, 169, 170, 173, 207
Fort Riley, Kans., 14, 133
Fort Row, Kans., 179, 191
Fort Saunders, Kans., 18
Fort Scott, Kans., 14, 21, 26, 31, 41, 51, 59, 69–70, 73, 76–77, 81, 134, 158, 207, 213
Fort Sumter, S. Carolina, 26
Fort Titus, Kans., 18, 49, 51
Fourth Kansas Infantry, 39, 48, 52, 53, 63, 86, 118, 163, 165, 168–69, 180, 213; consolidated, 216; reorganized (First), 184–85; reorganized (Second), 206, 208–10
Fourth U.S. Artillery, 159

Frank, Mrs. Andrew, 196
Franklin, Kans., 18, 51
Frémont, John C., 3, 7, 57, 58, 72, 86, 87, 97, 114, 121, 129, 147–49, 242, 245; emancipation proclamation of, 104
Frontier Guard (Fort Scott home guard), 30
Frontier Guard, Lane's, 26–28, 129
Fugitive Slave Act, 6

Gamble, Hamilton, 222
Gardner, Joseph, 51
Gardner, Kans., 58, 132
Gatewood, James M., 172
Geary, John, 18, 38
Gibbon, John, 159
Gibson, Garrett, 40, 75, 178
Gibson, Pvt. (Union), 206
Gilpatrick, Rufus, 54, 55, 126, 134, 193, 259
Gordon, Si, 160, 161
Gordon, Simeon B., 209
Goss, Benjamin F., 179
Gower, Zacheus, 41, 186, 194, 216
Grand Army, Fremont's, 118, 121, 149, 220, 242
Grant, Ulysses S., 34, 246, 248
Green, Martin E., 86–87
Greeno, Harris S., 74, 75, 83, 133
Greusel, Nicholas, 248–49
Gunn, O. B., 178
Guthrie (rebel), 89
Guthrie, Abelard, 10–11, 233–34, 237

Hall, Willard, 222
Halleck, Henry W., 4, 7, 154, 155, 159, 160, 202, 210, 212, 214, 215, 223, 225, 236, 241–42, 245, 247–48
Halpine, Charles G., 212, 214, 216, 242–43
Hamilton, Charles, 21–22, 43, 90

Hampton, Va., 90
Hannibal & St. Joseph Railroad, 29
Harney, William S., 7
Harpers Ferry, Va., 20, 26, 79, 80
Harrington, Stephen R., 129
Harris, Arnold, 28
Harris, Charles, 104, 126–27
Harris, James H., 65
Harrisonville, Mo., 45, 46–48, 243
Hartman, John, 194
Harvey, James M., 53, 65, 168
Harvey, Elijah E., 40, 93, 165, 168–69, 216
Hayes, Josiah E., 48, 57, 180
Hays, Margaret J., 243, 244
Hickman Mills, Mo., 113
Hildreth, By, 183, 203
Hill, Edward, 111–12, 158
Hill, J. E., 175
Hill, William H., 46
Hinds, Russell, 23
Hitchcock, E. A., 214
Hobo, Philip, 112
Holden, Mo., 197
Horne, Daniel, 219–21
Howard's Mill, Mo., 127
Hudson, Joseph K., 50, 181
Hughes, John T., 78
Humansville, Mo., 127, 128, 129
Humboldt, Kans., 59, 84, 86; Sept. 8 sack of, 83; Oct. 14 sack of, 132
Hunt, James S., 99, 127, 149, 170
Hunter, David, 27, 118, 129, 147, 148, 149, 155, 159, 160, 161, 167, 168, 179, 192, 200, 201, 202, 204, 207, 208, 210, 211, 222, 223–24, 224–25, 229, 230–33, 235–36, 242, 245
Huntoon, Andrew J., 77, 87, 111, 134, 174, 182, 195, 198–99, 204
Hurd, James, 203
Hyatt, Thaddeus, 51

Iatan, Mo., 29
Independence, Mo., 29, 111, 112, 114, 180–81, 213, 239
Independent Battalion Cavalry, 179, 208
Independent Mounted Rangers, 57
Indian Home Guards, 193; First Regiment, 253; Second Regiment, 199, 253, 256–57
Indian Territory expedition (1862), 251
Indiana Legion, 189
Ingalls, J. J., 9, 10
Insley, M. H., 178, 259
Iola, Kans., 179
Iola Battalion, 179

Jackson, Claiborne Fox, 29–30, 128
Jackson, Jeremiah, 22
Jefferson, Ohio, 50
Jefferson City, Mo., 30
Jenkins, Gaius, 19, 167
Jennison, Charles R., 4, 21, 23, 24, 40, 41–42, 43, 44, 45–46, 47, 50, 56, 57–58, 74, 75, 81, 83, 86, 98, 110, 119, 151, 168, 173, 179, 181, 182, 197, 208, 213, 241
Jewell, Lewis R., 66, 76, 84, 253
Johnson, E. B., 198
Johnson, Hamilton P., 39, 40, 65, 88–89
Johnson, Lieut. (Union), 123
Johnson (rebel), 125
Johnson, Waldo P., 99
Jones, Lieut. (Union), 182, 209
Judson, Charles O., 30, 41, 84, 133, 172
Judson, William R., 256

Kansas: 1859–60 drought, 23; geography of, 13
Kansas Brigade, 3, 210

Kansas City, Mo., 29, 48, 110, 168
Kansas-Nebraska Act, 14
Karnes (rebel), 60
Kerr, R. H., 259
Kille, Clayton, 206
Killen, Thomas P., 179
Kingsville, Mo., 122
Kirkwood, Samuel, 79–80
Kossuth, Lajos, 50

Ladd, Erastus, 64
Laiguanite, Giuseppe, 58, 260
Laing, John M., 210, 216
Lamar, Mo., 66
Lane, Anna, 16, 19
Lane, Ellen, 16
Lane, George, 229–30
Lane, James Henry: brigadier commissions offered, 33–35, 225; at Bull Run battle, 37; career following Kansas Brigade, 257–58; challenges to Senate seat, 35–36, 188–89; divorce of, 16–17; elected to U.S. Senate, 26; emigrates to Kansas, 16; forms Frontier Guard, 26–28; Great Southern Expedition, 116, 200–201, 219–38; Indiana political career, 16; Mexican War, 16; Kansas Territory political career, 17; leaves Kansas Brigade, 158–59; major general of Kansas territorial militia, 18, 21, 54, 167; physical description, 15–16; "Proclamation to the People of Western Missouri," 94; relations with regular army, 62–63, 109–10, 113, 114–15, 118–19; remarriage, 19; sack of Osceola, 106–108; speaking style, 8–10; suicide, 258; takes command of Kansas Brigade, 61–65; war aims of, 6, 7–8, 25–26, 28–29, 37, 62, 66, 70, 80–81, 85, 88, 96, 109, 115, 149–50, 186–87, 200–201, 229, 230, 245–47
Lane, James H., Jr., 16
Lane, Jane, 16
Lane, Mary, 16, 19
Lane's Addition, 12
Larnard (Union), 66
Larzalere, Alfred, 206
Law of War, 5–6, 249
Lawrence, Kans., 11, 16, 17–18, 19, 22, 38, 63, 151, 178, 258
Learnard, Oscar E., 213
Leavenworth, Kans., 38, 39, 62, 168, 221
Leavenworth Mercantile Association, 200
Lecompton, Kans., 11, 18
LeRoy, Kans., 59, 86, 190, 192
Lewis, Reese, 171–72
Lexington, Mo., 85, 86, 113, 160, 166; siege of, 97
Liberty, Mo., 65; U.S. arsenal at, 28
Lightning Creek, Kans., 59, 83
Lincoln, Abraham, 7, 19–20, 27, 33, 34, 116–17, 147, 155, 214, 215, 221, 224, 225, 226, 231–32, 235, 258; and Fremont's emancipation proclamation, 104
Lincoln, Abraham (slave), 157
Linden Mills, Mo., 149
Little, John, 22
Little Osage, Mo., 67
Little Osage River, Kans., 48, 64
Livingston, Tom, 83, 132, 133
Locke (rebel), 105, 161
Lockhart, John, 209
Lone Jack, Mo., 114
Loring, H. Gray, 259
Lovejoy, Owen, 186
Lupton, (Union), 175–76

Lynde, Edward, 207, 237
Lyon, Nathaniel, 3, 29–30, 34, 41, 48, 57, 58, 60, 241, 247

Manning, Richard, 161
Mansfield, Kans., 42
Mapleton, Kans., 87, 111, 134, 183
Marais des Cygnes massacre, 21–22, 43
Marini, Luigi, 58, 260
Marmaton River, Kans., 56
Martin, Bill, 63–64
Mason, Aleck, 129
Mathews, John, 59, 83–84
Maxson, Thaddeus, 41, 80
McCall, J. N., 259
McClellan, George, 34, 200, 222–24, 228, 229, 236
McCulloch, Ben, 60, 70, 84, 155, 174
McDonald, Lieut. (Union), 206
McDowell, William, 152
McGee's Addition, 110
McGinnis, William E., 186
McKinstry, Justus, 118, 148
McNeil, R. W., 67, 68, 69
"Mechanic Fusileers," 227, 229
Medical care, in Lane's Brigade, 77, 134, 165–66, 195–96
Medill, Joseph, 234
Medoc, Mo., 66, 133
Mefford, David, 210
Mercantile Library Association, 230
Merriam, Francis, 79
Miller, Adoniram, 185, 186
Miller, Capt. (Union), 173, 186
Miller, George A., 84
Miller, J. W., 212
Mills, J. H., 100
Missouri State Guard, 3, 29, 30, 34, 41, 43, 58, 60, 67–68, 70, 78, 86, 88, 162–63, 174

Mitchell, Pvt. (Union), 206
Mitchell, Robert B., 31
Moneka, Kans., 183
Montevallo, Mo., 127, 133
Montgomery, James, 20, 21, 22, 23–24, 38, 39, 41, 42–43, 53, 56, 57, 59, 70, 74, 76, 113, 128, 159, 162–63, 168, 172–73, 195, 203, 206, 216, 255
Moonlight, Thomas, 52, 65, 67, 68, 74, 88, 99, 100, 121, 122, 159–60, 180, 205, 210, 217
Moore, Andy, 203
Moore, Henry H., 73, 76, 77, 95, 98, 104, 119, 124, 127, 129, 149, 153–54, 156, 176, 177, 178, 179, 194
Moore, H. Miles, 120–21, 124, 126, 182, 183, 193, 194, 195, 196, 203, 204, 205, 206, 259
Moore, L. D., 24
Morris, Isaac, 44
Morristown, Mo., 88–89, 179; sacked, 45–46, 89
Morse, Lieut. (Union), 76
Morton, governor of Indiana, 188
Morton, P. G. D., 179
Mound City, Kans., 31, 32, 39, 41, 42, 44, 48–49, 50, 55, 56, 66, 168, 178, 182, 183, 196, 203
Mount Vernon, Mo., 57
Mule raid, 73–74
Mulligan, James, 97
Mylins, Lewis H., 172

Navoni, Luigi, 58, 260
Neosho, Mo., 128
Neosho Battalion, 179
Neutral Lands. *See* Cherokee Neutral Lands
Nevada City, Mo., 60

Newgent, Andrew, 156
Newman, Albert, 206
Nineteenth Indiana Infantry, 187
Ninth Kansas Cavalry, 179
Ninth Wisconsin Infantry, 208, 213

Offley, R. H., 118
Olathe, Kans., 58, 174
"Old Jim Lane" (song), 12
Opothleyahola (Creek chief), 190–92, 231
Orahood, John W., 209
Osage Indians, 59, 69
Osage Mission, Kans., 59
Osage River, Mo., 122
Osawatomie, Kans., 90, 151, 163, 165, 169, 172, 174, 186
Osceola, Mo., 98, 123–25, 166, 172; skirmish at, 99; sack of, 99–103

Paine, E. A., 248
Palmer, Henry E., 90, 100
Paola, Kans., 44, 127, 132, 168, 216
Panipakuxwe (Fall Leaf, Delaware chief), 121
Papinsville, Mo., 82, 83, 98; sacked, 176
Pardia, Marcellia, 204
Parker, J. A., 183
Parrott, Marcus J., 259
Parsons, Luke, 186
Peabody, Everett, 81, 85, 86, 97
Phillips, J. A., 216, 217, 218
Phillips, William B., 256
Pinks, Allen, 52
Platte City, Mo., 29
Platte River bridge, collapse of, 78–79
Pleasant Hill, Mo., 121–22
Plum, Levi (alias of John E. Stewart), 51–52
Plumly, B. Rush, 106–107
Pomeroy, James M., 58, 260

Pomeroy, Samuel C., 26, 27, 36, 58, 188, 214, 215, 234, 237
Pope, John, 87, 118, 241, 248
Potosi, Kans., 175
Pottawatomie Creek, Kans., 166
Price, Sterling, 40, 41, 60, 73, 78–79, 113, 114, 127–28, 148, 155, 163–64, 166, 172, 174, 208, 245; 1864 raid of, 199, 255, 256, 257, 258
Prince, William E., 41, 44–45, 48, 52, 57, 59, 61, 62–63, 65, 81, 82, 85, 116, 210, 214
Putnam, Elizabeth, 54
Putnam, Nancy G., 54

Quantrill, William Clarke, 43–44, 51–52, 182, 211–12, 254, 258
Quapaw Strip, 13
Quigg, Matthew, 48, 122, 180
Quincy, Ill., 52, 62, 86, 230

Rabb, John W., 156, 160
Rabb's Indiana Battery, 156, 168, 208, 213
Rains, James S., 70
Randlett, Reuben, 211–12
Raney (rebel), 105
Ransom, Wyllis C., 41, 119, 172, 216
Reader, Sam, 161
Refugees: Indian, 192–93; rebel, 21; Union, 31–32, 42, 44, 56–57, 59, 103, 132, 155, 161–62, 174, 177, 202
Rhodes, Elnathan, 193, 194
Rice, Benjamin, 44
Rice, Edward M., 196
Richardson, Albert D., 8, 21
Riggs, Samuel, 64
Riley, Thomas, 193
Ritchey's Mill, Mo., 127
Ritchie, John, 45, 47, 48, 53, 64, 69, 74, 86, 87, 90–94, 105, 116, 120–21,

149, 162–63, 166, 169–70, 199, 256–57
Robinson, Charles, 3, 25, 30, 31, 33, 34, 35–36, 44, 57, 58, 72, 115–18, 169, 175, 178, 184, 205, 207, 210, 217, 241
Rogers, John, 83, 209, 216
Rose, William, 40, 283n34
Ross, John, 251
Row, John R., 179
Ryan, James, 195

Sac River, Mo., 127
Sage, James, 161
Salomon, Frederick, 251
Saloon smashing, Mound City, 183
Santa Fe, Mo., 57, 216
Sawyer, Michael, 193
Schurz, Carl, 28
Scott, John W., 183
Scott, Samuel, 23
Scott, T. M., 254
Scott, Winfield, 6, 188
Scudder, Thomas, 169, 198
Seaman, Henry C., 49, 52, 56, 59, 66, 67, 76, 112, 129, 182
Searight, Joseph, 175
Second Kansas Cavalry, 218, 254
Second Kansas Colored Infantry, 244
Second Kansas Infantry, 31, 95, 217
Second Ohio Cavalry, 207, 213
Second South Carolina Colored Infantry, 255
Sedgwick, John, 121
Seminole Nation, 190, 231
Seventh Kansas Cavalry, 168
Seventh Missouri Infantry, 179
Shanghai, Mo., 171
Sheldon, E. B., 198
Sherman, William Tecumseh, 4, 6, 7, 29, 108, 171, 223, 246
Shoemaker, John, 59

Sigel, Franz, 41, 118, 148, 242
Sixth Kansas Cavalry, 41, 53, 84, 98, 132–33, 171–72, 207, 208, 213, 252–53; reorganized (First), 185; reorganized (Second), 216–17
Smalley, Frederick A., 176–77, 205, 206
Smith, Mary W., 50
Smith, Obediah, 98, 104
Smith, Robert, 160
Smith, Verres Nicholas, 240–41
Snyder, Col. (rebel), 102
Snyder, Eli, 22, 43–44, 49, 52, 56, 193
Soldiers' Relief Society, 112
"Southern Kansas Jayhawkers," 41
Southwest Battalion, 24, 64
Southwick, Albert, 79
Speakes, Joseph, 161
Speer, John, 17
Springdale, Iowa, 79
Springfield, Mo., 57, 58, 128, 155, 174, 208
Spring River, Kans., 133
St. Joseph, Mo., 29, 51, 159, 160
St. Louis, Mo., 29
Stanfield, Thomas, 105
Stanton, Edwin M., 214–15, 217, 232
Stanton, Frederick P., 35–36, 188
Stearns, George Luther, 31, 42, 50
Steele, William, 45
Steen, A. E., 73, 74, 166
Stephenson, Samuel, 196
Stevens, R. S., 215, 216, 224–25
Stewart, John E., 21, 49, 50–52, 56, 59, 63–64, 66, 67, 111, 112, 176, 193–94. *See also* Plum, Levi
Stinson, Sam, 110
Stockton, Job, 28
Stockton Hall, 57, 115, 220, 221
Stringfellow, Jacob, 240–41
Sturgis, Samuel, 44, 87, 95, 97, 107, 112, 113, 123, 124–25, 215, 237

Summers, James H., 86, 169, 170, 178, 197, 207
Sumner, Edwin V., 121
Swingley, Leonard J., 42, 43
Sykes, Josiah, 175

Talbot, Col. (rebel), 132
Tenney, Marcus de Lafayette, 200
Tenth Cavalry, Missouri State Guard, 89
Tenth Kansas Infantry, 216, 251–52, 256
Terrill, Chauncey, 89
Texas Rangers, 175
Third Kansas Infantry, 39, 52, 63, 86, 115, 163, 165, 168, 178, 181, 199, 204, 206, 208–10, 213; consolidated 216; reorganized (First), 184; reorganized (Second), 204–205
Thirteenth Wisconsin Infantry, 207, 208, 213
Thirty-ninth Ohio Infantry, 87
Thomas, Lorenzo, 229, 233, 236
Thompson, M. Jeff, 29
Thompson, Samuel C., 40, 209
Thrasher, Luther, 165, 176, 177, 206, 214
Thurston, Orlin, 76
Tippie, Michael, 194
Tives, Capt. (Union), 206
Topeka, Kans., 219, 220, 257
Trading Post, Kans., 86, 87
Trego, Joseph, 7–8, 59, 66, 69, 76–77, 86, 95, 105, 111–12, 114, 122, 124, 159, 162, 177
Tremont House, 229
Tremont Temple, 187
Triplett, Oliver, 183
"Troops in Kansas," 167
Truman, Harry, 239–40
Trumbull, Lyman, 223
Turkey Creek, Kans., 86

Twelfth Kansas Infantry, 220
Twelfth Wisconsin Infantry, 208, 213
Twenty-fourth Indiana Infantry, 149
Twenty-seventh Ohio Infantry, 87
Twenty-third Indiana Infantry, 87
Twiss, Charles P., 49, 52, 56

U.S. Reserve Corps, 45, 81
Union League, 258
Updegraff, W. W., 186, 260
Upton, William, 161

Vansickle, John H., 169, 170, 176, 195, 205
Vansickle's Independent Scouts, 169, 170, 176, 177, 178, 205, 210, 216–17
Van Horn, Robert T., 45, 47–48
Vaughn, Mr. (rebel), 101
Vaughn, Mrs. (rebel), 101, 107
Veale, George, 57, 73–74, 121, 210, 216
Veatch, "Squint-Eye," 159
Vecchi, Achille de, 58, 65, 260
Verdigris River, Kans., 86, 179, 191

Wade, Benjamin F., 37, 222
Wakarusa War, 18
Wallace, (civilian), 172
Walnut Creek, Mo., 42
Walnut River, Kans., 86, 191
Walsh, Hugh, 92
Ward, A. T., 127, 132
Watson, Greenville, 40, 65
Weapons, of Lane's Brigade, 52–53, 67, 84, 173, 186
Weaver, Stanton, 203
Webster, Daniel (slave), 157
Wed, George W., 260
Weed, Dr., 234
Weed, Thurlow J., 242
Weed, T. J., 225, 227, 260

Weer, William, 36, 38, 39, 45, 47, 48, 59, 65, 73, 94, 113, 129, 168–69, 180, 216, 217–18, 251, 256–57
Weidemeyer, John, 99, 100, 103–104
Weston, Mo., 29, 159, 160
West Point, Mo., 44, 86, 87, 98, 173, 179, 182, 243
Westport, Mo., 213
White, Lieut. (Union), 160
White, Richard, 158
White House, 27–28, 232
Wilder, A. C., 178, 260
Wilder, Capt. (Union), 82
Willard's Hotel, 28, 186
Williams, Henry H., 116, 175, 176, 196, 199, 203, 206, 251–52
Williams, James M., 45–48, 49, 52, 53, 56, 60–61, 66, 67, 73–74, 113
Williams, J. J., 126
Wilson, Henry, 37
Wilson's Creek, battle of, 60, 178, 217
Winthrop, Mo., 166
Wise, Henry, 79
Wood, (rebel), 66
Woodruff, William, 86–87
Worthington, John I., 202
Wright, Clark, 155
Wright, Jasper, 177
Wyandot Indians, 121
Wyandotte, Kans., 50, 165, 169

Yeager, Dick, 132

Zulavsky, Casimir, 50, 76, 77, 196, 206